In Search of Ali Mahmoud

Also by Vivian Gornick

WOMAN IN SEXIST SOCIETY
(co-editor with Barbara Moran)

In Search of
Ali Mahmoud

An American Woman in Egypt

 *Vivian Gornick*

Saturday Review Press/E. P. Dutton & Co., Inc.

New York

Published simultaneously in Canada by
Doubleday Canada, Ltd., Toronto.

Library of Congress Catalog Card Number: 72–88651

ISBN 0–8415–0242–0

Parts of this book appeared in an altered form in *The Village Voice.*

PRINTED IN THE UNITED STATES OF AMERICA

Design by Tere LoPrete

For Bess—with all my heart

In Search of Ali Mahmoud

"I'm going to Egypt," I said.

"Are you crazy?" my closest friend said.

"They'll never let you in," my editor said.

"I'd think that one over if I were you," my brother said.

"My dear young woman, you will be watched continually, you will never be allowed to do what you want to do," a French diplomat at the UN said.

"Egypt! What the hell has *that* got to do with anything?" a liberated woman said.

"That's simply marvelous!" a Persian writer I knew said.

"You are betraying the Jews," my mother said.

"For God's sake!" I yelled at my mother, having said comparatively little to everyone else.

"They'll kill you!" my mother hissed.

"Why would they do that?" I asked quietly.

"Because we are at war with them, my clever daughter."

"*Who's* at war? I'm an American national. I'm not at war with Egypt."

"Oh, God," my mother said, her anger giving way to weariness, and she suddenly looking older, much older. "You are such a fool."

Is she right? I thought. Am I such a fool? Does she know more about the dominating portion of my identity than I do? Can she tell, although I cannot, that I am only a Jew in the world? Is everything else that I am of no account once I land at Cairo Airport?

But then I remembered the words of Françoise, my lovely French bird of a friend who, having spent six years in Cairo, said to me, "Nonsense, my dear. You'll never get past being a woman."

And then again, the UN diplomat, barely controlling his distaste for my American boldness so obviously rooted in amateurish naïveté, speaking with great evenness: "You are an American *journalist*. That automatically makes you suspect. And into the bargain" (he raised his cold blue eyes to the ceiling) "you are a *Jewish* American journalist." Then suddenly turning all existentialist politics: "Why are you acting like a child? Don't you understand? Don't you know what's going on there? We are at war. We are *all* at war. There *is* no peace. There will never be peace. There are only temporary truces—everywhere. Everyone knows, even as they are signing, it is only a matter of the right time."

Dear God, what *am* I doing? I thought, leaving the UN that gray January day, wandering aimlessly down First Avenue in the general direction of home. How did all this start? Are they *all* right? Or is any of them right? If some of them are right, which ones? I am a woman. I am the American-born daughter of Russian Jews. I am a journalist. Are all these fixed elements of identity an outrage to the Middle East? Something to be spit out as quickly and as brutally as possible? Or, on the other hand, something to be spitefully neglected as of no value and casually sacrificed should the need to do so arise? Ali Mahmoud, where are you? I need you. *Now.*

But I know very well where you are, and I know why you are there and I am here, and when I remember all that, *really* remember, I know why I am going to Egypt, and the strength of that knowledge comes coursing through me like some purification of the blood, purging me of the fear induced by the ignorant opinions of self-important Cassandras, and in the deepest part of me I am urged again to take my risks as they flow directly out of my own experience.

I met Ali Mahmoud in 1969 in Cambridge. He was a graduate student in physics, a Fulbright scholar from Cairo, here on a joint U.S.-Egyptian arrangement whose prevailing condition was that the two governments would give him his Ph.D. provided that he would return to Cairo to teach physics at a university there (in this case, Al Azhar, the oldest Islamic University in the Middle East). When I met him he had been in the United States for four years. Four soul-wearying years. We lived together for six months.

It would be nice to be able to say that I first went home with Ali for the illicit pleasure of sleeping with an Arab, acting out of the dark and irresistible root perversity that drives us, in a multitude of forms, to give ourselves to the enemy, thereby taking him into ourselves; into that hidden central region where alone one discovers the wild limits of power and survival, grinding our lives for a moment against the steel edge of ultimate risk. It would be nice to be able to say all that. But the fact is, and in the necessary silence of my frightened heart I knew the fact was: I went home with Ali because he was *only* an Arab.

My meeting with Ali Mahmoud struck me as providential. For me, then, it was a time of terror and release, of breakdown and renewal, a time of enormous hope and painful fear. I was in sore need of comfort. But where—and how—in that desolation of American "cool"? One night in a student bar there came the perfect answer: an Egyptian physicist.

I was profoundly between lives. I had left my husband, my home, my job. I had had what amounted to a revelation concerning the insubstantiality of my life, and every foundation of entrenched opinion upon which my actions rested was crashing up all around me. When I wasn't talking frantically I was weeping copiously. But when Ali Mahmoud sat down in that bar to talk to me he electrified a source of power that had remained intact: I was an American Jew, and any way you wanted to slice that it came out better than being an Egyptian Arab. More important than better: it put me in control. From Ali's eyes there flowed velvet warmth, from his mouth there issued childlike wisdom, from the entirety of his body, accommodation. All qualities which we make use of in fear and despise in strength. I could handle this easy.

How can I describe what discovering Ali Mahmoud was like? Or what discovering him made me discover in myself? How can I explain what it was like to find in him all the expected clichés of Arab character, yes—but somehow, none of them adding up to what they were supposed to add up to?

Was he warm and childlike? Yes and no. Warm to those who responded to him, perfectly cool to those who did not. And the words, when you listened carefully, those childlike words of wisdom were shot through with an irony that was startling in its preciseness.

He shared quickly and unthinkingly whatever he had with whomever he cared for. But he was a profound materialist, responding to what he could see, hear, touch, taste and feel in his gut—an approach to life that struck him as eminently reasonable. He had no patience with abstract needs of the soul, and psychoanalysis seemed to him the plague of America.

He was the most sensual man I have ever known—and yet, he had not slept with a woman in more than a year because the sexual directness of Cambridge women shriveled his soul, and muted his desire. The ceaseless American quest for sensuality puzzled him. "The point," he used to say, "is to *restrain* your passions and concentrate on *work*. Otherwise, we are lost."

"I am not an excessively intelligent man," he often observed, "but I am a patient man." Oh, that patience of his. A hundred times I have seen him, when his gorge—or his panic—was rising, set his mouth and his eyes and start all over again. His patience kept him going through four years of the most unutterable loneliness, depression and humiliation. His patience kept us together when my explosive angers would surely have torn us both to pieces. His patience kept alive in him a proportion of need that was repeatedly in danger of being choked to death by the mechanized and obsessive obstacle courses that must be run by any who would avail himself of the American Ph.D.—obstacle courses that brought him to his knees more than once. His patience, in short, gave him the considerable strength of character that was his.

Nonetheless, it was the quality of his intelligence that was one of the two facts of Ali that ultimately took me to Egypt. Certainly, he was not an intellectual. Ideas, as such, never held his attention. He did not enjoy thinking abstractly, and so of course he didn't do it very well. But he had an amazing intelligence of the emotions. He was capable of grasping and describing the elements of emotional behavior with great clarity, great distinction, great detail. In fact, it was the details he observed and enlarged upon that were the key to the almost systematic nature of his understanding. His observations were made not in a void of separate perceptions but, as though cradled in a body of knowledge that lived deep within him, they came rather like atoms being pulled off a molecule. As a result, his emotional responses seemed strongly *rooted*, and were highly developed.

This emotional sophistication perpetually amazed me and I used to say, "How do you know all this stuff, where did you learn it?" And he would reply, "My father died when I was a child and I was raised almost entirely by my mother." Which only proved to me that he hadn't a clue as to *why* he knew what he knew; that he could describe but he could not analyze; that he could observe but he could not reflect. Nonetheless, rooted in ignorance or not, this emotional understanding of Ali's was one of the strongest threads of the strand that bound us together. It was, for me, more than pleasure, more than comfort, more than stimulation. It carried within it the seeds of that living intelligence that pushes back the darkness and allows us to breathe deeply for a moment.

The other "fact of Ali" that made me curious about the exotic country of his birth was that he began to grow extraordinarily recognizable to me. In two ways most particularly did his life come to seem like some strange echo of my own.

We could talk to each other in a particular way that neither of us could ever talk to Gentiles: joke and laugh, size up a situation, exchange exasperating-mother stories, talk of "them" as opposed to "us," relate joint family barbarisms, refer to "the ghetto." It was, of course, peculiarly and startlingly, the camaraderie of the outsider.

Perhaps, it was as well the camaraderie of Semitic roots, but if so then only in the sense that it was the camaraderie of a Moslem and a Jew who, in this most Western and Christian of centuries, were outsiders together.

Then, and this was the clincher, there was our mutual need and appetite for the city. We were both so entirely children of the city, and at that, very particular children of the city. Which puzzled me. I, after all, was the daughter of working-class immigrants. I'd been raised in the dense, poor streets of the Bronx where intelligence is sharpened on city shrewdness and anxiety and laughter and hunger, and the pure dizzying *detail* of life in those streets teaches you how to angle for your bit of the whole business. But Ali? Surely he was the son of aristocratic Egyptians. After all, there were only aristocrats and peasants in Arab countries, weren't there? How was it that he seemed to have been brought up in the same way and on the same kinds of streets that *I* had experienced? How was it that his formative perceptions seemed so very much like my own? We used to walk for hours, Ali and I, telling each other stories of childhood and shaking with laughter over the uncanny sameness of it all.

Once we went camping in the Sierras. We drove into those lovely California mountains late on an early summer afternoon and began looking for a suitable place to park ourselves. We found one on the bluff of a high grassy embankment that hung out over the strong tumbling river where men had excitedly panned for gold a hundred years ago. At the bottom of the embankment, close to the river's edge, another camp was struck and in it was a solitary man with a panel truck fixed up with a bed and a makeshift kitchen. We, of course, didn't have half the things you were supposed to have when you went camping—a flashlight, matches, a covering in case of rain—and the man in the panel truck had everything. We struck up a conversation with him, he gave us everything we needed, and told us he was a typesetter in the composing room of the San Francisco *Examiner* and that he just had to get away sometimes; just *had to*. I don't know why, but as we talked something wild seemed to come into the typesetter's face and I became convinced that he was unhinged; do what I would I couldn't shake the thought that in the middle of the night . . . He had an enormous butcher knife hanging on the inside door of the truck and later I kept saying to Ali, "Is it normal for someone to take a knife like that on an ordinary camping trip? I mean, does that seem *normal* to you?" But Ali only laughed and said I was crazier than the man in the truck.

Anyway, we camped, cooked, ate our supper, and prepared our sleeping bags for the night—me still thinking about the California lunatic down the hill, and Ali himself beginning to look a little anxious as the light started drifting out of the sky. He looked around casually—oh, so casually!—and said to me, "What do you think about the bears around here?"

"The bears?" I blinked at him. "What the hell should I think about the bears?"

"Do you think there are any close by?"

"Jesus, I don't know. I haven't thought about that." After all, how many kinds of impending disaster could I keep my mind on at once?

"Don't be silly," I said. "There are people camped all around here. And we haven't left any food uncovered. That's what you're supposed to do, right? Not leave any food out that will attract them?"

"Yes, I suppose you're right," Ali said, but he didn't look too happy about the whole thing.

We took off our shoes, doused the fire, crawled into our bags . . . and couldn't fall asleep. We tossed and turned, talked, fooled around, and finally I dozed. Suddenly, a noise, and I jumped awake. It was Ali climbing out of his sleeping bag.

"What are you doing?" I asked in alarm.

"I'm going down to the car to get those flares in the trunk!"

"Flares? What for?"

"Never mind what for. *Bears*, that's what for."

"You mean you're leaving me here all alone for that maniac to come and get?"

"Listen," he said. "I can handle a psychopath. It's the damned bears I can't stop thinking about." And he trudged down the hill, miserable and sleepy, with that poor maligned typesetter's flashlight in his hand, returning after an interminable time with the two flares. He then climbed back into his sleeping bag, taking the flashlight with him, and lay there face up, black eyes round and alert, a flare clutched in each hand. Suddenly, he looked exactly like every boy I'd gone to City College with, boys who also could handle psychopaths, but *bears*! I began to shake so with laughter that I almost rolled off the embankment.

And then, from out of nowhere, as though it had been flying around in the sky waiting for the appropriate moment to dart into my head, I thought: *What is this Cairo like that it could produce a City College boy? What is it really like?*

My friends in Cambridge kept telling me that Ali was an exceptional man, that you couldn't really conclude anything about Egypt from him—after all, look at the other Egyptians in Cambridge. (And indeed, the Egyptians whom Ali knew did seem like caricatures of Middle Easterners; however, Ali himself could not bear most of them, associated only in the most limited sense with his compatriots, and told me that in Egypt he wouldn't have known any of them.)

But I knew that something was wrong with the analysis of my friends because I knew that Ali was *not* an exceptional man. I knew that he was no free spirit in rebellion against his culture; on the contrary, he was a deeply conventional man whose soul pined for the order and goodness of middle-class life and the blessed anonymity of socially shared behavior. Thus, what was in him, to some degree and in some combination, must be common to Egypt.

We parted—well, what's the difference how we parted? It was a mess. We knew, but we could not bear to know, so we simply said that I was going back to New York to put my life in order, and then we'd see.

At Christmastime of that year Ali came to New York.

There were *some* funny things. Like my mother: "An Arab in *my* house? Never."

But he came anyway. For a huge dinner on Christmas Day.

"If we're having an Arab we might as well have Christmas, already," my mother said.

"You've got the whole thing wrong, Ma. He doesn't have Christmas *either*."

In the end, of course, my mother was impressed and delighted with Ali—and very confused, although she managed to scramble out of her confusion: "Listen, I never said there couldn't be an *exception*."

But, mainly, it was a forlorn time for us; we knew that this time we would be saying good-bye for keeps. I remember that it was bitterly cold that Christmas and Ali suffered terribly as we wandered the New York streets like two orphan children, choosing to lug our unhappiness through the city rather than sit alone with it in the painful privacy of my apartment. One day we were walking up First Avenue and we stopped to examine an elaborate holiday display in a large, glittering liquor store. As I was looking at the bottles in the window I casually asked Ali if he'd heard from his mother lately. He said yes, he'd just had a letter before he left Cambridge and he pulled out of an inner pocket one of those tissue-thin Egyptian envelopes I'd become so familiar with.

"For no reason at all," said Ali, "she's suddenly become obsessed with the idea that I am going to remain in this country." I looked up at him for a moment and then back to the window. He opened the envelope, pulled out two thin sheets of paper covered with Arabic writing and read out loud to me: "I fear for you, my son, when I think of you remaining in the United States. You *know* what they think of us."

I remember as though it were yesterday: I was staring at a bottle of Gordon's Gin decorated with a red satin ribbon, and I never stopped staring at the bottle as Ali read those words to me, and so he never knew that the words had the effect of a needle going straight into my brain, producing an opening the size of a pinpoint that nevertheless refused to close up. I could not—then or ever—erase from my mind the image of a woman sitting at a desk in a room in Cairo writing those words to her son in Massachusetts, and somehow encompassing in them a profound understanding of loneliness; an acute self-awareness; an intelligence that quietly came to the heart of the matter. Things started whirling and turning and tumbling in my mind . . . *I simply had to go and see what this Cairo was all about.*

One year later, almost to the day, a New York book editor approached me and asked me if I'd like to go to the Middle East and write my impressions of the Arabs. Without blinking an eye, as though I'd known all along it would be coming, I said, "The Middle East, no. Egypt. Only Egypt." I told the editor about Ali Mahmoud. I explained that there were thirty-five million Egyptians living in Egypt, most of them *fellahin* (peasant-farmers), less than 1 percent of the population an educated urban middle class. It was that less than 1 percent I wished to describe. It was Ali Mahmoud's family I wished to discover, and make real to Westerners. I wrote a proposal, the editor agreed, we signed a contract—and the nightmare of friendly advice began. All of which came to an end when I simply wrote to the U.A.R. Interests Section at the Indian Embassy in Washington (Interests Sections are part of the elaborate charade that is played when diplomatic relations have been formally broken between the United States and another country) and said, "Look. I'm Jewish. I'm American. I'm a journalist. I want to go take a look at Egypt." The Egyptians in Washington immediately replied, "Of course. Whatever made you think we don't admit Jews? By the way, you're not a pro-Zionist writer, are you?" Within three days I had a visa, and within two weeks, in February of 1971, I was on my way to Cairo.

I called Ali before I left. He was flabbergasted, then overjoyed. "Can I bring you anything from Egypt?" I said.

"No," he said sadly. "What can you bring me? Can you bring me Cairo? Can you bring me my mother?"

PART ONE

I delayed calling Ali Mahmoud's mother, Soad, for a day. I remembered Ali saying, "Will my mother welcome you! She'll *surround* you. After all, you are coming directly from heaven, directly from her son." I wanted twenty-four hours alone in Cairo before people began directing my attention.

I had arrived at midnight, anxious in the plane. Yet, when I stepped into the lighted airport space just inside the darkness holding Cairo back beyond my reach, I felt oddly reassured. It was only late February but the air was warm and gentle, alive to the touch. Impossible to be frightened in it.

Once inside the airport building anxiety returned, doublefold. Unlike the airport buildings of Europe—all clean, well-lit plastic glamor—Cairo Airport was dim, lit only by weak neon lighting, the halls and corridors an institutional green, and with the look of having been hastily appropriated. Everywhere, not groups but *masses* of people, and masses of confusion. People seemed to be racing around wildly in the grip of the most fearful distraction. And the people were almost exclusively men. Men everywhere—clusters and clusters of them, hardly a woman in sight—and the men all dark: dark skins, dark hair, dark glasses, dark uniforms. Everyone in a uniform of some sort, and all those uniforms milling, shouting, leaning urgently toward one another, pouring whispers beneath the din into momentarily receptive ears, and everyone looking anxious, somehow as anxious as I felt. I can still remember that look of anxious, distracted worry that filled the hall with an urgency whose origins I could not hope to fathom. My heart sank. I couldn't help thinking: They know I'm American, yes, but they should only know . . .

I stepped up to Passport Control, papers dropping from my disorganized hands, managed to get my passport across the counter to the sunglassed uniform behind it, and felt relief flooding me when the uniform spoke.

"Ah, the lady is American! Welcome to Egypt. Welcome."

It wasn't his words, it was his voice. His voice was full of a surprising warmth—a *dry* warmth—that instantly set me at rest. And so it was with the next man, and the man after him, and the one who followed him. As I moved from one counter to the next, passing through that interminable line of customs checkers, one Egyptian after another dispelled the anxiety that the silent, unknown appearance of things had created. They all joked and flirted and clowned a bit, and there was in their words, in their gestures, in their tones, a warmth dry and light, too easy to be sinister, too humorous to be threatening, and I thought then: In this place I might be confused but never frightened.

My passport came back to me in good order, my baggage was waved on unopened, I signed two or three pieces of paper declaring my worldly goods in Egypt, passed through customs, and on out of the building. In the back seat of a taxi I leaned against the half-opened window into the warm wind. It cooled quickly as the driver drove very fast down wide dark roads into the suburb of Heliopolis, past Nasser's floodlighted mosque-tomb, and straight into the center of the half-darkened city.

I awoke in the clean-but-ratty *pension* room and stepped out onto a stone balcony for my first look at Cairo. There, below me, in the brilliant sunshine, lay the Nile, alive beneath a thousand pinpoints of light: deep, wide, blue-green, on its lovely banks palm trees low and tall, arching gracefully toward the alluring water as far as the eye could see; and bridges everywhere spanning the river, and busy intersections on either side of the bridges, and out in the river the beautiful park-island called Gezira; and over and above everything the astonishing noise of honking automobile horns that seemed to go on forever, almost as though people were driving with one hand on the wheel and one hand on the horn. The noise was deafening, and somehow ludicrous. What on earth was it all about?

I dressed and went down to the *pension* desk one floor below my room. The young man behind the desk was named Mahmoud and if there was anything I needed, anything at all. . . . Mahmoud had faintly troubled brown eyes and was about thirty coffee-colored pounds overweight. Although it was already very warm in Cairo I remember he was wearing a flannel shirt, a gray and maroon woolen pullover and a shabby blue pin-striped suit jacket buttoned tight across his bulging chest, as though it was necessary for him to wear everything he owned when he left his house each morning. His voice was soft and beads of sweat stood on his nose.

"Would you point me toward the center of town, please?" I said.

Mahmoud nodded politely, took a tourist map down from cne cf the cubbyholes behind him, and quickly mapped out a route for me. I thanked him, pocketed the map, and stepped out onto the street.

Mahmoud had said it was about a twenty-minute walk into the center of Cairo; my destination was Midan el Tahrir (Liberation Square). As I walked, my eyes darted hungrily about. The streets were filled with high stone buildings: old, narrow, close together, decorated with carved balconies and elaborate facades, all washed in a kind of yellow-gray clay, all shabby and disintegrated, the city having here the unmistakable look of decayed grandeur. Before each building entrance there was planted a narrow, free-standing brick wall about six feet high and two feet wide. (Later I discovered that these walls went up after the 1967 War and are meant to act as a measure of protection in the event of Israeli bombing. They stand before nearly every building in Cairo.)

I walked on. The people began to multiply rapidly, and also the shops . . . hundreds of tiny shops, mainly looking like open rectangles cut out of the walls, lining the streets, their painted Arabic signs worn or streaked on the space above their doors, their wares a mysterious mixture for me to sort out, crowded with people coming, going, buying, selling: cigarettes in wall cases, food in huge brass pots, electric lights being tested between two bricks in a wall, stacks and stacks of flat oriental bread in glass and wood cases, men drinking coffee at little tables set out on the sidewalk, pyramids of dusty canned goods, sweets being fried in deep brass dishes on marble counters, men ironing clothes behind cloth-covered tables in a hole in the wall, women walking wrapped in shroud-black with gleaming gold in their ears, men dressed in the long *gelabyas* (the traditional Arabic dress) of every color and condition, two-wheeled carts topped with open wooden frames and colored glass roofs and filled with mountains of steaming food, matches and jewelry laid out on handkerchiefs on the broken pavements, goats and donkeys threading their bowed-headed way through the crowds, everything coming faster and faster, thicker and thicker, and then suddenly there it was. Midan el Tahrir.

Midan el Tahrir is often shown in books on Cairo; in the photographs it is a polished circle of walkway with grass and flowers in the center, and wide traffic lanes all around, surrounded by the heart of downtown, business Cairo—the major airlines, the American University, the principal municipal buildings, shops of all kinds—everything looking neat and prosperous. What it looked like to me as I now stood at its edge:

Half the pavement broken up, rising dust steaming up on every side of the square continually; thousands of people without end moving in every direction conceivable around it, across it, over it, behind it; tram lines obviously bent on collision courses slamming toward one another; three lines of traffic running counter to one another, continuously in motion; nine thousand Fiats, donkeys, trucks, carts, bicycles darting every which way, matched only by the people who keep coming and coming and coming, also darting every which way. And the cars honking, honking, honking.

I stood there, unable to move, watching. The terrible look of poverty everywhere pierced me: the shops dense and filthy, the people looking like wretched peasants, the animals sickly, the children in rags, and everything moving with tumult and noise and the most fearful commotion. If it had a horn it was honking, if it had a whip it was cracking, if it had a voice it was yelling. The din was stupefying. And where were they all rushing to? And again, the sense of men everywhere, and women almost nowhere. Clusters and clusters of dark men: moving, talking, hurrying, many in *gelabyas*, some in dark blue or brown suits, and again, as at the airport, somehow transmitting a vague sense of worry—whether the suits were good or shabby, the men manicured or dirty, whether running or walking calmly with briefcases, all looked slightly breathless, edged with distraction, *worried*; the crowds and crowds of worried dark men . . . I stood there, transfixed.

It was now late and I was hungry. Mahmoud had said if I wished to eat something I should look for a café on the square called Astra. I spotted it now on the other side of three lines of tram tracks and after an abstracted moment of "How do I negotiate *this*?" my New Yorker's blind belief in the power of providential behaviorism asserted itself and I plunged in, weaving and leaping, halting and lunging, until I was on the other side of the square, directly in front of the café, right next to the American University and opposite a large municipal building called the Mogamaa.

The Astra was a long high-ceilinged room with frosted-glass windows and a few dozen tiny marble-topped tables scattered all around. Clearly, it had once been painted that institutional green so favored by government paint distributors the world over, but was now overlaid with the deep dirt of long, helpless neglect, its windows and walls streaked out of all original appearance. The men behind the food counter and at the cashier's desk and those waiting on tables looked exhausted, expressionless. I stood before the fly-smeared counter and stared down at finger-length cheese and meat sandwiches that looked encrusted; various kinds of salad that looked moldy; balls of fried bread crumbs containing God knows what; and I thought: If I touch any of this stuff I'll be dead before I reach the end of the street.

My entrance to the café confused the very black *gelabya*-clad waiters and the counterman, as well as the cashier; they buzzed around me. What was all the fuss? I wondered. Finally, I made it clear that I wished a cup of coffee, and—with a shrug of many shoulders—I was ushered to a little table in the middle of the room. The coffee was brought, I was left alone, and I looked around. Then I understood: I was literally the only woman in the place. Men in twos and threes and fours sat all around me drinking coffee, and talking. I thought: The waiters need hardly have worried—at least not here at the Astra. So intensely self-absorbed was the atmosphere in that room.

The men in the café were dressed mainly in the familiar, slightly shabby blue or brown suit, and three out of five wore black-rimmed glasses. Many had briefcases or books or newspapers with them. In some profoundly urban sense they seem oblivious to their surroundings. They leaned across the little tables toward each other, staring into each other's faces in a rapt, concentrated manner. Each man seemed to speak intently, almost urgently, lighting cigarette after cigarette. Each man's hands moved in expressive accompaniment to his words, and the faces of all were remarkably mobile, altering swiftly in successive attitudes of laughter, sobriety, concentration, rebuttal. No one seemed to take the conversation lightly. It was almost as though their very lives depended on the things they were saying; as though it were a matter of utmost importance that they communicate their thoughts *right now* in the most precise way possible. It reminded me at first of those conversations that go on among students or political radicals or artists late in the evening in all-night cafeterias in New York. But these men were neither students nor radicals, certainly not bohemians, and as I watched them my sense of irony began to evaporate. There was about these men a compelling quality. They seemed besieged, almost; as though flung about by pressures too great to bear, too vital to ignore; as though the city lived intensely within each one of them, and had become an anguishing frustration too intimate to name, too threatening to absorb; as though each one spoke out of need, terrible need, and the worry out on the street was here, too, inside each one of these shabby brown suits, filling the Astra Café with cubic force. Suddenly I found myself thinking: This isn't New York, this is more like some dusty, twentieth-century version of Dostoevsky's St. Petersburg. This is Russia between the wars, this is Chekhov country, this is good and ordinary men living inside a pressure cooker while the boyars look on and tell each other it'll never happen here. . . . I sat staring at the men in the Astra Café long after my coffee cup lay empty and forgotten on the little marble table.

Behind Midan el Tahrir, district after dense district unfolded, moving away from the river towards the city's desert edge. I wandered in a daze for the rest of the afternoon through crowded, dusty Arabic streets, speaking not a word, listening to the strangely soothing sound of a city living out its day in a fiercely foreign language.

In the evening I ate my dinner at the *pension* and went to bed early. The next morning I called Ali's mother, Soad Hamamsy, and Egypt began.

"Hello? Hello? Soad? Is that you?"

"Ah, *Vivi*-yaan! We have been waiting and waiting for your call! Where *are* you? We will come immediately."

"I'm in a *pension*." I gave her the location.

"Ah, yes. I know the place. Remain in your room. My son-in-law comes at one o'clock and we will then come for you."

"All right. Perhaps I will go for a short walk, but I will make sure I am back here at one."

"No! Do not do that. Stay where you are. It is not good for you to wander about by yourself. You will surely get lost."

"Well, that's all right. I can't get *that* lost."

"No! Please! Do not leave the room. Never mind. I know a way. We will be there at *eleven* o'clock. That is only one hour from now."

"No, no. Don't trouble yourself. I won't leave the room. Come at one."

"*La.* No. It is nothing. It is no trouble at all. We will be there at eleven."

I hung up and sat staring at the telephone. Her voice was wonderfully clear, and full of British English. But why on earth was she so fearful of my wandering about by myself? She had sounded as though I might actually be in danger simply walking about the streets. But from what would the danger come? From whom? And from where, in the sunlight of downtown Cairo? Soad's words, had I but known, were my first glimpse of the anxious shadows that flicker continuously in Egypt, licking at the minds of Cairenes, especially at the minds of Cairene women. Women who, surrounded by a thickness of home-bound life, find danger lurking in every solitary motion, every slight loneliness.

They came at eleven o'clock sharp, and sat in the *pension's* little dining room waiting for me: four of them, forming a right angle on hard-backed chairs against the green, streaked walls, two against one wall, two against the adjoining wall, upright and silent until they caught sight of me, then all in motion at once. An old woman, small and wrinkled; a younger woman, gray and middle-aged; a somewhat square, very dark, youngish man; another man in early middle age, who bore a remarkable resemblance to Robert Benchley: a bit below medium height, entirely round, small brown eyes, narrow nose and lips, pencil moustache, black fringe of hair surrounding a bald head, character in a fat chin that wobbled firmly.

The old woman was Soad, a bit of a shock to me as the picture I had seen of her in Cambridge showed a much younger and more forceful-looking person. The woman before me was almost tiny, her face a mass of wrinkles, her iron-gray hair combed tightly back and twisted into a bun at the back of her head, her eyes nearly colorless, covered with the film of uncertainty one sees in the eyes of people who have been suddenly overtaken by age; but the features in her face, slim and fine, revealed former beauty, and her eyes became clever and focused the moment she began to speak. She wore a shapeless black coat, slightly shabby, and she carried a black leather bag that hung by two narrow straps from her wrist. These straps pressed into my back as she embraced me, speaking a rapid-fire English that seemed to bind itself about me, even as her arms held me fast.

"Welcome to Egypt! Welcome! Welcome! Ali has given me *strict*—oh the strictest!—instructions to see that you are cared for, that you get what*ever* you need, that you go wher*ever* you want to go, that you see all and learn all and become acquainted with all that we have to offer in this Egypt of ours, that our entire family shall be *altoge*ther at your disposal and that we must do our very best to see that your slightest wish is granted." She pulled her head back, her arms still holding me, and laughter came into her eyes. "And all I ask is that you will sit with me one or two days and tell me about Ali Mahmoud. Is that agreeable to you?"

Everyone began to laugh at once and the dark, younger man said, "One or two days, *Om-Ali*? ° One or two months is more like it."

Soad threw her head back and laughed like a child, releasing me at the same time. Then she half-turned toward the others and said, "Now, already I have impolitely kept you from my family. This is my sister Samiha" (the other woman came forward shyly, hugging me briefly and saying, "Welcome, welcome" in the embarrassed accents of one who did not speak English) "and this is her son, Captain Magdi Al-Amir" (the younger man shook my hand, saying, "Welcome to Cairo, Miss Gornick") "and this is the Captain's friend, Mr. Fawzy Amr" (Robert Benchley came forward and in clipped British English said, "Welcome, madam, welcome").

I turned to the younger man. "Are you a captain in the Army?"

"Heaven forbid!" He laughed. "No, I am a police official."

"My dear madam," said Mr. Fawzy Amr, "no one who is actually doing something for Egypt is in the Army."

Soad didn't like that at all. She pursed her lips and said, "Come, come. We are not going to discuss policy her first five minutes in Egypt. There will be plenty of time, heaven alone knows, for *that*. Now, my dear. What are your plans? Do you wish to remain here in this *pension*, or did you have it in your mind to settle in other quarters?"

"No," I said. "I can't remain here. I was hoping to find an apartment of my own."

"In that case, may I make a suggestion? The Captain and his mother occupy a very spacious flat in Garden City, and in that flat is a spare bedroom, absolutely separate and most comfortable. Why do we not go right now to examine it, and if it suits you, you are welcome to it. After all, why should you waste your money, you are not really a rich American, are you?"

I had not expected anything like this for an answer, and I was at a loss for a ready response. On the one hand, it was all so easy; on the other . . .

° "Mother of Ali." A woman is often called "Mother of ——" (her eldest son). Om-Ali, coincidentally, is also the name of a famous Egyptian dessert.

The police captain, as though divining the cause of my hesitation, said, "Really, it is as my aunt says, comfortable and separate. I am away from Cairo nearly half the week, and my mother goes to Alexandria almost as often. So in effect, the flat would be yours much of the time. Why don't you come and have a look?"

With many thank-yous and not-at-alls on all sides, we set out, then, to see the flat. In the street in front of the *pension* we all piled into an old Mercedes-Benz and within minutes I was being driven through an entirely different section of Cairo from the one I had walked through the day before. Here, the avenues were wide and quiet, filled with blocks of apartments and large handsome old-fashioned houses, nearly all sandstone-colored. Palm trees reached into the sky and when I peered up at them through the windshield I saw they were shot through with sunlight at their tops. Black iron gates surrounded many of the houses, and between the houses and the gates masses of brilliant foliage, scarlet flowers, purple vines, all covered with the dull gleam of the sun. I kept turning and turning in my seat, my head a whirl of sunny reaching palm fronds, sensual warm air, dazzling sandstone. The houses were a cross between 1930s modern and some European notion of Moorish stony splendor. I wanted to laugh—it was impossible to take them seriously—and I delighted in the look of things.

"Where are we?" I asked.

"This is Garden City," the Captain answered. "The old British Governor's Residence is not far from where I live. The English built this part of Cairo, and lived here right up until the time they left, twenty years ago. Now, it is ours," he said, an ironic edge in his voice.

"Most of these houses are embassies," I suddenly realized, noticing golden plaques announcing Embassy of Sweden, Embassy of Morocco, Embassy of Italy, nailed onto half the iron gates.

"Exactly," the Captain said. "When the English went their houses were too big for Egyptians to keep up. So, *embassies.*"

The Mercedes-Benz came to a halt before a large buff-colored building with rounded corners and yellow iron shutters on all the windows; it stood opposite the gardens of the Indonesian Embassy, and down the curving street was a swatch of glittering Nile. Inside, the lobby was all stone floors, narrow stone steps and gold metal banisters. To the right of the entrance, affixed to the walls, were three rows of little wooden mailboxes with glass doors and an apartment number painted on each door. To the left was a stone bench built into the wall; two men in white turbans and brown *gelabyas* sat on the bench. They instantly jumped to their feet as we entered the building, nodding their heads in a kind of bowing motion and saying, "*Salaam, salaam.*" ° We all filed past the doormen, walked up one short half-flight of stairs, stopped before a massive wooden door decorated with a gold plate that bore Arabic writing (the name of the family) and entered a very spacious apartment that lay almost entirely in darkness. The lights went on and we were in a large foyer furnished with a small couch, one or two chairs and a coffee table. The couch was imitation zebra-striped leather and the coffee table held a vase full of plastic flowers.

The Captain moved swiftly to the left of the foyer and switched on the lights in an imitation crystal chandelier affixed to the ceiling of an oversized living room filled with overstuffed maroon-colored pieces of furniture with yellowing antimacassars pinned to their backs and arms, the kind of furniture that filled my parents' house when I was a child. When I looked closely, sure enough, there was the familar dim gold thread design in the maroon material. On the long floor lay three beautiful Persian rugs and at the far end of the room a magnificent antique desk. The entire left wall was taken up with long, graceful windows filled with tightly closed shutters. Beyond those shutters, I knew, lay balconies and the brilliant Cairo daylight.

We all sat on the maroon furniture, grouped around a glass-topped coffee table with lace doilies placed beneath the glass, and the Captain called sharply, "Sayeda!" A thin, slight girl, very dark with liquid eyes, appeared, dressed in a long blue-striped gown. I was asked: Tea or coffee? Tea. Sayeda disappeared, and seemed to reappear almost instantly with teacups, a teapot, milk and sugar on a lovely silver tray. She poured the black tea through a silver tea-strainer into each cup and withdrew from the room.

We drank the tea, everyone jabbering a great deal at once, Soad asking about my trip, Mr. Fawzy Amr saying madam four times in each sentence, the policeman telling me he would be grateful if I

° One of the many variants of the Arabic greeting (others are *ma'salaam* and *salaam waleikum*), it means hello, how are you, good day.

stayed so he could practice his English, Samiha bobbing her head at me and repeating, "Welcome." Tea over, we rose at once and proceeded down the hall to inspect the proffered bedroom. We passed a darkened dining room on one side of the hall and the narrow dimly lit kitchen where Sayeda was cleaning a primitive-looking stove on the other. Then three bedrooms fanned out at the end of the apartment. These rooms were a joy to behold: the shutters were open, and there was light, golden light, pouring into them. The furniture was, as they used to say, blond. It was like stepping into a 1932 budget movie. Beds, end tables, wardrobes, bureaus—all blond.

The bedroom being offered me was, as promised, comfortable and slightly separated from the other two, large enough to contain twin beds, a loveseat, a massive art deco wardrobe with a mirrored dressing table inserted in its center, and a window that looked out on the Indonesian gardens. Everyone stood around the room watching me take it in. As I moved about, opening drawers, looking out the window, switching on lamps, I began to feel that to say no would be a slap in the face, and indeed, when I said yes, it looked fine and I would be glad to accept their offer, it was as though a single exhalation of relieved breath from the four of them filled the room.

"Thank you very much, Mr. Al-Amir," I said.

"Please, Miss Vivian. Magdi. No Mr. Al-Amirs here. And you are most welcome. I hope you will be comfortable and entirely at your ease here. Well" (turning to the others) "*that* is settled."

Soad put her arms around me saying now I was one of the family, Magdi's mother beamed, and Fawzy Amr said it was time for lunch, and the Captain and I must honor him with our presence at an informal meal at his home; later in the day we could claim my luggage from the *pension* and by nightfall I would be fully installed in my new home.

It all seemed extraordinary, and yet at the same time entirely natural. I had the odd sensation that I was caught in some peculiar confusion of lives; as though something from another time and place had drifted into the atmosphere; for an instant I smelled nostalgia, curious and intense. Was it childhood I was being reminded of? No, not exactly. Home? No, that wasn't it either. . . . What? The whiff of indefinable familiarity drifted away; yet I couldn't shake it. I felt caught; fooled; puzzled.

No one in New York would act as these people were now acting, and yet I could not escape the sensation that they were remarkably like my own family. Was it that I thought this was how my mother would have acted had she been Egyptian? Perhaps. But that wasn't really it, either. What was being raised in me? It was almost as though I was experiencing the memory of something that had never actually happened. I didn't know, I simply didn't know.

We seemed to be leaving the city, and I turned to Fawzy Amr in the back seat of Magdi's Mercedes. "Where do you live?" I asked.

"In Heliopolis," Fawzy said, straining forward over his fat belly, his thick little legs widely separated on the narrow floor of the car. We watched together as Magdi drove, fast and honking, leaving the quiet villa-filled streets of Garden City quickly behind him, swooping down on one radically changing Cairo neighborhood after another—villas becoming high, narrow buildings, buildings becoming crumbling shops, shops becoming tumbledown mud houses—threading his way finally through streets that had given way to dirt lanes alive with women in black, men in *gelabyas*, donkeys, goats, ragged children, dozens of glass-topped carts offering a variety of foods, coming at last onto a wide broken street that lay in the shadow of the ancient walls of the city, and moving then onto a road headed for the Mukkattam Hills, Cairo's natural northern boundary, and the smell of desert beyond. We drove swiftly along for a time, passing an extraordinary cemetery filled with tombs that looked like houses (one of the famous Egyptian Cities of the Dead) and in the warm wind filling the car I asked Fawzy why he lived such a distance from the city.

"Ah, Heliopolis is lovely, Miss Vivian. Lovely. There one can *breathe*, as opposed to Cairo where the air is a stinking offense! And the *crowds*, the crowds destroy a man's mind! Also, I happen to like my wife, and my mother does not happen to like my wife, and so we put as great a distance between the two lovely ladies as we possibly can. Peace! Peace is everything!"

Magdi turned to me: "I also live in Heliopolis."

"What do you mean?"

"My wife and children live in Heliopolis. I am divorcing my wife, so right now I am living in the flat in Garden City, but I have lived in Heliopolis for ten years."

We drove in silence for another fifteen minutes and then we were winding through the streets of Heliopolis, which looked like Garden City, only more so: wide, sparsely populated streets filled with sandstone villas, palm trees, poinsettias, heliotrope and sun streaking brilliantly through the green-and-mustard-colored streets. Here, more than ever, the look of an old-fashioned movie about the British in the Middle East: the houses vast baroque fantasies, indulgences of Europeans in the desert; monumental sand carvings and George Brent on the veranda. I felt like giggling.

We pulled up before a high iron gate half covered in vines; beyond, a square yellow-gray house five stories high with square balconies jutting out. Fawzy told me the house was a block of flats built only a few years ago, but it looked no different than houses I'd been told were seventy-five years old. We walked down a narrow path inside the gate, climbed four flights of stone steps to the wooden and glass door that unlocked Fawzy's castle, and stepped into a large rather dark room with frosted-glass doors all around. Fawzy began shouting into the hidden recesses of the house. Immediately, three children came running from around an open doorway to the right I had not immediately seen: two boys and a slim little girl, dancing eagerly about Fawzy, shouting, "Poppy! Poppy!" Fawzy laughed delightedly as the children climbed all over him, saying in English, "Stop it! Stop all this. We have an American guest. What will she think of Egyptian fathers and their uncontrollable children. Hm-m-m? Hm-m-m?" The little girl, for whom the English had obviously been spoken, immediately became quiet and stood before me, calm and polite. She stretched out her hand and said, "How do you do. I'm Sohair. I am *so* pleased to meet you."

Sohair's English was as delicate and dignified as she. She was nine or ten years old, very slim and straight, with deep-set shining black eyes and black hair pulled back behind her ears, tied at the neck and falling between her shoulder blades like a silky black snake.

Fawzy said, "Sohair, this is Miss Vivian. She is a friend from America, a friend of Uncle Magdi's cousin, Ali Mahmoud. Do you remember Ali Mahmoud?"

"Of course I do not remember Ali Mahmoud," Sohair said gently.

"I was only four years old when he went away, Poppy." Her tone was clearly that of one attempting to save another from his own foolishness.

Fawzy rolled his eyes at me. "Oh. Of course," he said to his precocious daughter. "How stupid of me." And then: "Come. Come. Why are we all standing here in this most unaccommodating place?" And he led the way through the glass door nearest us on our left into the Amr sitting room.

The room was square and high-ceilinged with a gray stone floor, gray plastered walls, two gray-shuttered windows, and gray-shuttered french doors that led out onto a balcony. Among the furniture were three or four pieces to sit upon, all at such great distances from one another that the room looked half-empty: two wing chairs under the windows, covered in gray-blue imitation brocade; against the opposite wall a couch with a highly curved back covered in the same material; against another wall a massive mahogany sideboard, very old-fashioned and ungainly upon its high clawed legs; against its opposite wall on one side of the french doors a small high table with a double-doored drawer in it: on the table a shortwave radio; on the other side of the french doors a hard-backed chair with an upholstered seat, looking like a cut-out against the gray wall. All in all, the room looked like the natural setting for a turn-of-the-century family portrait. Clearly, Fawzy's economic and social circumstances were a number of cuts below those of the owners of the Garden City flat.

We all sat down, Magdi and I in the wing chairs, Fawzy and the children on the couch, the little boys shyly hiding their heads in their father's lap. In a few moments, a woman entered the room and Fawzy rose to introduce his wife, Mona, and to explain rapidly that Mona spoke perfect French but her English was nonexistent.

Mona looked like Fawzy's daughter, not his wife. She was a woman of perhaps twenty-five, small with a slim sexy body, short brown hair, sallow skin and the slightly flattened, slightly thickened features that are unmistakably Egyptian. She was wearing a light blue nylon sweater, a plaid skirt that stopped at her kneecaps and scuffed pointed-toe black high heels. She looked like a tired, slightly sloppy American typist of ten years ago, and I expected her behavior to reflect the faintly sullen expressionlessness with which she had entered the room. But when Fawzy explained me to her, her face was suddenly transformed by a smile of deep swee'ness and she came forward eagerly to shake my hand and make me welcome in her home.

Magdi now had the children all over him. An amazing change had taken place in him. No sooner had he entered Fawzy's house than he seemed visibly to relax, and the formality of the morning disappeared. He laughed a great deal now—a high, piercing laugh strangely at odds with his dark solidity—over what I couldn't tell as the bantering was all in Arabic.

"These children," Magdi said to me in mock sternness. "Terrible. Terrible."

Mona sat on the couch, smoking: her legs crossed, swinging the one off the ground, her toes hooked around the black shoe half off her foot. Fawzy sat beside her, stiff and fat, his eyes almost beady, watching me watching everything.

"Fawzy, what sort of work do you do?" I asked.

"Quality control, madam. I am in charge of quality control in a paper plant. A wretched business. Truly wretched."

"Why so?"

"Ah, madam. The days when a man could take pride in his own effort are gone in Egypt, entirely gone. Socialism, madam." (Fawzy struggled forward on the couch.) "Socialism is the *scourge* of the earth, and now it is the scourge of Egypt. The government guarantees every job in my plant. No one cares. No one takes pride in the work. No one *works*. My superiors are vain and corrupt, insufferable in their incompetence. And those below me are *criminal* in their negligence."

"Well," I said lamely, "all these things take time. After all, these last twenty years are the first in two thousand that Egypt has ruled herself. Surely," I laughed, "you're not saying things were better under the British?"

Fawzy's eyes became beads of fever; his cheeks puffed out as his lips tightened; he strained at his collar and his arms quivered with the effort to remain still. He took the plunge: "Yes, madam! That is *exactly* what I am saying. Under the British there was order and pride and work done beautifully. Beautifully. Now, under these creatures of Satan, these despots that only the Middle East could produce, life in Egypt is an *offense*, an offense against God and man."

"Enough of that nonsense," Magdi said curtly. "Let's eat."

Mona motioned with her arm toward the doorway as though to say: All is ready. I only await your pleasure. We all stood and trooped out of the sitting room, across the dark room-sized foyer and through a glass door on the other side. Here, also a square high-ceilinged room with shutters tightly closed against the bright broad day, the room entirely lit by electric light. On the long mahogany table surrounded by high-backed upholstered chairs the "informal" lunch was laid out: large plates of fried chicken, mounded rice, stacked flat bread, stuffed grape leaves, lettuce-and-tomato salad, vegetables in meat and tomato sauce, fried potatoes. There was enough food for fifteen people.

We seated ourselves and Mona reached over to the sideboard behind her for a stack of soup plates, handing one to each of us. At that moment a woman who looked as though she'd just finished scrubbing every floor in the house entered, carrying a tureen. She set it down and Mona began to serve.

Fawzy leaned over the bowl, sniffed, and began to beam.

"Ah, this is a rare treat," he said happily. "In honor, as it were, of your most welcome arrival in Egypt, Miss Vivian. *Molochaya!* The first of the season. Here. Try it. Now, you must put lots of rice or bread in it, almost so that you are eating rice or bread soaked in *molochaya*. The *molochaya*, as you see, is like a green grass soup. It is a plant, boiled in water, with lots of garlic; the longer it is cooked, the better it tastes. This is a true Egyptian dish, one we are all extremely fond of."

I hated it. Fully expecting to enjoy myself, I took a heaping spoonful of the stuff into my mouth, and nearly spit it back into the bowl. It was a thick gelatinous substance the texture of mucus, slimy and disgusting to me. A moment of panic, while the awful stuff glued itself to the inside of my mouth, then: I swallowed.

"Oh," said Sohair quietly. "I believe Miss Vivian does not like *molochaya*."

Mona stared wordlessly at me.

Fawzy became very agitated: "Take it away. Take it away from her. Now, now. Do not be distressed. It is an educated taste. You must not eat anything you do not like. There is plenty for you to choose from. Plenty."

Magdi glowered. "What? You do not like *molochaya*? Inconceivable. These Americans!" He brought all his fingertips together and raised them to his mouth. "They have no *taste*. No taste whatever."

Fawzy laid down his spoon and regarded his friend in silence for a moment. "This man," he said to me. "This man, madam, is a beast of the first order, capable of un*believ*able brutality. But," he looked blissfully at his friend, "I cannot do without him. What is to be done? I simply cannot do without him."

Mona, meanwhile, was silently heaping my plate with chicken and rice and grape leaves and salad. I ate heartily, grateful that I liked everything else on the table, not putting down my fork until I felt more than full.

"What?" said Fawzy, eating nonstop himself. "You must eat more. Why, you have only eaten a few spoonfuls."

"Really, I can't eat any more," I protested. Fawzy looked so hurt that I took up my fork once more.

"Miss Vivian, you eat like a bird," he said when I had finished a second plate, and indicated that I would not go on.

"I can't, Fawzy. I'm stuffed."

"Just a bit more," he pleaded, while he kept shoveling heaps of rice and bread soaked in vegetable sauce down his own throat. "Just finish the food on your plate." I looked down. My plate had been refilled.

An hour and a half after we first sat down to eat I struggled to my feet, and left the room. I was searching for a sink to wash my hands in and opened a glass door I thought would lead to a bathroom. Instead, I found myself in an extraordinary room, a room that was small and bright (the shutters unaccountably open), and filled to overflowing with books. On shelves, on tables, on the windowsill: books from floor to ceiling. Some in good condition, some in bad condition, some neatly piled, some flung one on top of another, some covered with dust, some carefully wiped clean. I went closer. There were books in French, books in German, mainly books in English. There were Balzac and Stendhal and Maupassant, as well as Gide and Rousseau, and Tolstoy and Dostoevsky in French; there were Austen and Hardy and Hume and Strachey and Maugham and

Churchill; there were Twain and Steinbeck and Hemingway; there was an account of the Napoleonic expedition to Egypt tucked in between two German economics books, and there were Alan Moorehead's books on the Nile, as well as Julian Huxley's writings on the Middle East. The room was unmistakably Fawzy's. It *looked* like him: fat and disheveled, full of appetite and disconnected opinion . . . and something else, too. An odd mustiness, some curious stillness at the center of the room I could not identify, something off-center and hidden away, something beating its wings in a cage no one is looking at. The sensation had come upon me swiftly, and caused me a surprising pang, sharp and stilling. For, generally one feels nourished and at the warm center in a room full of books.

I withdrew quickly, closed the door, finally found the bathroom, and later joined everyone in the sitting room for tea. Magdi and Mona were on the couch, speaking Arabic intently to each other. The children were playing together, and Fawzy sat in a wing chair, smoking. I fell into the other wing chair and said lightly, jerking my thumb in the direction of the little room, "I see you are fond of books, Fawzy."

Fawzy jumped as though he'd been shot. "Ah," he said, "you have discovered my little library, my most impoverished excuse for a library. Fond of books, madam! *Fond* of books." He leaned forward, one fat, oddly delicate hand on one thick little knee. "They are my life," he said with dramatic quiet, "my very life." He stood up and walked quickly over to the mahogany sideboard on the other side of the room, flinging the doors open as he reached it. In place of china, glasses, silverware, liquor bottles, whatever one finds in such a piece of furniture, there were books, dozens of books stuffed into the shelved spaces of the sideboard. Fawzy stood before his books, looking at them, then at me, then back at the books. "Hm-m-m? Hm-m-m?" he said excitedly. He rushed over to the table on which the shortwave radio sat, his cigarette in his mouth, ash spilling onto his shirt front as he knelt before the little table and with both hands pried open the doors beneath the flat surface. Books spilled onto the floor. He stood before them, again looking at the books, then at me, then back at the books. I followed his gaze in amazement, looking at the books, then at him, then at the books. He was like an alcoholic suddenly revealing all his secret places for stashing the precious forbidden stuff—and I couldn't tell if he was asking me to admire his cleverness in acquiring such cunning storehouses, or if he was in the throes of bitter admission to a shameful compulsion.

"Fawzy!" Mona cried, rolling her eyes to the ceiling and slapping her knee, as if to say: There he goes again.

"Ah, Fawzy has found a friend," chimed in Magdi. "Is Miss Vivian as interested in books as you are?" and the handsome police captain, suddenly looking dark and forceful and utterly philistine, threw back his head and laughed.

Fawzy was silent, panting slightly, his head bobbing rapidly from his books, to Mona and Magdi, to me, and back again. He sat in his chair and looked at me for a long moment.

"You see, madam," he said woefully, "I am alone. Utterly alone. You have come here to write a book about Egypt, yes? Well, then, put that in your book. Yes, you must put *that* in your book. A man in Egypt who loves books is alone, alone, alone."

Magdi and I drove back to Cairo in the dying sunlight.

"You mustn't take Fawzy too seriously," he said as we were passing the City of the Dead. "He is a wonderful man but he loves to make people think he is a miserable creature, misunderstood by everyone around him. But I assure you, we—his wife and I—understand him very well."

"How old is his wife?" I asked.

"She is twenty-six," he said, and threw me a sharp look. "And he is forty-three. Something strange to an American? They have been married ten years, and believe me, they are very good for each other. Mona was a girl just out of school when Fawzy married her. She knows nothing of the world, nothing. But she is intelligent and she understands her life very well. She knows very well how to manage both her house and her husband. There are many women like Mona in Egypt. Many. And Fawzy? With all his 'intellectual' moaning and groaning he is like a baby. He is *entirely* useless in a crisis. Not only will he instantly go into a panic but he will not stop until he drives *you* into a panic. Believe me, he cannot even boil water, and if he should cut his little finger . . . He needs Mona, and he knows it. I love him, I love them both, they are more like my family sometimes than my own family."

"What is *your* wife like?" I asked.

"She is a good girl," he said quickly, "a very good girl. She is beautiful, educated, she speaks three languages, she comes from a good family, she is half-European, she is a good mother to the children, and—she is a good girl," he ended lamely.

"Why are you divorcing her?"

"Because she gives me no peace," Magdi burst out unexpectedly. I turned full in my seat to look at him. His face had grown darker and he was evidently trying to control himself. He swallowed whatever it was that was trying to swallow him, looked shyly at me, and laughed. He spoke again, more calmly now, but with an intensity that took me by surprise and made me ache for him.

"I guess it was all my fault, really. I guess I spoiled her from the very beginning. I gave her everything I could. And she wanted more, and more, and more. And finally she asked for what I *could* not give. Not to her, not to anyone." He looked as though he could not puzzle out his own thoughts. "Not even to myself," he said.

The telephone woke me, ringing and ringing through all the empty rooms of the apartment in Garden City where I lay sleeping for the seventh morning in a row. It was Soad calling.

"Now, my dear Vivian," she pealed, "you are in Egypt one week already and you have taken your lunch with us only once. This condition must be corrected at once. If you have no urgent plans today you must come here."

"Yes," I mumbled, still half-asleep, thinking: *Lunch? Why lunch?* (It had been difficult for me to adjust to the fact that the main meal in Egypt is lunch at three in the afternoon, not dinner at seven in the evening.)

"Yes, Soad, I'll be there. I'll come at two."

A week has gone by. An incredible week filled with Hamamsys. It is as though they have all formed some huge circular net, and I have fallen from a great height, and am bouncing now on the bottom of their hospitality. They are everywhere: if one lets go even for a moment, there is another waiting to catch me.

Soad is the queen mother. She, at sixty-six, is the oldest of six living children; her sister, Leila, is the forty-three-year-old baby. In between there are two other sisters—Magdi's mother, Samiha, and Haifa—as well as two brothers: Monir, an engineer in his early sixties, and Salah, an elegant fiercely proud man in his forties whose business was nationalized ten years ago. Around these six there is gathered a pride of husbands and wives, and a wilderness of children. Everyone has been married at least twice (divorce—easily acquired by Moslem men—and death take an incredible toll in Egyptian marriages), and children have issued from every single attachment formed. Nearly all of the Hamamsys live in Zamalek.

Zamalek. It is a section of Cairo located on Gezira Island in the Nile, somewhat like Queens in relation to Manhattan. Once, I suppose, it was an idyllic suburb of some sort: one crossed the bridge into Zamalek and left the city behind; certainly, this was true for the British, who lived here in great numbers from 1875 until they left Egypt in 1952 when Nasser came to power, and here built the country clubs they (and now the Egyptians) called "sporting clubs," the most famous among them being the elegant Gezira Sporting Club planted in the midst of a huge, lovely, somewhat jungle-ish park on the edge of Zamalek. Her Majesty's Army officers must be turning over in their graves at the thought of the fat Egyptian matrons who now sit lolling at the edge of the club's pool while their engineer–doctor–factory-foreman–Army-officer husbands prance about the tennis courts and drink whiskey-and-soda at the bar. (In reply to which most Egyptians would say "*Inshallah.*" [God willing].)

Zamalek itself—older than Garden City—is also a mixture of former European grandeur and Arabic street life, as well as Egyptian middle-class life. While there is a good deal of new building going on now in Zamalek, its streets are mainly filled with fifty-year-old villas, gardens, and five-story blocks of flats, all spacious and well made with stone floors and lovely glass, high ceilings and carved balconies, hanging mosses and curving palm trees in the gardens—and all weeping with neglect and disrepair, and the memory of a time when a colonial owner would determine upon a particular effort at repair, and that effort would bear fruit.

On the business streets of Zamalek moves the vivid stream of Arabic life whose particularities are available to the eye in a way they aren't in the dense dusty streets of downtown Cairo; Shara Hassan Sabry, the major street of Zamalek, actually wide yet oddly narrow in the mind, dotted with fruit stores before which are piled gleaming pyramids of oranges, pears, bananas; open rectangles in which men and boys sit patiently sewing the intricate designs on embroidered *gelabyas*; bakeries from which there perpetually floats the smell of freshly baked bread: both the flat oriental kind and the long, narrow, soft "french" kind; shoe stores; cigarette kiosks; ice-cream stands; stationery stores; windows with bolts of cloth gracefully unrolled; little stand-up restaurants before which are planted the charcoal-broiling *sha-werma*° works. And everything overlaid with a thickness of dust and grime, and the rushing movement of Cairo.

Just off Hassan Sabry, in a narrow, quiet street where ragged and well-dressed children play ball together and men push broken-down Mercedes, and a *gelabya*-clad man irons clothes in a hole in the wall, and the air is somehow still and warm, and the languid smell of the nearby Nile comes drifting toward you, is the house in which Ali Mahmoud was born and raised. Here, Soad Hamamsy has lived for more than thirty years, through two marriages, one revolution, and innumerable births, deaths, and crises. Here, she raised her children, lost her husbands, said good-bye to the British, lived through the turmoil of the last twenty years, and now writes to her son in the United States.

Soad's home is a five-room flat on the fourth floor of a tall gray house with an ornate facade whose entrance is down a narrow stone path off the street. The elevator in the house—like all the elevators in Cairo—is an open-work wire-cage affair that ascends but does not descend (it must be called down from the first floor). On the fourth

---

° A huge hunk of lamb stuck through a thick iron spit and placed before a vertically standing bed of coals; as the spit turns and the lamb cooks, slices are shaved from the meat and served up as sandwiches in small soft rolls. *Sha-werma* comes from Syria, and Egyptians often say it is the only concrete result of the short-lived union between Syria and Egypt.

floor you ring the bell before the scratched wooden door to the right of the elevator and Soad or her daughter Gasbia, or one of Gasbia's children, or Soad's sister Samiha, or Gasbia's husband "the Doctor," or an old servant will open the door to admit you to a tremendous central hall (or *salon*, as Egyptians call it), high-ceilinged and stone-floored, one wall of which is covered with long, frosty windows that do not admit any real light, and three walls of which are covered with doors leading to all the other rooms in the house: three bedrooms, a sitting room, a dark primitive little kitchen, and a large bathroom. In the middle of this central hall there stands a long table covered with a tired piece of oilcloth: on this table the family takes all of its meals. Off the bedrooms and the sitting room are stone balconies that look down onto the gardens below. When Soad first moved here she could see the Nile from two of her balconies, but she will point now to the two tall houses across the garden that have wiped the lovely river off the face of her view.

Soad lives in her flat with her daughter Gasbia, who is Ali's half-sister, Gasbia's husband Ibrahim, and their three children. Gasbia's children occupy the bedroom that was Ali Mahmoud's, and one of the real questions in Gasbia's mind is what will happen to all of them when Ali comes home.

Gasbia, also, is a shock to me when we meet. Ali had spoken often of her, and although there had been a bitter edge to the humor with which he had described their lifelong feud, I had imagined her to be cool, slim, willful. The woman who throws her arms around me in a shriek of welcome when I first come to Soad's flat is very small, very fat, her dark skin coarse and somewhat mottled, her features like those of a hook-nosed, sad-eyed American Indian. She is as unlike Soad in appearance—who is very light and looks European—as she is unlike Ali Mahmoud—who is all olive-skinned smoothness. (Until the day I leave Egypt I will continue to be amazed at the variety of color and feature that ranges across nearly every Egyptian family, running from pure African to pure European in a single set of brothers and sisters.) Gasbia's looks are even more alarming as her little fat body is dressed in a pair of brilliant blue stretch pants and an acetate cerise print overblouse, while her face is heavily adorned with pancake makeup, black eyeliner, blue shadow and deep red lipstick. On her wrist there is a gold bracelet, around her neck a gold chain and in her ears gold hoops.

"Welcome! Welcome!" she shrieks in a strangely hoarse voice, her eyebrows drawn together in an inexplicable frown of worry. Has something happened? I wonder. But, no. I will soon discover that this expression is Gasbia's constant companion.

Gasbia's husband Ibrahim, a druggist invariably referred to as "the Doctor," comes straggling out of one of the bedrooms, in bare feet and his undershirt, hastily buckling his pants belt over his huge belly. Ibrahim, a large fat man, is startlingly "pretty"; his skin is a rich, smooth, yellowish-brown; his eyes are large and liquid-dark, thickly fringed with black velvet lashes; his cheeks, nose, and mouth, small and well made. Below his nose a narrow black moustache, on his head thick black curly hair just beginning to thin at the crown. He looks forty-five and Gasbia looks fifty; actually, he is thirty-five and she is forty-three.

Ibrahim's voice is a slow, dolorous whine in complement to Gasbia's hoarse shriek. "You mo-o-ost. Call on us. At enny-time," he says in heavily accented English, his eyes blinking rapidly. "En-n-ny . . . time. Whatever you need. You mo-o-ost call. You. Are one of the family. Now." Gasbia stands beside him, dancing about on her little feet, nodding eagerly. "Yess, yess, yess," Gasbia shrieks softly. "One of the family now!" What a couple they make. She looks like a pig, he looks like a bear. Why do they seem so well matched? Within minutes I am stung with guilt at my ungenerous thoughts. They are so good-natured! They are all over me in a welter of kindliness, offering me food, love, transportation, entertainment, sightseeing tours, relaxation, instruction (don't-buy-anything-without-us-we-can-get-it-for-you-wholesale). Anything. Anything. Nothing is too good for Ali's friend from America. Children, come kiss Auntie Vivian! Nahed, bring cake! Bring tea! Bring! Bring! Bring!

Ibrahim works five days a week from eight in the morning until two in the afternoon at a pharmacological factory on the road to Heliopolis and six nights a week from seven to ten at one of the largest nationalized drugstores in downtown Cairo. Gasbia is a secretary at the Hilton.

"Ah, it is a very hard life," Gasbia complains. "We must work,

work, work, Poppy and I, just to keep the roof over our heads and bread in our mouths and the children in the German school. People think we make a lot of money, but they do not understand! It costs me two pounds a day to keep the house running. *Two pounds a day!*" At the incredulous thought of two pounds a day her voice rises to a positive frenzy.

Ibrahim, on the other hand, is not as interested in complaining about the financial difficulty of his life as he is in giving me the benefit of his expert advice.

"You mo-o-ost not write only of the upper classes," he says in his slow, ponderous whine. "You mo-o-ost inspect all the ways of life in Egypt. All the ways. You mo-o-ost not know only the upper classes." I look at him—sitting in his undershirt at the oilcloth-covered table in the large hall in this apartment that looks as my peasant grandmother's apartment would have looked had she lived to make that great social leap from the immigrant's initial slum dwelling on New York's Lower East Side to a four-room apartment in the Bronx—and it takes a moment to sink in: Ibrahim means himself and his family when he says the upper classes. In time, it will become abundantly clear to me that the Egyptian definitions of middle class and upper class are very nearly as blurred as the American ones are; that people whom I would classify as lower middle class or even, in some instances, working class—by virtue of their tastes, ambitions, values, not to mention their incomes—consider themselves of the middle class; that, in fact, anyone who speaks English in Egypt—that is, anyone with any education at all—is automatically of the middle class, undershirts and oilcloth-covered tables notwithstanding.

But it is only when we are in the car, he and I, driving back to Garden City that first night, that Ibrahim dares broach his real subject:

"Do you wish to know only official Egypt or do you wish to know the secret ways of Egypt?" When he says "secret" I don't know what he means; but his voice is positively sly so I strain to figure it out fast.

"What do you mean, secret ways of Egypt?" I ask finally.

"Well." He smiles smugly. "In Egypt the men cannot know the women, and the women cannot know the men. So there are special flats where men can know women, and women can know men. Some men *own* these flats. I have ways of gaining entrance to one or two of these flats. Would you like to see them?"

"Do *you* own one of these flats?"

Ibrahim looks quickly at me, his sallow face blushing in the lights of the bridge; we are halfway across the Nile at this point.

"Ah, madam," he sighs, "that is a dangerous question in Egypt. A most dangerous question." And I know that he doesn't own one of the flats and this conversation seems suddenly sad and shabby rather than merely lecherous.

"We have whorehouses in America, Ibrahim," I say. "I don't really want to see an Egyptian whorehouse."

"Are you interested in the hashish?" Ibrahim goes on blandly.

"Not right now, Ibrahim. I'll let you know when."

The entire Hamamsy clan contains just such a range of bizarre contrasts as exists among Soad and her daughter Gasbia and her son Ali. In personality, occupation, economics, taste and politics they are—as many Egyptian families are—as different, one from another, within their Egyptianness, as it is possible to be. For instance, take Salah.

One morning during the week, when Magdi was in Cairo, the doorbell rang in Garden City and vigorous steps came clicking down the stone hallway toward our bedrooms. Magdi was in the bathroom and I was at the mirror in my room combing my hair. Through the mirror I saw in the doorway behind me a man standing there, asking if Magdi was at home.

"Yes, he is," I said. The man was tall and slim, with narrow handsome features set in his entirely bald head. He was wearing a dark-blue pin-striped suit cut in the English manner, with a vest and a cravat beneath his jacket, a snowy white collar, pearl-gray gloves, pointed-toe black shining shoes, and he held a walking stick in one hand. His eyes were green and amazingly clear, somewhat like flattened marbles. They looked as though they had the power to penetrate at will whatever they fell upon. Yet, oddly enough, there was in them an expression of expectation, as though the man behind those eyes was waiting for something; but waiting like some great cat: tense, wary, highly controlled.

"I am Salah," the man said. "Ali's younger uncle. Perhaps Ali mentioned me to you in America? He worked for me once, on a small piece of land that I own."

"Oh, yes!" I said with relief. I *did* know who he was. Was *this* what he was waiting for? "Of course I remember you. Ali spoke often of how you all made a farm out of a piece of desert, and the *work* it took to do it."

Salah looked pleased. His stern face was split by a smile, and he said, "Ah, yes. I taught that boy how to work! Because I demand *perfection*. Something very few people in Egypt know anything about. *Perfection*. I set him a problem to solve on the land, and he knew he must work until that problem was solved—to perfection! But come, come." Salah was removing his gloves, finger by finger, and moving away from the doorway. "Come into Magdi's room where we may sit in comfort."

I followed him into the bedroom on the other side of the hall where a low table and chairs were set before the window. Here, when Magdi was home, we drank coffee in the morning and tea in the evening.

Now, Salah sat down on one side of the table, carefully straightening the crease in his trousers as he crossed his legs; I plopped into the chair opposite him.

"Ah, America is a wonderful country," he said, "a wonderful country."

"Oh?" I said.

"Don't you agree?" he said.

"It has its points," I said.

"Ah, one is never grateful for what one has. I spent five years in America, five wonderful years. I learned everything there was to know about American production. The men I worked with! Wonderful. Wonderful. There is nothing those men set out to do that they cannot do. Nothing. Organization. Precision. Decision. That is America! I came back here and I set up a factory; I used what the Americans had taught me: not to follow blindly but to adapt your methods to the available material and labor around you. I took American methods and I made them work the Egyptian way. I didn't try to bring in machines that no one would know how to operate. No! I taught Egyptian men how to do the jobs of machines and I put more men to work in my factory than five other businesses combined could do. And it worked beautifully. Beautifully. That factory was my whole life, I worked day and night. I was everywhere at once, night and day, night and day, seeing to a thousand details. My wife—I was married then—was very jealous. She thought I was out with other women. But no. I was in the factory. And then . . ." Salah paused dramatically, flicked a cigarette from a package, tapped it gently on his sleeve, lit it and looked up at me. "And then," he said, "they took it all away from me, and they threw me out."

I stared at him.

"You cannot believe it?" he smiled ironically. "Believe it. Believe it. It is true of half of Egypt. They took what *I* had built, and they threw me out. And I *knew* them. I knew them all. I was an officer in the Army at the time of the revolution. I knew them all."

"What have you been doing since then?" I asked after a long moment.

"Egypt is now a country in which human rights count for nothing," Salah went on exactly as though I had not spoken. "*Nothing.*"

Magdi walked into the room, wrapped in a terry-cloth robe, rubbing his thick wet hair with a towel.

"Salah!" he said with pleasure.

I looked up at him. The variousness of Magdi's looks never failed to amaze me. Sometimes, his features were thick and squat, his lips almost purple, his skin dark and lightless, unbelievably ugly. And sometimes, as now, when he was advancing toward the brilliant light of the window where we sat, his face was incredibly smooth, coffee-and-milk colored, his eyes rich and brown and magnetizing, and he a force in the room.

"My dear Magdi," said Salah, obviously equally pleasured by the sight of his nephew. "I have come to invite you to a birthday party."

"Whose?" said Magdi, still intent on rubbing his scalp.

"Monir's. He is sixty-four years old this Saturday. I do not know if I would choose to celebrate such an unwelcome age, but he does. Or rather his wife does. So you are all invited for the evening."

Magdi laughed, and pulled up a chair beside us.

"How are things going, Salah?"

Salah looked speculatively at his nephew, and made his decision: "I believe I am about to win my case," he said quietly.

"No!" Magdi's voice was astonished.

"Yes! Would you believe it. They seem ready to recognize my rights. I received a letter today directing me to appear at the Ministry next Thursday and indicating that my case was about to be reviewed favorably." Salah turned to me. "As you are a stranger here, I will relate the details to you. For ten years I have been fighting the government. I wish them to recognize the fact that I must be given a job at the same level of money and responsibility as the one at which I stopped working. And now, for the very first time, they seem ready to listen. I would *not* give in, and now they seem ready to concede. All these years I have refused to work as they wished me to work. I went away and I threw myself into work on the land. How lucky for me that I had the land! But now it appears that I may come back, after all!"

Magdi ordered Sayeda to bring tea, and congratulated Salah vigorously. He asked many questions about the case, but in a noticeably distant and discreet manner: odd in the midst of such intimacy. In a while Salah stood up, brushed off his jacket carefully, and said he must be going. After the door had closed behind him, Magdi and I sat drinking our tea.

"I am the only one he still comes to see," Magdi said. "Because, you know, once, when he owned his factory, everybody gave him great recognition, and *now* . . ." He shrugged his shoulders. "But I still listen to him exactly as though it were yesterday. He was everything to me once. I followed him everywhere, I dressed as he dressed, I even spoke as he spoke. When he ran for office the whole family went wild, but none more so than I."

"What kind of office did he run for?"

"He ran as the representative from Garden City to our so-called Congress, the Arab Socialist Union. We worked like dogs, all of us, and he would have won, he would have won. He *did* win."

"What happened?"

"Nasser didn't like Salah. At the last minute he produced another candidate and instructed everyone to vote for him. That was the end. Salah was finished. He retreated then to the farm, and almost from the world. He stopped speaking to people, he went nowhere, I don't think he even has women anymore."

"No, I don't think so either."

Magdi looked quickly at me. "He is very handsome," he said.

"Yes," I said, "but his looks are dreadfully cold, there is no warmth, no sex, nothing alive in them."

"You are right." He sighed, and lit a cigarette.

On the following Saturday Magdi and Samiha and I went to Zamalek to Monir's birthday party.

Monir's family occupied an enormous apartment on the ground floor of an ornate four-story building two blocks away from Soad's house. Across the hall from Monir lived Monir's and Soad's sister Haifa with *her* brood: her second husband and three grown children (each the offspring of a separate attachment), one of whom was married and now lived in the apartment with his wife and infant son as well. The two families, naturally, mingled together often. Which is not to say that they *liked* each other, necessarily. Only that they *saw* each other continually.

When Magdi and Samiha and I walked into Monir's house on Saturday the party was in full swing, dominated by that unmistakable look of a family gathering: the same face stamped out on male, female, young, old; children running about underfoot; food continually being passed around; the young talking with the young, the old with the old, occasionally a young woman pulled onto a sofa by an elderly uncle.

I would never have taken Monir for the brother of the elegant Salah; he was a bald-headed man of medium height, very light skin and the body profile of a bowling pin; his features, in a heavily lined face, were large and craggy, touched with warmth and sensuality, and his watery blue-brown eyes were merry and kind as he shook my hand, pulling my arm through his in one fluid motion, welcoming me to his home with "My dear, we must have a long conversation about the United States! Why do they *hate* us so?"

Monir's living room was large and high-ceilinged, its paint a deeply yellowing white, its furniture as dated as the furniture in

Garden City but older, shabbier, its light bare and harsh. (The Egyptians look very favorably on functional overhead lighting—half their rooms are lit by a blue-white bar of neon that is attached above the doorway; this neon satisfies in them the same taste for "Western modernity" that makes many of them adore station wagons and Formica furniture when they come to the States; the neon lighting, in time, became for me a clue to the taste, position and acculturation of the occupants of many Cairo apartments.)

There were Hamamsys everywhere, scattered through the salon and thick in the living room. Soad was there, as well as Gasbia and Ibrahim. Salah, of course, and Monir's wife, Tu-Tu, a lady in her fifties of dyed black hair, red red lipstick, harlequin glasses and frantic gaiety. Monir's daughter, Aischa, a very thin young girl with delicate features and a mournful manner—looking rather more Spanish than Egyptian. Aischa's brother, Mohammed, twenty-four and in the Army, but looking like a stocky, ruddy-faced sixteen-year-old, awkwardly protective towards his sister, uncomfortable among the adults. A tall, thin, ascetic-looking man named Kamel who was identified as a widowed cousin, close to Monir's family. Kamel was said to be an under-secretary in the Ministry of Foreign Affairs.

Then there was Haifa: a lady in her late forties, she had light skin, dark hair, a bearing full of faded stylishness and a subdued manner. Two of her children stood beside her: Nabila, the daughter of Haifa's present marriage, and Fouad, the son of her first marriage. There was also Soad's youngest sister Leila and her husband, a heavy man in a pin-striped suit with a gray crew cut, flashing rimless glasses, and a limp. He was a doctor. The couple was known to the family as "Leila and the Doctor." Leila was forty-three, and like her sister Haifa, another faded beauty, she, too, seemed curiously silent. Her eyes were dull and lifeless, her face seemed imprisoned behind some lifelong defeat; she wore, unaccountably, a blond nylon wig of upswept curls that simply sat there atop her motionless face. She was very cordial to me, shaking my hand warmly between her two hands, while her eyes struggled to light up. Her husband, the Doctor, smiled distantly at me from across the room.

Monir pulled me down onto a sofa briefly. "Do you know, a few years ago I was on a train in Switzerland," he said. "I met some Americans in the train and we began to talk. When they heard I came from Egypt they said they had always wanted to come to Cairo to see the crocodiles in the Nile. I said to them, 'Crocodiles in the Nile! The only time I have ever seen a crocodile in Egypt was in the Cairo Zoo!' Then they wanted to know about the camels in the street, and was it true the traffic stopped for them! Why do they *persist* in this madness? You *must* tell me."

Magdi laughed beside me, and rescued me.

Monir's wife, Tu-Tu, fed me *felafel*° and thrust one of the widowed Kamel's children onto my lap.

In the distance, I heard Gasbia's hoarse shriek. . . .

Nabila, Haifa's daughter, approached me. She was a large bold-looking young woman with a great aquiline nose, beautiful dark eyes and long dark hair, fashionably straightened. She wore a midi skirt and leather boots. She was twenty-one but she looked twenty-six. "Tell me," she said, "what is Women's Liberation all about in the United States? Why are the American women rebelling? They have *everything*. Here, in Egypt, we are slaves, but in *America*!"

Haifa heard her daughter's words in passing, and stopped to speak with us. "It is true what Nabila says," she said. "Women *are* slaves in Egypt. But in America! Oh, what a wonderful country that is. You know, I lived in California for four years. We were a great success in America. No one who met me would believe that I was Egyptian. No *one*. They thought Egyptians are savages. I used to give little lectures once a week to ladies in Los Angeles, explaining my life as an Egyptian woman to them. . . ." Her sadly quiet face suddenly lit up with nostalgic laughter, and Nabila and I waited for her to return to us. When she did it was with a knockout. "They fell in love with us," she said to me, her hands clasped in a rapture of memory. "They just fell in love with us! And they were very sympathetic to our cause, too. You know," Haifa leaned confidentially toward me, "they don't like the Jews in America, either. Yes, that's *true*. They don't like them, *either*. The Jews own America. Everybody knows that. And everybody hates them for it."

My head felt like it was on fire. Suddenly, I could hear again the words of Soad and Gasbia, who had taken me aside that first day in

° A peasant food made of ground beans and vegetables, shaped into small balls and fried in deep oil.

their house and said, "Ali has told us you are Jewish. Believe me, it means nothing to us, nothing. But not all people are as broadminded as we are. Some people are quite stupid about this matter. Especially these days. So, please. Tell no one that you are Jewish. Not even the other members of our family. Simply forget about it. No one, after all, is going to ask you if you are Jewish, and there is no need to volunteer the information." Words I had really, fundamentally, dismissed in an atmosphere I had thus far not felt as threatening.

Now, listening to Haifa, the words became a loud echo in my head. But, I calmed down, were they really any worse than words I'd heard in Arizona or Nebraska or on the subway in New York, for that matter?

"You know," I said now to Haifa, "the people in America who hate Jews hate Moslems, too. I wouldn't trust those Americans who tried to be friendly to you by telling you they hated Jews."

She stared at me, nonplussed. She had presented her words as an offering of friendship, why was I responding like *this*? Uncontrollably, my head turned away, almost without any direction from me; I caught Magdi's eyes on me. Grateful, I returned to the two women and said, "Excuse me, Magdi wants to speak to me." Nabila's eyes swung instantly to Magdi, who smiled at her. I looked back at Nabila, ready to bring our uncomfortable conversation to an end with an automatic smile; but I stopped, startled by the handsome girl's eyes. They were fixed on Magdi, filled with an unmistakable hunger. What is *this*? I thought.

"What is it?" said Magdi. "You look upset."

"Do I? Not at all. No, no. Everything's fine, your aunt Haifa is a strange lady. . . . What goes with you and Nabila?"

Magdi flushed. "She is my cousin. I have known her all my life. When she was a little girl I carried her about on my shoulders. And now, I must avoid her."

"Are you in love with her?"

"Not at all. But she is with me. So I do not visit my aunt as often as I used to. Besides, they are all slightly mad in that family. It is just as well I do not go to them. Have you spoken yet with Fouad?"

"No. Why? What is Fouad like?"

Magdi smiled mysteriously. "You will see. Speak to him. And then just imagine him living across the hall from Salah."

At that moment the door slammed open and all eyes turned. In the doorway were three people: a man, a young girl, a baby in the girl's arms.

"Here comes Amr," said Magdi. "He is Nabila's half-brother; the son of her father by another wife. No actual relation to Fouad, but Haifa raised them like brothers. The girl is Amr's wife, Mirella. They also live in the flat across the hall."

The women swarmed around the girl with the baby in her arms, cooing and oohing and tsking. The man extricated himself from the circle and came towards us. Magdi stood up, and they clasped each other in a warm embrace, kissing on both cheeks, and slapping each other's backs many times.

"Amr, this is Miss Vivian. She is a friend of Ali Mahmoud from America."

Amr said, "Hello. Hello. It is a pleasure to meet you. A pleasure."

Amr looked fantastically healthy, and there was about him a kind of smooth, round-cheeked good nature. He and Magdi spoke in rapid bursts of Arabic, excusing themselves to me in English every few seconds; it was only "business" they were speaking of.

Within the hour I found myself in a remote corner of the salon, standing with a plate of food in my hands facing Fouad, who also stood with a plate of food in his hands.

Fouad looked like an American college student. He wore blue slacks, a V-necked green woolen sweater and a blue shirt beneath the sweater. His eyes squinted behind thick glasses and his nose was small and so short that it pulled his upper lip slightly towards it.

"Did Ali ever speak to you about me?" he asked in a soft halting voice. "I lived for a number of years in the United States. In Washington, D.C. Perhaps he mentioned that? But then again, I was back in Egypt before he went to Cambridge."

"No, I'm afraid I don't recall his speaking of you. What were you doing in Washington?"

"Studying." Fouad smiled ruefully. "What else does an Egyptian do in Washington?"

"Studying what?"

"Mathematics. At the American University. I teach now, at one of the universities in Cairo. What are *you* doing here?"

"Well, I've come to live here for a few months and write my impressions of the people I meet."

"A few months!" Fouad said excitedly. "You expect to understand Egypt in a few months? You will write nonsense! Like every other Westerner who comes here and thinks he understands the entire country after sitting in the Hilton for a few weeks and talking to the people at the Gezira Club bar. Ah! It is *disgusting.*" His eyes squinted at an alarming rate.

"Take it easy," I said. "I didn't say I was going to write the definitive work on Egypt. I said only that I would write of the people I met."

Fouad stared at me. Then he slumped against the wall, looking out toward the living room in front of us. "Well, you will never arrive at any significant conclusions, even about the people you meet, if you stick only to my family."

"Why is that?" I asked calmly.

"Because there is nothing of the spirit of Egypt in them," he said bitterly. "They are the greedy, useless, unfunctioning bourgeoisie of this country, full of petty selfish concerns. They are unable to see what is happening right before their eyes. They hate and fear the only things that can lift Egypt out of the Middle Ages." He stared angrily at his relatives. "I hate them. I hate them all. Can you imagine a man like Salah understanding the revolution that is going on here? All he knows is *they* took his factory away from him. And even Soad. She is the most honest of all of them, yet even she is an ignorant old woman who places a far greater value on her ability to understand than it deserves. They are useless, all of them.

"When I first came home from America I thought I would go mad. The only one I could talk to was Ali. He was five years younger than me and just beginning the university but he was the only one who understood anything. I used to run over there and talk, talk, talk. I would follow him around the room while he ate and keep talking until he got into bed, pulled the covers over his ears and yelled at me to go home and sleep." Fouad laughed, a tight, slightly hysterical laugh, and pushed his slipping glasses up onto his bridgeless little nose. He seemed almost mesmerized by his own speech. I felt that no answers, no agreements, no interjections were necessary from me. Let him go on. Just let him go on. And he did:

"You all hate Nasser. You are all so fond of telling us what a dictator he was, what a police state Egypt is, how individual rights have been destroyed here. Democracy is dead in Egypt. *Democracy!* How ridiculous! Yes, democracy for Salah and Monir and all the rest of them." He jerked his head toward the living room. "They are the kind of Egyptians who hate Nasser. But go talk to workers and peasants and students!

"But nobody—no matter how much he hates him—can ever forget that Nasser nationalized the Canal. And nobody outside of Egypt can ever understand what that means. . . . They took thousands of Egyptians out of the villages—under the whip—and made them dig that canal. Fifty thousand Egyptians died, and then bit by bit they stole the whole thing from us. Bit by bit, as you know, Britain lent money at exorbitant rates, and took her pound of flesh in the Canal. To be a nine-year-old child hearing those things! And to hear it all your life! You can never understand what it meant to us, and you can never understand what Nasser came to mean because he got it back for us. And even the Egyptians didn't really understand what he meant until the Sixty-seven War.

"What happened here on June ninth and tenth in 1967 can never be forgotten by anyone who lived through it. If you were in Cairo then, and you closed the shutters and remained in your flat, and just listened to the radio you might have thought it was all a planned demonstration. But if you were out in the streets then you saw, and you knew that something fantastic was happening, something that had never happened before.

"For two days the radio had been playing the Koran continuously: those parts connected with the prayers for the dead. This built up, and built up, and built up. And then Nasser came on, and he began to talk. And it was terrible. Terrible. It was not as if a country had been defeated. It was as though a people had died. I sat there, listening, holding my head and saying over and over again: My God, my God, my God. I didn't know what to do. I couldn't stay in the house. So I went to the university. Just to see some people I could be with. And we sat there, some of my students and people I work with. And then something began to happen. To this day I don't know how, or what it was, but we felt a *need*, and we picked up a flag and we began to walk toward the governmental palace. And suddenly, other people were walking, too. Secretaries in high heels and old men and peasants. They began to walk, too. And now there was only one word: *Gamal stay! Gamal stay!* It wasn't *him* we wanted so much, as some proof that the country was *alive*, that we weren't dead, that we could rise from this horror and start over again. And every man, woman, and child in Cairo felt it that day. They all felt that Gamal was a symbol of their ability to remain alive as a nation, as a people."

The outburst was at an end. I waited. Then:

"What do you do with yourself now?" I asked quietly. "I mean, since the war."

"Nothing, really," Fouad answered just as quietly. "I work. I talk to my students. I wait. You know, I cannot think about myself anymore. Really, I can't. My personal troubles or happiness seem so *unimportant*. I can never forget all the suffering in the world. So much of it. I mean, *really*, how can I care for myself? I meet girls. They are pretty, they are sympathetic. From time to time one of them catches my attention, but . . . Besides, I think I have lost the ability to love."

We stood there. Suddenly, there were no more words to speak; and yet we did not move; it was as though the words that had passed between us held us in place.

Then Soad was standing there with one hand on each of us. "Children," she said. "It is good to talk, but there is a *party* going on. Come and join us now. The people want to have the pleasure of your presence." And she began to pull us into the living room. As she moved off, ahead of us, Fouad said, "See? They cannot bear it because they know we are talking seriously. It will be impossible to talk further now." He twisted his head about, looking in various directions. "Where is Aischa? Have you seen her? I must see her about something." As he was about to wander off, I said, "Will I see you again? I'd like very much to visit the university with you."

"Certainly," he said. "You are staying with Magdi, aren't you? I'll call you there." And he disappeared into one of the darkened recesses off the salon.

I joined the rest of the family, but I heard nothing for the rest of the evening, unable to shake free of Fouad's words; they echoed in my head and had become a pressure on my heart.

At last, Magdi rose from his chair and said, "Come, we must be going now." Samiha and I rose dutifully to our feet, and after many kisses on both cheeks and cries of *"Hamdulallah!"* (Thank God!) and *"Ma'salaam!"* and promises to call and come and go and meet, we were finally out on the cool, quiet, very darkened Zamalek street.

An hour later, Samiha in bed in the flat in Garden City, Magdi and I sat in his bedroom, drinking tea and discussing everyone at the party.

"Your Aunt Haifa has some interesting ideas about Americans," I said.

"She is a very stupid woman," Magdi said. "And her husband is an animal. Need one say any more?"

"Her children are, indeed, an odd assortment: Nabila, Fouad, and Amr. What a crew! Nabila's a spunky girl. I liked her. And Fouad knocked me out."

"What do you mean, knocked you out?"

"I mean I found him very impressive. He spoke like an impassioned socialist, and he moved me. He spoke of what Nasser really meant to Egypt, of what had happened here in 1967 when Nasser tried to resign, of how the war had seemed like the death of a people rather than just a military defeat."

Magdi nodded over his teacup. "That is true," he said equitably. "All too true. It was as Fouad says."

"He also said that if I remained only with your family I would never capture the spirit of Egypt," I said, picking up the silver tea-strainer in one hand and the teapot in the other. "That I could never find out what was really happening in Egypt if I talked only with them. He seems to hate Salah in particular."

"The spirit of Egypt!" Magdi spit out. I was looking down at my teacup. The harshness in his voice, without the signaling change in facial expression, startled me, and I looked quickly up at him. Magdi's face, usually somnolent in repose, was something wonderful to see when it suddenly became animated with anger or annoyance. His eyes grew so dark they gave the illusion, almost, of being rimmed in black. His jawline tightened and his wide lips and nose seemed fine and carved; in these moments, he looked as though he had stepped from an Egyptian temple drawing: a warrior returning from battle, with some incontrovertible truth sunk deep inside him, behind eyes that were steady and would never again be other than dry.

"The spirit of Egypt!" Magdi said again. "They all talk about the spirit of Egypt, these socialists. Where is it? Who's got it? The spirit of Egypt is never in anyone you know. Did Fouad say he'd call you? Of course, he did. Well, he never will. Not because he wouldn't give five years of his life to go on talking to you, but because he is *shy*. *That* is the spirit of Egypt! The man has feelings, the woman has feelings, and no one expresses them. Ever. *Friends* do not express their feelings. Everyone is shy. I was, too. But when I lived out of the country I rid myself of this misery. Now, when I care, I *speak*.

"Let me tell you about Fouad. He is a thirty-five-year-old virgin. He goes nowhere, he knows no one, he is always alone. He hates the family and hardly ever joins a family gathering. He spoke so long to you only because you are a stranger. He hates his mother and his stepfather but he lives with them because it is free. He buys absolutely nothing but books. He is a *collector*." Magdi brought all the fingertips of his left hand together, in the air, and shook them. "Ninety percent of these books he doesn't read. But he cares for them as though they were his children. Sometimes he can't sleep because of all the plastic bindings on the books. He starts choking, they are taking all the air in the room. But no one, not even his mother, is allowed into his room to clean, and he locks the door when he goes off to his classes. He will spend nothing on anything. He is a glutton. If it is free he will eat until he is sick. He is infuriated if his opinion is opposed. He makes fifty pounds a month and pays no rent at all. He learned nothing in the States about the country, and made no friends. He went to the movies twice. Once someone took him and then he had to take the man who took him. He loves only the company of the very young. When he came home he spoke only to Ali. Now it is Aischa whom he instructs. . . . He once did a terrible thing. When he came home, after five years, everyone wanted to draw him back into the family again. My aunt in Jordan has two sons, neither of them now in Egypt. One of these sons went at the request of his father, who is a mathematician, to ask Fouad if he had a certain book. Now, my aunt's husband did not need this book, he did it only to draw Fouad closer. The boy came to Fouad's room and knocked on the door. The door to this room has two parts, an upper and a lower. Fouad came to the door but opened only the upper part. The boy spoke to him and delivered his father's message. Without looking through his books Fouad said, 'No, I do not have it.' The boy became distressed and begged Fouad to let him into the room, perhaps he could find it. Fouad refused, saying it was his right to refuse admission to his room to anyone at all. The boy went home in tears."

Magdi remained silent. He opened his mouth as though to continue, but then clamped his lips shut. I sat there, speechless. A light silence entered the room and covered us like a thin summer blanket. We drank tea, grateful for the mechanical gesture.

"Isn't there anything about him you *do* like?" I said at last. Magdi looked genuinely surprised.

"But of course I like him!" he said. "He is my cousin!"

The Nile. Everyone loves it. Everyone loves it *equally*. Magdi loves it as much as his servant Sayeda loves it. Magdi needs the river as much as Sayeda needs it. In the evenings in summer Sayeda walks along the river because there is no other place in Cairo to escape the heat of her choked little room in Giza. In the evenings in summer Magdi goes to a special childhood place on the river because there is no other place in Cairo to escape the melancholia that begins to plague him when the weather turns hot.

The Nile lives in Cairo as few great rivers live in other cities. Someone once said that the Thames was liquid history. The Nile will never be history, really; certainly not in the sense that history is a record of past passions. The men and women who walk along the banks of the Nile today are the true descendants of seven thousand years of living, thrashing history; if their ancestors were to come to life tomorrow they would, *gelabyas* and black-rimmed eyes aside, recognize in them the essential Egyptian.

There is something else about the Nile. To stand at its edge is to experience the astonishing sensation that you can almost chart the river's course through the entire country. I have never felt the binding power of a river as strongly as I have felt it standing beside the Nile. I could literally *feel* the river connecting Cairo with that whole burning mysteriousness of Upper Egypt in the south, and the green open rushing toward the Mediterranean in the north . . . and the woman walking past me here on the river, just as we are both passing the Hilton Hotel, with a tank of bottled gas on her head, her back magnificently erect inside her long black *milayeh,*° her figure filled with an ancient lesson, her entire being a cut-out against the moving life of the Nile, that woman is the binding material.

I walked this morning to Soad's house in Zamalek by way of the Nile. Leaving Garden City, I walked two blocks from Magdi's house to the river then turned right, walking up, up, up through the city along the riverfront that is called the Corniche, past the old British Governor's Residence, past the Nile Hotel, the Semiramis Hotel, the new Shepard's Hotel, the Hilton Hotel, the Arab Television Building, and finally, along the incredible edge of the medieval slum of Boulac. (Which is something like a walk from New York's Park Avenue at Fiftieth Street to Park Avenue at One Hundred and Fiftieth Street.) Here, where the river was intersected by Boulac, I turned left and crossed the Twenty-sixth of July Bridge (that ugly green iron monster I would come to love for no damned reason at all and which caused my heart to lift each time I crossed it on foot or in a car). That walk seemed to me a microcosm of a walk through Cairo: from the old colonial wealth of Garden City, through the new colonial wealth of the American hotels, right back into the vast and treacherous poverty of Boulac where the streets swarm with a crippled kind of cunning, and an ancient life that seethes beneath the rake-off.

On the other side of the bridge: the large thoroughfare that extended into Zamalek. I walked down this thoroughfare for a few blocks to Hassan Sabry Street (at this juncture now named rue Brazil but still called Hassan Sabry by Cairo taxi drivers). As I walked along Hassan Sabry I suddenly remembered Françoise, and an address she had given me before I left New York. "There was a bookshop there," she said. "I worked in it for years. The man I worked for was *fantastic.* Go and see what has happened to him."

Françoise. Her life had begun as the daughter of a vigorously bourgeois French family, and led her with short strong bird-hops

---

° The traditional Arabic dress for women: a single length of black or white cloth wound around the head, shoulders and body, and falling directly to the ground.

through an unhappy Parisian marriage, six years alone in Cairo, years of marriage to an American classics scholar, and now, the exhausted peace of a loft in Hoboken, New Jersey. Our paths had crossed during her Cambridge period (and mine), and somehow or other we had kept distracted track of each other ever since. I always felt a peculiar blend of peace and tedium when I went to visit Françoise. Wherever she went, however often she moved from one ramshackle apartment to the next, however dreadful were her rootless circumstances, she always rebuilt her home into a cozy and beautiful nest—to hold anew the little bird. When I think of Françoise's houses I always see brilliantly whitewashed walls, very green plants, strong sunshine, pewter pitchers, Beatrix Potter books, strands of exotic jewelry on the walls, a shining oak table, unusual prints, French biscuits, a white china coffeepot, a bedspread that will be in fashion in two or three years; and of course, her knitting. Françoise's knitting that is indeed an act of creation. She knitted the loveliest things: skirts, sweaters, jackets, coats, full of delicacy and design, the kind of stuff that should have been selling in Henri Bendel's, and thirty years ago *would* have been selling there, but today it simply wasn't economically feasible for them to buy her things. That was really Françoise's story. She was, in her essence, thirty years out of date. Her touch was the lightest, the most graceful, the most unerring I have ever known—and it was completely dislocated in the New York of the 1960s.

Perhaps that is why Françoise's mind became genuinely engaged only when she was telling stories of the past. Her stories were like her knitting: stitch by jeweled stitch they added up to a design of extraordinary subtlety, but one had to wait with educated patience for the pattern to make itself obvious. And I, with the temperamental impatience of my culture, could never wait.

When I knew I was going to Egypt I rode out to Hoboken to visit Françoise: to remind her of her years in Cairo and to ask for some "real" advice.

"You can forget about being Jewish," Françoise said, pouring tea into large blue-and-white cups. "It will mean nothing in Cairo. It is being a woman that will be *terrible*." (She said the word in French.) "You cannot imagine! The sounds they make! The touching! The places you cannot go! The contempt for the foreign woman! The contempt for the Egyptian who takes up with you! *Terrible. Terrible.* And you know, my dear, the years I was in Cairo were some of the worst: 1946 to 1952. After the revolution, being a foreigner and a woman together was very difficult, very difficult." She shook her small, birdlike head and her eyelids drew themselves forward over her bulging green eyes as they always did when she was stirred. We sat at the oak table and she sipped her tea, but I could see she wasn't really in Hoboken anymore.

"When the revolution came," Françoise mused, "I was really in trouble. I never *was* in Egypt properly, you know. I came with a tourist visa, and when I wanted to stay I had to prove I was working, and every year I had to prove it all over again, and every year it grew more and more complicated. After the revolution I feared not only deportation but . . . who could tell? People seemed to be disappearing every day. And the man I worked for was a Communist, and although I never knew what was going on in back of the shop, who would believe me? I lived from moment to moment for two years. Finally, they called me down and this awful Army man who had been *torturing* me about my visa, and implying always that if I would consider certain propositions he would consider giving me a permanent visa, he was there at the police station. He said to me, 'Madam, we have a dossier on you this thick. You have forty-eight hours in which to leave Egypt.' What could I say? Dossier? What dossier? It was a nightmare, an absolute nightmare. To clear up six years of life in forty-eight hours! Oh, I can't tell you. The things I left behind, the people I lost and was never able to find again. (You see, so many people were seen from day to day, from appointment to appointment. You never knew where to find them, only where you were to meet the next time.) My servant, Hamid, cried for twelve hours. Finally, he arrived at the house with a kilo of halvah and a bottle of oil. 'Eat the halvah and drink the oil, madam,' he wept. 'It will make you ill and they will not be able to make you leave.'

"I looked at the halvah and the oil and I said, 'Hamid, not if I knew I was going to the guillotine.' "

"Françoise, it sounds awful. Why did you want to stay there so long as it was?"

"I loved it," she said simply. "I felt as though I had come home in Egypt. You know, my dear Vivian, I am *hardly* a candidate for mystical experience, and yet in Egypt I often had the strange sensation that I was living a second existence. That I had *felt* once before in this same place. I dreaded leaving. Sometimes, I would have nightmares in which I was being forced to leave the country. Then I would wake up, sweating, my hair wet, and I would look wildly around me until I realized I was in bed in Zamalek and the lemon tree was there outside my window and all was well. . . . You will love it, I know you will. It will be magnificent no matter what has happened there these twenty years. Two things you must do in Cairo: buy silver in the bazaar and eat sweet lemons. You have never in your entire life tasted *any*thing like Egypt's sweet lemons. Meanwhile, I will look through all my old things and before you go I will give you the names and addresses of the people I remember best. God knows where *any* of them are now. But still, you can try." And she had done just that. I had left New York with about twenty names and addresses, each of which had been accompanied by a history that had taken thirty minutes to deliver, and none of which I could remember the next day.

I had not yet tried to locate any of the people on Françoise's list, but now as I walked along Hassan Sabry I suddenly remembered: Twenty-eight Hassan Sabry. That's where the bookstore was. That's where Françoise's marvelous Abdullah Ibrahim was to be found.

It took me half an hour to find the address because Hassan Sabry at this point on the street was rue Brazil, and the house I was looking for was no longer 28 Hassan Sabry but 7 rue Brazil. Finally, I found it and there *was* a shop at 7 rue Brazil but it wasn't a bookshop, it was an art gallery, an art gallery devoted to Egyptian and Arabesque paintings and objects and furniture, beautifully arranged under wooden arches and on white stucco walls. The place had grace and style and great charm, and I felt happy walking into it. Inside, three or four people walked around looking at paintings, jewelry, furniture; they looked like wealthy foreigners. At an old carved desk sat an immensely fat woman with a beautiful face and sexy brown hair that was graying. Beside her, sat another woman: plain, with fading reddish hair and watery blue eyes. Over them both hovered a thin black man in a flowing *gelabya*, and they were all having a terrific fight in Arabic. I stood before the desk waiting for the fight to come to an end, and for the fat woman to acknowledge me. When the argument showed no signs of abating (I had begun to recognize the obsessive quality of Egyptian arguments), the fat woman suddenly jerked her head in my direction and said with some distress, "Yes, madam? What is it? What can I do for you?"

"I wonder if you could tell me when this shop was last a bookstore, and where I can find the man who ran the bookstore?"

The fat woman with the beautiful face sat back in her chair and stared at me, her face having suddenly undergone a transformation: her large oval eyes had become flat and snakelike, her features looked both drained and excited at the same time.

"The bookstore was closed ten years ago," she said, "and the man who ran it has been in Paris for fifteen years. Why? Did you know him?"

"No, but I know someone who used to work for him, a Frenchwoman now living in America, and she asked me to look him up."

"Françoise," the woman said instantly.

"Yes," I said excitedly. "Did you know Françoise?"

"Yes," she said. "I knew her." She stopped. I waited. "How is Françoise?" she said finally.

"She's fine," I said, my voice softening unexpectedly. It was as though the fat woman and I were alone in the gallery, the sounds around us suddenly turned off. She continued to stare at me, her eyes curiously hooded, and I remember thinking: What is she seeing? What is she actually looking at? She shook herself and her eyes came into genuine focus on me.

"It is impossible to talk now," she said. "Can you come back another day?"

"Yes, of course."

"Good. Come the day after tomorrow at four o'clock and we will talk."

I nodded and turned away from the desk. "By the way," the woman called after me. I turned. "My name is Lizette Abu Shady." I returned, shook her hand, and gave her my name.

Out on the street again, I hurried on toward Soad's house, late now for lunch.

Soad and I sit drinking tea in the sitting room. It is five o'clock and the rest of the family are sleeping after the heavy meal we have all just consumed, but I cannot sleep and it is unthinkable for Soad to sleep while I am her guest. Besides, it is a chance for us to be alone together—just the three of us: me, Soad, and Ali.

I sit on one end of a red imitation brocade love seat; when I lean back my head touches the curved gold-and-white painted frame that surrounds me. Soad sits at the other end of the love seat; her short legs off the ground, her body turned toward me, her gray hair straggling a bit from her usually neat bun after her long labor in the kitchen. Our teacups are before us on a plastic tea tray on a marble-topped table. Sun streams through the shutters partially opened in my honor. Soad speaks, straining hard out of her inbred politeness to pretend that this is a conversation while she indulges herself in talk of Ali:

"We loved each other com*pletely*, that boy and I. After all, his father died when he was two years old, and my entire *life* I knew that I must give him every opportunity, every chance, every *way* to become the man I knew he could be. I worked, I watched, I taught him *discipline*. I took care of the house, I went to work, I kept an eye on the servants, I prepared his dinner with my own hands, I saw to it that he studied when he should study. And," she beams at me, "he did very well. *Very* well." Suddenly her face falls, and all her years crowd in on her as the animation drains away. "But now," she continues quietly, "now it is really awful. Five years in America. Five years . . ." Her eyes grow old, old, that familiar film of uncertainty spreads thinly across them. She struggles to become cheerful for me. "That is a very long time, five years, is it not?" Her laugh is dry and brief. "But it was necessary for him to go. Absolutely necessary. There was no way for him to advance here in Egypt, and he said to me, 'Now, Mummy, it will be very hard for us to be separated from each other but we must face that difficulty. The man who stands still soon finds himself left behind, and you do not want that for me, and I do not want that. So we will bear this burden of separation for a short while in order that I may advance my life.' And I said to him,

'My son, *definitely* you must go.' But when he left my arms and went forward toward the plane I felt that my brain was ice and a knife had been plunged into my heart. I would surely have sunk to the ground if there had not been Gasbia on one side of me and the Doctor on the other side. I kept waving and saying 'Good-bye, darling! Good-bye!' but I could see nothing anymore, nothing. . . ."

The memory of her ordeal strengthens her. Soad straightens up, her back suddenly ramrod stiff, her eyes behind their dimness gazing with quiet command off into some private distance that penetrates the wall on the other side of the room, directly opposite us. Her fingers pluck blindly at her throat. We are quiet for some time. She speaks again.

"Once, about a year before he went to America, I came home from work one day, and as I turned the key in the lock, the door pulled open and Ali swung me off my feet and whirled me around, oh many times, before he let my feet touch the ground. I laughed and laughed, although I never knew what was the cause for this jubilation. 'Mummy,' he said, when I had caught my breath, 'you have had no pleasure in your life. Only hard work. Now, Mummy, I want to give you some pleasure. I want you to pretend that you are my girl, and I will do things for you instead of you always doing things for me. You must have some *pleasure*, Mummy.' "

At six o'clock Gasbia and Ibrahim came into the room, both in pajamas, wiping sleep from their eyes. It was difficult for Ibrahim to return to the world of consciousness; he sat rubbing his belly silently, his eyes blinking like a rabbit's, his mouth chewing on nothing. Gasbia immediately began shrieking softly, calling to Ibrahim's sister in the kitchen to bring some tea.

Ibrahim's sister, Za-Za, was visiting from the village where she still lived with Ibrahim's parents. She was newly married and preparing for her "wedding" here in Cairo, under the supervision of Soad and Gasbia. It was through Za-Za that I first learned of the three-part process that is marriage in Egypt.

The first step is a formal engagement party that is like a wedding party in the United States. This party is, in essence, an announcement that courting is about to begin between this man and this woman ("girl," as the Egyptians euphemistically put it; God help her if she is a "woman"). According to ancient custom the man and the woman at this point hardly even know each other, have certainly never been alone together, and if the marriage is an arranged one they may never even have met before. Of course, most Cairenes claim this is a thing of the past, that the engagement party is merely a traditional formality, the man and the woman now, in modern Egypt, having known and chosen each other, and then announced it to their families. But the fact is the percentage of men and women who have privately known and freely chosen each other is very slight, confined mainly to the most advanced of university students. On the other hand, between the most ancient and the most advanced, lie a thousand combinations of approach to the desperate business of marriage.

After the engagement party comes a period of courting during which the engaged couple are meant to learn to know and understand each other—although they are still never alone; this perceiving of each other taking place in the company of relatives and friends. In other words, the man may now come to the house twice a week to sit in the front parlor with the girl and her mother. At this point both man and woman have the right to call the whole thing off. If they survive the engagement period, and when the proper time comes (that time usually is determined by money), they enter into a ceremony of marriage that is performed by a Moslem *sheikh* or a Coptic priest and registered in the proper governmental bureau. The woman is now given a certain sum by the groom's father with which to purchase her gold. (A woman's gold is crucial in Egypt. She must have earrings, or a set of bracelets, or neck chains, whatever she chooses, so long as it is solid gold. Thus, one sees peasants who own nothing but the *milayeh* on their backs with solid gold in their ears.) However, the marriage is not consummated at this point, and the man and the woman both remain living in their respective parents' homes. The consummation will take place only after a home has been found for the couple—which in Cairo is no easy matter; the frenzy over flats must be seen to be believed. (A joke around Cairo goes: "He: I love you. She: Have you got a flat?") This home must be suitably furnished in the most extraordinary detail: furniture, china, silver, curtains, linens, rugs. Then, and only then, can the "wedding" take place. All in all, the entire marriage usually takes from one to three years to accomplish.

Ibrahim's sister Za-Za had just had her marriage to Samir registered, and the entire family was now in the throes of finding an apartment for the couple, and furnishing it properly. The burden of this task fell to Gasbia and Soad, as Ibrahim's father was a senile old man, and Ibrahim had become the titular head of the family; Za-Za and Samir, incredibly docile creatures somewhat inept at doing these things for themselves, were apparently grateful for the Hamamsy assumption of responsibility. So, Za-Za was often to be seen at Soad's house for days and weeks at a time while the business of getting her properly married slowly proceeded.

She came in now with fresh tea on a tray, and I looked at her for the second or third time since I'd met her that day. Za-Za was twenty-two years old and she was fatter than Gasbia and Ibrahim combined. Her breasts were huge and seemed to jut out nearly a foot from her chest. She was rather tall, and wore a long shapeless housedress with no sleeves from which large rounded arms hung. Her face was pretty, round, light-skinned and amazingly smooth; her brown eyes were calm, utterly without expression; her hair was tucked into a kerchief. She said little but giggled a great deal. She looked more like a Russian peasant than an Egyptian peasant, but beyond doubt a peasant. When I later met Samir I quailed. He was small and thin, warm-brown, his head hung at a shy, appealing angle; he was as quietly alarmed by the world as Za-Za, and they seemed to cling together. I could not imagine them in bed together, but Soad assured me that there was passion building between them and if the family didn't get them properly married soon only Allah knew what would happen.

We drank tea yet once more, and Ibrahim slowly announced to me that he and Gasbia were invited to a party that evening and would like to take me along.

"They are people of the highest standard," he droned at me. "The highest standard. The lady is an actress, very famous now in Egypt, and it will be very good for your research." (*Resairshes*, he said.) "You must come."

"Why thank you, Ibrahim, I'd love to come," I said. "What time is the party?"

"It is at approximately ten o'clock. First I will go to the pharmacy, and you will return to your home to change your clothes."

"What's wrong with what I'm wearing?" I said. "I would wear this to a party at home."

"No, no," Ibrahim said, alarmed. "These are people of the highest standard. You must put on something for the evening."

"Yes," said Soad. "We are a bit more formal here in Egypt than perhaps you are in the United States. Why do you object? The Captain assured us that you have evening wear. It will be no great difficulty to return you to your home. The Doctor will take you and bring you back."

The Captain had assured them I had evening wear!

"Of course, Soad. If you wish me to change I will do so."

Two hours later I had changed my clothes in Garden City and was sitting with Ibrahim in the pharmacy in the middle of downtown Cairo waiting for him to take care of whatever it was he had come to take care of.

The pharmacy in which Ibrahim works is located in downtown Cairo, on the edge of the Bab-el-Louk district, two blocks from the great Bab-el-Louk market, and it is open half the night. At eight o'clock on this particular evening the drugstore was full. Long lines of people extended perpendicularly from the counter, which ran the length of the large rectangular room, and behind which half a dozen men stood busily filling prescriptions.

The drugstore reminded me of the Astra Café. The walls were cinder blocks painted institutional green, the windows were streaked plate glass, the floor looked as though it had *originally* been made of discolored stone; three bars of weak neon were the only light in the long sad room. But this place had a different kind of filthy, neglected, anxious, out-of-date look than the Astra. This had the look of the inexperienced revolutionary bureaucracy, the look that says: We're just barely in control. If we take time out to clean up the place the whole operation may go down the drain. The people standing on line seemed to occupy a kind of vast vacant space in which they waited half-heartedly for what they needed. The men behind the counter mainly wore an expression of neutral weariness, but some seemed the embodiment of the officiousness one finds in small men suddenly placed in the position of being able to withhold from people something they want badly.

Ibrahim ("Dr. Ibrahim" to all the men behind the counter) stood behind the counter, at some distance from the others, riffling through a batch of prescriptions. The lines of people, looking mainly as though they'd been standing in this dim light for half a lifetime, were quiet. There were peasant women in black *milayehs* with infants at their exposed breasts, men in rags and turbans, others in shiny blue or brown suits, two or three high school students, two Sudanese gentlemen, impeccably dressed. Everything moved very slowly. While I sat there no one seemed to advance toward the counter, much less get what he had come for and leave.

Suddenly, a man came rushing in, looking fearfully distracted. He was somewhere in his late thirties but he was dressed like a very poor graduate student: frayed cuffs, a shabby V-necked pullover, soles and heels worn nearly to the ground. His face was broad and dark, but his features fine. His hair was very black and straight, swept straight back off his forehead, and behind thin rimless glasses his eyes were very expressive. He came directly to Ibrahim, speaking and waving a piece of paper at the same time. Ibrahim kept on riffling through his prescriptions. The man shoved the piece of paper beneath Ibrahim's nose and finally, without looking up, Ibrahim replied. The man stared haggardly at him for a moment and rushed out.

"What's up?" I said to Ibrahim.

"He is having nervous breakdown," Ibrahim droned.

"Right *now*?"

"Yes," Ibrahim said, and all I had of him were his black velvet lashes lying calmly on his smooth brown cheeks as he returned to his papers.

In five minutes the man was back, looking more distraught than ever. This time Ibrahim looked up at him. The man waved the paper at him once more, speaking very excitedly as he did so. Now Ibrahim grew impatient. He barked something at the man, and the man ran out once more. Ibrahim would gladly have gone directly back to his papers but as I was straining half out of my chair toward him he felt obliged to say something to me.

"He is having depression," he sighed. "He wants something this night. What he wants I do not have here. I told him, 'Call this place, they have it.' The place is closed. So he comes once more. I send him to another place."

Ten minutes later, the man was back, now looking as though his eyeballs were about to disappear into his head. Ibrahim got up and stood behind his counter. The two yelled wildly at each other for a full three minutes and the man with the depression looked as though he were seeing hell in Ibrahim's face. Finally, utterly dazed, he lurched out of the drugstore and Ibrahim said cheerfully to me, "Is nothing. We have many like him since the war." He meant the Sixty-seven War. When a Cairene says "the war" he always means the Sixty-seven War. The electricity failed just then. (The lights go out twenty times a day in Cairo—no one blinks an eye or drops a word.) Ibrahim continued. "But we deal with it. We must. So we do."

Ibrahim wanted Gasbia to take a taxi and meet us at the drugstore, but she refused. So we climbed back into the ten-year-old Volkswagen that Ibrahim drove around in and returned to Zamalek. Gasbia was waiting for us, all made up and dressed to the teeth in her gold jewelry and a pink wool suit two sizes too small, and essentially more sporty than the clothes she'd made me change out of. She climbed into the car, and off we drove, retracing our steps entirely and then driving across the Nile onto the island of Roda, the second of the two islands in the middle of the river, and into a district filled with buildings either newly inhabited or still being built. We drove along an unpaved street filled with piles of dirt lined up before the new buildings. (There are many such districts in Cairo; they resemble building sites all over Europe and the United States, except that in the West the dirt will be shoveled away in a few months and the streets paved; in Cairo it may take three years; everybody runs out of money in the middle of everything.) The building we stopped before was the usual concrete block to be found all over the world, except that inside the doors were lovely dark wood, and within the apartments wooden molding framed the walls.

The apartment we entered was the home of a twenty-three-year-old actress who was currently becoming famous in the Egyptian movies; in fact, today was her twenty-third birthday, and this was her birthday party. The rooms beyond the doorway were filled with people, talking, dancing, drinking, erupting into sudden shouts of laughter.

"She is a goo-oood friend," Ibrahim said in his inane pomposity, but as we stood there, just inside the door, I saw that both he and Gasbia were overcome with shyness. Clearly, they didn't know a soul.

"How does Ibrahim know this woman?" I asked Gasbia in a low voice.

"She comes to the pharmacy," she said.

"Oh," I said.

The place was fixed up like a whore's idea of heaven. Red velvet curtains hung in every doorway in sight, and appeared, for no reason at all, on various parts of the walls as though framing (non-) existent windows. The curtains all curved down and were caught up in a great loop. Where there were no curtains on the walls there hung a dozen or so wooden plaques, some shaped like cocktail glasses, some like the silhouette of a naked woman, some like that of a kitten, and all with a piece of calendar art vividly sketched into their centers. There were masses of red carnations and white lilies in *papier-mâché* vases everywhere, looking like floral arrangements at a funeral. They were so startling that for a moment I was completely dislocated. Have we wandered into the wrong party? I speculated idiotically. (In time I would become used to the flowers: at every party in middle-class Egypt—weddings, birthdays, anniversaries—one finds these gruesome bunches of lilies or carnations tricked out in red or white satin ribbons, making me think they're about to uncover the body in the next room.) The rooms were lit entirely by overhead bars of neon that turned everyone and everything a kind of sickly blue-green.

But, the people. Oh, the people.

The men were all in dark suits with white collars vivid against their own natural darkness. Many wore dark glasses. They were old and young and middle-aged, some heavily handsome, some with faces full of character. They spoke with animation, a drink in one hand, a cigarette in the other, and gestured expansively. They seemed filled with a warm, coarse confidence, an exaggerated sense of themselves, a theatrical laughter, a caricature almost of the actor's preening self-consciousness.

In this room, however, for the first time since I'd been in Egypt (and for the last if I only but knew it), the women dominated the room. They seemed to be everywhere. They were all *large*: tall and voluptuous, as well as full-running-to-fat. Many wore "fashionable" blond or brown nylon wigs composed of huge curls and waves. Their features were often very pretty in a coarse porous way, and they were heavily made up, their eyes outlined with kohl in the ancient Egyptian fashion. They wore long dresses of black velvet, or blue satin, or red moiré, heavily trimmed in gold or silver, and they all seemed to be conducting the most casual conversations at the tops of their lungs. They looked like a cross between a parody of Melina Mercouri and those hideous *papier-mâché* masks used in the modern theatre to indicate grotesquerie. Looking closely, I could see that half the women in the room were old enough to be the mothers of the other half, and then I realized they *were* the mothers of the younger women. It was astonishing to see here in this room a kind of living preview of what was coming as well as what had been. In every daughter was the future mother; in every mother the vanished girl.

A young woman detached herself from the crowd and came lurching toward us, gesturing with exaggerated sensuousness in a half-drunk, half-deliberate manner. Her breasts, three-quarters exposed, heaved and trembled toward us; her hips swung to the left and then to the right; her hands, hanging from limp wrists, flopped in the air. She was tall with a very pretty, strangely "mature" face, lovely clear skin, a voluptuous body, and a blond wig of curls that fell to her shoulders. She wore an extremely tight gown of pink satin with ropes of false pearls that draped around the neck of the dress and encased her arms as well. She looked like a woman of thirty-five about to usher in her last year of full ripeness. Decay shimmered just inside the lovely skin over the smooth fleshiness. The woman was our twenty-three-year-old hostess.

When she got close enough she threw her arms around Ibrahim's neck and, screaming and laughing, planted a huge lipstick print on his cheek. Gasbia nearly went through the ground, looking like a desperately embarrassed dwarf in the king's court. Ibrahim blushed fiercely and tried to laugh, a man of the world. I just stood there.

We were led to three chairs set up in front of one of the many tables loaded with food and drink. A man filled three plates with a mess of food and stuck them in our hands, and there we sat, watching the people of the highest standard. No one said a word to us, and we said not a word to anyone. I was happy to be left alone to watch. What the hell. It was open theatre.

When I think back on it, this party was the only one I was ever at in Egypt where there was a lot of drinking. At most parties in Egypt, people *eat*, and keep on eating. But these, after all, were *movie stars*, and like movie stars anywhere, each one considered himself or herself the best bit of theatre going. So, one drank to fulfill one's theatrical promise, and the music got wilder, and the laughter thicker, and food fell from nerveless fingers, and sometimes the owners of the fingers kept following the food, until both were sprawling in a sticky mess on the floor, everyone laughing hysterically. There was much double-cheek kissing among the men and exuberant embracing as someone came or went. Then someone yelled in Arabic—this whole party was in Arabic—"Play the old songs!" and someone picked up a guitar and began to strum old Arabic peasant songs, and there was much weeping and heart-clutching.

What was great in the midst of all this madness was the sexiness of the women, the older women acting as sexy and drunkenly self-assured as the younger women. Women of fifty behaved as though they considered themselves as desirable as their twenty-five-year-old daughters. And, indeed, they were, the men caressing and courting them as often as they did the younger women; and the older women responding or ignoring, accepting or repelling, with the same degree of lustful vanity that their daughters displayed. If I had gone up to one of these bewigged Melina Mercouris and said to her, "Listen, where I come from they put you in a closet when you pass thirty-five, and any woman who then acts as you're acting now does so out of nervous desperation, and everyone feels contempt and pity, like doesn't she know her *place*," she would surely have looked at me as though I were mildly retarded, and if she could have she would have replied, "But I do not understand. I am alive, no? And while I am alive I have sex, no? And while I have sex I desire, no? And while I desire I am desirable, no?"

I never again in Egypt saw women quite like that, but I never forgot those women, either. To this day, when I recall that party I feel pleasure, and somewhere inside myself I am crowing. Because there it was in all its blowsy, full-blown possibility.

I couldn't wait to get home to Garden City to tell Magdi about the party.

Magdi. My dear friend Magdi.

He is short, Magdi, a powerfully built, barrel-chested man: a squat, muscular, healthy animal. At all times he gives off a powerful sexual force; a man who gives the impression of going through women like a sharp knife moving effortlessly through soft bread.

When I first began to know Magdi I thought him rather a universal type than an Egyptian, especially; the type being that of the man involved with the glamor of his own virility. They seem the same the world over, such men: utterly inert when they are not working, fatuous and bored, hopelessly in love with the care and feeding of their superb physical selves—rather like actors or prizefighters—responding only to the sexual attention they feel is their due, the whole being justified by the magnificent performance they will give once they go into action. There is a great deal of this sort of thing in Magdi. He is interested in nothing, really, besides his rather specialized police work. He lies about the house, spends long hours in nightclubs, will respond only to conversations dealing with personalities and the analysis of emotions.

Yet, Magdi is also very perceptive, with a wide-ranging sense of protectiveness and deep feeling for Egyptian life. He said once, "My wife wanted to send the children to German school. One word I spoke: *No*. They go to Arabic school. This country is like a sinking ship. If we do not all get behind her, where will we be? I love Egypt. I am proud to be an Egyptian. So I will *be* one. My children go to Arabic school."

He has been my invaluable mentor, guide, and friend. I talk over everyone and everything with him. He corrects, he balances, he adds, he soothes, he encourages. Especially, he encourages me to go and do alone, to be as independent of the family as possible, to discover for myself. He admires my independence and he enjoys talking to me; he likes a woman like me, he says. But, he tells me, he would never marry an American. "She must be Egyptian," he says. "If I marry again, it will be as a true Egyptian man. She must obey me in everything. In my house there is only one voice. Her *opinion*, yes, but mine is the decisive voice. And she and she alone must cook my dinner and prepare my clothes and care for my house." But he is looking at me defiantly as he says this.

Magdi has a girlfriend, a twenty-two-year-old secretary named Naha; he has been sleeping with Naha since he left his wife. "I was nervous, terribly nervous," he says. "I suffered too much over this divorce! Naha's smile was something *wonderful* to me then. She laughed and she was gay and she cared for me always. . . . It is good between us." He smiled cynically. "She does her job and I do mine. But I would rather put a bullet through my head than live in the same house with her."

Naha is often at the house, although she never spends the night, returning always to her mother's home, never even bringing Magdi to visit her married sister: he waits in the car when he drives her to her sister's. She is a vivaciously pretty girl, big and full, extremely sensuous-looking; in a few years she will be coarse. She is already jealous of Magdi, given to scenes and tears, and occasional accusations. She is angry that I am living in the flat in Garden City, and—although she is essentially good-natured and wants to be friendly toward me—overcome with resentment in my presence, sullen and silent. Magdi begins to grow irritated with her. What the hell, he is practically saying out loud, I left *one* crying wife, what do I need another one for? Be gay! Or get out. Privately, he tells me that Naha is pregnant and must be aborted. After he sees her through the abortion he is thinking of ending it.

I am growing used to Magdi. More than used to him. We have told each other immense amounts about ourselves; each confession increases the quickening sympathy between us. And then, drinking coffee and reading the newspapers with him in the morning, drinking tea and talking the whole day over with him at night, has become very seductive to me. Despite his essential fatuousness something is growing between Magdi and me, something that frightens me. Desire.

Something strange last night. A bit of trauma that keeps whirling and tumbling through my head today; a curious dryness that layers my throat at the instant of remembrance; a confusion in my soul. For the first time in my life, fear brought on by the peculiarity of my being Jewish. Brought on, but not actually *caused* by it.

Gasbia and Ibrahim insisted I visit their friends Esam and Mediha. Mediha works with Gasbia, and Esam is a lawyer; they live not far from Soad's house in Zamalek. Mediha is a very withdrawn woman, nervously quiet and sweet; although only in her late thirties she is hopelessly faded, her eyes almost as colorless as Soad's. She runs back and forth with food, and attends to their two young sons. Esam, on the other hand, is lovely in his openness, very European-looking (rather Hungarian or Czech), speaks perfect British English and is deeply polite, with an innate delicacy that sets him apart from the other three. He has been in many places—England, America, France, Yugoslavia, all over Egypt and the Sudan—and he is eager to talk.

We sat in the "salon"—Gasbia, Ibrahim and I lined up on a hard, stuffed little couch, Esam on a stuffed chair facing us, Mediha nervously leaping up from her kitchen chair every fifteen minutes to bring tea, pastries, sandwiches, olives; in the stripped-down glare of overhead lighting a mysterious excitement passed between me and Esam as we talked, the other three quickly becoming silent background to our excluding conversation. It would be months in Egypt before I figured out the source of that excitement; the excitement of a man in the rare company of someone who shared what in Esam's life could only be considered esoteric knowledge.

We spoke of the countries we had both traveled in, of the difficulties of various languages, of the peculiarities of custom and provincial life in different places, and we laughed a great deal over Esam's attempts to speak a Yugoslavian dialect after two days in the country. He was most interesting, however, when he described Upper Egypt. Coming to Upper Egypt for the first time in his life as a grown man, he discovered the southern region of his own country almost as a foreigner would; but of course, Esam qualified, he was peculiarly well equipped as a Cairene born and bred to understand the meaning of that strange and haunting part of Egypt. He considered it the most fascinating place he had ever been to.

After a while, Esam asked me where I came from; that is, where I *really* came from, knowing that all Americans come from somewhere else. I told him that my parents were Russians, that my father came from a village and my mother from a city in the Ukraine, and that they had met in their twenties in New York and married there. Forgetting myself, I said carelessly, naturally, almost parenthetically, "But, of course, they were Jews as well as Russians." Too late, I remembered where I was and that Gasbia and Soad had asked me not to tell anyone I was Jewish. Hastily, I prepared to pass on. But Esam did not let it go. Excitedly, he leaned forward in his chair, his eyes widened and he said, "What did you say? What did you say? Joos? You are Joos?"

A chill fell on me as I heard those words. His voice was not threatening. Worse. It was fascinated, as if by the discovery of some unexpected freakishness, not quite human but extremely interesting. I did not at once reply and my silence dropped into the silence that suddenly surrounded me. I can still remember the quality of that silence. Silence that lasted only a few moments, I am sure, but fell with the force of a slow-motion dream and seemed, literally, to shine with a heavy shining stillness, as though it were composed of particles of dust of a peculiar brilliancy that had gathered themselves into thick clouds dropping on us, muffling us. Then Gasbia, her low shrieking voice forcing itself desperately through, said, "No, no! Don't be silly. Your father is dead. Your mother doesn't want to go to . . . You are *not* Jewish. You have nothing to do with that!"

"Of *course* I'm Jewish!" I cried reflexively, and then, with a sudden quick rush—curious! almost as though a void were being gratefully occupied—I was filled with pure terror.

I knew that in actuality these people (this kindly, decent lawyer!) and this place would not—could not—harm me. I kept saying to myself: There is nothing to be afraid of. There is absolutely nothing to be afraid of. But I was out of control. Waves of fear kept rising like nausea in me.

Some part of me knew, even as it was happening, that I was being irrationally overcome, that there was no proportionate relation between what I was feeling and what was actually happening, and afterwards, when I was home lying in bed, trying to figure it out, my mind a jumble of fragmented images and memories, it occurred to me that I would have perceived things differently had my own anxieties and irrational fears not leaped directly out of me to meet a moment that had appeared, I now realized, not threatening but dreadfully isolating.

It seemed to me, then, that if I had been more self-possessed than I in fact was, that is, if I did more thoroughly own myself, if there were no shadows of humiliation and painful dishonesties, no fearful half-thoughts and bewildering compulsions within me, if I were free and clear inside, I would have instantly assessed the situation more accurately, I would have known the exact dimension of true danger, and I would not have experienced the inflated terror I did feel, a terror that spoke to God alone knew what. And that panic. That nauseating panic! As though I were guilty, irrevocably guilty of being in the wrong place at the wrong time, and having been found out, only the worst could befall me, only loss and defeat and some unspeakable destiny could now follow.

So that's it, I thought calmly, lying in bed in Garden City. That's how it all *really* works.

In the Indonesian garden a gnarled black man in a *gelabya* and a white skullcap clips brilliantly scarlet flowers. In the street just below my window another man wearing ragged white balloon pants that go down to the knee and a black vest over a collarless white shirt marches behind a two-wheeled cart calling softly, "Bottled gas!" In the distance the Nile sparkles in the early March sunlight. The smell of freshly baked bread comes drifting up from somewhere down below. The streets are quiet and empty, the buildings of Garden City with their neat, rounded corners like a hard-edged painting in the clarifying light. . . . A perfect day for an abortion.

Naha came early this morning with Mona. She sat in a maroon chair in the living room, sullen anger on her face, while Mona flopped on a couch beside me and Magdi paced the floor, glaring at each of us in turn. He was frightened, and wished himself well out of the whole mess. Naha, on the other hand, as though she knew she was about to be discarded, was fighting with tears and anger and fierce looks to bring Magdi to her side; it was difficult to tell if the actual ordeal before her frightened her, she was so busy punishing Magdi. . . . Later, Magdi, in an utter confusion of self-defense, said to me, "She was very rude to me. Very rude! I cannot tolerate that."

The plan was: Naha and Mona were to go off to some doctor's office in Cairo for the abortion, Magdi was about to leave for Alexandria, and I was asked to remain in the flat to greet the women on their return. Naha would spend the day in Magdi's bed and return to her mother as late in the evening as she dared.

And so it all happened. At one o'clock in the afternoon the bell rang and I admitted an exhausted Naha leaning heavily on Mona's slight, sturdy frame. I took her other arm, pulled it across my shoulder and together we all steered a wobbly course down the hall to the bedroom. Naha undressed and crawled into bed. Mona took Naha's underwear and her slacks and disappeared into the bathroom. Sayeda made tea and silently brought it to the bedroom. Naha slept, Mona and I tiptoed about, the afternoon passed.

When Naha awoke, Sayeda was sent out to a restaurant and returned shortly with large packages of *kabob*, salad, bread and *tahina*° all wrapped neatly in white paper and string. Mona sat on Naha's bed, and I sat at the small table near the window. The two women on the bed looked like high school girls who had played hooky and were now giggling as they ate, enjoying their stolen time.

Early in the evening, Fawzy arrived. He came rushing down the hallway and stopped precipitously in the doorway to the bedroom, his jowly chin quivering, his eyes quick dark beads darting about the room in all directions, trying to grasp as much of the situation as possible before he had to speak. Naha looked up at him from her pillow, her dark eyes bold and flirtatious, her laughter a mocking triumph. Fawzy's hands slapped his thighs, and his eyes rolled to the ceiling.

"A child!" he said to me. "She is an absolute child."

Fawzy came and sat in the chair opposite me, and called to Sayeda to bring coffee. "I could not rest the entire day," he said, patting his

---

° A kind of thick paste made of crushed sesame into which Arabs dip bread; it is also used as a salad dressing.

forehead with a large linen handkerchief, "thinking of *her*. Anything can happen, after all, with these things, and what is one to do then? Hm-m-m? Hm-m-m?"

"Well, nothing did happen," I said. "She's fine, so relax."

"Yes, yes. *Relax*. What an American word! There is not its exact equivalent in the entirety of British English." His eyes returned to the bed, where Mona lay merrily stretched out on one hip, and Naha snuggled down under the covers, her black eyes huge with smug laughter. Fawzy stared sternly at them both, but they continued to laugh; undone, he, too, began to laugh, with his tongue caught between his teeth, emitting a kind of strangled hiss. ("T-s-hisssssss," went Fawzy.) "Ah, well," he sighed at last, wiping his eyes with his linen handkerchief, "better this than marriage, I suppose."

"Why do you say that, Fawzy?" I asked. There leaped into my mind the memory of the night Fawzy and Mona and Magdi had taken me to the Salt and Pepper, Cairo's most expensive night club; at one point in the evening Fawzy and I had been sitting at a table, while Mona and Magdi were out on the dance floor, giggling together like two children. Fawzy followed my gaze as it fixed on them, and suddenly he had said, "You are wondering why I took as my wife one so young, are you not?" "No," I'd said, startled, "not at all. I wasn't thinking that at all." Exactly as though I hadn't spoken, he continued. "She was an orphan. Yes, laugh if you wish, but that is the exact truth. Her father first lost all his money, and then he died. She was left with nothing; at sixteen her life was over. I saved her from all that. Yes, madam. I saved her." His eyes had rested lovingly on Mona.

Now Fawzy was saying (with the two women on the bed jabbering in Arabic it was almost as though we were alone), "Ah, lovely Vivian, you cannot mean that! Marriage, after all, is an irrevocable step, one with fierce consequences, whether taken lightly or in need."

"But, Fawzy," I said maliciously, "don't you believe in love? Don't you believe that if two people love each other they can overcome the strains of marriage and make their connection a happy and a necessary one?"

Fawzy sat regarding me in puffed silence. His thin lips drew together into a line pasted to his lower face, then they opened as though in need of air. His cigarette burned unheeded in his left hand.

"This is a very grave question, madam," Fawzy finally spit out, "this question of love and the family. One that cannot be dismissed casually. Hm-m-m? But," he said, leaning forward to squash his wasted cigarette, "we shall give it a try."

Fawzy usually calls me "lovely Vivian" and his manner is gay and flirtatious. But when the conversation turns serious his soul is up for grabs. His eyes become black beads. His mouth spits out clipped phrases. And I become "madam."

"Let us face the facts, madam," he continued. "As they are in life. The moment a man is married and secure of the woman" (his eyes darted to Mona) "love vanishes. And it is replaced by mixed affections. Composed mainly of respect. Admiration. A sense of the other's generosity. Forgivingness. Behavior in a crisis. And so on and so on. Very soon, these mixed affections, madam, give way themselves." (His eyes moved again to Mona, swinging her legs, talking fast.) "And are replaced, madam" (eyes sliding frantically toward the non-English-speaking wife once more) "by sheer habit." (He stopped completely for a moment.) "Sheer habit. Then the life is more hell than heaven, madam, regardless of how wonderful or unique or passionate the two people may have been at the beginning of their marital journey. They must continue to face each other during a succession of days and nights in which they no longer *wish* to face each other. Their household life is a round of mechanical responses, happily broken by a little tragedy now and then. That, my dear madam, is marriage. Of course, what justifies it all is the children. One's view of the passionate partner shifts to the children, and one's loving obligation to them. The family becomes everything. Everything. And the children will grow up and wish to marry and nothing on this earth—not a single solitary influence—will avert the will of that renewing delusion."

We both remained silent. Madam had absolutely nothing to say, shocked by the depth of resignation in Fawzy's voice. And, as one, we both looked at Naha. It was so easy to read her face: Now! Now that all this trouble is behind me, now that I am gay once more, *now* Magdi will marry me.

Who or what on earth could ever successfully convince her that if Magdi *did* marry her, in a few years . . .

At the end of Garden City, on the river's edge, is the bridge to Roda Island. You cross that bridge, as you do every bridge in Cairo, in a sea of traffic: cars, bicycles, pedestrians, donkeys, everything moving forward in a deafening swarm of darting vehicles and honking horns. Oh, those horns! Those horns that have begun to haunt my dreams and alter the rhythm of my speech and insinuate themselves into my every bit of consciousness.

"You are really ridiculous on this subject," Magdi had said to me one day as we were tearing along in the midst of it all, on a street headed for the Kasr-el-Nil Bridge. "We have many things to contend with here," said he, driving with one hand, honking with the other. "I *must* use my horn as much as I do. Now, take that fine gentleman over there" (pointing to a deadpan Arab in a trailing *gelabya* on a donkey in the right-hand lane). "If I do not use my horn he might suddenly decide to enter my lane. Or that one over there" (a turban on a wobbling bicycle to the left of us). "Or them" (three men, arms linked, strolling amidst the cars). One thing about Cairo traffic—it's very democratic; everyone walks without batting an eyelash in the middle of the gutter no matter what's happening; me too, now. I'm sure I'll get killed my first day back in New York.

So Magdi went hurtling along, honking away for dear life, headed directly for every pedestrian in sight (the favorite Cairo traffic sport), convinced that he was only taking rational stock of the situation. But I am now equally convinced that Cairenes honk in order to be sociable, in order to make contact. I have seen taxi drivers honking like crazy until you look at them; then they grin and stop. (Ah! They're just *lonely*.) I have seen cars honking at each other until one horn or the other breaks. I have seen cars driving along in absolutely unchanging circumstances for ten or fifteen minutes, then for no discernible reason, one will suddenly start honking. One day a Fiat honked out "Mary Had a Little Lamb."

The entire matter was sealed for me one day at the Hilton. I was passing along the back of the hotel and a number of little black-and-white Cairo taxis were lined up in the driveway. One, I noticed, was blocking the free passage of the driveway, as the taxi driver was talking to a departing passenger. Suddenly, I heard a short, sharp, vicious car horn and before I could really grasp my own thoughts I was thinking: That's not a Cairene. Sure enough, it was an American car with three Americans in it right behind the taxi, and they meant *business*. I realized then that the sound of the Cairo honking is never angry, never hostile, never really irritated, only excitable and childish, full of surface temper and desire for attention.

Carried along on just such a tide of traffic, you cross into Roda, and keep moving across the island with its densely packed streets spreading out to the left and to the right until you are on the ramp of another bridge, this one the widest and loveliest of all of Cairo's bridges. No matter what the weather, the river below this bridge is always *shining*: so wide, so expansive, stretching, stretching in a lush endlessness that swells the heart, and produces pleasure as open as the merging elements all around.

At the end of this bridge you are in Giza. A thousand years ago Giza was a village nine miles distant from the city limits of Cairo, dominated by the great pyramids built by the Pharaohs. The pyramids are still out there, at the end of the Pyramids Road that now bisects a Giza that has moved slowly up the river to meet the growing city, and is today a section of Cairo.

You move slowly through Giza, a strangely mixed section of extremely wealthy streets and a kind of mad, sprawling street life. There is something wild in Giza, something I can never figure out, but I always feel as though I am about to have a fatal accident here. And, indeed, there are more bus and automobile crack-ups in Giza, I think, than anywhere else in the city.

And then you are out of Giza, out of the city, and on the Pyramids Road, and everything in you opens up to the smell of freshening air, the wide road ahead, the density of Cairo behind you, the excitement of possibility that always comes as one heads out into open country; and there, in the distance, are the pyramids, those triangular miniatures on the horizon that grow larger and larger until they fill the sky around you, and you dutifully think Serious Historical Thoughts, whizzing by, passing the lovely canals that stretch to the north and to the south of the east-west road, canals that take your breath away, with their tender green trees and fields leaning toward the narrow channels of water, looking as though they have not changed in five thousand years. And at last, you are genuinely free and clear of the city, and out in the countryside, heading north into the Delta.

I am with Salah on this soft Friday morning (Friday is the Moslem sabbath, and Friday in Cairo is like Sunday in New York); we are going to "the land" (Salah's farm). The farm can be reached in two ways, but we take the agricultural road to Alexandria instead of the road that runs through the desert, as I, a foreigner, am not permitted on any desert road, from which the majority of Egypt's military installations are visible. We drive down wide dirt roads lined with hanging mosses and eucalyptus trees, an occasional peasant on a donkey, a barefoot woman in black balancing a water jug on her head, a car honking down the dead center of the road, chickens scattering wildly. In thirty minutes we are turning right onto another, narrower road surrounded by fruit trees and the deep smell of silent sunlight; we are on Salah's land. "The land" is twenty-seven acres of desert that Salah has turned into a productive farm of fruit trees and beanfields. He has owned these acres for a number of years but it was not until his factory was nationalized that he turned his aggravated energies to the land. Once he did, there was no turning back; he would not rest until the land had been bent to his will; until he had "created" something; until he could turn his aristocratic head in a dozen directions and feel his reflected self. (Of course, Salah would not quite describe his desire to farm as I have done. . . .)

The car comes to a halt near a fork in a road that bisects the fields of the farm. Nearby, in the field closest to the car, is a kind of arbor, vines strung along a frame of poles providing a natural roof over the cleared space in which an earthen bench has been carved and a wooden table set up.

"Let us take our rest here," says Salah, "and then I will show you the entire farm."

Salah wears a white full-sleeved blouse and white cotton slacks. He now removes his shoes, rolls his pants partway up his legs, and announces with satisfaction, "Now, I am on the land!"

We sit in the arbor, feeling the warm silence all about us. I feel an extraordinary peace, one I associate with desert lands. There is some deep, sunny, horizontal quiet here rooted in warm sand, some endlessly extending presence of the land that is enormously satisfying.

In a while Salah takes my hand and begins to lead me out of the arbor and down the road to our left. He indicates the direction in which his prize piece of machinery—the English pump that is at the center of his entire system of irrigation—is housed. It is our destination, and clearly it will mean making a huge square around the fields of the farm, so that I will have seen half the place by the time we get to the pumphouse.

We walk for a while in silence down the wide sandy road, on either side of us an even thickness of fruit trees. "These are all oranges, peaches, and pears," says Salah. At the end of the road directly ahead of us, about half a mile in the distance, is a line of trees tall and wispy, tossing themselves up in the air. The trees are slim and fragile, very beautiful against the desert.

"They are there to break the wind," says Salah. "In winter the wind is terrible here. And look, look at the fields below the trees. See the blue and the white of them?" Yes, he is right. The fields are covered with tiny white and blue flowers. "Those are deliberately planted to keep the fields in readiness. I cannot plant the fields but I will not let them lie fallow."

The road curves to the right and we follow it. Now we are surrounded by low plants in even rows in fields to the left and to the right of us. The sun is stronger here and I feel it soaking through me. The rows are so even!

"Squash, peppers, lettuce," Salah says solemnly, walking with his hands clasped behind his back. He is telling me of the long, continuous labor that these fields represent, of the days and nights and endless hours of back-breaking work and attention to detail.

We come now to a narrow irrigation canal running through the fields. As we draw closer I see two peasants bending low over the flashing green water, poking at something in the bottom of the canal. They are sitting on their haunches, their knees wide apart, dressed in white cotton *gelabyas* that balloon out across their spread-out bodies; their faces are as dark and gnarled as the trees; their heads covered with the familiar white skullcaps that come down to the tops of their ears; one of them has a cigarette butt in his mouth. When they catch sight of us they jump to their feet, addressing Salah as *bey*° and touching their hands to their foreheads for me. We nod and continue. "Two of my boys," Salah says proudly.

In a while, the road curves once more toward the right; we are making the second turn in the square; the land begins to change, rising slowly, almost imperceptibly, then leveling out, with the sky very wide and the shallow desert beyond, and on the horizon before us a low squared-off concrete building, with steep concrete steps on one side of it and a flat rooftop terrace, all flat, sharp, clean edges.

As we approach the building I see the long, even, concrete canal half-filled with water that surrounds the building on two sides; it has about it a look of extraordinary orderliness and reassurance, almost like an illustration in a technical manual rather than the actual three-dimensional thing itself. Salah leads me up the stairs first; we will descend to the pumphouse afterwards.

On the roof of the building we stand, surveying Salah's domain. Here, seen all at once, is the farm, which we have just walked across. Indeed, it is glorious. Row upon row of the most evenly planted trees and field after field of lush fruit and vegetable plants, all looking miraculously the same, all separated by tiny ridges of exactly the same height. It looks like the kind of farm one sees in California, the kind of farm that is made with the use of expensive and complicated machinery.

"And I have done it all with my boys!" Salah says, triumphantly. He leans against the edge of the terrace roof, his head a bronzed dome in the sunlight, his eyes defiant green, his clothes arrogant white. He looks startlingly alone in the world. For the first time, I feel in his face, etched against this land that is now his entire life, the lonely strength and mute frailty of this oddly aristocratic man. Something in Salah is continually being rebuilt with the same patience and dogged single-mindedness with which he has built this California farm here in the desert outside of Cairo . . . but at what cost? at what cost?

We descend to the pumphouse, and there it is. His prize, his

° The feudal form of address to a person of high standing, the equivalent of "master" or "sir."

trophy, his wife, his mistress, his best friend: the English machine, gleaming with polish and wiped carefully clean. He explains at great length exactly what the machine does to accomplish canal irrigation of the farm, caressing it as he speaks, unable to keep his hands off his love. I keep nodding at what I assume are the appropriate moments. I don't understand a word he's saying.

We leave the pumphouse and continue down the fourth side of the square, back in the direction of the arbor. In these fields to our right are the mango trees, most of them very young and green.

"It takes ten years for a mango tree to mature," Salah says, "although one can pluck fruit after three years. Mine are still very young. But I do not let the fields waste while the mango trees are growing. I have planted beans here. Come, let us go into the fields. I believe my boys are working here this morning."

"How did you learn all this, Salah?" I ask. "After all, you were a manufacturer."

"I read a book," Salah replies triumphantly. "And I followed it to the minutest detail. If the book said mango trees must be planted eight feet apart, it was eight feet apart. Not seven and a half feet, not nine feet. Eight feet. And I did it by being here day and night for months, for years! Watching over my boys to make sure they did exactly as I wished. It meant walking over these fields continually, watching to see that everything was being planted and pruned and plucked in exactly its right time, that disease was being prevented, that not too much water or too little was being released into the fields, oh, thousands of things! But I did it, and now you are walking on the finest farm in Egypt. And I did it with men, not machines. Men, and patience. You see, *that*—if they would but listen—could be the secret of Egypt."

We were walking now through the fields, row after row after row of bean plants with tiny mango trees evenly interspersed among them, all neatly separated by little ridges of sandy dirt. And here were Salah's "boys," bending, plucking, overturning. They were about fifteen or twenty peasants ranging in age from eighteen to sixty, all dressed in the white *gelabyas* and skullcaps, all moving about like gentle silent specters. We came to a peasant crouching over a tiny campfire, and Salah stopped.

"We will sit here and take tea with him," he said. "You have never in your life tasted anything as delicious as the tea these peasants make in the fields."

The man smiled shyly at us, and beckoned to us to seat ourselves on the little ridge before him. He set up a tiny scaffolding of twigs over the fire and placed a tin can with a loop of wire across it. Then he began to stir the liquid in the tin can, talking all the while to Salah.

"What is he saying?"

"He needs more money for the boys. Always the same story."

The tea was ready very quickly. The peasant took a tiny teapot from a packet of black oilcloth behind him. He poured the tea into the pot, and then produced three small, slim glasses, all curved outward at the top like an inverted bell. Lifting the pot high into the air he allowed a thin stream of golden tea, poured from this great height, to fill each glass. Then he handed one to Salah, one to me, and took one for himself. We all drank. The tea was magnificent: rich, sweet, aromatic. I felt happy drinking this tea, and I consumed many glasses, to the endless satisfaction of Salah and his "boy."

Salah lit a cigarette and leaned back on his elbows. "Ah, it is good to be here! Very good. It is a cleansing of the soul to walk in my fields and to talk to my boys. They are so simple, so happy, so without desire for the world outside."

"Salah, you sound like an American white Southerner of a generation ago."

Salah looked puzzled for a moment. Then his eyes lit up and he threw back his head in a huge laugh. "I see what you mean," he said gleefully. But he sobered up quickly. "But no, it is not the same thing at all. Our peasants are very different from your blacks. Their wisdom is simple but deep; if they reject the world it is out of a belief that that world is really not as good as the one they have here. Believe me, they do not comprehend the revolution at all. It is not *their* revolution. What is happening in Cairo means nothing to them. Thay cannot really sense any of it. See this man here?" He nods in the direction of the man bending once more over his tea. "A few weeks ago he said to me, '*Bey*, tell me, are the Russians the sons of the pashas?' 'Why do you ask me that?' I asked him. 'Well,' he said, 'we were trying to lift a very heavy box in the village last week, and we could not do so. A Russian was there, and he picked it up in his arms as though it were a baby and carried it for us.'

"Now," continued Salah, lighting another cigarette, "this man knows that the pashas, who were Turks, were white-skinned and very strong. So he concludes that the Russians—who are white-skinned and very strong—must be the sons of the pashas. And this, after twenty years of socialism on the radio!"

"None of this means a damn thing, Salah. The real question is: Would you under any circumstances change lives with this man?"

"Would I! In a moment! In a moment!"

"What's stopping you?"

"Well." He stopped short. "Well . . . I simply *cannot*. I have too many responsibilities. Too many. . . ."

Late in the afternoon, we returned to Cairo by way of the desert road. When I remonstrated with him, Salah shook his head and said, "No, no. You will see. They will not stop the car when they see me go by. They know me. You will see. After all, you are with a very important man!" But the self-mockery had an acid taste to it: and never more so than when things turned out as he had predicted they would. As we passed the checkpoint he merely waved to the two soldiers standing on the side of the road. They waved back, and we continued on without stopping.

On Monday afternoon, Soad called.

"We are going tonight to choose Za-Za's furniture. It would be a most useful experience for you, to see where the furniture is made in Cairo, how it is sold, and so on and so on. If you are free, the Doctor will call for you at seven o'clock."

They came at seven-forty-five: Ibrahim at the wheel, and Soad, the three children and Za-Za, all crushed into the back so that I could have the comfortable seat in front. We drove madly through Garden City, into the district called Kasr-el-Ainy, past Midan el Tahrir, through the heart of fashionable downtown Cairo, toward the Opera Square, and then off to the right down narrow, twisting streets, choked at this hour with traffic leaping, pushing, pulling, cursing, needing to get it *done*: all around, men in *gelabyas* sitting at tiny round copper tables set out on the sidewalk or just inside a large open café, talking, playing a board game, smoking through a great length of "rope" attached to a bubbling bottle; children playing a street game the equivalent of tag; mothers pulling the black *milayeh* closer around their mouths, still managing to give a child standing before them a tongue-lashing; men at steaming carts dishing stuff up by the light of a tiny kerosene lamp attached to the frame of the cart; the Koran and Om Kalthoum (Cairo's legendary singer; a waif from the village with an extraordinary peasant voice, she began more than fifty years ago to dominate the world of Egyptian music; to this day she is adored by the poor of three generations and, now seventy, she sings in person in Cairo on the first Thursday of each month) blaring down pitilessly from a thousand radios to blend with the honking shouting din.

We came at last into a quieter street where much the same was going on but at a greatly reduced rate, the cafés thinned out, the radios rare, hardly any children in the road; here, two or three old men around the copper table in a store doorway, only now and then someone smoking. Before an open, deeply lit doorway on this street Ibrahim stopped. Two large rooms were instantly apparent, standing side by side on the street: one a regular store, the other a kind of open garage fixed up as a workroom. In one the furniture was made, in the other it was sold. I looked into the open doorway before heading for the store, and saw standing, waist-high, at a tremendous table covered with wood shavings, about six or eight boys from twelve to fifteen years old; they had a chest of drawers on the table and were busily planing, sanding, applying glue from a sticky black pot; I stared at them; it was now eight-thirty in the evening.

We entered the store—all of us—and the three men inside bowed and smiled, greeting all as though they were old old friends, or, at the very least, distantly related.

"Do you know these men?" I whispered into Soad's ear.

"No. We have never been here before," she replied.

The rooms of the store were not large enough to have all the furniture spread across the floor. As a result, furniture was stacked to the ceiling so that the place looked like a warehouse rather than a showroom. But we managed. The salesman followed us around with a long stick and when Soad pointed, he placed the stick high up against the piece she indicated and all of our attention was directed thither. There were two kinds of phony French provincial furniture, there was a great deal of 1930s blond, and one angular bedroom "suite" known as "modern." For a full hour Soad and Ibrahim argued the good and bad points of each piece of furniture and haggled with the salesman exactly as if they had already decided to buy (when, in fact, Soad told me they were just looking and wouldn't dream of buying this night). Everyone's opinion—including mine— was solicited. Everyone's, that is, except the bride's. Za-Za hung back, her cow eyes dark and silent in that moon-smooth face, clutching Gasbia's baby girl to her huge bosom, laughing now and then with the other two children: a huge child-nurse inexplicably playing this bewildering role of bride.

When Soad turned to me for the fifth time and asked me what I thought of a dining-room set, did I think it would be easy to clean (the big concern is the dreadful, eternal thick dust that blows in off the desert into every crevice of Cairo, and will the furniture be easy to dust off?), I grew very uneasy and I said what did it matter what I thought, it was Za-Za who would have to live with it. She ignored me, saying absently, "Of course, of course," her mind on fifty other things. But I pursued.

"Really," I said, "why isn't Za-Za allowed to pick her own furniture?"

"But, my dear!" protested Soad. "Of *course* she can pick her own furniture. She can say no to anything."

"Accepting or rejecting what you choose is not the same thing as choosing something herself," I countered. For some reason, the sight of Za-Za hanging back at the end of the parade while Ibrahim and Soad decided on the stuff she'd have to spend the rest of her life with embarrassed me dreadfully; I could not let it go.

"Well," Soad said, a bit bewilderedly, "we must have *some* rights. After all," she laughed with good-natured amusement, "*we* are paying."

I returned to Lizette Abu Shady's art gallery in Zamalek this afternoon, a day later than I had said I would come. Now it is late at night and I sit here at the antique desk in the living room in Garden City, Samiha asleep down the hall, Magdi away from the city, and I, perfectly still inside, a thick strand of concentrated response that muffles the immediacy of this room, this neighborhood, the city even. I feel caught by the sharp memory of those few hours spent with Lizette Abu Shady; a memory filled with an oddly voluptuous melancholy; a melancholy that slows down the rhythm of my breath, and produces a soft pain behind my eyes. Something about the lady at Number Seven rue Brazil has pierced me and pinned my attention. . . .

When I enter the gallery she is sitting alone behind the same antique table she sat behind the other day. She is very short and very fat, somewhere in her fifties. She wears a shapeless blue dress, an old black sweater across her shoulders, and scuffed shoes. She appears unconcerned, beyond it all, surrounded by her flesh. But in the middle of her jowly ruin of a face she is beautiful: smooth cheeks, a narrow finely made nose, marvelous eyes, and that sexy brown-gray hair falling like Marlene Dietrich's smooth helmet halfway to her shoulders.

Those eyes of hers: large, brown, finely rimmed, smooth surfaces; utterly calm; frighteningly calm; they seem to sink, behind their smooth brown surfaces, to some lightless depth not available to the public. They stare off into space a great deal when she speaks, approaching but not quite crossing the flat edge of bitterness; they give to her face an aristocratic aloofness, making her seem almost unapproachable; one feels her distance must be respected, one must justify disturbing the withdrawn equilibrium of that dead brown calm.

And yet, if you stick with her long enough, if you keep talking, keep asking questions and waiting for answers, you see that there is in those eyes not a void, not a human coldness, but rather a gathered spiritual toughness whose heart you are looking directly into; a toughness that took years to grow itself, and terrible things to grow itself on; and you know that those eyes attest to a genuine legacy of experience.

Lizette Abu Shady broods. She sits in her beautiful art gallery that was once the bookshop Françoise worked in and that the marvelous

Abdullah has fled from, and she broods. Like a hooded, unblinking turtle: she broods.

She has two smiles: one is controlled, one overcomes her. The controlled smile is small, tight, cynical, causing the upper lip to curve away almost in a snarl. This smile Lizette uses as a mannerism, accompanying the many casually hopeless observations she makes. The other smile is open, surprised, with the light of responsiveness taking her against her will. This smile is caused by the person she is speaking with; it comes out of the unexpectedness of human communication, it takes her completely by surprise, she is thrown off guard, and all the expectation of adolescent possibility is suddenly alive in her, shining with deep suddenness in the face of this brooding, compelling woman with the flat hooded eyes sunk in all that rooted flesh, those eyes that have watched . . . what? how much? how long? where and with whom? and for what?

Bit by bit, she speaks. It doesn't really matter what she says: when, in answer to which question, what observation, silence, flicked cigarette, call for coffee, easy pause, dry stare, deep memory, distant laughter, recalled fears . . . it is all of a piece her speech, it is an atmosphere, a substance; it is the sense of the woman, the flavor of her history, the peculiarity of her very Egyptian bind.

"Yes, Egypt is changing," Lizette says, and she stares across the room. "Faster than she could have believed possible. Oh, if you talk to those who lost in the revolution you will hear: Everything is terrible, it was never worse, you can't get meat, can't make any money, on and on.

"I know what I'm talking about. I could have been one of them. My family *is* one of them. . . ." She looks off for a long while, drags her eyes back to my face with difficulty.

"After all, I was one of the 'white' people. My parents were Greeks, my mother is Christian, we speak only Greek in the family, to this day I can't read or write literary Arabic, although of course I speak Arabic fluently. I was born in Cairo and raised to believe that the Egyptians are dirty and stupid. When I finished high school I was packed off to New York City for a proper education." She smiles that tight, cynical, little smile of hers. "After you came here the other day I began thinking about New York for the first time in years . . . it all began to come back to me . . . Columbia University, International

House, the American students, the elevated trains everywhere—that was 1936, are those trains still there?

"They wanted me to stay, everyone wanted me to stay: scholarships, money, marriages, professorships they offered me. . . . But I came back. My heart is Egyptian.

"I believed in socialism for Egypt long before the revolution. Oh, it is an absurdity! Democracy for Egypt! Where? By who? *For* who? In a country that is ninety percent illiterate peasants who will run the democracy? It would be the same old story—a democracy for the few. Egypt *had* to go left. And, of course, the time was right, history was with her, who on earth could make a capitalist revolution in this day and age?

"So they went left. But you see, it was *their* revolution, they didn't like any other brand of revolutionary. . . ." She sinks deeper into her skin, her eyes go flat, even the tight little smile disappears, she broods inside the memories . . . the room is evaporating, the time blurs . . . she returns with a start.

"So they tortured the Marxists. They pulled us out of our homes, out of our lives, out of our universities, out of all our talk, talk, talk. We were the enemy in their midst, we received the knock on the door at three o'clock in the morning. . . . That is when Abdullah fled. But we who remained, we were hauled off to the dungeons in Cairo, and then out to the camps in the desert.

"Yes, I know something of the police state. My husband was tortured, and he died in prison in 1960 when my daughter was two and a half years old. He was forty-seven, a professor of history and economics. A wonderful man. Very, very intelligent . . ." She is fading away again, the eyes going . . . but she speaks her bemused thoughts. "I remember my family almost died when I married him. He was an Egyptian Moslem and my aristocratic Greek family was horrified. The first time they came to the house, my husband sat in his chair and he took his shoes off as many good Moslems do in their own houses. My sister turned pale. . . ." Lizette shakes her head violently, her lovely hair puffing out all around her face.

"Many were tortured. But only fifteen were killed. He was one of them. Actually, it was a very bloodless revolution. . . . Now, many of them are out of prison. Some even holding high positions.

"But, *still*, I support the revolution. Still, I think it was the only way for Egypt. The Egyptians denigrate themselves. But they do not see themselves as I do. They are a very intelligent people. Not very scientific, perhaps. Perhaps not very good at those things. But I watch them, these very intelligent ones, growing right up out of the streets. . . . And today a porter's son goes to the university. . . .

"Now I sit here: a failed bourgeois, a failed Marxist, a failed wife. I will never marry again because if I did my husband's family could take my daughter away from me. I am finished with all that, finished. . . . I surround myself with beautiful things, I raise my young daughter, I no longer argue with my family. It is very quiet here now. Very quiet. Zamalek is a good place to grow old."

I cannot stop seeing her face before me, the marvelous eyes, the lovely hair, the two smiles, the hooded turtle body, the wild compression of contradictions that is her life, her essence, her Egypt. It turns and turns in my mind, falling and tumbling into different shapes, like threatening shards in a kaleidoscope and, idiotically, one fixed image returns and returns: the image of Lizette saying, "I never learned to read and write Arabic."

Oh, this Egypt, where everyone speaks three languages with a facility amounting almost to national genius, but Arabic was never compulsory! Where native Egyptians could grow up, their colonized souls trilingual, Arabic an oddly fragile connective, a sweetly thickened thread invisible in the air of occupation, a dream of personal history, haunting and difficult to grasp, a struggle for identity from which one falls back in joy and despair. . . .

The morning tosses itself out, brightly scattered and filled with the hurrying promise that is the streets of Cairo at the beginning of the day. I am walking from Garden City into downtown Cairo, and the pleasure I take in the scene all about me is tinged with a peculiar kind of familiarity, one born in the suddenness of delayed recognitions; and there is in me now as I walk through Cairo a sense of other places, other days, of a connectiveness in my life strung like telephone wire across the globe.

For weeks I have been overwhelmed by the massive poverty, by the thousands and thousands of Cairo poor walking, running, sitting, in their rags and their *gelabyas*, on their donkeys and carts and bare sore feet; the thousands and thousands of people whose lives seem subhuman to me: all these *gelabyas*, all these bare feet and dusty brown faces, all these people to run and fetch and carry and clean, all these blind and half-blind, crippled and bandaged; these streets and streets and streets of packed, huddled humanity amidst filth and decay and neglect, this incomparable throwback to the teeming Middle Ages.

And suddenly this feeling—this revulsion—has begun to alter, to lose its strength, and drain away from the surface of my mind. Partly, I think, because that dumb, sluggish misery one expects to accompany this kind of life is simply not present in Cairo. People are constantly *moving* and doing and carrying on: exactly as if they had someplace to go, and something to do, exactly as if it all mattered.

One day I found myself saying: It's just like New York. And I realized on the instant that what I had said was true. Cairo *is* like New York. Not, obviously, in terms of the quality of its population, but in terms of the quality of its energy: compulsive, full of hunger and anxiety, and above all, longing. Cairo, like New York, is in pain, but *alive*.

It is *not* like New York—dear God, not at all like New York—in the sense that New York has not been able to deal with pressure without becoming brutal, whereas Cairo . . . oh, not Cairo! Something in Cairo hangs on. There is an endurance of spirit here that touches and excites, a melancholy sweetness in the determination not only to survive but to remain human as well.

One day I was swinging along Kasr-el-Ainy, a wide crowded street full of shops and houses, headed toward downtown Cairo, the street I am on right this minute. On that other day, a boy of about eight or ten, dressed in rags from neck to knee and dragging a goat by the ear, passed me on the street. The boy turned to stare at me, and as it happened, I turned to stare at him at the same time. We stood there—staring at each other—and then, at precisely the same moment, we both burst out laughing.

I have never been in a peasant country where my stare was not answered either with total expressionlessness, or with low-keyed fear or hostility. When that boy with the goat laughed the particular quality of Cairo crystallized for me. The boy and I were equals at that moment—no mistaking it—simply because we were exchanging total human recognition, and because it had obviously not occurred to either of us that the other one didn't have that recognition coming. It is this human recognition, extended to all, withheld from none that—regardless of what happens in the houses—is felt in the streets of Cairo. I have seen evidence of it fifty times a day since I have been here, and felt the extraordinary atmosphere such a quality creates, an atmosphere inundated with affection, and alive with the helplessness of compassion.

If the word for London is decency and the word for New York is violence, then, beyond doubt, the word for Cairo is tenderness. Tenderness is what pervades the air here. Tenderness is what you feel in the streets, in the offices, in the conversations, in the humor, in the music, in the way men embrace on the streets, in the way people rush to help if someone stumbles, in the way a woman smooths back her servant's hair, in the way food is offered, in the way the harshness of a political conversation is suddenly undercut with a gesture of the hand or an expression in the eyes; in all these ways sympathy forces itself through ritual politeness and emotional shyness and dehumanizing poverty, and the recognition of this sympathy rather than the frightened denial of it creates the shrewdness of emotional intelligence that dominates this strange Moslem city on the other side of history. *That* is what I am now perpetually aware of. That is what makes my heart light this morning and carries me without fear down streets I have never been on, into districts I am unfamiliar with, into places where I am the original stranger.

I have passed from the wide boulevard of Kasr-el-Ainy into Midan el Tahrir, through the battering clang and din of the square, knocked about in the dust by five hundred rushing Cairenes, into Soliman Pasha Street, headed for Midan Soliman Pasha, Cairo's most elegant square, and somewhere beyond it, Sharif Street, and on that street a store I am looking for. The store is the Standard Stationery Company; it is the only place in Cairo where I can get the particular typewriter ribbon I need.

Coming onto Midan Soliman Pasha—really a large traffic circle in the center of which, as in every other square in Cairo, stands an oxidized bronze statue of the patriot for whom the square, inevitably, is named—I spot Groppi's, the hundred-year-old European bakery-café that is famous even outside of Cairo, and pushing through the crowds, I am on the other side of the square and headed in the general direction of Sharif Street which I found my way to once before. I keep walking along the street that is filled with expensive shoe stores, import shops, dry goods, bakeries, *sha-werma* restaurants, a movie house, the blare of Egyptian songs, the honking rhythm of traffic, policemen in black or white military uniforms, their arms moving like semaphore signalers in place of traffic lights, women shopping, men rushing to business, boys from twelve to sixty going at a dead-run with small tin trays covered with tiny coffee cups, glasses of water and the little brass pots in which Turkish coffee is made, others selling junk jewelry off racks standing against buildings, picking at you as you go by, old men in hopes of a few piastres rushing to open taxi doors when they have already been hailed by someone else, women in black or white *milayehs* sitting yogi-fashion on the ground, often nursing an infant, their hands wordlessly outstretched, peanut vendors standing before their carts whose tiny chimneys are smoking and whose paper cone containers are stacked high, bending perilously in the slight March wind.

As usual, what I am most aware of is the men, the men with each other, dominating the landscape of the street. Everywhere men walk, arms linked or, often, holding hands, as lovers do in the West: two students, two peasants, two lawyers, two importers; a grandfather and a young friend; a man of twenty and another of forty; two boys of twelve; two men of thirty; two twenty-year-olds with their arms locked around each other's necks. . . . They move like figures in a Chagall painting, doe-eyed and leaning softly toward one another, almost as though not touching the ground; the street seems full of this dark, soft, dancing cleaving together of the men. And when two friends meet on the street, and there is a sudden outcry, and the two men clasp each other strenuously, give each other bear hugs and kiss each other on both cheeks, it is almost as though a rhythm were being broken for the sake of replenishment. . . . I cannot understand, really, why I feel strengthened watching the men with each other; why *they* seem strengthened: strong in the fragility of the human embrace.

I am lost now. I stand somewhere, not sure I'm still on the street I started down, looking up at buildings I don't recognize at all, my precarious sense of direction now utterly at sea. I adopt my usual tactic and remain firmly where I am.

"Sir," I say to a man in an old brown pin-stripe and thick glasses. "Sir?" The man stops, openly curious about the foreign lady, and stares full into my face as if amazed that I can actually utter words.

"Can you tell me how to get to Sharif Street?" I say, never doubting that he understands English.

"*La*," he says, shaking his finger under my nose. "*La eengleese, la eengleese.*"

Okay, okay, on your way, don't stand there waiting behind that open mouth and those black crystallized eyes for the foreign freak to perform.

"Sir, sir, oh sir."

"Yes, madam? May I help you?" Another pin-stripe, this one tall and self-assured: very black hair, warm olive face, white collar, bending toward me, an arc of fleshy kindness.

"Can you tell me how to get to Sharif Street?"

"Sharif Street. Sharif Street. Let me see now." Brows drawn together, finger on pursed lips, total concentration. "Yes!" triumphantly. "You go *this* way."

I have an odd sense that it is *not* this way, but rather *that* way, and I stand, puzzling, about to say: Are you sure?

"No, that is not correct," says another voice directly behind my right shoulder. I swing around, the arc straightens up, the voice is met head-on. It belongs to a tall boy of sixteen or eighteen, very thin, painfully thin, in a white slightly shabby collar, V-necked maroon sweater, clean dark cotton pants, with a student's notebook in his hand; his hair is slightly kinky, brown and clipped close to his head; his face is brown and bony with a large mouth and alert brown eyes behind horn-rimmed glasses. There is in those eyes an expression of amusement gentle but cynical, the characteristic of suffering intelligence. He looks like Gandhi's grandson, I want to ask him if he's Egyptian, what's he doing here in Cairo, say: You're right, Sharif Street is *not* this way, stay here and fight for it, we both know you're right, but this ignorant pin-stripe can convince us both he's right and we're wrong because he seems so much more at ease in the world than you look or I feel, but I'm with you, I'm with you . . .

"Oh?" I say to the boy. "Which way do you think Sharif Street is?"

"This way," he says without hesitation, his hand moving in the direction I had begun to suspect was the correct one. "I am going that way, I will walk with you if you like, and show you where to turn for Sharif Street."

"No, no," the pin-stripe says vigorously. I look into his face. I know he doesn't know where the hell Sharif Street is, but he's more than willing to take me by the arm and shove me in an unknown direction rather than admit his ignorance.

The boy looks at me, rolls his eyes briefly toward heaven, and says, "I assure you, it is this way."

"Yes, I believe you." And I turn to the pin-stripe, thanking him for all his help but I'll walk a bit in this direction and see if I don't find the place I'm looking for.

"Where are you going on Sharif Street?" the boy asks, walking swiftly beside me down the sunny crowded narrow street we have turned onto, neatly sidestepping sitting beggars, darting boys, stalled carts, shoving shoppers, while I am barreling into everything, trying to follow his lead, I can see already he's a professional walker in this city, and I must concentrate so hard I am getting a headache.

"I am trying to find the Standard Stationery store," I say, elbows out, breathing quickly.

"Oh yes," he says. "I know it well. I will show you exactly where it is."

"Oh thank you! That is very kind of you. I'm not taking you out of your way, am I?"

"Not at all. It is directly on my way."

"I *knew* that man didn't really know where Sharif Street was."

"No." The boy smiles. "But you see, he wears a good suit and he carries a case and I . . ." His shoulders shrug and his hand passes downward to indicate his appearance. "How could *I* know where Sharif Street is, and he not know?" We both laugh and look directly into each other's eyes. I like this boy. Oh, I do like him!

"Excuse me," he says, "are you English?"

"No, I'm American."

"American! How wonderful. I know only two Americans. They come to the library all the time. I work in the library, and we talk, the Americans and I. Perhaps you would like to meet them?"

"Perhaps. What are they doing here?"

"They study. You know, all foreigners come here to *study*. They think they come to study Egypt and Egyptians. They bury themselves in libraries. They read about the Pharaohs. They read statistics from the government reports. They go to Khan Khalili. They go to the American University. And they go home and write about . . . *me*." He sticks a mocking finger into his chest. "But I do not find myself in these books. Never I find myself in these books."

"Well, I, too, have come to write about *you*." I laugh.

"Yes?" His eyebrows shoot up. "Will you come to the library?"

"No."

He slaps his knee in delight. We have arrived at Sharif Street. He points diagonally across the street. "There is the Standard Stationery store," he says. I turn to thank him and stretch out my hand to say good-bye. He takes it, and holds it briefly.

"Perhaps we could meet again?" he says. "I know so few foreigners."

I am about to say no automatically. After all, a pickup? What do I know about him? Where will it lead me? I look into the face of Gandhi's grandson.

"Yes, certainly," I say. "Let's see, today is Thursday. How about Sunday afternoon?"

"Excellent. I must work in the morning on Sunday. I am free after twelve o'clock."

"Let's meet at Groppi's," I say.

"That is very good," the boy says. "I will be at Groppi's at twelve-thirty on Sunday. Now, you must know my name and I must know yours. I am called Mohammed. Mohammed Fouad El Dine."

I tell him my name and we part, happy that we have not had to put a surgical end to the sympathy between us. I run across the street to the big European-style stationery store where I will purchase my typewriter ribbon, rejoicing in the unexpected rewards of my lousy sense of direction.

Soad's brother, Monir of the birthday party, called. He wanted to discuss United States policy with me, but would take me sightseeing so the pill would not be too bitter to swallow. Would I be interested in visiting the Mohammed Ali Mosque and the Citadel with him? I warned Monir that I was the wrong American to discuss "policy" with, that I knew nothing of politics, either in his country or my own.

"Of course, of course," he said abruptly. I laughed.

"No, I really *mean* it," I said.

We agreed to meet on Wednesday at ten in the morning. I would be waiting at the flat in Garden City for him.

Monir drove a white Nasr, the little Egyptian car that is actually a Fiat, and he drove it like a madman. I lurched around in the front seat, protesting silently to myself: He's too *old* to be driving like this! Looking over at the face beside me, attached to the hands and feet that now controlled my mortal destiny, I was struck as I had not been previously by the force and definition of Monir's features. I had been too lazy to think the last time I'd seen him and had dismissed him as a "kindly old man" resigned to decency instead of action. Now, watching him wrench the car in and out of gear, and feeling myself tearing along as though at the side of a hotrodder, the heavy Romanesque quality in the face of the sixty-four-year-old engineer became apparent to me, and I thought this was a man who would resign himself to *nothing*: the heavy rather hooked nose whose long sensual nostrils curved arrogantly when he cut off another driver, the lips that tightened into a thin bluish line when someone cut him off, the watered blue eyes that looked so blandly on the honking mayhem he was helping to cause—these were the features of a man who would think of himself as giving orders until the day he died.

"*Why* has the United States given us over to the Russians?" he cried exasperatedly, as the car raced across Cairo, headed for the desert edge of the city where the famous Citadel has rested with its back to the Mukattam Hills, facing the entirety of Cairo since the beginning of the thirteenth century. (Built as a mountain fortress during the reign of the medieval Moslem ruler Saladin, the Citadel is Cairo's most symbolic landmark: part of the first authentic attempt to make of the city a unified whole, protected by strong walls and impregnable defenses. Its symbolic power increased when later, in 1811, the tyrant, Mohammed Ali, had four hundred and eighty Mamelukes—Turkish lords of the Ottoman Empire—massacred within its walls.)

"What do you mean, given you over to the Russians?" I said,

thinking: Why am I even *saying* this. It's like learning how to ask for directions in French, and then not having the foggiest notion of what the reply is all about. What do I say after he *tells* me what he means? Lord, this is absurd!

Monir's reply was long, pointless, and informed by all the wearying postulations I have heard repeatedly since I have been in Egypt: if the Americans had only done thus-and-so at *this* time, then the Israelis would have done thus-and-so at *this* time, then the Russians would have *had* to do thus-and-so at that time. . . . I nodded in a number of places, but it was quickly clear to him that I really had nothing to say on the matter or, as he seemed to prefer to believe, that I was being politic, and refusing to say what I thought on the matter. Oddly enough, he gave over rather quickly, and to my intense relief we began to speak of other things. I asked him if he had traveled in the Middle East.

"Ah, you cannot imagine what the rest of the Arab world is like!" Monir said. "Kuwait, for instance. I spent nine years there. It was dreadful. Simply dreadful."

"When was that? What were you doing there?"

"Just recently. When the factory was nationalized and we lost everything. No money. There was no way to make money here."

"Were you a partner of Salah's? I didn't know that."

"Well, of course. We all had an interest in the factory. A great deal of my wife's money went into that factory. And we all depended on it. When Nasser took it we were finished. All of us. I had to go to work in Kuwait."

"What was it like? Living in Kuwait?"

"Hell. Absolute hell. Beastly hot. Nothing to do. And the women are animals!" he cried. "*Animals.*" His large expressive mouth was alive with agitated annoyance as he spoke, and his veined, splotched hands gestured wildly in the air.

"How are they animals?" I asked mildly.

"They care for nothing but orgasm. You meet them and instantly they are ready. No matter what, they immediately begin to unzip. They wear these very tight dresses with zippers on the sides as well as in the back. One zip, two, three zips: on the couch with her legs drawn up. And they care nothing for the person they do it with, only for the orgasm." Monir's face turned ugly as he spoke these words.

His features became contorted with an unforgivingness that seemed to seep up in him from some boiling depth.

And now, having driven at last through the dense Mohammed Ali district that surrounds its base, we were curving up, up, up on the long winding street that leads to the ancient fortress—heavy and solid with its history of fabulous treachery—and then we were within its magnificently thick walls. It is a monolithic place, this Citadel, within which sit a number of palaces dating back to the twelfth century, as well as the Mohammed Ali Mosque, built in 1811. The palaces have been converted into museums and to military quarters (the Citadel is now partially a military camp) but the mosque, of course, remains untouched. It sits astride the Citadel, too magnificent, too ornate to arouse a religious sense in me—just as the most beautiful cathedrals in Europe do not: rather they make me dance inside with the pleasure a child feels watching a fairy tale unfold on a stage. (It's the stripped, agonized, unforgiving places that reach out and sink a hook into me.) The Mohammed Ali Mosque, famous in Cairo for its beauty, is a marvel of alabaster walls, gigantic dome and very delicate minarets, stone fountains splashing in a dazzling open courtyard whose arabesque tile walls reach to the heavens.

Just inside the courtyard walls old gnarled men sat on their haunches holding out pairs of cloth foot coverings for the tourists who were loath to take off their shoes. All around us were throngs of tourists, Egyptian soldiers, guards in black berets and uniforms to match, men in *gelabyas* preparing to pray . . . everyone softly eyeing everyone else. The old men took absolutely no notice of the tourists whom they serviced, but when Monir and I walked up to them they rose in immediate recognition of the Egyptian engineer. Monir, all *noblesse oblige*, spoke in a kindly voice, offered a few piastres, oversaw my feet being laced into the foot coverings, and put on a pair himself. We wandered about the inside of the rug-covered place of prayer, enjoying it as we would an interesting museum, I so ignorant of the meaning of the designs in the wood and ivory work and of the rituals various objects represent that they simply glanced off the surface of my consciousness; it was all pleasing geometry to me; I felt like a barbarian. Monir offered a few sparse facts about the architectural history of the mosque's facade but he sounded like an ignorant guide with a few memorized bits he himself did not understand. After a while we left the mosque and began to wander around the high terraced spaces of the Citadel, coming at last to a large open place of observation from which the entire city could be seen, spread out on the floor of the desert below.

I felt the breath in my body suspend itself for a moment at the sight of the ancient city of Cairo, tossing itself out to the haze on the horizon: a thousand sandstone domes and minarets, a million crooked streets, squares without end, the teeming motion of people the size of ants, everything looking the color of earth, rooted in the sand, soft and losing definition in the glaring mist that hangs forever over the deserts. It was all so hot, and endless, and something of man chained to his own instincts, condemned to circle and circle forever in this remote desert. It was a spectacle that stirred and excited.

"Come, come." Monir tugged impatiently at my sleeve.

The good engineer seemed to be growing more and more irritated. Was this his habitual manner? Or had I done something to annoy him? Was it that our "political" talk had died prematurely? I felt puzzled, and yet detached. I could not give the matter my full attention. Let it unravel itself. . . .

Monir announced that we would go to Al Azhar, and then have lunch in the bazaar. Did I agree? Of course, of course, I demurely smoothing my short skirt over my knees as he let out the clutch, and kept his eyes on my legs.

He drove fast down the curving Mohammed Ali Street we had ascended slowly. Too fast. *Too* fast. I held my breath, and my foot pressed hopelessly on an imaginary brake. . . . At last, tearing across three neighborhoods hard by the desert edge, we came screeching into the huge square of El Husseiny that lies nearly at the foot of the Mukattam Hills. Oh, that square! I can see it yet. El Husseiny is dominated by a tremendous mosque that fronts one whole side of the square. To the right and left of the mosque, moving *in*, behind the mosque, is the ancient bazaar of Khan Khalili, those narrow twisted covered streets in which for a thousand years men have made and sold silver and amber, silks and brocades, leather and cotton, grain and spices, and gold, above all, gold. It is all still going on today exactly as it went on a thousand years ago: boys of twelve squatting on the ground, embroidering the incredibly complicated designs on fancy *gelabyas,* boys of eight turning beads on primitive whirling rods, men of eighty bringing out silver. . . .

The front streets of the quarter are filled with shops, crowded with American and European tourists, everyone buying, selling, hawking; the back streets climbing up, up toward the desert hills, filled with remnants of ancient mosques, harem windows, Fatimite houses, and on the streets beneath these magnificent ruins men, women and children who scratch the earth for the dust that will be their dinner.

In front of the mosque in El Husseiny lies a square that is alive—and never more so than at night—with an open market: strolling workers, picture-snapping tourists, bargain-hunting middle-class Egyptians, beggars by the thousand (almost all between six and fifteen), sellers of fruits and vegetables, candy, glassware, miniature Korans, knitted skullcaps, prayer beads, postcards, pots and pans, earthenware, Egyptian chewing gum, tremendous pans of the sweet, sticky pastry called *besbousa,* glass beads, combs, matches, *felafel* carts.

And in the distance, across the square, and on the other side of a huge traffic thoroughfare, stand the looming minarets and towers of the ancient mosque and university of Al Azhar. It is the oldest Islamic University in the Middle East, it has stood here since the tenth century, its influence on the life of Cairo is incalculable. Here, they came by the thousands, and still come, from all over the Arab world, to study theology, Islamic law, and Arabic. Here, men live as students for fifteen and twenty years, religious scholars supported by endowment. Here, the political and social power of Islam is woven into a tapestry of religious life, alive with ancient pain and structured comfort. Here, the sense of Allah begins, and out there in those streets it ends.

I stood there in the glaring sun of El Husseiny, surrounded by the dust and heat and stink of Cairo's rushing poor, looking up at the clean, powerful lines of the ancient university. Monir took a firm grip on my upper arm and began shoving his way through the crowd. Marc Antony among the rabble, he angrily waved off the beggars and hawkers and travelers who replaced each other swiftly as, one by one, they fell back from our path. At last we stood at the edge of the thoroughfare. I felt drugged by the noise and heat, the thousands and

thousands of milling people, the dusty light coming off the desert.
(Here, in this part of Cairo, I always felt as though the desert, in
some blind, sucking fashion, was reaching out for me.) Finally, we
were across the street and walking up into the courtyard of the
university.

The mosque of Al Azhar was the first place in which I felt the
beauty of Arabs in the presence of Islam. The mosque itself is
tremendous, cool and dark, like the inside of the most gigantic circus
tent ever constructed. It is filled with ancient tombs and niches and
arabesque, its floors covered with thick soft Persian rugs, brass
lanterns hanging everywhere. Oh, it was lovely to walk into this! I
felt that I was being received into some marvelous place of comfort,
gentle and accepting, willing to listen to anything. As my eyes grew
accustomed to the half-light, I began to see that scattered everywhere, standing in small groups, sitting on the floor in twos and
threes, leaning solitarily against pillars, were students and their
teachers: some in *gelabyas*, some in Western clothes, all in white-
stockinged feet. They spoke quietly, they listened intently. They
lounged, they read, they joked. One sat propped against a pillar,
daydreaming; another lay stretched out asleep, his hands locked
behind his dark head, his books beneath his hands, his white collar
open against his smooth brown throat; two more played a board
game while three others looked on silently. They seemed to be as at
ease here as they would be in their mothers' houses. A deep welling
comfort rose up, as though from the walls and the floor, soft and
human, easy and protective. There was no god of wrath in this house,
only tender spirit; as though man and god were joined here in the
mutual pursuit of respite.

Monir strolled quietly beside me, content to have me breathing
deeply where he, too, obviously, felt the full force of indefinable
atmosphere.

Out once more in the dusty sunlight, it was time for lunch.

"You will have a real Egyptian bazaar lunch," Monir said
promisingly.

"Wonderful!" I said eagerly.

Jesus Christ! I thought miserably, twenty minutes later.

Monir steered me back to the square at El Husseiny. From the
front of the square to the back—in other words from the sidewalk to

the mosque—on either side, the square was lined with shops selling food: *felafel, fetir, foulmedammis,*° whatever you wanted in the way of proletarian Egyptian food, you could find it here. Stuck in between there was also a bead shop, a cigarette kiosk, a large filthy café, a small restaurant, a leather goods store. It was into the little restaurant that Monir now led me.

The restaurant was a tiny blue and white place (blue paint, white tiles) with a long steaming counter directly on the left. The place was constructed on two levels to create more space and was now filled to overflowing with workingmen—all dark eyes, *gelabyas* and skull-caps—hanging off the sides of their chairs in some places. The waiters kept rushing by with large shallow plastic bowls filled with some steaming stuff. The bowls were all the same, and the same bowls were on every waiter's tray.

"Oh," Monir crowed, "I haven't had this since I was a boy!"

The man behind the cash register came rushing out when we entered, and led us to a tiny crowded spot on the upper level where room at a long table was instantly made for us, every eye in the place following us until we were settled. Without consulting me, Monir gave our order to the cashier, who waylaid a waiter and repeated the order to him.

"Now here," Monir then turned to me, "you eat only one thing. It is called *shourba kawarea*, and it is a kind of soup which is made with the head or the feet of the cow. It floats in the soup."

"The head of the *cow* floats in the soup?" I cried.

"Yes, yes," Monir said impatiently, "you will see. It is delicious. And very healthy. *Very* healthy. The marrow of the bone is full of calcium, and the soup itself is pure protein."

My stomach started turning and my heart began to beat violently. In my mind's eye, I kept seeing a plate coming at me with a cow's dead eyes staring up at me. What on earth was I going to do? How would I get past *this*?

When the waiter came rushing up the stairs with our bowls I was relieved to see only a viscous kind of soup lying in the bowl, with a

---

° *Fetir* is a strudel-like food eaten with powdered sugar or black honey or crumbling mold cheese. *Foulmedammis* is a kind of baked-beans dish, and *the* national food; Cairenes will rush around at two in the morning looking for *foulmedammis* the way Americans go searching for hamburgers.

great many whitish strips floating around in it. No wretched cow eyes. What Monir had meant was that *part* of the head or the feet would be in the soup.

The waiter plunked down the bowls along with a plate of flat bread and another bowl full of mounded rice. Like *molochaya*, this soup was eaten with lots of rice or bread dunked in it. And as with my first bowl of *molochaya*, I thought I was going to throw it all up. I ate some, and then began pushing it around in the bowl with my spoon. Monir was shoveling it greedily down his throat, but when he saw me floundering he turned in irritation and cried, "*What* are you doing? *That* is not the way."

Sadly, I remembered Fawzy and the *molochaya*: no similiar sympathy would rescue me now. Well then, let's get on with it. I began shoveling rice into the bowl, spoonful after heaping spoonful. Finally, I had a bowlful of soup-soaked rice. My face was burning, my arms ran hot and cold, my throat felt dry even though it was continually being wetted. I began to eat. It will never end, I thought, downing the awful stuff as slowly as I could. Never. I will be sitting here three days from now with this spoon in my mouth and this stuff before me, its level never diminishing in the bowl. Ah, this is really Dante's hell! I, a compulsive eater, I, who am hungry every twenty minutes, I, who scheme to walk past bakeries and ice-cream parlors, *condemned* to eat.

"Wonderful! Wonderful!" said Monir, leaning back in his chair, patting his bulging stomach blissfully. I lurched to.

"Yes," I said cheerfully. "It *is* good. But so filling! I can hardly finish it."

"You eat like a bird," he said, peering into my bowl.

"No, no." I laughed desperately. "Do I *look* like a bird?" (Remembering, too late, that in Egypt everyone thought I was *thin*.) "It really is simply too much. You know, Americans aren't used to eating such huge quantities of food." (God forgive me, I said silently.)

"You are in Egypt now," Monir said shortly.

Don't I know it. Don't I know it.

I'm still not clear about how we actually got out of there, but suddenly we were standing in the lovely glaring light once more; I was upright, and my hands, mercifully, were at my sides.

"Would you like to stroll in the bazaar?" Monir asked kindly.

"Yes."

We turned left, passed behind the mosque, and entered the narrow covered streets of Khan Khalili. I had been here once before with Gasbia, hustling after her fat little body as she dickered—on my behalf—over the price of slippers, silver, gold, jewelry, with shopkeeper after shopkeeper, although I wasn't buying, and only wished to walk through the thousand-year-old streets where life and craft had only accommodated themselves to the centuries, but never actually altered with them. . . . Now, Monir was enjoying himself watching me move slowly among the shops and stalls of the bazaar, peering in this window, leaning over that barrel, fingering some silken stuff, stepping neatly over broken cobblestones while sellers and artisans, hawkers and beggars, called to us every half-step. It was cool and vividly dark inside the bazaar streets, and we strolled slowly for quite a long while. Then, unexpectedly, we emerged into an open sunny street somewhere in back of the mosque, on the other side of the square. The street was lined with carts and stalls. I stopped before a cart filled with the beautifully knitted skullcaps worn by every man in a *gelabya*; the colors and designs were lovely and I began to examine first one, then another, then yet another. The man who sold the skullcaps crowded eagerly in on me. Monir smiled and asked me if I wanted one.

"Not really," I said, and lingered. "Well, perhaps. Ask him how much he wants for them."

Monir smiled at the man, and asked him the price of the caps. The man answered.

That was the last that anything made any sense.

Monir terrified the air with his shrieks. He stood there, fierce and murderous, before the amazed man with the skullcaps, his face literally purple with whatever one could call the emotion that had taken entire possession of him. His yells were mighty and went on without end; his eyes were sparks of fury carrying enough fire to inflict third-degree burns; the veins in his neck were blue ropes struggling to slip free of the imprisoning skin; his mouth—oh his mouth!—was a narrow, deeply-creased ridge of skin turned dead white, curling itself malevolently around his stabbing words.

All around us were gathered fifteen or twenty people from the bazaar who had come running. The man with the skullcaps had recovered his wits and his speech, and was now yelling back hotly. People on all sides restrained the two men, who seemed about to go at each other any minute, as clearly mere words would not suffice very much longer.

I was frantic. I kept pulling at Monir's sleeve, crying, "What is it? What is it? What did he say to you?" but he was beyond me, I doubt if he even heard me. Then I resorted to "Stop it! Stop it! Stop it!" hoping the phrase would produce a reflexive response to a familiar sound even if he couldn't actually distinguish the words. Then I realized: How can he respond to the sound of *English* in this passion? Finally, I figured Monir was simply going to murder the man at any moment, and I would be arrested as an accessory to the crime. I waited silently for events to unfold with fateful logic.

It was all over as suddenly as it had begun. The crowd managed to get between Monir and the wretched vendor of skullcaps, and five or six men were gently steering Monir away from the stall, speaking softly and rapidly to him all the while, never taking their hands from his sleeve and shoulder until he was well down the cobbled street, I stumbling along behind.

At last: "Monir, what on earth did the man say to you?"

He wiped the side of his face, looking off ahead, still in great agitation: "I asked him the price of the skullcap—which as you must know should be about twenty-five or thirty piastres—and he said, 'Two pounds.' He said that because he thought you were a tourist and *I* was the kind of Egyptian who steers tourists to the bazaar and then splits the profit with the vendor."

I stared incredulously at Monir. For *that*, this murderous ecstasy, this venom, this boiling fury. For *that*, this hungry need to annihilate.

From that moment on I feared and hated him.

We returned to the car in the square. As I settled myself in the seat beside him, Monir said, "Now, for a nice cup of tea at home!"

I looked at him. It was as though nothing had happened. His watery blue eyes positively twinkled at me, his face had relaxed into its normal sags and creases, his hands moved steadily on the gearshift, his feet smoothly let out the clutch and pressed down on the gas. He drove back to Zamalek with only his customary madness, speeding viciously, cutting other drivers out, cursing those he was abusing.

Back at Monir's house, in the front room where the birthday party had taken place, Aischa, Monir's young daughter, and Nabila, her cousin from across the hall, were sitting playing with a little girl and a little boy. They welcomed us gaily, and Aischa called for tea, rising at the same time to kiss her father.

I flopped into an overstuffed chair near the window, too confused in my spirit to decide whether or not I was glad to have the girls bombard me no sooner had Monir left the room:

"What do you think of Egyptian women?"

"What do you think of Egyptian *men*?"

"What do you think of Cairo?"

"Where have you been?"

"Where do you want to go?"

"You must come to the university."

"You must come to the club."

"How old were you when your father let you go out alone with a man?"

"Did your mother ever demand that you encourage the friendship of one you did not like?"

"What is it *like* in America?"

"Tell us. Tell us the truth. What does it *mean* to be an American woman?"

While we were drinking tea, Aischa's brother Mohammed wandered in, shaking his head and laughing at the two girls, whom he had been listening to in his room. "Do you think she wants to hear all this nonsense?" he scoffed softly. "And do you think you'll get free if she answers those questions?"

A bit after that, the door opened and in came Mirella from across the hall with her baby in her arms. She perched on the arm of a chair, trying to loosen her long dark hair from the infant's clutches, laughing softly, pleasurably. Another few minutes, and the door slammed open and shut again. It was Amr, the smooth-cheeked, round-faced husband of Mirella. He said, "Hello, hello, hello," and dropped into the chair beneath his wife.

"Well, what have you been doing with yourself?" he asked me.

"Oh, nothing much. Seeing Cairo, I guess. Concentrating on your incredible family."

"Incredible? Why incredible?" Amr laughed.

"I'm beginning to think I need meet no one outside of this family to write about Egypt."

"Oh, that would be too bad!" Amr said, sitting upright. "Yes, that would be too very bad. These people are not typical of Egyptians, not typical at all."

"Why do you say that?" I also sat upright.

He slid back down in his seat and began playing with his wife's hair, so long that it hung down onto his shoulder. He smiled into her hair, and didn't answer me.

"Why do you say that?" I repeated. He looked shrewdly at me, turned away again, then spoke.

"For one thing," he said quickly, "there is not one who will speak the truth to you. Not one who will tell you what he is really thinking."

"Oh, Amr!" burst out Aischa. "That is ridiculous! They are no more or less honest than anyone else in Egypt. You are not to believe him, Vivian. They are a good family for you to get to know. They will teach you something about a certain kind of *very* typical family."

"Perhaps," Amr said, and closed his lips tightly. But he could not contain himself. "But if you stick only to the Hamamsys you will have a very unbalanced picture of this country. *Very* unbalanced."

"She is not going to know only Hamamsys," Aischa replied, irritated. "For God's sake, Amr, she is only just starting!"

Amr said no more after that, but he continued to smile a slow, almost secret smile, and his eyes, grown suddenly alert and intelligent, told me he certainly had volumes more to speak.

The door opened once more, and in came Kamel, the under-secretary who was the widowed father of the children in the room and cousin to the Hamamsys. He seemed startled to see me, then advanced politely to shake my hand and welcome me once more to this house. Kamel was a strange-looking man: tall and thin, almost bony, with a narrow skull concealed beneath a curving brown cap of hair; his eyes appeared to guard a quietly controlled intelligence. Almost at once he was preoccupied with his children. When Aischa told him what Amr had said to me, he laughed and said shyly, barely looking at me, "Well, it is certainly true that you must meet as many kinds of people as you can—students, working people, all sorts—I would not be as hard on the Hamamsys as Amr has been."

I waited, but that was it. A most politic statement from a most cautious relative.

It was getting late and I was preparing to go. Amr stood up, and excused himself. I saw him disappear down the hall into a room near the front door. I stood up too, saying I was going to look for my jacket, and followed Amr into the room. He was bending over a telephone, his back to the doorway, when I spoke.

"I wonder if we could get together by ourselves sometime, Amr."

He whirled around, blushing fiercely. His eyes seemed to contract and dart out at the same time; obviously, he was doing some fast, silent calculating.

"*Hamdulallah!*" he whistled sharply. "You really *are* serious."

"Sure I am." I grinned. "What did you think? You'd get away *that* easy?"

He threw back his head and laughed; then suddenly caught himself and looked quickly at the doorway.

"What's up?" I said. "Are we doing something wrong?"

"No, no," he said hastily. "But it is better we keep this to ourselves." He was scrawling on a piece of paper. "Here is my office number. I am there between ten and two every day. Call me. And we will talk." He pressed my arm and hurried out of the room.

Salah took me last night, at my request, to an Egyptian nightclub to hear oriental music and see oriental dancing. He'd be more than glad, he said. He hadn't been to one of these clubs himself in years. We drove out to Giza, then onto the Pyramids Road, which is Cairo's "strip." The road is lined as far as the eye can see with garish neon signs all announcing the delights that await at the end of the lit-up driveways leading to over a hundred nightclubs. We stopped at one called The Arizona. A large dark Arab in a white turban and a brown *gelabya* piped in black led us inside to a heavily curtained foyer, and then beyond, into the club itself.

The place was cavernous and bathed in a dull red light. In the dimness I could make out huge fake gold columns standing everywhere in the room, a few hundred small tables placed all over the floor and, directly ahead of us, a large lighted stage. The atmosphere was something of a cross between a shopping-center nightclub and a casino in a Catskill Mountains hotel. On the stage a European-style band was sawing away at an American tune and a man in a white shirt and brown pants was putting six overweight women through something that resembled chorus-girl paces. I couldn't help thinking that they'd all seen Gene Kelly in *Marjorie Morningstar*, and that was *show biz* to them. It was ten o'clock in the evening. Nothing in these clubs started until close to midnight. What was going on onstage was a rehearsal of some sort. The fact that the club was actually open for business, and people like us were beginning to wander in, obviously meant nothing to the maestro on the stage and his resigned chorines.

Salah and I (Salah *breathing* upper-middle-class aloofness) were seated at a small table facing the center of the stage. We sipped Scotch, and watched as the club began to fill up: Egyptian civil service workers, businessmen, factory foremen in blue or black suits with big stomachs, thin moustaches, and slicked-down hair; behind them, their wives, girlfriends, mistresses, bursting out of sateen dresses, swaying slightly on spike heels. People shouted and waved as large tables filled up, and friends were recognized halfway across the gigantic room. Bursts of high-pitched laughter split the air. It all began to look like New York's Puerto Rican Fourteenth Street on Saturday night. The warmth in the room billowed and flowed. I felt good inside; amused and charitable. At twelve-thirty three or four men elaborately served us a third-rate dinner: which Salah and I solemnly consumed.

At last, the show began. First surprise: instead of being replaced by oriental instrumentalists, the music was to be provided by the European-style band already on the stage. They began to play and I experienced a jolt: somehow, the lovely oriental sound became *kitsch*, coming as it now did from violins and saxophones instead of the large-bellied *oud* and the thin reed instruments that make the distinctive Eastern music. . . . Why? I thought. This wouldn't be happening in *New York*. . . . It was the first time but certainly not the last of the evening that that mute astonishment rose up in me.

As it happens, I am a lover of Eastern music: the primitive and repetitious sound speaks to something deep inside me. When I was in college my friends and I spent many evenings at the Greek nightclubs on Eighth Avenue in New York, hypnotized by the whining sensuality of the music and the slim sad belly dancers whose movements built to an unbearable pitch of sex and heat, irresistible in its melancholy joy. I had come to Egypt expecting the belly dancing in Cairo to be even more exciting, naturally, than it was in New York. This, after all, was the real thing. I could hardly believe my eyes as the show at The Arizona began to unfold.

The first dancer came bouncing on stage. She was shockingly fat. She wore a green-and-gold version of the traditional harem costume, except that her midriff was covered with a diaphanous material in the green of her costume. I thought it was because she was so fat, but I soon learned that all the belly dancers—by law—had to have their midriffs covered: an edict of Nasser's.

The girl now on the stage smiled extravagantly at her whistling, clapping audience and went through twenty minutes of boring, mechanical gyrations, during which her flesh shook fiercely instead of grinding rhythmically. Then suddenly she was gone. Another one, not so fat, not so bad, but still quite plump, still quite mechanical, took her place. For the next two hours, the dancers replaced each other every twenty minutes, each one getting a little better than the last, but not a single one with the ability to bring the dance to the climactic pitch I knew it could arrive at. The girls were extremely sweet, almost *wholesome*, singularly unsexy. Their audience laughed, clapped, whistled, called up all *kinds* of suggestions to them: there seemed to be an almost filial rapport between performer and customer. At last, on came Sohair Zaki, one of Cairo's top belly dancers and the star performer at this show. She was slimmer than the rest but still not slim, and certainly her dancing was more expert and more talented than that of the others who had been jostling around on that big empty stage. Her heart-shaped face was even sweeter and *more* wholesome than the faces of all who had gone before her. In other words, what made her a star was that she was just like everyone else—only more so.

Belly dancing under socialism! Of course, afterwards when I was railing against the show to my Egyptian friends, I was laughed at and told I was naïve, that traditionally belly dancers *were* fat . . . but the hell with that stuff!

"How do you like it?" Salah leaned solicitously toward me.

"It's a helluva lot sexier in New York," I said ungraciously.

"Really!" his green eyes opened wide, and he subsided to contemplate the marvels of the decadent West.

A male singer took over as master of ceremonies after the dancers were through, and the singers began coming on. The singers—men and women—ranged from tired to beat-up. Only one woman, Laila Kamel, was good but even she didn't really hit the stride that carries you away.

What was strangest—and most amusing—about what was happening on the stage was that everyone—the singers, the musicians, the m.c.—acted as if it were a rehearsal. They'd walk around the stage when they got bored, talk to the drummer for a while, come to the front of the stage to peer across the footlights looking for friends and relatives, wave happily when they found them . . . and the audience loved it all.

The best, the funniest, the warmest and most vital part of the entire evening was the audience. Absolutely determined to feel abandon, the men carried on like demons, waving, laughing, shaking handkerchiefs in the old sexy manner, coming on to the performers; the women in the audience got pretty raucous too. . . . But they knew, they knew. And at two o'clock in the morning they *proved* they knew.

A little girl—obviously known to the performers—was suddenly plucked from the audience and hauled up onto the stage. She stood there, her hands knotted together, her ankles crossed, staring shyly out over the footlights. Then the music was struck up, and this child—surely no more than eight or ten—began to dance as no belly dancer there had danced all night. In absolutely asexual innocence, the little girl in a matter of seconds re-created the whole compelling sexuality of the dance, moving her body with the cruel, knowing removal of the dancer who watches in detached fascination as her body reveals its own power even to her, simultaneously attracted and repelled by the response it arouses.

The crowd went crazy, and the little girl watched with an extraordinary expression of distinterest on her face as her body did its work. The whole thing was wild, and strange, and very exciting. A man in the audience beckoned the girl madly to the edge of the stage. She moved—still dancing—cautiously forward and when she got close enough the man bent nearly in two in order to kiss her hand, almost sobbing with joy. . . . And the crowd rose as one in a shout of approval. Egyptian sexiness was *saved!*

After that it was as though the atmosphere shifted into another gear. Nothing could top what had just been done, so why bother? At about three o'clock the m.c. beckoned someone up from the audience. A girl in her early twenties—very tight kelly green rayon dress and a hank of dyed red hair—jumped up on the stage and began to dance. She was simply dreadful. The m.c. laughed, embraced her, really *enjoyed* her. And so did the crowd. What became apparent—as it does over and over again, all over Cairo— was the pleasure with which Egyptians greet the appearance of sensate joy. The sheer good nature of it all!

At four in the morning Salah and I tottered out of The Arizona—performers and audience still going full tilt.

We were both very tired but Salah suggested a cup of coffee at the Sheraton and I agreed. As we sat, stirring the steaming liquid in our cups, I casually said to him, "By the way, I didn't know that Monir was a partner in your factory." The remark had been meant to fill a lull in the conversation. The response to it amazed me. The tired Salah flared up, his nostrils going dead-white, his voice harsh and bitter: "Did *he* tell you that? He's a liar, a damned liar! That factory was mine, entirely mine. He tells people that he lost all his money when Nasser took the factory. The fact is that he lost all his money *gambling.* He came back from Upper Egypt a broken man because he gambled everything away . . . and now he gambles all of *us* away."

On Sunday night at seven o'clock the two-year-old cease-fire between Israel and Egypt came to an end. I sat with an assorted group of Hamamsys in Giza on an enclosed terrace overlooking the Nile and the pyramids in the home of "Leila and the Doctor," Soad's youngest sister and her husband. When the president's announcement came over the radio I was the only one in the room disturbed by the news.

"Well, we are at war," the doctor said gaily. He caught sight of my face and began to laugh. "My dear, don't look so upset! You are at war in the *Middle East*. That is like no war anywhere else in the world. Nothing will happen! I assure you. Nothing!"

We had come at two in the afternoon, Magdi, Samiha, and I. Soad and Gasbia and Ibrahim and the children were already there. Also, there was Leila's sister-in-law, a tall pregnant young woman whose husband, a brother of the Doctor, was in the Army, stationed at the Suez Canal. Leila had invited us all for lunch, and to stay on to hear Sadat's seven o'clock broadcast.

The children ran around in a fearful racket with Leila's three young daughters. Not the slightest attention was paid. It was as though nothing were happening. When the noise level rose to a din someone yelled briefly at them, and they subsided into symptomatic silence. Within twenty minutes the cycle had begun to repeat itself. (The leeway given to Arabic children is a phenomenon: until eight or ten years of age they run absolutely riot, with no visible restraints placed upon them; then, suddenly, as though a door clangs shut inside them, they become docile, respectful adults of twelve or fourteen, utterly obedient to their elders.)

The Doctor limped into the room, smiled briefly at everyone and settled himself carefully into the most comfortable chair in the room. Leila, lounging in suburban white pants and her blond wig, seemed oblivious of his presence. He, in turn, when he had occasion to address his wife, did so in a voice that seemed permanently tuned to short-tempered irritation: a dull, nagging sound, somewhat like toothache. (Later, when I asked Soad about them, she said quietly, "He came to ask for her hand. She was the youngest and the most educated of all of us. She had learned so much that no one was good enough for her. At last, she was growing old. She became frightened and she married him. He knows she does not love him and he cannot bear it. He does not love her *either*, but he cannot bear it that she does not love him. It is an ugly business, their marriage. None among us speak of it.")

At four o'clock lunch was served. We ate industriously for nearly half an hour without a stop, then everyone fell back, bloated and groaning.

Salah walked in, looking most slim and disdainful of the prostrate bodies all about him. He carefully held the crease of his pants as he settled himself into a hard-backed chair and, although Leila instantly placed a plate of food before him, he chose to tap a cigarette against his forearm for a prolonged moment while a kind of absent smile played on his face. Then he looked at the food . . . and lit his cigarette.

"We are much honored," Soad said sarcastically so that only I could hear her. "Salah rarely comes to family affairs. Perhaps it is your assured presence that brings him here. Nothing makes him happier than to be among foreigners. They hate Egypt, he and the Doctor." As though he had heard her, and wished to support her image of him, the Doctor leaned toward me, asking me how I was enjoying his country. I smiled and said everyone was extremely kind. His lips drew back from his teeth in what I suppose could loosely be called a smile. The late afternoon sun shone into his glasses, making him blind.

"Have you noticed the continuing presence of our famous leader in Egypt?" he said evenly. "Although he is dead nearly a year?"

"Yes, I have," I replied. "There isn't a wall in Cairo that isn't plastered with his picture."

"Yes," the Doctor said, leaning back in his chair. "We love him. We love him. Put that in your book," and he began to laugh, a choked high sound that became a giggle. "Tell the world," he said, now giggling almost uncontrollably. "Nasser has taken everything from us—and we still *adore* him. You understand me?" He leaned forward from the waist up, his stiff leg straight out before him, his eyeglasses glinting appropriately, his mouth now a grim line. "We *hate* him," he hissed. "From our very depths we *hate* him."

"And that," said Salah triumphantly, carefully recrossing his legs, "is the opinion of an educated man!"

Everyone remained heavily silent. Magdi shifted around uncomfortably in his seat, but said nothing. When I looked at Soad I saw that her eyes had lost their focus and she was going off into one of those private distances of hers.

Leila and her sister-in-law had been whispering together in a corner and now the two women excitedly announced that we would make *Om-Ali* for dessert.

"No!" shrieked Gasbia. "You cannot make it!"

"Yes, yes, yes," said Leila, clapping her hands together. "For the first time in my life, I will have *Om-Ali* made in my own house. She is very good at it" (pointing to her sister-in-law) "and it is her pleasure to make it, especially for Miss Vivian."

"Oh," I protested automatically, "not for *me*. But what is *Om-Ali?*"

"It is a most wonderful thing," said Soad, smiling. "It is made with broad noodles and much milk and sugar, and it all becomes a kind of hot pudding. *Dee*-licious!"

The two women hurried off to the kitchen to see which materials they had for the making of *Om-Ali*, and which the children must be sent for.

Outside, the light had suddenly gone out of the early March afternoon, and the electric lights of Giza had begun to come on, all around the Nile, spreading out to the distant skyline. The pyramids disappeared into the growing blackness beyond, and Cairo seemed like any other city after dark. Inside, we each turned on the light nearest us, and the conversation shifted slightly in tone.

Soad settled herself upon a daybed placed against the wall facing the terrace windows. She was uncomfortable with the pillows behind her back, and removed them, tossing them to either side of her. One she held onto, and placed upon her lap; but she soon seemed equally uncomfortable with the pillow in that position, too; she then pressed it to her breast and folded her arms across it. There. *That* was it.

Ibrahim began to speak of Ali, the missing son, remarking that Soad was holding the pillow to her breast as though it were her child. Was she trying to replace Ali with a pillow?

"But she is holding the pillow as though she were suckling an infant!" protested Gasbia cheerfully, as if that clearly explained there was no relation between the pillow and her long-gone half-brother.

Soad blushed with pleasure, happy to be the object of this kind of attention, and she laughed—oh, that laugh!—with a lightness and a girlishness that rushed up into me, and my own heart sang.

"Perhaps you are both right," she said warmly. "Perhaps I *am* suckling an infant here, and perhaps the pillow *is* Ali. And why *not*, may I ask? Why, indeed, not?" And she held her head back and high upon her suddenly straight, slim neck, her eyes looking aristocratically down under half-lowered lids at her audience; then, quickly, she collapsed into merriness. "Say what you will," she said, laughing at herself, "a mother's heart is not to be questioned!" Her volatile face changed once more, turning dreamy, and she half-lay against the strewn pillows, now lost in a bliss of spoken fantasy. . . . "Oh, it will be heaven when Ali returns. Really heaven. I can see it now. I will rise in the morning to make his breakfast. He will go off to the work. I will take care of his things myself—no servant shall *touch* them, even. In the evening when he returns I will make his dinner, and watch with delight as he eats. . . . Afterwards, we will sit and talk. . . ." She was rolling, almost voluptuously, on the daybed, pressing the pillow closely to her breasts.

Magdi spoke for the first time. "Those are the words of a lover, not a mother, *Om-Ali*," he said dryly.

Salah, who had all this time been watching his sister shrewdly through his cigarette smoke, turned to me and said, "These men, the sons of women like my good sister here, are called *son of mother*. Egypt is full of them."

Soad laughed and laughed, gleefully agreeing with them both.

It was now six o'clock. Leila and her sister-in-law had been in the kitchen nearly an hour. I walked down the hall of the flat to see what they were up to.

"What's happening?" I said, as Leila, the sister-in-law, and three of the children bustled around the small, smoky kitchen lit by a single naked overhead bulb.

"Oh, it is coming along, coming along," said Leila distractedly. She was as uneasy in a kitchen as I was. Only the young sister-in-law seemed to know her way about.

On top of the stove two large shallow pans were filled with broad noodlelike strips that were each being lightly fried. On the counter beside the stove stood a big heavy casserole dish. Into this dish layers of the fried noodles were being placed; over each layer a thick, sugary, milk mixture was poured. When the dish was filled it would be baked in the oven.

"How long does this whole thing *take*?" I asked. The sister-in-law thought carefully. "About two and a half hours," she said cheerfully.

"Good God!" I said. "Two and a half hours just to gobble it down in ten minutes!"

"Yes," giggled the Doctor behind me. I whirled around. "We make *Om-Ali* to while away the time," he said, and roared with laughter. "To give ourselves a sense of life. For, here in the Middle East, men are cheap and time is no object. Shaw said that, and it is still true. . . . Yes, yes. Put that in your book, put that in your book," and he continued to laugh like a madman.

At ten to seven the radio was turned on. All resettled themselves as though they were suddenly in public. Salah recrossed his legs, brushed off his suit jacket, and said casually, "And now we are about to hear how our glorious armies are ready at any instant to crush the enemy and return victorious to Great Cairo." Magdi laughed, but Ibrahim and the women only smiled quietly.

When Sadat's voice came on the air everyone leaned forward, silent and intent. I felt very nervous, but I sat quietly, knowing that no one was going to interrupt the train of his or her thought to translate for me. The president's voice droned on for more than half an hour, his phrases delivered in a low, even key. I began to relax. How could he be saying anything *bad* in that voice? After a while, when the Arabic showed no signs of letting up, I rose and went into the kitchen. Leila and the sister-in-law were preparing to remove the *Om-Ali* from the oven.

"Don't you want to hear the president's speech?" I said to Leila. She raised her bewigged head from the oven, and looked at me.

"Oh, that," she said, and her hand pushed impatiently at the air. "Whatever he says, believe me, we have heard it all a thousand times already. Either we *will* fight, and be victorious. Or we will *not* fight, and be superior. Either the mad-dog Israelis will attack us, in which case we will drive them back to the gates of Tel Aviv. Or they will not attack us, and therefore we will triumphantly prove that they are afraid of us. . . . It is always the same thing. Believe me, it will be no different this time. Oh, look! The *Om-Ali* is ready. How wonderful it looks! Now *this* is real, my dear."

When I returned to the terrace it was all over. The radio was turned off and they were all speaking excitedly.

"What did he say?" I asked Magdi, and nearly lost my balance when he told me that the cease-fire had come to an end.

"My G-God," I stuttered, "why did he do *that*?" at the same time that the Doctor was merrily saying now we were at war.

"He says Egypt can no longer continue in this state," Magdi said, lighting a cigarette. "We cannot go on living neither at war nor with peace. He says the situation is impossible. Now it must be one or the other."

I felt stricken. My heart was beating like a drum, my throat felt too dry for speech, the future seemed suddenly black, and the immediate filled with danger.

"What is the matter?" Magdi said mockingly. "Are you afraid for your life?"

"No," I said, and realized only then that it was true, I wasn't afraid for my life, it didn't really seem possible that I would die, or even that Cairo would be bombed, only . . . only. Only what? Some dread began to fill me, some desolation of the American soul, childish in its disbelief, frightened in its ignorance. I had been so *certain*. It was *inconceivable*. War? Why, that was *madness*! I had needed so badly to believe that the "policy-makers" were rational men and women of good will. Now, suddenly, I sat there, cold and tired, engulfed by all the old convictions of doom and annihilation every political announcement in the world had produced in me since the age of ten. Only this time I was at a *total* loss: unable to marshal my feelings, unable to locate "the enemy," unable to know exactly where the barricades were set up, and which direction the danger was coming from. I was a Jew in Cairo. On the eve of a possible Israeli invasion. The people in this room were like family to me. The Israelis who might fill the sky *were* family to me. . . . I shook myself.

"No, Magdi," I said. "I'm not afraid for my life. It is only that I suddenly see how hopeless the whole thing is. How utterly hopeless."

Magdi shrugged his shoulders. "We will live through it. We will live through everything."

Sadat's ultimatum absorbed thus with twinkling speed, the conversation turned to customs and mail censorship, as it seemed likely that now government control on who and what came into and left Egypt would once again tighten up. Soad began to tell one hilarious story after another about mail censorship, the stories centering mainly on a nephew who insisted on writing to his friends abroad about "policy," and had had five letters in a row sent to the wastebasket and was now watched continuously. That seemed to knock Soad out: she nearly fell off the daybed laughing.

Soad told me I should write to my mother quite soon to let her know all was well with me, as any letter I sent from here on in would take from eight days to two weeks to arrive in New York, depending on how long the "authorities" chose to "detain" my mail. I began to feel ill, cut off from the world. I looked into Soad's face, and she looked back into mine. In her eyes there was a curious kind of reassurance: it was the sympathy of the fully initiated for the novitiate. . . . But I could see that her own panic had long since subsided into philosophy. I felt more alone than ever.

I didn't hear anything after that; the talk all around me was reduced to a background buzz, dark and unfocused; my brain was filled with its own buzz. The *Om-Ali* was served, but I hardly remember what it tasted like.

At nine o'clock Magdi rose and said we must be going. Samiha instantly gathered herself together, and I, with great relief, did the same. We drove in silence back to Garden City. Cairo looked darker than ever, and I realized the city's lights were deliberately not being turned on. Dear God! Was it possible? Could I actually end my life in a shattering blaze of Israeli bombs?

Samiha retired almost immediately. For the first time since I'd come to live here I was too depressed to sit drinking tea with Magdi at the end of the day, and I also excused myself and went to my room. I threw myself full-length upon the bed and stared up at the ceiling. In a few minutes, lying down became intolerable. I leapt up from the bed and began pacing the room. Suddenly, I couldn't stand up, and I sat violently down on the edge of the bed, my head in my hands. Inside, I was beginning to feel desperate. Loneliness welled up in me, like some solid material filling my head, my chest, my arms and legs. I was often subject to such attacks of depression. They came like malaria, from a source that remained often dormant but apparently indestructible. This was the first time in Egypt. . . .

Magdi came to the door of my room. He looked deeply tired, and restless too. "Come inside. Have some brandy with me," he said. I looked at him, trying to figure out what I was willing to say to him. I quickly decided: nothing.

"Okay," I said, surprised at the shakiness of my voice; I had assumed myself still essentially under control.

I sat at the small table near the blackened windows in Magdi's bedroom in the glare of the overhead light. He poured golden-brown liquid from a green bottle with a small square Arabic label on it into two tea glasses and handed one to me: *Salud!* I gulped mine down; the liquor stung my throat and brought tears to my eyes, but my chest felt instantly warmed, and as though that sickening wall of lonely feeling was about to be penetrated, broken up . . . I should have known better.

Magdi began to talk, and I was required to listen and respond. I could hardly hear what he was saying. His voice seemed to be coming from a long way off. I couldn't shake loose from myself. Do what I would, the depression clung like pieces of magnetized stone to my insides. I felt as though some invisible membrane lay on me like a second skin through which I could see him moving and talking, even vaguely hear his voice, but I could not make out the words. The overhead light shone down without pity, fixing me in my chair into some vast, isolating space. A great buzzing silence swirled about my head.

"What is the matter with you?" Magdi's voice broke through.

"Nothing," I said, struggling to speak calmly. "I'm a bit depressed tonight, that's all." And to my horror, I began to cry. Magdi seemed electrified.

"Dear God!" he cried, moving quickly toward me. "What *is* it? What is wrong? Is it something I have said? Or done? What? Speak! Don't cry! I beg of you, don't cry! I cannot *bear* the sight of a crying woman!"

"Oh, *shut up!*" I wailed.

Magdi smiled. "What is it?" he asked softly.

My tears still fell, hot and wet on my cheeks, but I strained to recover speech.

"P-poor Magdi," I stuttered, "surrounded by weeping women. All he wants is a little laughter, and look what he gets."

"Stop that nonsense." Magdi frowned. "Do you really think I am such an animal?"

"No," I said quietly. "Not at all. It's nothing, Magdi. I don't know why, but all of a sudden I feel depressed, terribly depressed." The tears began again, and I gulped like a child, struggling to stop, struggling to speak. "It's nothing, really, it's nothing. I often have these feelings at home. You wouldn't understand. You're never depressed."

He looked shrewdly at me. "What makes you say that?" he said. "How do you know I am never depressed? I am *often* depressed. I miss my children terribly. I miss my *flat*. I miss . . ."

The telephone on the bedside table rang. Magdi went over to the bed, sat down, and lifted the phone. He listened for a few moments, then said something in Arabic, then hung up. He remained sitting on the bed.

"That was headquarters," he said. "I am to come at midnight, to sleep there for the night. In the event of enemy attack . . ." He trailed off. That stopped me cold.

"My God! In the event of enemy attack, *what*?"

"Well," he said, yawning nervously and wiping his large hand across his tired eyes, "they will wake me, place a sealed envelope in my hands, and I will. . . . But don't be afraid. It is all nonsense. Nothing is going to happen. It is just that they feel, what *if*. They cannot forget 1967."

We remained silent, both of us. I brought Magdi his half-finished brandy and he sprawled on the bed, nursing the drink. I remained in my chair, staring at the floor. We were both miserable. Utterly miserable. Magdi said to me, "Come here. Lie down beside me. I promise not to make love to you."

I walked over to the bed. He moved away from the edge to make room for me. I sat down, then lay down. My body felt exhausted with the long effort at control. Magdi half-sat up on the bed, and put his arm across my shoulders, and with his other hand brushed aside the hair that had fallen against my eyes. At the kindliness of his touch I collapsed entirely. I buried my head in his shoulder and wept uncontrollably. It was as though some wild grief were wrenching itself loose from my gut, washing itself out of me, letting me breathe. I could tell from the quietness with which Magdi held my shoulder and stroked my hair that I was crying for both of us, and at last I could say to him: I am alone in the world, entirely alone, everywhere, always.

He pressed me close, close, and his hand covered the exposed side of my face, as though to conceal me.

"Yes," he said heavily. "I know. I know. It is the price that is extracted from us. The price we pay for civilization."

He turned and kissed me. We clung hard to each other, and for a short time then we were not alone, either of us. . . .

At eleven o'clock Magdi rose to dress and leave for police headquarters. I sat propped up in bed, watching him move around the room. He changed into a pure white shirt and the pants of a fresh blue suit. As he was brushing off the blue jacket he suddenly laughed out loud and turning to me said, "Perhaps I should take you along with me."

"Could you?" I asked gullibly.

"Wouldn't that be something!" His face was gleeful. "Me walking in with one of the enemy."

My head spun. He doesn't mean anything, I said to myself, he doesn't know what he's saying, he only means you're an American, don't say anything, don't say anything. And I said, "You know I'm Jewish, don't you?"

He literally whirled on his feet. His warm brown face turned ash color. His eyes darkened and widened. He looked: caught. We stared wordlessly at each other. Magdi stood, motionless, with his blue suit jacket in his hands. I sat, motionless, in the bed, the sheet in my hand bunched up around my chin. Then the silence in the room returned: it buzzed once more about my head, and shot painfully away toward Magdi, surrounding him, holding us together yet apart in a thick separating embrace. An eternity seemed to pass. It was exactly as though we both knew we must hold on as hard as we could, as long as we could, to this silence, this suspension, this thickness of air we held between our eyes; as though we knew that when the silence broke, life would come crashing in on us, and we were each destined then to rush, headlong, in opposite directions, fleeing each other.

"You're Jewish!" Magdi burst out. "Why didn't you tell me? You should have told me."

I pulled the covers closer around me, and searched around inside my throat for my voice. "Why? Does it matter that much?"

"It doesn't matter at all to me," he said excitedly, "but I may be watched now."

"Why would you be watched? No one in Egypt knows I'm Jewish. Only Soad and Gasbia." Suddenly, I remembered the day we had gone to the Mogamaa, he and I, to register my residence in his house with the police—but that was silly, how could they know anything, it was only in Washington that they knew. Magdi looked as though his brain was being wracked in an effort to order his thoughts.

"Did you ever tell any Egyptian official that you were Jewish?" he asked.

"No. Only the officials in Washington. I wrote to them when I wanted to come to this country. . . ." He stared at me again, then he began to pace the room, saying, "Let me think. Let me think," while I sat huddled on the bed and the harsh light glared down on us and all the 1930s blond furniture and the blackened windows, and the Nile glimmering distantly in the cold March moonlight.

He stopped pacing and said suddenly, "No one will ever say anything to me. I'll just suddenly be transferred. . . . Let me think. I must *think*." And he paced again. And stopped again. "I'll go to Central Intelligence! They're my friends. I'll just *tell* them." He looked directly at me. "You foolish girl. Do you think that letter just *stayed* in Washington? Don't you understand? It's the terrible power of the *informant* we fear here."

"I can move," I said miserably.

And he grew angry. "If you say things like that I will not speak freely to you. You know I like you very much, and want you to stay with me. You feel that? Or you don't feel that?" I nodded dumbly.

"Do not worry. Do not worry," he said, working hard to pull himself together. "It will all work out somehow. . . . Somehow."

And he went off—he who had been one of Nasser's special police—to guard the city.

I switched off the overhead light and fell into a black unconsciousness that lasted ten hours, burrowing greedily into sleep, released at last from the hopeful beginnings and grievous endings that had literally consumed this day.

The next day the sun was shining, Cairo was going about its usual noisy business, and the war scare seemed over: a fiction of the paranoid night that evaporated under the clear blue desert sky.

I rose at ten, dressed in the empty flat (Magdi not back yet, Samiha gone somewhere), drank the tea Sayeda had placed in my room on a silver tray, and set off to walk into the central part of town. As I walked I looked long and hard at the Cairenes. One could hardly credit the notion that half the people in this city had gone to bed last night thinking they might be blown to kingdom come by morning. Now, on this sunny spring morning that followed upon a night of politics and fear, they laughed and joked, seemed intent on business, rushed about buying, selling, honking, hawking. Somehow, it all would not cohere inside me. I found myself unable to think in sentences; thought forced itself through a series of disconnected word-messages: war . . . impossible . . . cheerful Cairo . . . brave . . . enduring . . . warm . . . soft . . . mindless . . . venal . . . brotherly . . . ignorant . . . Magdi . . . Jewish . . . who Jewish . . . which Jewish . . . dislocated . . . numb . . . a job to do . . . Ali . . . betrayal . . . necessity. . . .

The words tumbled, churned, bounced around inside me. I began to realize that a single thought was forming itself out of all these disconnected fragments I hadn't the energy to deal with. Or rather, it was a *realization* that was beginning to emerge; a realization that rather shocked me; shocked me because it seemed, suddenly, to come as no surprise; almost as though I'd been waiting for it, expecting it, knowing it had to come; the image that pressed itself on my mind was that of a crocheting needle hooking itself onto the threads necessary to make the next loop in the design: I was beginning to feel some peculiar distance inside myself when I heard the word "Jewish."

I had been truly stricken by Magdi's response to my "revelation"; nevertheless, even then, somewhere inside myself, in a place the size of a pinpoint, down deep in the dark, I was feeling some faint sense of removal I had never before known: as though the word "Jewish," which had always struck intimate flesh, was now hitting foreign flesh;

as though I were hearing "Irish" or "Italian"; as though it didn't have anything, really, to do with me; as though there was a slight case of mistaken identity here; it was, very nearly, as though a membrane of some sort had formed itself around the outermost layer of my consciousness and my immediate sense of my Jewishness had become trapped somewhere in the space between. For an instant there flashed through my mind: The body produces its own antibodies when attacked by foreign matter; nature anesthetizes for purposes of survival. But I pushed the thought away: it was too bizarre to contemplate.

Nevertheless, as I walked along busy Kasr-el-Nil Street, repeating the word "Jewish" to myself, it was as though that pinpoint of removal had swelled and was now the size of a nailhead.

No matter, I shrugged my shoulders. Examining my sensations carefully, and discovering that this "distance" was causing me neither pain nor discomfort, only a curious sort of numbness, I determined to ignore it, and go on my way. I could think about it tomorrow, next month, next year. If it came to that, I had my whole life to think about it.

At six o'clock I swung through the glass doors in Garden City, ran lightly up the steps, turned the key in the massive wooden door—and immediately wished I hadn't.

Magdi, dressed—like most Egyptians relaxing at home—in pajamas, sat in his chair at the tea table in his bedroom, reading a newspaper. I stopped for a fraction of a moment in the doorway, smiling hugely on my way to him. He looked up from his paper, and his eyes told me everything there was to tell. They were very polite, those eyes; mildly receptive, did so wish to avoid a scene, and-er-who, exactly, *are* you? Why are you rushing like this into my room, as though you had a right to be here? By the time I got to the chair my smile had frozen on my face, and I was feeling cold and dead inside. I stooped and swiftly kissed his cheek. He smiled and said, "Sit down. Have a cup of tea." With one hand he waved me into the chair opposite him, with the other he stifled a sudden yawn. He laughed, and stretched his arms far above his head, arching his back as he did so. "O-o-o-o-h-h. I am tired. I must take a nap, I must get dressed, Naha is coming in one hour, I must take the car to have it repaired, I must be at the airport for a little while tonight, and then I must go to Fawzy. . . ."

I said very little, and in thirty minutes left the house saying I was going for a walk. When I returned an hour later the flat was empty. I sat in one of the stuffed maroon chairs in the front room the entire evening, reading, in fever and dim misery. I felt as though I were three years old and my mother had been sitting in front of me with a spoonful of food for half an hour and, although I was hungry, I would not eat. And then, the moment I *did* decide to eat, someone came into the room and her hand with the food in it wandered away from me as she turned to talk.

But I am not three years old, I reminded myself, burrowing into the maroon chair, my legs pulled up beneath me, one hand a fist against my cheek. I am thirty-five years old. So I can't kick and scream and cry with anxiety and confusion and frustration and disappointment. I have to "deal" with things. Another of life's many opportunities to "cope," to be "mature." And so friendly of Magdi to offer it to me. . . .

Needless to say, this welter of confused self-pity would have its repercussions. Two days later, Magdi and I were having morning tea together in the living room. I had asked Sayeda to give me my tea there, and Magdi, alone in the bedroom, had come seeking me out with his old friendliness, exactly as though nothing had ever happened, neither our coming together nor our subsequent frozen politeness. We chatted, calmly enough, but I could hear that cutting edge in my voice I know so well, and have so come to dread: for I know what it presages. It is the more harmless end of a kind of defensive behavior that begins with irony and ends with an anger so viciously out of control that while in its grip I am capable of saying and doing things so wild, so brutal, that afterwards my head reels and my stomach turns in agony to remember, to remember. . . .

But, surely, all that was still a good way off, and now I was on my guard. But good Lord! what was *this*! Here was Magdi saying, "Why are you attacking me?"

For days now, Cairo has disappeared. I am sunk, entirely, in the weight of rejection, hypnotized by misery. Magdi's indifference is perfect: invariably polite, never moody, cheerfully friendly on the mornings he is here, not the slightest opening behind those wide expressionless eyes that I now feel as an impregnable wall between us. And I am lost and leaping, despair turning to anger somewhere deep in my gut, rushing up into my throat and out of my mouth, with each cutting response, each sarcastic observation, my entire being demanding: recognize me! Magdi's control is a direct measure of my own disintegration. I am humiliated, belittled in my own eyes, my energy drained. I sit for hours staring at a book that lies on the arm of my chair, forgetting to turn the page.

At last, I cry out, "You are hurting me!" And my directness disarms.

Magdi takes me in his arms and says, "It is no good. No good. I wish we could start over again. Let us forget what has happened, and not ruin our friendship. Believe me, it is better this way. No, it is *not* because you are Jewish! That worries me, but believe me, that can either be straightened out or not straightened out. It has not to do with *us.*"

"How can that be?" I ask coldly. "How can I believe—more important, how can *you* believe—that if I had not told you I was Jewish this would now be happening?"

Magdi stares at me. His eyes gleam, and in them is a soft cynicism. "We will never know for sure, will we," he says gently. "Perhaps the threat runs deeper than I am able to perceive. Perhaps if it were not for that, I would be willing to risk . . . But no, no. That is all nonsense! Really, it is. Come, let us try again. Let us simply be friends as we were before." We shake hands and vow to be straightforward again, and decent with each other.

But now the controls are off, and our attraction to each other comes creeping back, bit by bit. Three nights later, in the silent volatile darkness, we take each other again in blind, melancholy greed, our lust edged with a fear of tenderness so palpable it is very nearly a third person in the bed. I, of course, am on the brink of plunging into that tenderness. Magdi is not. The next day he disappears behind his eyes in the middle of a sentence, he announces Naha is coming when I expect to go out with him, he leaves the house without explanation, he picks up a newspaper when I enter the room.

Another scene. Another set of insane recriminations from me. . . . *Dear God! What is happening to me? How long? How long? And for what? For what, exactly?* . . . Clearly, Magdi thinks me mad. And then, at last, he grasps me roughly by the shoulders and says, "I *cannot* fall in love with an American. I *will* not fall in love with an American. I *am* not in love with an American."

Soad, my beautiful Soad. . . .

At times she is a wrinkled crone, her eyes dull and lightless, her face a withered skin, the years inside trapped, pinched, dying: she totters, stumbles, nearly, nearly she is going down, a humiliating second childhood swirling about her, reaching for her. At other times, she is a regal lady, her eyes all fire and majesty, flashing: *Never!* I am an *authority* in this world. An authority does not disintegrate, neither does it topple. If you wish to topple me, I promise you will come down with me, kicking and screaming, your eyes wide with surprise. In such moments, she is Natasha Ivanovna sitting in the cherry orchard—but with the guts to straddle both worlds.

"Don't believe him," she whispered fiercely to me after the Doctor denounced Nasser. "Gamal was *beloved*. It was slavery here. *Slavery*. And then Gamal came, and for the first time there was a chance to see an end to it. Yes, it is true, they took everything. But what could they do? It was misery on misery on misery here. If they looked up or if they looked down, if they looked left or if they looked right, if they looked south or north. *La.* There was no money. A'tall. A'tall. Noth-ing."

Soad folds her small delicate hands, coarsened and broken by sixty years of labor; they lie, like ancient birds at rest, in her black rayon lap; her back is straight against the round red brocade chair in which she sits. On a small marble table before her, her untasted tea. She waits patiently for me to speak. It is five in the afternoon. Beyond the open shutters the floating branches of a large backyard tree hang wearily over the balcony, cold in the dying sun. I turn on the tufted love seat to face Soad directly.

"Soad," I say, "I think I had better move to another flat."

"Why do you say that?" She leans forward in astonishment. "Is there something wrong? The Captain has not been offensive to you in any way, has he?"

"Oh, no," I say hastily. "No. Not at all. He has been my good friend. It is only . . ." I find it hard to speak the words I have come to speak, and I trail off, looking at my fingernails. But the woman beside me gives me courage, and I lift my eyes to look directly into hers. "Soad, I think Magdi and I are going to get into trouble if I stay much longer."

She looks at me for a long hard moment. She knows *exactly* what I am talking about. She resettles herself in her chair, arranging the black lace collar at her throat thoughtfully, and then she says, "Of course, it is only natural that you should wish to have your own flat. After all, you have your pride. Why should you not wish to pay your own rent? Everyone can understand that. Everyone in the family will understand that. We will see about it im*medi*ately. Do you think you would like to live in Bab-el-Louk? I know of a flat that is for rent there. In fact, it is a flat that the Captain nearly rented himself. It is on a high floor in a convenient section—very near to the pharmacy— not too expensive, I think it will be fine for you. Shall we inquire?"

"Oh, Soad! You are wonderful! I knew that you would rescue me." And we are hugging each other across the fat brocade arms that separate us. Soad sits back in her chair, her hands folded once more, her face suddenly unwrinkled, her eyes focused, her voice young and *purposeful.*

"You will find me a totally reasonable woman. I can listen to everything and, *yani,*° I have eyes to take it in, and flesh to feel it with, and ears to understand what is being said. That is because I have had to be com-*plete*ly self-reliant almost all my life. My married life, *yani,* was about three years altogether. Otherwise, com-*plete*ly alone, alone, alone. And could I ever think: I have a brother, he will

° "So to speak." Arabs use this word the way Italians use *prego*; it punctuates the speech of the most fluently English-speaking Egyptian.

help me with so-and-so? Or: I have a sister, she owes me so-and-so? I
could not. In fact, I had to do for *them*. I was the eldest. They looked
to *me* for everything."

She lifts her teacup and she drinks deeply.

Sometimes, in Cairo, one can cross six centuries in the space of
three neighborhoods. Yesterday, I did just that.

I set out from Garden City to walk through what Cairenes call
Misr Adima, the Old City. (It's *all* the Old City to me, but what is
meant by the term is that section of Cairo in which there still stands
the remnants of the original walled city of a thousand years ago.) I
walked along the lovely Nile Corniche for a short way, then turned
right on a street called El Sad El Barrany, and began climbing up the
hilly street, away from the prosperous riverfront and into the city.
After a while I came to the beginning of the old walls which stand
like broken dinosaurs on the curving streets. There are many open
arches in the walls and I could see people huddled in those
arches—tending fires, eating food, nursing children, staring, beating
donkeys, pushing goats along. Sometimes, in the distance behind the
arches, I could see the concrete blocks of flats the government has
put up for the people of the Old City: but they hardly made a dent in
me, so vivid was the image of the people huddled before me within
the shelter of the uncaring arches.

As I walked, the street began to give way, first to broken
pavement, then to no pavements at all, then to the look of a country
road. And still I climbed. By now I had an army of children behind
me, not begging, just amazed by my presence. I named a square as
my destination—Sayeda Zeinab; they nodded eagerly, and began to
lead me. We passed into a section that looked for all the world like
the outskirts of some remote village: an open dusty road, grasses
growing vaguely on the side, no houses at all, women in black with
babies at their breasts walking beside men atop donkeys. I kept
saying to myself: I'm in the middle of Cairo. We stumbled along
through the dust for an interminable time until I felt the beginnings
of some subtle change taking place all about me: a shack appeared in
the side of the road, further on an open cart stacked with boxes of

produce, then two men in a garagelike house hammering away at some horribly mashed piece of metal; in a while, the recognizable beginnings of a street again, not paved, but wide, and with houses accumulating on either side. The children and I walked faster now; we turned a curve in the road, and came full into a genuine village street with people, a few shops, two- and three-story houses, chickens crossing the road, and suddenly the sound of the Koran on the radio coming straight down on me from the top floor of one of those houses.

The religious chanting which, like the car-honking, pervades my consciousness in Cairo, pierced me at that moment as it never had before. I felt as though together, the children and I, had been struggling up for a long way into civilization and yes, it was true, it really *did* exist, and here it was. Everything in me went forward as goods and services and developed relations began to multiply before my very eyes. We rushed along then, the streets getting fuller and fuller, and everything coming faster and faster, and I was suddenly swept into a huge bazaar street crowded with shops and stalls and market carts and thousands of people pushing and pulling and we ended up at the mosque of Sayeda Zeinab, one of the children holding tightly to my hand, but suddenly pulling away from me, and three strange boys attaching themselves to me while cars and trams honked all around me and someone tried to sell me six plastic hangers off a cart, and the boys clung like gnats to me saying, "One piastre, lady, one piastre," and a lovely man in a shabby brown suit and black-rimmed glasses suddenly took hold of my arm, yanked me away from the boys, said in Cambridge English, "Are they annoying you?" (God knows what he said to them in Arabic), and walked me silently out of the mob, shaking hands with me and turning back in the opposite direction when he was sure I was okay.

I couldn't bring myself to tell the man in the brown suit that I really wanted to plunge back into all that madness in the square and eat *fetir* at one of those marble-countered holes in the wall near the mosque. After all, he was saving me. . . . So I turned, and walked halfway across the city, back toward the Nile and Garden City, having come full-circle back into the very particular inhibitions of polite society.

Now that I was moving, Magdi and I were once more the best of friends. On a Saturday night he went to visit his uncle Monir, and insisted I come along. Monir's front room was filled with family. That is, *male* family. I was the only woman in the room, except for Monir's wife Tu-Tu (Egypt is full of women who will go to the grave being called Tu-Tu, Za-Za, Shu-Shu), who did not sit down and take part in the conversation, but rather kept running back and forth from the kitchen, directing the serving efforts of a twelve-year-old girl who was producing a succession of small dishes of food as well as endless cups of tea and coffee. Salah was there, and Kamel the under-secretary, and smooth-cheeked Amr, and Monir's young son Mohammed. Gathered under the glaring light fixed to the high ceiling, sitting among the faded streaked walls on the clumsy old-fashioned furniture, they formed a striking portrait of what was once known as shabby respectability. Salah sat, back ramrod stiff, pants leg perfectly creased; Monir smoked, easy in a maroon silk bathrobe; Amr lounged, one leg thrown over an upholstered chair arm; Kamel stood near a false mantelpiece, looking very self-contained in his oddly pensive reserve; Magdi drank coffee, his dark eyes expressionless; Mohammed stood, then sat, then stood again, restless with adolescent anxiety. It was 1971 and they were a group of dark, solid Egyptian men. Yet I could not escape the impression that I had wandered into a Victorian tintype, brown and crumbling at the edges: something frozen and held back at the center of this room, attached to each of the men here with invisible threads, pulling like gravitational force, grouping and regrouping them for a portrait that remained nevertheless the same in its compositional design: closed, defensive, the gut pulled out, the edges sealed over, proud, silent, a melancholy steadiness in that massive flinching effort. . . .

The men spoke long and loudly, turning now and then to me to apologize for the Arabic. I smiled and nodded, but grew restive. It occurred to me suddenly to wonder if they would be talking Arabic were I an American *man*—and instantly I saw the true anomaly that my position in Egypt represented: I was here, now, because I was an

American; nevertheless, they were speaking Arabic because I was a woman.

Magdi and I went back to Garden City at midnight. We drank tea and separated for the night. At nine in the morning I heard the doorbell ring and Monir enter the flat. He was to drive Magdi to headquarters, as there was some family business he wished to discuss with him. I heard them both leave and I fell back into the sluggishness of interrupted sleep.

An astonishment. An hour after Magdi and Monir left the house the doorbell began ringing insistently. I wasn't going to answer but it went on and on, and finally I padded down the hall in my pajamas. In the doorway stood Kamel, the under-secretary.

"He's gone," I said. "Monir just drove him to headquarters."

Kamel seemed startled, and remained motionless in the doorway. Finally, he crossed the threshold and said gently, "I hope I have not disturbed you."

"Oh, no," I said sleepily. "Not at all."

He smiled and took my arm. "Come, let us sit down for a moment." I remember being slightly puzzled as he led me into the darkened living room: something strange in the air. We spoke on the couch for a few strained moments, and suddenly Kamel began to fall apart. His hands reached blindly, his lips whitened, the muscles around his eyes twitched. It was *me* he had come for!

"Your eyes, your lips," he moaned. "Especially your lower lip. I dreamed about it last night. Everything! Everything about you! I couldn't stop thinking about you from the moment we met, and then you came last night, and oh, you stayed so short a time, and then you were gone! I had to see you again, I had to. Everything about you. The way you talk, what you say, the way you look, even your *hair* is sexy!" All this time grabbing, biting, kissing, and me stunned, immobilized, fixated on: my lower *lip*???

Still, I did not really push him away, drawn, as though in a trance, by the insane energy of Kamel's groping hunger. I kept saying to myself: I really must put a stop to this, but it was *fascinating*. Something vain and curious in me wanted to see what would happen next. He thrashed about on the couch, buried his head, groaning, in my breasts, mashed my lips with his own. And then I began to grow frightened.

"Please!" I cried. "The family . . . I'm a friend . . . a *visitor* . . . stop it! Goddamnit, I said *stop* it." I tore away and stood quickly up. But I had set in motion something I could no longer control. Instantly, he was on his feet and clutching at me again.

"Don't be frightened," he babbled, "don't be frightened." Which of course terrified me. His eyes closed, his body swaying, his face literally drained white, he seemed about to faint, even as his fingers, now like steel, held me in a rigid grip. I remember thinking: What the hell is going *on*? He acts like he's just escaped after five years in a state penitentiary.

Then Kamel's fingers dug into the flesh of my arms, his head sank to my shoulder, and he cried in quick, high-pitched succession, "Oh! Oh! Oh! Don't let me go, dear! Don't let me go!" His body shook with the unmistakable convulsion, and on the front of his expensive blue pants the white staining fluid began to seep through. He fell away from me, sinking onto the couch behind him, muttering dazedly, "Forgive me. Forgive me." But his eyes were closed, and on his mouth a satisfied smile.

Shortly, he rose, straightened his clothes, begged me to assure him that I had not been too distressed by his behavior, and said he would not leave until I had promised to speak with him later in the week. I could hardly hear what he was saying by now, and mumbled yes, yes, anything, anything, just please go. *Go.*

I stood there in the hallway, staring at the door, my lips actually bruised purple, remembering that the family had full hopes that one day their reserved cousin would become a ranking minister.

I never saw Kamel again.

The flat Soad has found for me is at the edge of the Bab-el-Louk market in the heart of downtown Cairo, a seven-minute walk from Groppi's in Midan Soliman Pasha, ten minutes from Tahrir Square and fifteen minutes from the Immobilia Building on Sharif Street. The street is the width of an alley, dusty and unpaved, lined on either side with high stone buildings whose balconies are strung with washing and from whose windows the blare of radio-Koran and whining Arabic music floats continuously. Noise and tumult everywhere: laughter, honking horns, screeching voices, men yelling at recalcitrant animals, servants rushing to the market for the daily ration of food.

Upstairs, on the fourth floor of one of these buildings (to which we have ascended in pitch darkness in a creaking wire cage that I am sure will plummet momentarily to the ground) is the set of rooms that will be my home for the next four months. A high, narrow, dark apartment with stone floors, frosted windows, balconies facing south and east, an evil-smelling primitive kitchen with the usual single cold-water faucet and the tank of bottled gas beside the stove, a bathroom that looks like something out of the American Civil War, and the eternal looped curtains in every doorway, along with the tightly stuffed, squared-off, bulky furniture (always in green, brown or maroon—this time in maroon—and always four pieces too many in every room), set off by glass-topped tables, plastic flowers, imitation art deco on the walls, and the gloomy neon lighting.

No matter. I raced through the rooms, happy in the large front bedroom with sunlight pouring in when I wrenched open the shutters, and stood on the narrow balcony looking down onto the streaming street below, three barefoot little girls waving and laughing to me from the balcony opposite, and I with relief washing through me. Noise and gaiety, the excitement of the central city, the mixed blessings of solitude and relearned independence once more before me! How the Hamamsys had engulfed me! How weakening the voluptuous pleasure of living with Magdi had been! How good it would be to learn to be alone again! Why, it was almost like entering Egypt for the first time all over again.

The night before I moved from Garden City I met Amr in the lobby of Shepard's Hotel. Shepard's was, for nearly a hundred years, *the* colonial British hotel: visiting diplomats in Cairo stayed at Shepard's; businessmen, engineers, spies, soldiers—all met at Shepard's. In 1952 Shepard's—then located on Opera Square, near the

Ezbekiah Gardens, a lovely spacious part of Cairo in the 1880s—was razed during the fearful burning of Cairo that preceded Nasser's revolution. Subsequently, the hotel was rebuilt on the Nile, in a straight line with the Semiramis, the Nile, the Hilton, all the major hotels, and whereas once it had resembled a rambling white wooden English country house it was now a modern hotel of somewhat garish proportions, filled with blue tile, false-looking arabesque windows, and lower-middle-class tourists.

Amr was waiting for me in the high-ceilinged, dimly-lit cocktail lounge in Shepard's lobby. It was always remarkable to me, this matter of the difference between the Egyptians who frequented the Hilton or the Semiramis or Shepard's. Although I knew full well that the Egyptians who went to one of them went to all of them, nevertheless each hotel somehow accumulated a different atmosphere; in Shepard's it was distinctly less "colonial" than at the Hilton, but definitely more so than at the Semiramis.

Amr rose half out of his seat as I sat down at the small low table at the far end of the room. He looked altogether different tonight than he had looked in his uncle's front room. He wore a blue suit, a smooth white collar, a narrow black tie. He looked older, more serious, a man out in the world, no longer the moon-faced, sweet-natured man-boy lounging about the house. I realized then that I actually knew nothing about Amr. Who was he? What did he do? Where had he done it? *Why* had he done it?

"You know, Amr . . ." I said.

He was thirty-five years old, and a retired naval officer. In 1967 he had backed the wrong man and was one of fifty-four officers who went on trial for treason. He had spent two years in prison.

"It was wrong, the whole thing was wrong. They never knew how to fight a war from the very beginning. I said: Hit first and hit hard. But no one could make the decision. When we came back from the frontier and I saw the people in the city swimming and drinking coffee and going to the cinema I really couldn't bear it, and I said so at the trial. For whom? For what am I risking my life?

"I learned a lot in prison, and now—it is finished. I know my limits, something very few people in Egypt know. So now I am a businessman, pure and simple. I buy, I sell, I take pleasure in giving my wife what she wants and needs, and I am content.

"My family—they are all fakes. They love me because they think I hate Nasser. I am their hero, their martyr, because I hate Nasser and I went to prison for it. They are so stupid. I am a man of principles. I do not hate a man. What is Nasser? I knew soon he would be dead. In a year or in a hundred years, what does it matter in history? They think I did something they cannot do. So they spend their lives hating Nasser, and succeed only in destroying themselves. They think they are first in politics, first in economics, first in banking, and they are nothing. Nothing! There is not one among them who will ever speak the truth to you, ever speak directly from his heart. They cannot! They do not *know* the truth about themselves. They can never know it as *I* know it!"

He seemed agonized by his memories, and embittered by present truths. I found myself deeply touched. From there to feeling sexual attraction was not, of course, a very great distance to travel. . . . *Dear God! Am I going to go through every one of them in turn? Is it just the Hamamsys or is it going to be the whole country? All this angst and sex. Everywhere!*

As though he were reading my thoughts, Amr grinned at me, leaned his dark head toward my own dark one, and said, "What is sex? Nothing. It goes, just like *that*. But friendship lasts forever. So when I find one like you, whom I can talk to, I want it to be friendship. So we will fight it, yes?"

"You're damn straight we'll fight it," I said, and took a long swallow of my drink.

He looked at his watch. "Come," he said. "I'll take you back to Garden City. I must go to my office, now. We have many talks ahead of us, yes? There is no need to rush ourselves."

He drove a ten-year-old Cadillac, and he insisted on treating it *right*. We waited for the car to warm up.

"How long have you been married?" I asked, as we sat in the restful gloom of the old Caddy.

"Three years. Mirella was seventeen. I've known her since she was nine. I practically helped her parents raise her. So I *know* she is a good girl." He laughed. "Not like me. Mean and bad and complicated."

"Are you faithful to her?"

"Faithful," Amr sighed. "What does that mean, faithful? Let me put it this way. There are three kinds of unfaithful husbands: those who run after other women, those who take it only when it comes their way, and those who try hard to avoid it and who struggle with themselves and suffer afterward. The first is the worst, the second the next worst, and the last the best. Right now I am in the last category, but soon I will go to the second. I know it. It is the way with all men."

Back in Garden City, my mind full of Amr's confessions, I wandered around the empty flat. When Magdi came in, we drank tea uneasily on this our last night together. It was difficult for us to speak, difficult for our eyes to meet, difficult. . . . Needing to fill the sudden void, I began to speak of Amr and his odd political history. Magdi, restless and uncomfortable, grew sharp.

"He is a hero? He is *nothing*. The family felt sorry when he was arrested. They felt a child was going on trial. He is narrow-minded and cunning. You will see. When the war came, and the chief of staff was deposed, Amr came to me in Alexandria and said, 'He will be back, stronger than ever, and I'll be with him.' He went to the chief's house and slept there. He thought that was really something special. He didn't know they *all* slept there. Then came the chief's suicide, and all close to him, or apparently close, arrested. . . . Amr once wanted to marry my wife's sister. I said no."

We sipped our tea in complicated silence. I didn't know it then, but it was the last time Magdi was to guide me in the fine Egyptian art of double exposure. From here on in, I was on my own.

PART TWO

The apartment in Mohammed Sidki Street seemed so different now that I was alone in it. Shadows loomed everywhere, and when I sought to dispel them, neon lighting bathed the rooms and halls in a gloomy green light that soon made me long again for the semi-darkness. The toilet wouldn't flush, the stove wouldn't light, the shutters wouldn't open. There was no refrigerator. The desk stood in a dark well before the dining-room window that looked out on the side of the building where the street was narrowest and least traveled; the effect, at the desk, was that of sitting in a prison cell. Thin, cheap curtains flapped in all the doorways, the slab of marble beside the kitchen sink was perpetually cold and dirty, an inch of Cairo's ever-present dust lay on everything.

That first night I fell into despair. I wandered about the apartment in a genuine panic of loneliness. It was as though I had entered Egypt twice, the first entry having been a fraudulently lulling one; now, this second entry, *this* was the genuine coming into Cairo. I was alone as I had never quite been alone before. It was not like New York where there was always some way to break the spell of the bad times, make the contact that dissolved the pressure. Now there were no thirty-two best friends to ease the pain when it came, no gossip

and distraction and reassurances of love from the hundred fragments
of life and people that in no way cohere, but no matter! they must
pass for the real thing. . . . Now there was not even Magdi Al-Amir.
Now there was no one but me. Now there was nothing for it but to
fight it out alone. Now there was only the sharp awareness of
wanting to plant myself, a stranger in someone else's life, and say
gimme, gimme, gimme.

The doorbell rang. I rushed eagerly into the hall. Magdi! Soad! I
had wanted to be free of them, oh I would be so glad to see them! In
the dark outer passage stood two little girls, barefoot and in ragged
dresses. They stared at me with round eyes, and the bolder of the
two—also the older—spoke up, gesticulating energetically while she
spit out a number of rapid-fire Arabic sentences. I stared at them in
dismay. Suddenly, it dawned on me that I knew no one in the house
who spoke English. Mrs. Lutfallah, the woman who had rented me
this apartment, and who lived on the first floor, spoke only Arabic.
We had smiled extravagantly at each other and said "*Salaam
waleikum*" and "*Ma'salaam*" many times, but it was Soad who had
actually conducted our business. Everyone I had seen coming up in
the elevator today had clearly spoken not a word of anything other
than Arabic.

"I do not speak Arabic," I said to the little girls. They returned my
stare, waiting a decent interval before the one who had spoken spoke
again: repeating, it seemed, exactly whatever it was she had said
before. I struggled around inside my head, finding at last the words
in Arabic to say I didn't understand Arabic.

"*Ana mishafham Araby,*" I said loudly, in an American accent so
thick that the children continued to stare at me until I saw the light
of comprehension go on suddenly in the older girl's eyes and she
stood there, bobbing her head eagerly in my direction, laughing
delightedly at my feeble attempt at communication. She reached out
and took my hand, pulling me through the open doorway into the
hall, towing me behind until she stopped at the apartment directly
facing the elevator and vigorously rang the bell. Behind the tall
narrow glass and wood halves of the door identical to mine only a
dim light shone, and there was a long moment of quiet after the bell
had been rung. I began to withdraw but the girl, her hand still in

mine, shook her head silently. At last the door opened and a thin black man in a white *gelabya* and skullcap stood in the doorway. The girl spoke to the man and he disappeared into the dark interior of the apartment, reappearing very quickly with a fat young woman in pajamas, her thick kinky hair pulled up into a bun on top of her head. Her face was very round, yellow-brown, and strikingly beautiful. The young woman bent her luminous brown eyes to the child, and they spoke rapidly in Arabic. Then she turned to me.

"The little girls have come to welcome you," she said in blessed English. "How do you do? My name is Fatma Shanawany. Are you the American who has rented the flat?"

"Yes!" I said. "Oh, yes. Yes."

"Come," she said, taking my arm and moving out into the hall beside me. "Forgive my sleeping-wear," pointing to her pajamas, "let us see the flat. Do you need help? Do you know where to shop for food? Do you have a servant to clean for you? Do you wish my servant to go to the market this night? Have you anything to eat or drink in the flat?"

"The stove," I said weakly. Anything to keep her in the flat for a while.

"The stove," she repeated quickly. "Does it not function? Have you bottled gas? Did they not supply you with a tank?" and she was rushing ahead of me into the narrow, high-ceilinged kitchen with the two little girls giggling behind us.

The stove was a two-burner gas ring propped up on a low metal table; neither burner would light. My new neighbor went quickly to work, rolling up her pajama sleeves, examining the gas tank, lifting the inner parts of the burners out, poking, blowing, cleaning, lighting matches without end, standing back, peering sharply, starting all over again; me standing next to her frowning intently as though I were learning something; the two little girls giggling in the doorway; the kitchen feeling like an air-shaft in which we were all somehow suspended, working like intent little moles. And Fatma Shanawany talking, talking, talking all the while.

"Have you just come from America? Will you stay long in Egypt? Why have you come? Will you occupy the flat all alone? Do you have friends in Cairo?" And I answering as fast as the questions come, with Fatma's magnificent eyes widening into huge circles, her eyebrows rising, and her clear soft voice saying "Really!" to everything I say.

"Oh, my dear, I am so glad you have come to live here!" Fatma laid an impulsive hand on my arm. "We shall be friends, yes? I will help you to manage this peculiar Egypt of ours, and you will improve my English, yes? German is my first language, you see. My English is rather weak."

No sooner said than done: within fifteen minutes Fatma and I were confiding our life stories to each other, she all the while poking about with the stove, her round brown arms soon smudged with grease, her falling hair being pushed up on her forehead with the back of her hand, her fingers continually striking matches.

"Married twice!" said Fatma. "A journalist! Ah, I think it must be a very wonderful thing to be an American woman. You are free! Free to travel, free to marry or not to marry, free to dress as you like. Here we are not free. Oh, no, my dear, the Egyptian woman is not free a'tall. A'tall. My husband, he is a good man, a *very* good man. But he is not modern. He is very conservative with me. I wish to make a trip to Germany. German is my *language*. I work for a German engineer. He would take me when he makes a small business journey. My husband says: No. That is all. *No*. Why? I say. But it is finished. He does not reply."

"Why did you marry him?" I asked. Fatma's eyes were calm and steady, and very direct. They rested on me a moment, as though gauging what my response would be before she spoke.

"We are Nubians," she said. "We must always marry each other. When I was seventeen my father came to me and he said, 'Here are four relatives. Choose one.'" Fatma laughed conspiratorily. "Secretly, I was in love with my husband who was one of the four. But none knew of this. None!"

"How long have you been married?"

"Eight years. I have now twenty-six years. An old woman with two children! My husband is forty-one. Think on it, my dear. Forty-one! But not a *young* forty-one. He works too hard, too hard. He is a doctor. Oh, my dear, they are never in the house, doctors. Really, it is something terrible!"

"Do you still love him?"

"Yes," she said simply. "We understand each other very well, he and I. But he is too conservative!" She lit another match and held it to the still recalcitrant burner. "Never—no, never, my dear—since I am married am I permitted to wear a dress without sleeves. Never have I bathed in the ocean. Never may I go to the cinema in the evening with my sister. He says, 'All are watching.' And that is the end of that. 'The life is changing,' I tell him. 'All are doing what you do not permit me to do.' 'The life may change,' he says, 'but not for *my* wife.'" She lifted her eyes to the ceiling in mock despair. She laughed again. Her laugh was an intelligent chuckle in her throat; it made her nose wrinkle.

"My sister is becoming engaged in two weeks," Fatma said. "You will come, yes? No, no, my dear. Have no fear. A foreigner is an honored guest. You have not yet seen a Nubian engagement party, have you? Good! And this is a very *special* party." She looked directly into my eyes once more. "It is my youngest sister who will marry. She marries a 'white' Egyptian. She is the first woman in our family to do so." Fatma laughed her intelligent, tickled laugh. "All are opposed. All are watching. All want to do the same." And with that she triumphantly lit the stove.

And so we began, Fatma and I, our long neighborly warmth, eyeing each other in the months to come with a mixture of exasperation and affection: moral distaste and emancipated anger. And once again, I was saved from the ultimate aloneness.

Lovely, comic-mournful Mohammed. He is twenty-three years old, a devoted Moslem, lives in the densely poor district of Shobra, attends a government-run institute for city planning, and works mornings and evenings at the Egyptian Library. At the library Mohammed receives twenty piastres a day for six hours' work, bringing home one pound and twenty piastres a week. When he graduates from the institute he will work as a draftsman, under a five-year contract to the government he had to sign in order to get free training, for twenty pounds a month. In Cairo, this wage is referred to as "the famous seventeen pounds." Every university graduate goes to work for twenty pounds a month, bringing home seventeen: the equivalent of approximately forty American dollars. (Here, in this single statistic, one has the entirety of Egypt's crippling economics, for no one can survive without drastic help on seventeen pounds a month. It is a sum that will perhaps purchase—just barely—food, public transportation and cigarettes. It will not pay for a flat, clothes, shoes, taxis, books, a weekly restaurant dinner, or any other incidental expenses. Thus, no university graduate can live alone, much less marry, without financial support for a good many years from his family.)

Tall, skinny, young-graceful, horn-rimmed glasses, a gently cynical smile on his mouth and in his eyes—that is, when his eyes are not large and anxious—Mohammed is always depressed, bowed down as he is by the transcendental questions concerning "the meaning of it all" that he constantly applies to his twenty-three-year-old state in life.

Mohammed is also very funny, incapable of not observing himself with the rich, self-mocking humor of the ghetto. One day on the street we ran into a friend of his, shorter by a head and rounder by a foot than Mohammed. The young man mopped his sweating forehead while he spoke swiftly and urgently up into Mohammed's calm thin face. Mohammed nodded attentively, hearing his friend patiently out. Then he leaned down toward him, and in English said, "I know four languages. In any one of them, or in all of them, I can tell you: I have no money."

Oh Mohammed, how wonderful you must be in Arabic.

This is our third meeting. We walk rapidly along Kasr-el-Nil Street, headed for the Opera Square, then the Library, and then out towards the Mohammed Ali district. We are going to climb to the top of the Citadel today. Mohammed holds me delicately by the upper arm, steering me cautiously through the crowded streets, pushing me forward, pulling me back, avoiding collision with donkeys, carts, automobiles through the split-second expertise of a born survivor-on-the-streets. Our heads incline toward each other. Something there is between me and this boy, some sympathy present almost from the first moment, flowing deeper and wider each time we meet. We have sat in Groppi's for hours, our heads close together, listening to the sounds of intimacy. Intimacy! That extraordinary mystery that appears without warning and for no *real* reason. I feel as though we are leaning into each other, Mohammed and I, bound loosely by a depth of peace and intimate affection that is strong, and grows stronger hourly. If he were a bit older he would probably insist, but since he is just as he is, he takes his cues entirely from me, and is glad to have this exotic lady in his life; for me, he is curiously healing.

Today, he is moody and depressed. "I do not work," he says plaintively. "Two days now, I do not work. I don't know. I am tired. Tired in my *mind*. I am unhealthy tired! I want to change the life. I don't know how. How will it happen? It *cannot* happen! I want to go away. Away from the life, away from the people. The noise in Cairo!" He smacks his forehead. "I cannot *think* anymore. Perhaps, if I could get away for a while, I could have some peace, and then I would come back." He is silent for a moment as we pass the book stalls fronting the Ezbekiah Gardens. Then, insistently: "How can I find a good girl? In Egypt it is impossible to know a girl. First one marries, *then* one knows. I cannot do this. I cannot! On Tuesday I did not work. I came to Groppi's. I hope that you are there. You were not. . . . I wander. Today, I am *happy* in the morning. I will meet you! I feel—what is the word?—*relief* when I speak with you."

He is hustling me past a block-long open café, filled with workmen "drinking a cigarette" (smoking the waterpipe), sipping tea, eating *felafel* sandwiches. The men gape at me, and I hold back, laughing, safe with Mohammed beside me: I want to gape, too. Mohammed understands and laughs with pleasure. He puts his hand on my head and says with wonder, "Standard Stationery Store."

We pass through the streaming ancient streets of the Mohammed Ali district, and begin the long hot climb up the winding dusty road to the Citadel. The last time I was on this road I was whizzing upwards in Monir's car. Now, as I walk, my legs begin to give out and Mohammed pulls me along, reminding me of all the undernourished Moslems who have trudged up this road to reach the mosque at the top, not to mention the eighteenth-century Mamelukes who rode cheerfully up this path to their deaths, lured by the promise of a good meal from the baroquely barbaric Mohammed Ali, patron of said mosque, Cairo's first authentically Moslem tyrant.

The sky is brilliant, the mosque glitters, the old men fawn, the tourists tour, the beggars beg, the black uniformed guards glower uncertainly. Policemen in Cairo are dressed either in black or white uniforms. The "blacks" are known throughout the city for their stupidity. "Never ask directions of one in black," I am told repeatedly. "In fact, ask *nothing* of them. Walk a few more blocks until you find one in white." But it is the black ones who seem to be everywhere: the menace of a country that must put its legions of illiterate unemployed to work—in a uniform.

Mohammed and I circle the mosque, heading for the open Citadel terrace behind it. A black-jacketed guard stops us. He questions Mohammed, jerking his head in my direction. Mohammed answers him. The guard says something further. Mohammed's face pales. He withdraws a card from his wallet and offers it to the guard. The guard stares at it. I am sure he cannot read. He glowers some more. He says something further. Mohammed nods and turns away, back toward me. He does not take my arm, but rather walks stiffly at my side.

"What is it?" I ask.

"He says I must register at the Ministry of Tourism," Mohammed answers shakily.

"What are you talking about?"

"He says I cannot accompany you about the city if I do not register my name and yours."

"What did you tell him? Didn't you tell him that we are friends? That we know each other through mutual acquaintances? Surely you didn't tell him we met on the street!"

Mohammed hangs his head awkwardly on his slim fine neck, his bony jaw twitching in the shadowed sunlight. He points with his forefinger to his head.

"Cut it off," he says mournfully. "Guilty. I am one guilty stupid boy."

"Oh, God!" I say in exasperation. He looks quickly up at me.

"You are not very sympathetic to mistakes, are you?" he says ruefully.

"No, Mohammed." I grin. "I'm not. I'm a first-class American bitch."

He nods sorrowfully, one more unavoidable thrust of fate he must acknowledge. After all, it should be his lot to know a *sympathetic* exotic lady?

"The hell with it." I laugh. "Let's just forget the whole thing. When we walk away from here he'll never see us again."

"He has my name," Mohammed mourns.

"Damn! It's incredible. He would never have dared to approach you if you had looked like a doctor to him."

We sit brooding on the edge of the terrace, drawn by the magnetic view of the ancient city spread out on the earth-colored desert floor below us: a thousand years of dusty intrigue, earthbound passion, convoluted wisdom and endurance muddling around down there among the maze of streets, squares and minarets rising with mad imperiousness into the desert haze. And up here we sit: the boy from Shobra and the girl from the Bronx, a pair of brown eyes and a pair of green eyes gazing out, hopelessly separate, strangely mingled, lost somehow together in the immediate threat of uniformed authority: I as powerless as he, he as bitter as I.

Later, we race down the road we have ascended so slowly, and soon we are mingling gaily in the ancient poverty of the Mohammed Ali streets. Once these streets were a treasure of fabled Egyptian degeneracy, now they are only stone poor. . . . I want to buy some *felafel* at a greasy open window. Mohammed yanks me away. The man in the window throws back his head and laughs. I do the same. Mohammed puts his hand on the back of my head.

"How old are you?" he asks.

"Thirty-five," I say.

He stops dead in his tracks. "No! I cannot believe this. *Twenty-five.* No more. You cannot be. You look so young. You laugh like a child."

"That's it, kid. Thirty-five to the penny. You know, in America we never age. The life. It is so *good.* We grow younger and younger. And when we die they bury infants."

"Perhaps you will teach me, yes?" Mohammed says, laughing and hugging me. "How not to grow old?"

"I'm afraid not, Mohammed. Egypt is no country in which to learn that particular lesson." And we tramp on back to Groppi's where I have to fight with him to buy him a lemonade.

How good the Egyptians are to each other: a gentle ministration of the poor to the poor! The tourists complain about beggars in Egypt, but no tourist will ever put out as many piastres as any barely employed Cairene is destined to part with in the course of a single week. Everyone is petitioned, and sooner or later everyone gives. Mohammed, for instance, always responds to some ten-year-old with his hand out, some ancient derelict, some wordless woman with a baby slung inside her *milayeh*. With an existential shrug of his poor-student shoulders he distributes the piastres in his pocket. And Mohammed is not uncommon.

The other day I was in a taxi on the Corniche. It was hot and the windows were open to catch the river breeze. At a red light, a seven-year-old in ragged knee pants and a dirty white shirt appeared just below the driver's window. The driver said *la* sternly, but the kid kept on wheedling. The driver said something, and a look of cunning came over the child's face. He replied, and within seconds he and the driver were both clearly engaged in a battle of wits. Finally, the driver laughed out loud, and dug into his small store of coins. You've got to take a ride in a Cairo taxi to know what that means. A Cairo driver works fifteen hours a day, sweats like a pig, makes about twelve pounds a month, feeds six to eight people, and his cab, inevitably, is festooned with at least three sets of Moslem prayer beads: his last desperate hope of warding off the evil eye that besets him on all sides. And yet he gives: he gives cigarettes, matches, coins. He gives to the ragged children, the trembling old men, the wordless women.

And it is this way everywhere: the hurrying men in shabby brown or blue suits, the housewife out shopping, the university students, even the rushing coffee-boys: all frown briefly, all try to disengage themselves, but in the end, more often than not, all give. And they give *gently*. Gently. Almost, the giving is a caress. Almost, it is a self-comforting gesture, a helpless compassion, a shrugging admission of shared destiny.

This gentleness in the streets of Cairo! It never ceases to amaze me. I have literally never seen anger here, the kind of anger that is a commonplace in the streets of New York. Take the traffic. The traffic in Cairo could unhinge a saint—in New York it would surely create mass apoplexy—and yet no one is ever really driven to fury over it. The bridges over the Nile become maddening bottlenecks at least twice a day, usually at two in the afternoon and then again at nine in the evening. Thousands of cars crawl along, sometimes for an hour at a time. Every now and then some driver obviously says to himself: The hell with it!—and simply turns his car around in the middle of his lane, nosing toward the opposite lanes of oncoming traffic. Within seconds fifty people are following his lead, and a gigantic snail-like creature of turning Fiats has been formed, hopelessly entangling *everything* for hours to come. In New York such an action would instantly produce large-scale certifiable madness. In Cairo, you look into the faces of the drivers caught in this mess and you see: a patient weariness, an ironic smile.

Once, here in Mohammed Sidki Street, an old man on a cart being drawn by a donkey was traveling slowly dead-center down the middle of the narrow street. Behind him a Mercedes-Benz crawled along for a few minutes and then began to honk wildly. The old man continued as though he heard nothing. The Mercedes horn seemed to go berserk. The old man finally turned his head—ever so slowly—in the direction of the noise; he turned back and continued on as before; after an interminable time, and apparently for no particular reason, he edged over to the side of the street. I turned, then, to look at the driver, convinced I would see a face etched in frustration and rage, purple veins standing in the neck, eyes bulging in the head. Not a bit. The handsome heavyset man at the wheel saluted the old man on the cart, and smiled winningly as he edged his big German car past the donkey.

The doorbell rang last night at ten. Fatma Shanawany stood in the darkened hallway, her head bending into the light of my open doorway.

"Come," she said in a quick low voice. "He has just arrived. You will take tea with us."

I nodded, picked up my keys, closed the door behind me and

followed her down the hall and into her flat. Just inside the doorway is Fatma's "salon," a small square foyer with two thick maroon couches, small end tables for teacups and ash trays, a threadbare Persian carpet on the stone floor, and the soft gloom of weak neon lighting over all. On one of the couches sat a man in striped pajamas with gray woolly hair and the face of an American black who might have gone ten rounds in a boxing ring once or twice in his youth. Dr. Walid Shanawany rose to his feet, sent his newspaper drifting down to the floor, and stretched his hand out to me.

"How do you do, Miss Gornick. It is a great pleasure to meet you at last," Fatma's husband said in perfect Cambridge English, and the dour flattened features in the black face came alive with such suddenness and such influencing kindliness that there flashed through my mind: No wonder she still loves him. The tired doctor had a pair of light brown eyes that seemed to be the natural home of all the reasonableness in the world and I thought Plato was right, a reasonable man must be a good man.

Dr. Shanawany motioned me to the couch opposite him, and we both sat down while Fatma disappeared into the kitchen to prepare tea.

"Do you always work this late?" I asked.

"Yes," he said, passing his hand quickly across his eyes. "By day I am a military doctor, and by night I am a doctor of the more straightforwardly poor." He laughed, and held his hands out before him, palms up, in the classical what-is-one-to-do gesture. "And you?" he asked. "How are you getting on here in Cairo?"

His voice struck a note that to this day I cannot rightly identify but which, that night, left me suddenly with no reserves at all. To my surprise and horror I found myself saying, "I'm terribly homesick."

Walid lit a cigarette and peered thoughtfully at me through the rising smoke. "I don't believe in homesickness," he said, and while his words were faintly chastising his voice was infinitely comforting. "Loneliness, yes," he said, "but not homesickness. If you are working well you will not be homesick. Home is inside yourself. Inside your sense of doing something worthwhile. When you see yourself doing your work well, then you cannot be homesick."

"You're right," I said ruefully. "Precisely right. That is exactly what's happening to me. A month in Egypt and I feel lost. . . . lost somehow in my sense of where my work is going, or *if* it's going, or what my observations are leading to, and what am I *doing* here, anyway?"

"Oh, my dear young woman," Walid said. "You will feel that way a thousand times before you leave this Egypt. A thousand times! But be brave. Hold on. And hold *out*, as you Americans say. It will come. I assure you, it will come."

"Yes, my dear," Fatma said softly, appearing with a tea tray in her hands. "Listen to one who pined for this filthy Cairo—*pined*, I tell you—through three years in London." Her eyes laughed tenderly at her wise husband who suddenly blushed.

"Well." Walid laughed. "That was different. After all, I am not suggesting that she go happily into *exile*. Of course, if she were preparing to remain here forever it would be another matter."

"Another matter, indeed," sniffed Fatma. "He could not bear to extend even one more year in London. There are many, my dear, who could settle, and gladly, in Europe, in America, in Australia. But not Walid. Oh, no, not this Walid. He must have Egypt. With all his complaints and all his hardships here, he must have this dirty, hopeless Egypt."

"You see, I am *Nubian*," said Walid softly. "Nubians cannot *live* outside of Egypt."

The irony of Walid's patriotism bore down on me. Nubians are the Egyptian blacks. They are a race of people whose origin is mysterious (they speak a language unrelated to any other in Africa), and they have lived in the villages of Nubia (set in Upper Egypt between Aswan and the Sudanese border) for more than a thousand years. Nubians are known for their passionate attachment to their land, and for their earthy music. Walid is a third-generation Cairene. His grandfather came to Cairo seventy-five years ago, almost as an emigrant would cross the ocean, and before he died, his pride in his grandson, the doctor, was unbounded. For the Nubian in Cairo has always lived as a displaced primitive in an urban culture; he has worked, mainly, as a servant or a gateman or a crude laborer, and his opportunities for educating his children have been nonexistent. (Now, of course, a Nubian's children, like all others, may go to the university at government expense.) Egyptians are fond of telling me that there is no racism in Egypt. Nothing "a'tall" like your situation in America with the blacks. We love our Nubians. In fact, they are the gentlest, kindest, most direct, honest, uncomplicated people in the world. Rather like little children? I say, and the Egyptian looks at me, puzzled. Would you marry one of them? I say, and he draws back with a nervous laugh. My next-door neighbor is a Nubian surgeon, I say, and the Egyptian is astonished.

We drank our tea, and spoke idly for another twenty minutes or so, until Walid's face began to turn gray with fatigue. Then I stood and we all shook hands and wished one another a good night. It was a ritual—this ten o'clock tea—we would repeat many many times during the months ahead, and one I associated always with comfort, comfort reaching deep inside me, restoring my internal balance often when it seemed to tilt dangerously, comfort. . . .

Lizette Abu Shady hung a one-man show in her gallery this week and invited me to the opening on Saturday night. The paintings were the work of Fouad Anwar, a painter and professor of art who enjoys a small reputation here in Cairo; his work is in keeping with Lizette's determination to celebrate native art in her gallery.

Hassan Sabry Street was dark and quiet except where a pool of light spilled out from Lizette's open door onto the narrow pavement. Inside the tiny gallery about twenty people were gathered: stocky, middle-aged, ill-assorted men and women, all looking vaguely Middle European rather than dark Egyptian; people laughing and talking in the manner of those ill at ease in their scattered daily lives, grateful to be collected here together, if only for a few hours: they were old leftists of one sort or another.

Lizette greeted me warmly and immediately pulled me toward a tall gray-haired man in the center of a group of five or six people. "Fouad," she said gaily in a very loud voice. "Meet an American journalist. Tell her how good you are, and persuade her that Egyptian art is about to take the West by storm." To me, she whispered, "He is deaf. Speak directly into his ear." Then she rolled her eyes briefly to the ceiling as though to say: What I have to deal with here! and she disappeared into the crowd.

The gray-haired man turned his surprisingly sharp-featured face

toward me, and as he did so I saw the entire shape of his head: weird.
It moved with difficulty on his neck, as though a steel plate were
embedded in it, and its back seemed sliced flat rather like a character
out of Dick Tracy; as a result, the gray hair stood in a pouf above a
high, deeply lined forehead, and the European features seemed
squinched toward the front of the face. The eyes were weak and
blue, but piercing by virtue of the determined, somewhat glinting
stare the painter turned on the object of his immediate attention.

"Ah, madam!" Fouad Anwar said in a whispery voice. "It is
possible so beautiful a woman is also intelligent enough to be a
journalist?"

"Oh," I said dryly, "in America all *sorts* of wonders are possible."

"Ah, but *no*," the painter said, taking me by the arm and
immediately disengaging both of us from the group. "You have a very
special sort of beauty, uncommon I am sure in your own country as
well as in mine. There is a mystic intelligence in your eyes. Yes,
mystic."

Dear God! I thought.

"That is most extravagant of you, Mr. Anwar," I said with my best
theatrical frost, "most extravagant. But I would so much rather see
your paintings than talk about my beauty—mystic or otherwise."

"Ah, you are a cold, hard woman, I see," Fouad Anwar whispered.
"A cold, hard woman. But no matter. There is fire and ice in you.
You will inspire me!"

"Yes," I said, looking around uneasily. "Meanwhile, I'm going to
look at the pictures."

"I will accompany you."

"Oh, no! Please. Go back to your friends. Besides, I love to wander
around galleries alone."

He took me by the arm as though I hadn't spoken. He hadn't
heard me. Or (I looked at him suspiciously) was he using his deafness
conveniently? No matter: there was no way out. He began guiding
me from one painting to the next. The pictures were vaguely
surrealist, vaguely folkloric, generally uninteresting. Done in blues,
greens, yellows, they were dominated by the ancient Egyptian image
of a creature half-human, half-beast: the body of a man, the head of a
bird; the body of a woman, the head of a calf. Sun and fire, circles of
veiled heads, kneeling primitives, rituals of sacrifice, rituals of rebirth

floated through the blue-green-yellow wash, as though the last fifty years of world art had never happened.

Fouad Anwar spoke in a dry, whispery voice, explaining each symbolic detail in his paintings to me in a language that grew more and more abstract, more and more frustrated as his English plainly failed him. Then, suddenly, in desperation, he would declare in the middle of a sentence whose beginning I couldn't remember anyway, "You will inspire me! Yes, you *must*. I need your inspiring beauty. I need it to warm my cold and bare existence, to inflame a new image, a new *urgency* in my work! You cannot refuse me! No! You cannot! It is not for you to refuse. Your beauty is being called into the service of *art*. It no longer belongs to you."

There flashed through my mind the improbable image of some hulking New York painter making this speech. I became panic-stricken: giggly laughter began to rise uncontrollably in me.

"Let's have a drink, Mr. Anwar," I said quickly.

"What?" he said distractedly. "What you say?"

"A drink," I said loudly. "A drink. I want a drink." I sounded like an alcoholic about to have a seizure.

"You are thirsty?" Anwar said, all worried Egyptian hospitality.

I stared at him. I *was* an alcoholic. "Yes," I said eagerly. "Thirsty. I am thirsty."

We turned back into the crowd. A man—black-eyed, black-haired—came toward us.

"Fouad?" he said. "I must be going soon."

"What?" the painter said irritatedly. "Speak Arabic! After all, *you* are not an American journalist." And he turned abruptly away from us.

The man looked uncomfortable and smiled anxiously at me.

"You must forgive my brother," he said. "He is very tired now. Very tired. Sometimes when he is tired he seems rude. But he is really a good man. A very good man."

"Is he your brother?" I said, astonished. "My God, he looks pure European and you look pure Egyptian."

"There is no such thing as pure Egyptian," the handsome Egyptian said sadly. "But, come. You wish something to eat? Something to drink? Ah, but first you must know my name. I am becoming rude myself. I am Engineer Samir Anwar, brother of Fouad Anwar. And you are . . . ?"

I told him my name and we shook hands. Engineer Samir Anwar. In every respect he differed from his brother. He was stocky, solid, conventionally Egyptian handsome; his eyes were soft and vaguely anxious, his manner shy and deferential, his movements now steady, now uncertain. Every action seemed to contain an afterthought. But food and drink for the American lady he could gather swiftly and surely. He moved to a buffet table and came back quickly with a loaded plate and a glass of red wine.

"Won't you join me?" I said, taking his gifts.

"No. Thank you very much, but no. No, thank you," said Engineer Samir Anwar with a troubled expression in his soft dark eyes. "I have much stomach troubles this day. I cannot eat or drink." Of course, I thought. This guy *would* have an ulcer.

I sipped the wine and ate some stuffed grape leaves. The crowd was beginning to disperse. Lizette and Fouad Anwar moved toward us. The painter spoke rapid Arabic to his brother for a few minutes. Then he turned to me and in his hoarse, whispery voice said, "You have refused my offer to make you immortal. Nevertheless, *I* will contribute to your work. Would you like to see how the painters of Cairo live and work? I can take you tomorrow, if you wish, to an ancient and most beautiful house in Cairo where my friends and I have our studios. It is one of the great Mameluke houses still left in Cairo. The government has turned it over to the painters. It is something you will not see again in the world. Will you come?"

Well, I thought, what, after all, can happen? He's deaf and I've got fifteen years on him. I can surely outscream and outrun him. . . .

"I'd be delighted, Mr. Anwar."

"Good. I will meet you exactly at noon in Groppi's café." He shook hands all around and walked out the door with two men and a woman.

"May I see you to your home, Miss Vivian?" Samir Anwar asked politely.

"Why, thank you very much, Samir," I said. "That would be fine."

I collected my bag and a book, kissed Lizette good-bye, and walked through the door that Engineer Samir Anwar held firmly open for me.

It was early April and once again the soft, warm night took me by surprise. Spring had flooded Cairo, and the velvet night air flooded me as well. I seemed to spend a great deal of time these days on one moonlit bridge or another, leaning down over the Nile. One night last week it was like midsummer in New York. I stood in the middle of the Kasr-el-Nil Bridge looking down at the moonlit river. It was hot and lush, the air full of jasmine, the atmosphere voluptuous. I was caught for a long while by the sensuality, and then began to weary of it, sickened almost by its too-sweet quality. Suddenly, I felt the city behind me, that whole struggling effort going on in all those winding streets and dusty alleys, and in that instant I saw how the Nile and the streets pierce and suffuse each other, and how in that penetration lies the melancholy and the sweetness and the depth of Cairo, and I felt for the first time that charge of feeling that Cairenes have for their city, whose dimensions are real and full of life's ugly beauty, and for the first time, too, it struck me that my emotions were in danger, that it might hurt to leave here. I could see that I would never grow comfortably immune to the sensuality of Cairo, that it could never simply become some cloying sweetness I'd had more than enough of: the anxious harshness of the city was inextricably mixed with the sweetness, and thus the dosage was just diluted enough so that one came back for more and more until finally the addiction was completed, and one was hooked. Hooked on Cairo.

I'd been thinking about this phenomenon for some days now, and wondering obscurely about resistance. But now as I walked through the door into the April night with Engineer Samir Anwar I breathed deeply and thought: To hell with it. I'll think about it tomorrow.

"Let's walk across the bridge," I said. The man at my side nodded agreeably and off we went, down darkened Hassan Sabry Street, turning left into the main road that led onto the Twenty-sixth of July Street Bridge.

As we walked, Samir questioned me eagerly—but always politely —about myself. I told him all, all (except that I was Jewish; I wasn't in the mood for that particular complication now), and he devoured my replies like a thirst-ridden man finally at a stream of water. And then I questioned *him*.

He was thirty-four years old, this barely bulky man with a head of tight black curls, warm sexy eyes, a boyish face easily worried, easily fatuous, ready to break into childish anxiety at any moment. He had only this year returned to Cairo after ten years in the desert as a reclamation engineer.

"Ten years," he said, shaking his head in wonder as we walked across the bridge. "Ten years away from society. It is amazing to me, even now, that I could have passed those years. Almost it is as in a dream. . . . And yet, they were good years. The loneliness became something *known*, something I could deal with. And the desert has its own satisfactions. The stillness was never a prison out there. Not as the stillness inside my head is, sometimes, here in Cairo."

"I know what you mean," I said. "I lived once in the American desert. The solitude opens up. It becomes an enormous surrounding comfort. But the solitude in the city is a confusing and painful thing."

"Exactly!" He beamed. "Here, I am alone inside my head too much, too much. I go to the work. I return to my flat. I take my dinner with my brother. I take a coffee with a friend. My mother is dead. . . . I am alone, always I am alone. The city *distracts* me. And yet, I cannot return again to the desert. No. Not again." We were in the middle of the bridge. I stopped and leaned over the railing, watching the water gleam and glide through the moonlight.

"It is so difficult, the life," sighed Engineer Samir Anwar. "To find a woman with whom there is passion and . . ." (he struggled for the right words) "and a mental structure as well. I always find one or the other, never both. But you know?" He put his hand over his blue-suited heart. "I am a very sensitive man, I want both. Yes, I *cannot* settle."

I nodded sympathetically. I had often been involved in the same search myself, I said. I understood the bewilderment, the grasping at shadows, the indefinable hunger.

"Yes," Samir said eagerly. "It is a whole *mechanism*. Loneliness, contradictory needs, always being alone inside one's head." He took my arm and held it close against his side as we continued to walk. He seemed almost to throb with the excitement of the conversation.

"A woman like you," he said. "You must be the perfect woman. You are beautiful, you are strong, you are free in your thoughts . . ."

You are an easy American mark, I completed the thought silently for him.

"Not at all," I said briskly. "In love I am not strong at all. I am full of jealousy and insecurity and always act badly."

Samir smiled wistfully. "Ah, but these are the components of a woman with deep emotions. The woman with deep emotions is always weakened by love. Even by the *appearance* of love."

That sounded pretty good so I said nothing, and we walked off the bridge in silence. We turned right onto the Corniche and continued to walk along the river, going "downtown," as it were, in the direction of the Hilton and the parallel center of town.

Suddenly, Samir announced that he was engaged to be married. I looked sharply at him.

"Something strange, yes?" he said, his mouth laughing but his eyes dreadfully anxious. "That I should be engaged but still speak of such loneliness? I will explain it to you. I met this woman through my uncle. Her mother is a distant cousin of my uncle. She is twenty-six years old. She is an economist. She is intelligent, yes!" He nodded his head violently as though this statement was part of an ongoing internal argument. "But, I do not know," he went on. "I go twice a week to visit her, and I sit with her in her mother's front room. . . . We speak, yes. But we do not *really* speak." He stopped walking suddenly and turned full to face me. "Do you know? I feel I know *you* better than I know her. She is, I don't know, her mentality is bounded, it is not free like yours. She says not what she feels but what she thinks I wish to hear. That is the life here. I wish it were otherwise. I wish I could be with one like you . . . but that is the life here."

"Don't marry her," I said. "It does not need to be the life. Egypt is changing. Find a woman who is changing with it."

"I cannot," he said, shaking his head miserably. "That is the life! Egypt is changing, yes, but by the time it *changes* I will be old and dead."

"Samir, why don't you take me to visit your girl the next time you go to see her. I would love to meet her." He looked at me in panic.

"Oh, I could not do that," he said. "She would not understand. How I know you. What is our relationship."

"Why not?" I said. "I'm an American journalist and I wish to meet all sorts of Egyptians. Surely, that is legitimate enough."

"Well," he said feebly. "Perhaps. We shall see. I will suggest it the next time I visit her and I will telephone you if the prospect is bright."

At the Hilton we left the river, and walked into the center of the city. In fifteen minutes we were before the huge iron gate that fronted the house on Mohammed Sidki Street. We shook hands, and Engineer Samir Anwar swore solemnly to call me the following Wednesday night after he had made his habitual Tuesday visit to his lady economist.

Half an hour later I was drinking tea with Fatma and her twenty-year-old cousin Samiha. I described my evening to the two women, and repeated faithfully everything that Samir had told me. Fatma and her cousin exchanged significant glances. Samiha laughed and shrugged her slim shoulders.

"He is a damned liar," Fatma said calmly. "If he really wishes it, why he did not marry a colleague at the university, or a woman he meets at work, or one he has slept with? He likes to tell you that he wishes the life were free, and the woman so-and-so, but it is not true. He wishes nothing of the sort. They are all the same. They all say they wish the women were free, but if they meet one who is they spit on her, and go off to look for one with whom they sit in the front parlor."

The following Wednesday I waited in vain for Engineer Samir Anwar's call. I never saw or heard from him again.

The next day at noon, however, there was weird, deaf, unappetizing Fouad Anwar huffing into Groppi's.

"Come, come," he whispered, "the taxi is waiting. We will take our lunch at the studio with my friend Farouk. Is that agreeable to you?"

The taxi wound through dusty, noisy, noonday Cairo out to the edge of Khan Khalili. There, it was dismissed and Fouad went tearing through the narrow bazaar streets with me hustling along behind him. At last, he plunged into an alleyway and we came out on the other side of the bazaar facing the hilly streets that climbed now toward the desert edge of the city. Up, up, up we went, each street giving way to one that looked increasingly more barren than the last.

Old! I never knew what old streets could look like until that afternoon. The very stones in the street looked bleached with age, the houses began to look like caves, the people in the streets like members of a more ancient race than the one back in the center of Cairo, the donkeys starved, the food rancid, the children stunned. But Fouad Anwar didn't seem to notice anything special, and when he waved to an old man or tossed a child in the air or carried a woman's basket some distance the people didn't seem to notice their condition either.

At last, we ducked into another narrow, sandstone-colored alley, and through an open archway, and we were in a large central courtyard with flagstone on the ground, green plants all around, a network of crisscrossed iron gates everywhere, and rising up out of the courtyard, on all sides, walls of the most marvelous carved-wood arabesque screens covered with tiled decorations, and stained glass, and carved openings for windows. It was a treasure and I feasted. This house had belonged to a Mameluke merchant: one of the special breed the Turks had brought to Egypt to implement their rule. Five hundred years ago in this courtyard women of the harem peeked out from behind these screens and orders were sent down into the garden through these openings and cotton in great bales bundled off through this archway.

Fouad called out loudly: a man and a woman came running, the man wiping food-stained fingers on his pants, the woman doing the same on her apron. They beamed when they saw Fouad, and bowed shyly to me. Fouad told the man to run and bring *kabob* and salad and bread for four.

Upstairs, in a room with a fifteen-foot ceiling, a mosaic floor with a decorated well sunk in its middle, walls made of intricately carved wood, ivory and stained glass, niches of richly colored tile, wrought-iron hanging lamps, sun dancing in kaleidoscopic patterns, Fouad and I sat with the painter, Farouk, and an adoring art student named Mediha. The girl spoke no English. Farouk struggled to communicate with me. He was slight and serious, soft in his manner, yet authoritative. They played Arabic music on a phonograph, and when the caretaker arrived at a dead run with many neatly wrapped little packages of food, we ate and laughed, and they explained their work to me, and I thought: Yes, what else are these ancient rooms good for?

Farouk showed me his work. His paintings, too, were dominated by a folkloric obsession. Many of them showed peasant women in elaborate veils with earthen houses and palms against the sky behind them.

"When did you do these pictures?" I asked Farouk.

"Last year. In the village," the kindly painter said.

"What village?"

"Khalil. It is the village of my father."

"Where is it?"

"To the north. About forty-five kilometers from Cairo."

"Do you go there often?" Suddenly I was eager. "Do you think you could take me there?"

"I go once a year. But, yes. Yes, I could go again soon if you wish to see Khalil. How lovely it would be for them. They have never seen a foreigner, not once in their lives. Do you really wish to go?"

"Oh, yes! But do you think I will be able to? You know, it is illegal for a foreigner to travel anywhere in Egypt except to Cairo or Alexandria, and to Aswan on the train."

"No, no," Farouk protested, eyes closed behind thick glasses. "There is nothing military in my village. No one can object to your coming to the village."

"Listen, Farouk," I said, "what you call military and what your government calls military might not be exactly the same."

Farouk stared at me, shrugged his shoulders, raised his eloquent painter's hands palms up in the air before his chest, and generally indicated that if I didn't want to go, that was up to me, but I was acting like an overcautious American fool.

"Well," I said lamely. "Let's make preparations to go, anyway, and I'll try to find out if I am taking a risk."

We agreed that we would plan for the following Friday, and I'd be in touch with him during the week.

Fouad grew restless. He wished to show me *his* studio. Farouk looked at him, a smile of unmistakable contempt in his eyes. . . . So, it was a regular routine, after all. Well, get it over with, get it over with. I stood, and we said our good-byes, the non-English-speaking girl smiling and nodding, smiling and nodding.

Down a narrow corridor, through an open archway, onto a terrace overlooking the garden, then through another archway, another corridor, and into a room dazzlingly like the one we had just left. Imagine. This palace had been the home of a merchant.

The room was filled with paintings and drawings very much like the ones that had filled the walls of Lizette's gallery. I began to turn and wander. . . . The unhappy man with the flattened head and the dim hearing threw his arms about me, and began babbling once more about my beauty. I disengaged myself and said flatly no. He babbled again, and groped once more. I grew angry. When all was at last exhausted he threw himself down upon a narrow daybed at the end of the studio. He remained quiet. Quiet. He locked his hands behind his head, and stared up at the ceiling. I remained where I stood, motionless, silent. A brooding silence spread across the room. Fouad Anwar's eyes roved in the silence. They lit upon his paintings. I saw then how deafness could be used like a drug: cut off the struggle to hear, listen, respond, and the world retreated rapidly, leaving the deaf man in a state of undisturbed inner musings. That mystic intelligence Fouad thought he saw in my eyes now seemed to transfigure his own face as he half-lay, half-sat upon his little bed, surrounded by the vast richness of half a millennium of Arabism; the living history of his race, his country, his very thought seemed to soak through him as he lay musing, his body still, only his eyes alive and interpreting. Suddenly, he spoke:

"The Egyptian people are haunted by the mythology of their past and the influence of foreigners. . . . These two things have separated them from their lives, and created their tragedy. . . . But they are a people with great spirit and a marvelous intelligence. They felt themselves always slaves so they could not make the effort, the mechanical effort, to do the work. But because they were intelligent they dreamed a passive dream and spoke an abstract language that grew out of that dream . . . tempered by the mythology and the foreigners. . . . Now they begin to be different. The Egyptian peasant. Always before you said to him, 'Are you happy?' and he said, 'Yes.' He was a slave, he expected nothing and feared everything. Today, he takes from the government, he is an owner, and you ask him, 'Are you happy?' and he says, 'No. I want more.' His life was separated before, and his songs completed his life. Do you know, those songs have stopped . . . completely voluntarily. The poetry people came seeking in Egypt you will find no more. . . . All gone. . . ."

He stopped speaking as abruptly as he had started, and jumped suddenly to his feet. He moved quickly about his studio, gathering things: a paintbrush, a little box, a length of canvas. He would take these things with him. Abstractedly, he looked about. Ah! There was some cord, and there paper. He seemed, literally, to have forgotten that I was in the room. And why not? I thought as I watched him: rough, bemused, melancholic, resentful. What, after all, was I? A woman. After all that poetry, a *woman*?

At the very last moment, with his hand on the door, Fouad turned roughly and motioned to me to follow him. We left the room silently, traversed the garden silently, down through the oppressive hilly streets, back into the bazaar and in twenty minutes a taxi brought me to my door.

I never saw *him* again, either.

"Don't go," the *New York Times* man said from the other side of his desk in the Reuters office in the Immobilia Building. "Last week an American architecture student was picked up because he was making sketches on top of the Mohammed Ali Mosque. You've got to weigh your needs carefully before you make a move like that. You could be out of this country within twenty-four hours."

"Khalil-al-Souk?" said the man at the Arab Press Center, where I had registered as a visiting journalist. "Where the hell is that? No, no, we're not saying you definitely can't go, only we must check it first. If it is in a certain direction, no you cannot go. If another, perhaps. . . . You must understand. We are at war."

Farouk and I went to the Cairo railway station. We walked into the office marked "Police-Tourist Station" and Farouk leaned over a desk behind which sat a slim, doe-eyed, black-moustached young man in Army fatigues. They ranted and raved at each other, cutting the air with syllables that sounded like attack weapons. I was sure I was being arrested, and Farouk was fighting to keep me out long enough to make a phone call. Then he turned to me and said, "It is fine. We go on the ten-forty-five train," and the police officer was smiling, and nodding a slow steady nod at me. It turned out I could travel by train to Khalil with no problem whatsoever. It was only if I wished to *drive* that the situation would get a bit sticky.

In the exhausted-looking buffet room of the station we had bitter Turkish coffee served to us by a black Arab with a sweet smile in a dirt-on-white *gelabya* and turban, and then we moved across the large station of drab stone decorated with blue-tile arabesque to the third-class car of the waiting train. ("My God," said Fawzy Amr later when I told him of my trip. "You went *third class*?" I couldn't really explain to him that while Farouk had been living for three years off a government grant that allowed him to teach one day a week and paint the rest of the time, he had been raised in Shobra, and it would take a dozen one-man shows in Paris and New York before he would lose his third-class instincts. And what the hell. It was twenty piastres round-trip, and third-class once around was okay with me.)

On the streets of Cairo the poor are diffused, but here in third-class they were dense and concentrated; looking like a bazaar of five hundred years ago, the train was packed with women who were masses of silent wrapped black topped by large staring eyes, and men dressed in bundles of what looked like discarded Army burlap. The car was a long, yellowish, high-ceilinged cylinder, its dirt vivid and timeless, its seats broken and scarred, weary as though it had been shuttling war refugees around the country since time immemorial. Jammed together on the broken-down seats, holding bundles of all kinds, people leaned from the filthy windows, crossed and recrossed aisles, leaping over countless knees, passed waterpipes, boxes, bread and cigarettes back and forth at a great rate, in a kind of complicated bartering that seemed to be an exchange of one set of rags for another. And as usual, the great hullabaloo that accompanied every transaction in Cairo. What was most astonishing about third-class was the constant attack by hawkers of all kinds, pushing determinedly through the car, each and every one of them looking exactly like the bedraggled passengers themselves. Everyone— hawkers and hawkees—treated the assault like some great, humorous game. But I could never figure out what was happening and needed constant translation. Within minutes all the *gelabyas* around were trying to explain things to me, and, as usual, from the most unexpected-looking faces would come—English.

A terrible shriek went up suddenly from the far end of the car and I jumped nearly two feet out of my seat. A small mass of white shirt, brown face, and dead-black hair beside me came to giggling life. I looked down at a boy of twelve or thirteen and said, "What's happening?" expecting no answer. In correct English the boy said, "The man is selling twenty oranges for ten piastres." I said, "Of course. Why else would he be screaming like that?" The kid broke up. He rapped his books against his knee and laughed and laughed. Two minutes later the same shriek split the air again. I looked at the kid. "Twenty-one oranges now," he said. "Still ten piastres?" I said. "Yes," he said. I looked around. Everyone was laughing.

In a few minutes someone came through selling stale candy; after him: glass beads; after him: matches and combs; after him: a fruit drink from a huge jar with a silver spout strapped to a heaving back; after him: a boy of fifteen or sixteen with no legs, hobbling along the car floor amidst all those hawking legs, yelling God would enrich our lives if we only gave to him. Meanwhile: nobody bought, everybody laughed, the number of oranges kept going up, lungs remained in excellent condition, the philosophical mien of the passengers increased, and the dust of Cairo gave way slowly to the dust of the strangely shapeless countryside that began to replace the straggling city outskirts framed in the train windows.

We were traveling north into the Delta land where the Nile has fertilized the soil. It was a day of swirling dust and wind, one of those duststorm days that precede summer in Egypt, and the clouds of dust that came up and died down created a kind of grayish-yellowish haze over everything, giving an eerie look to the flat land and the lines of palm trees swaying hopelessly on the horizons that seemed to come and go as, one by one, villages rose up and then fell away, leaving me with a train-window impression of great networks of earthen houses in dirt lanes that moved away from government-laid concrete stations on which peasants in trailing black and bare feet and with heads supporting everything from baskets to water jars to tanks of bottled gas were massed, always moving, always looking urgent. . . . Then suddenly there would appear a mile or so of fields, fields that took my breath away: brilliant, marvelously green fields full of the richness of the earth, and a love of the Nile and its outpouring of life leaped up in me once more.

After an hour and a half of this, Farouk suddenly pulled my sleeve and said, "We get off now." We were handed down among five or six people and I was in Khalil-al-Souk, with only a forty-minute walk ahead of me. (*Souk* means market. Beside the station was the market; forty minutes down the road was the village of Khalil.)

We started. Behind us came a caravan—from the market, from the train, from the school just letting out: children, donkeys, farmers, women with babies—all of us going down the road which cut a wide path through flat fields that edged out to the horizon, along which the eternal palm trees moved, giving shelter from the wind, and various kinds of nurture. The fields looked scrubby, and the people who walked beside me poorer than those in the city. Two out of five children had some dreadful eye disease, the men were all in rags, and women swathed in black sat in the road selling motheaten oranges, with their legs stretched helplessly before them. Everything in me was sinking. There are ten thousand villages in the Valley of the Nile. More than twenty-five million Egyptians live in them. Khalil—everything that now lay before me and ahead of me—was only a fraction of the life that repeated itself endlessly to the shores of the Mediterranean, to the borders of the Sudan.

But Farouk didn't seem depressed, and I began to concentrate on the pleasure of the walk. The road was flat dirt, just the kind I like, and the air was sweet, and the oranges, when we bought them, proved to be delicious tangerines, small and sweet inside their shriveled skins.

As we walked into Khalil, my spirits lifted considerably. An irrigation canal increased the depth and thickness of green in the fields, neat whitewashed buildings (Ministry of Culture buildings, it turned out) appeared, and the houses looked, somehow, more complicated, the people more involved in the business of the day, than I had thought they would be. The village was actually very large and I could see that it was spaced out, rather than bunched together. A density of houses and streets, then suddenly open fields, then off at an unexpected angle another group of houses, and so on for quite a distance in a number of directions. It gave off a feeling of openness and relief.

And now Farouk's relatives came forth from the little crowd milling in front of us across a narrowing road emerging from one of those small groups of houses surrounded by broad fields edged with sky and palm trees. A number of men, ranging from eighteen to forty, in various states of Eastern and Western dress, were grouped around one woman. The woman was Farouk's sister, Sayeda, who had come up from the city the previous day. Sayeda was a Cairo secretary whose husband had been in Kuwait for a year. (Egyptian marriages in every station of life are punctuated by these separations. In search of work and money, husbands, and sometimes wives, are often compelled to spend from one to three years away from their families in countries like Kuwait, Saudi Arabia, and the Sudan.) She was all dressed up in a wiglet of curls hanging from the back of her head, a blue nylon sweater drawn tight across her heaving bosom, a black skirt with an uneven hemline, fat varicose-veined legs wobbly on high black heels, and about three pounds of makeup on her face. On New York's Fourteenth Street, she would have been a hustler; here, in the village, she was a lady from the city. But Sayeda's manner, unlike her appearance, was soft and vague. The men around her were much more definite. There was Mohammed, the young schoolteacher cousin, dark and muscular, dressed in a suit jacket and bare feet; Ahmed, the thirty-eight-year-old uncle whose house was our ultimate destination, and who was dressed in a flowing *gelabya* and the kindliest silence I have ever experienced; Mustafa, another cousin—twenty-five or -six—squat and vigorous, on leave from the Army; and a few others who dissolved into the crowd.

I, the foreigner, as it turned out, was not really the main attraction. Farouk had not been here in nearly a year, and every man within twenty feet leaned hand over hand to embrace him, or shake his hand, or attract his attention. Clearly, the boy who had grown up spending all his holidays in this village and had then become a painter in Cairo was a celebrity, and the object of the most amazing affection. Throughout that long day, wherever we went, men, women, children—all would greet him in one way or another. Farmers coming home dog-tired from the fields would dismount from their donkeys and reach out to embrace him, a smoky sort of tenderness in their eyes; children would yell and dance wildly around us until he put out a gentle hand to touch their heads; women smiled and bowed, moving backwards away from him, holding their veils before them. At first, I thought they were all relatives. Then I thought: Farouk does sort of remind me of *The Idiot*. Perhaps this is primitive awe of saintly spirit. But soon I saw that there actually was nothing worshipful in all this attention, nor anything intensely personal. It was simply that he was one of them. He had gone out, and he had come back, and now, in his presence, his absence was being *recognized*.

Mohammed, the schoolteacher cousin, was to be our guide. As we prepared to start out, with the entire village gathered around us, he and Farouk had a short conference. Then Farouk said to me, "Come. We go first to Mustafa's house. We take a cup of tea there." "I don't want a cup of tea," I said. Farouk looked steadily at me. I figured: I've got him. He doesn't know enough English to argue with me. His fingers pressed into my arm ever so slightly. "We go to Mustafa's house," he said. And the whole village seemed to understand what had happened, and to approve.

We all trooped off, across a narrow stream, a dusty field, past a cluster of houses, and came to a large wooden door in a shapeless earthen house. Once inside, we seemed to be in a kind of courtyard with a few doors and open doorways in its sides. We were whisked through another door and installed in a small room with a high ceiling, crumbling walls of streaked whitewash, two stiff couches, a rickety cardboard table, the famous blue-painted windows (almost all the windows in Egypt are painted blue since the 1967 War as a measure of blackout protection against Israeli attack), and a tiny transistor radio lying in some sticky mess on the table, vying for space with the flies. We all sat down: me, Farouk, Sayeda, Mustafa, Mohammed, Ahmed, and three more men I never did identify. For the next hour we sat there, hardly saying a word. That is, they hardly spoke to one another, and no one could speak to me, except to say in English, "Welcome to you"—and to keep on saying it and saying it.

Finally the tea came, and it was, as I knew it would be, delicious. It was the same strong sweet mint tea that Salah Hamamsy's worker had made for me that day on his farm, and it was being poured from a great height into slim glasses just as Salah's man had done, and I knew I was about to feel very happy drinking it. I drank many glasses of the stuff that morning in Khalil and everybody was much pleased with me.

After the tea I asked to see the house and was eagerly taken through it. I realized suddenly that I was being reminded of New Mexico, where I had once lived for a year. Like the houses of the American Southwest, this one, too, was all adobe; the rooms were built around an adobe courtyard, the ovens were open constructions in the unroofed central space, an adobe staircase led out onto another level constructed on the flat roof above. But it was all so much more primitive than New Mexico that I experienced dismay. There were animals of all kinds in the courtyard, wandering through the rooms, part of the household; the women cooking were masses of black huddled on the ground like specimens of human life older than anything to be seen in the most remote part of America or Europe; there was no system of sewage or water conduction at all; a hole in the ground behind a rude wooden door was the toilet and washing was done at a shallow earthen well in the courtyard while someone held a waterjar over you.

Upstairs, on the roof, it was suddenly beautiful. From here you could see the entire network of houses spreading out in continual single-wall connection—like a game of dominoes—against the fields and the sky, and the warmth and the light of the day went right through me, and the adobe all around seemed suddenly a heroic effort against the harshness of life and the indifference of the earth. (This is a sensation that overtakes me again and again in Egypt: everything will seem hideously primitive, and then suddenly I feel I am at the center of the original impulse toward civilization.)

That entire day I was dragged around to about ninety-two relatives.

"Look, Farouk," I said, as we were being taken through some cousin's beanfields ("Green *foul!*" Soad said back in Cairo, "you had green *foul*"), with Mohammed in his suit jacket and bare feet leading the way through this line of men working in the fields, and veiled giggling girls with lunch baskets on their heads, and donkeys who kept pushing me off the row, and me struggling with a swollen bladder. "Look, Farouk," I said, "one more cup of tea and I'm going to lose control before I get to that hole in the ground." Poor Farouk.

"Try to understand," he said patiently. "If we do not go to that man's house when he sees me here and he invites me, the next time I come, he and I, we must both *avoid* each other." So on we trooped: from uncle to cousin, from aunt to niece-in-law, from mother's uncle to sister's nephew; and as we went I began to realize that Mohammed was the comic of the village. With each visit he seemed to get looser and funnier, and I began to regret intensely my lack of Arabic. Every time he opened his mouth, a roar went up from the crowd whose numbers increased from house to house, and I figured that much of his humor consisted of puns, facial expression, irony—all delivered with perfect timing. But how could I enjoy it? Farouk's translations were long and painful, as the translation of a joke often is. And besides, I knew that Mohammed was really Buddy Hackett in disguise, and who could translate *him*?

The English teacher—an uncle—was something of an intellectual. He greeted us, standing in his beautifully kept herb garden in a spotless green-and-white striped-shirted *gelabya*, smoking a Kent. A spare, ascetic-looking man with green speckled eyes in a narrow, delicate head, he sat us all down in a circle facing the garden, ordered tea and Coca-Cola, and cut us all small spring plants to hold and to smell as though they were flowers.

When the Coca-Cola came I raised the familiar green bottle to my thirsty lips (here I *did* fear the water), and as I did so, the English teacher said to me, "You are really from New York? But New York is very good to the Jews, is it not?" I sent a stream of Coca-Cola back into the bottle, and said in some confusion, "Oh, I wouldn't say *that* exactly." "Yes," the English teacher persisted. "I have heard. New York is a castle for the Jews." Clearly, he wanted some statement of denunciation of American policy toward Israel from me. Well, I thought, I'll play *his* game. I remained silent. Totally silent. I stared out at the garden, at the desert, at the palms, at the sky; and when I returned to the English teacher he was thoughtfully lighting another Kent.

At first, the sight of the women drove me nearly crazy. I could not bear to look at them, their condition was like a knife going through me. Huddled masses of black with hands sticking out, holding veils tightly in place, sitting on the ground with babies at their breasts, or walking with the eternal water jar on their heads. They seemed worse off than anyone else—men, children, or donkeys—a total renunciation of consciousness. But that proved to be nonsense.

In an aunt's house the women suddenly gathered around me and I said to Farouk, "Ask one of them to give me her veil for a moment. I want to look more closely at it." (The veils were black, with a red bead in the center of the top part that fitted across the bridge of the nose, and a chain that extended from the bead up across the forehead, disappearing into the hair beneath the headscarf.) When my request was translated, the women stared at me, and then, as one, they threw back both their veils and their heads and roared with laughter. Then they pulled their veils down more tightly than ever, and wrapped their heads closely in their scarves. In a moment I saw that they were parodying themselves.

Suddenly, one of the older women came directly up to me, pulled me from my seat, and taking from behind her one of the long, ragged, black velveteen dresses they all wore, threw it over my head; then came the veil fitted into place by this loose chain cap that is placed on the head with the bead at its center holding the veil down; then many black scarves wound around my head and shoulders. All this was done with much laughter, but done very *gently*, not at all as though I were a freak to them, and when their work was done they dragged me off to a mirror. I guessed I would look as incongruous in their clothes as I thought they would look in mine. Not at all. Except for the color of my eyes—lighter than any Egyptian's—I looked exactly like them. In an instant the clothes had absorbed me entirely, and I had become a *fellaha*. I felt genuinely shaken by the image in the mirror and I kept thinking: It's all such a close call. All of it. I had the unmistakable feeling that every woman in that room was thinking the same thing.

At last we ate. Returning late in the afternoon to Ahmed's house, we washed elaborately at the well in the courtyard with towels and soap, took a short walk on the roof, and came down to the little sitting room where two boys rushed in shortly, holding a huge flat basket which they dropped on the table. Everyone gathered quickly around the basket which contained *fetir meshaltet*. (*Fetir* is sold in Cairo but everyone dismisses it as a bad imitation. "You haven't eaten *fetir* until you've had it in the village," the Cairenes say, and are they right.) The *fetir* is a cross between strudel and noodle pudding. It is made by rolling out circles or squares of dough, very very thin, and then throwing them back, again and again, upon themselves, thus forming many layers of the stuff and squaring it off, spreading it with butter and baking it in the earthen oven until it is crisp, hot and brown on the surface, and soft and cooked within. It is eaten with black honey or a mold cheese that is crumbled like salt on the *fetir*—and it is fantastic.

You eat *fetir* by grabbing. Everyone stood around the basket, grabbing as fast as he could. I wasn't as quick as the others—after all, they were pros—and soon they were all looking out for me. Someone would grab a particularly crusty-looking piece and push it into my greasy hands. I would protest, then give up and eat it. This went on without a stop for a full fifteen minutes. Then, without any preliminaries, when everyone's stomach was bulging and the basket was thoroughly massacred, the meal was abruptly over. (It's just like the Bronx, I thought.) We all collapsed on chairs and now Ahmed's wife, the lady who had made the *fetir*, put in her first appearance.

She was very pretty, with smooth soft skin and large black eyes, her face marked only by some creases in the skin around her eyes that were filled with dirt, thus making her look somewhat criss-crossed by black seams. She wore all the usual black clothes, but her headscarf was decorated with little colored glass beads and in her ears were huge golden hoops with a blue bead close to the earlobe. I thought she was about thirty-five. It turned out she was twenty-eight, had eight children, and was pregnant with the ninth. She sat down beside me, her veil thrown back over the top of her head, and began shyly to try to communicate with me. I liked her immensely from the start—some *vigor* in her being very attractive—but of course the attempt to speak to each other was a lost cause.

Her attention began to wander more and more toward the men. Mohammed was now making joke after joke about the meal, and its effect on all of them, and clearly, Ahmed's wife wanted to join in. Politeness toward the guest in her house kept her by my side. Slowly, I turned more and more toward the other women sitting near me, until at last, unable to resist any longer, my hostess turned her chair into the circle of men, planted her feet far apart on either side of her pregnant stomach, wiped her mouth with the end of her black scarf, pushed her veil further back on her head, and was off. She talked as fast as any of them, she delivered opinions that were listened to, she made jokes that were laughed at, she doubled over at other people's jokes, her husband blushed and was pleased with her. She was entirely in her element, entirely equal here in her own house, entirely a woman of whatever substance this life had to offer. I delighted in her, and I thought longer and harder about her than about anyone else I had met that day when, back in Cairo, oppressive memory-images of the primitive village life struggled up in my mind for days on end.

Toward six in the evening I wanted out, and I wanted out *now*. Suddenly, I felt I had to get away, that I couldn't stomach another moment of the alternating waves of familiarity and remoteness that had been attacking me all day long, as though I'd been tasting some strange food that I felt I could acquire a taste for in time, but right now was making me ill.

There was a seven o'clock train back to Cairo, as well as a nine o'clock one.

"Farouk," I said. "Let's make that seven o'clock train."

"Oh, we cannot do that," he said gently.

"Why not?" I said quietly.

"Well, that would mean leaving right now, right this minute."

"So?"

"No, no. It all takes much time. They would never understand if we all of a sudden were gone."

"Farouk," I said, my normal hysteria rising in me.

"No, no," he said softly, but with absolutely no give. I knew I was trapped. I sank back inside myself, repeating over and over: Patience is one of the rewards of age.

After six more cups of tea in six more houses, we found ourselves finally in the thick country darkness on the last adobe veranda, with a mob of people gathered around, drinking watery cocoa this time, and eating peanuts and oranges by the light of two kerosene lamps, Mohammed's jokes still coming thick and fast, with him periodically booming a self-mocking "Welcome to you!" at me, and an odd peace on everything, and in me, too—now that the struggle for self-mastery had died a twitching death. In the half-light, I saw Farouk's face and on it a strangely deep smile.

"You didn't really want to make that seven o'clock train, did you?"
I asked.

"No." He laughed. "I didn't."

"Why not? I know that you've been as bored as I many times
today, and certainly you must be as tired."

He leaned back in his chair, threw an arm across the low earthen
wall beside him, and said, "I *enjoy* it. I enjoy it all, even the
boredom, even being tired. I want a *full* day, the most full it can be. I
want to have it all while I am here."

Of course, I thought. He really feels this place, feels it deeply. He's
feeling what I used to feel in New Mexico when New Yorkers would
come to visit, and the complicated pleasures and realities of the
repetitious life escaped them, while those same pleasures and
realities had become alive and focused for me. How absurd of me not
to have seen what he must be seeing.

How absurd, indeed.

On Saturday night Fatma's youngest sister became engaged to the
"white" Egyptian. Fatma left early to help with the preparations,
and her brother came at seven o'clock to escort me to the family flat
in a square just on the other side of the Bab-el-Louk market. The
smallish, somber rooms were decorated with wreaths of flowers and
red satin ribbons; the front room had been cleared, and was entirely
bordered with small, hardbacked chairs on which sat a row of silent
relatives. At the far end of the room sat Fatma with her three-year-
old son on her lap, her blue satin dress climbing up over her heavy
knees, her beautiful face expressionless; beside her sat Walid, stiff in
a high white collar and a brown wool suit. The engaged couple were
nowhere in sight, nor were Fatma's mother or younger brothers or
sisters. The people on the chairs were heavy, dark uncles, their lips
pursed in narrow lines of disapproval. Beside one of the men a very
old black man in a white turban and a *gelabya* sat nodding: the
grandfather. The women were the uncles' wives: middle-aged, in
shapeless black or red dresses, dark and also silent; but their silence
vacant, not disapproving.

"What's going on?" I said to Fatma as I dropped into the empty seat beside her. "It's more like a funeral than an engagement party."

Fatma nodded grimly. "I have just had a most severe argument with my uncle," she said. "They disapprove of this night. Why, they say to me, she cannot wait until your brother completes his studies and returns from Moscow? He comes in the summer. Why is there all this rush? What is the meaning of it?"

"Why should she have waited until your brother returns? What is the significance of that?"

"My father is dead. My oldest brother is the sole male authority in this household. Before he left for Russia he was most opposed to Raga's relationship with Samir. He said he would never extend his approval, and he disowned her as his sister. Raga grew ill. She would not eat, she could not sleep, she cried the entire day and night long. My brother grew distressed and relented, but would not discuss the matter further. He went to Moscow and Raga soon pressed my mother to write to my brother and receive his permission to become engaged before he arrived in Cairo. My brother was much worried by his studies, and also he knew that he would be relieved of the responsibility should she become engaged while he was not here. So he sent his permission. Now my uncles realize that something strange has occurred, and they disapprove. . . . Oh, really! I cannot bear all this pressure. My sister has caused much troubles for all of us." Fatma turned her back to her husband, and lowered her voice. "Walid was furious. He forbade me to see Raga. He said to me, 'Your brother is in Russia, and therefore *I* should have been consulted in this matter.' Later, Raga realized she had made an error, and she invited Walid to take part in the negotiations with Samir's family. But Walid would not relent. No, never, my dear. His pride is too stubborn, too stubborn. He said to me, 'Who is there for me to deal with? Children! Women and children! With these I do not deal.' "

Fatma fell silent, shifting the uncomfortable little Mohammed on her lap. She stared snakelike at her uncles, and they stared back. Suddenly, she whispered to me, "I would not have done as she has done. Let somebody else be the first! I would be the second but not the first. No, no. I do not approve of what she has done."

I stared at her. Beneath the intelligence, and the articulate defiance, there lurked a conservative heart. Why, Fatma really *was* proud of her husband's restrictive love!

And now, Raga whirled into the room with her white Egyptian in tow. The girl glowed with black snapping eyes and a chin held very high; her young body encased in a tight pink dress, her black hair straightened and lacquered after three hours in the neighborhood beauty parlor, her fingernails blood-red, her big feet in white satin pumps, she came forward into the hostile room, pulling her prize with her: a thin young man with soft, sad doe-eyes, confused, and looking as though he wished only that all this trouble would magically disappear, and how, after all, had he found himself in this position? Oh, life was really too hard, too very hard!

In a little while the doorbell began to ring, and ring, and ring. Friends of both Samir and Raga crowded into the room, and the emotional atmosphere grew diffused. Trays of fruit drinks circulated, and food appeared on the table in the salon. Then the musicians arrived; five young men with *ouds* and guitars and reed instruments and tambourines, and the magic energy of Nubian music (very reminiscent of West Indian calypso music) overtook the room. The sound of Nubian music is high, delicate, distinct, fraught with a rhythmic repetition that whirls and dips and deepens and is entirely mesmerizing. Joy, pure sensate joy, is at its heart, a drunken innocence, an irresistible pleasure: one is *alive!* What, on this dusty hot earth, could be better?

For hours and hours the musicians played; people swayed toward the music, fingers clicking, legs jumping, eyes shining, mouths singing. Everyone ate and drank and laughed, and even the grim uncles seemed to unbend. Raga had gotten away with it: seducing her relatives with their own earthy tradition, she had managed to become engaged to her white Egyptian. Things would never be quite the same again in *this* Nubian family.

Mohammed and I continue to meet: three meetings, four, five . . . always the same odd quiet, closeness, humor, wordless acceptance between us. We wander, we take the trams and buses, we eat in bazaar streets—*koshry, felafel, halvah*°—stuff and places I experi-

---

° *Koshry* is a peasant dish, made of rice, bits of pasta and fried onions, found in poorer quarters all over Cairo. *Halvah* is a famous Middle Eastern sweet made of crushed sesame.

ence with no one else. He drags me tenderly through it all, and I lean, lean, lean into this sensitive, intelligent, moody boy who gives me such strange peace and creates in me an atmosphere of desire rather than desire itself.

Mohammed has been begging me for two weeks now to come home to Shobra with him, and today, a Thursday afternoon, is finally the day. We meet at Groppi's at noon, and rush for the bus in Midan Bab-el-Louk. It is only with Mohammed that I would brave the buses of Cairo. Wheezing, lurching, grinding hunks of scrap-iron on wheels, the castoffs of half a dozen nations ("Here we have the Western bloc," Mohammed says, pointing to a red-and-white bus, "and here we have the *Eastern* bloc," pointing to a blue-and-white bus), the buses are at all times jammed with a thousand sweating bodies, leaping on and off while the bus is still in motion, angling desperately for a bit of breathing space, pressing together with a great hue and cry. The mere *thought* of making my way alone on one of these jobs. . . . But with Mohammed pushing me on, pulling me off and encircling me in between, I am able to go inert and give myself up to the lurching motion, the shrieking passengers, the oddly pleasurable sensation of being batted around inside this human din where no alertness is required of me, no straining watchfulness. Ah, it is so good, now and then, to become a child again!

The bus lunges away from the square, and goes batting out past Midan el Tahrir, past Boulac, past one neighborhood after another, headed toward the outer limits of the city; the streets all come together, the dusty broken pavements, the streaming crowds, the broken-down shops, the children and old men begging, the mosques, the tenements, the food carts: street after street after street of Cairo poor, until suddenly we are in Shobra, and unbelievably, it is even worse than what we have been traveling through. Mohammed, of course, has been noticing nothing: what, after all, is there for *him* to notice? Through the din, the crowds, the dirt—looking more than ever like Gandhi's grandson, the inside of his head filled with his own pressing thoughts—Mohammed quietly shouts in English at me.

"The people. They do not give my mi-i-nd rest. They make me crazy. I will not bear it."

"What do you mean?"

"All of the people here in Egypt, they work but they do not work.

I, too, work, but when I work I must work *well*. I cannot do as the rest do. So in the library they hate me." There is a funny little crooked smile Mohammed always smiles when he is being ironic, and he smiles it now. "They will always hate me," he yells confidentially. "Wherever I go. I will work, and they will not, and they will hate me. And in time I will change. Not they will change. *I* will change. And for this I am afraid. I am afraid before my God." Oh, the self-importance of a twenty-three-year-old soul! Yet, he suffers, and he reminds me, he reminds me. I can feel again with Mohammed all those dark, tossed days in the wilderness of the Bronx when I wandered the streets, locked inside my head with a nameless misery that seemed to stretch forty years into the distance. And no one to *understand*! And what did it all *mean*?

Shobra. Magdi once said, "I had a dear friend, a *most* dear friend. He lived in Shobra. He never *left* Shobra. Finally, I said to him, 'My dear friend, if I must come once more to Shobra, *once* more, we will no longer be friends.' "

There are literally a million people in the streets of Shobra. All the insanity of Cairo is concentrated here in this density of falling-down houses, broken-up shops, distintegrating sidewalks. People, donkeys, cars, bicycles, piled, pell-mell, one on top of another, the streets an endless rising of dust and racket. The head spins and never stops spinning.

Mohammed pulls me along Shobra Avenue, yanking me out of the way of children, carts, beggars: boys racing with coffee, trays of sweets, pots of food, freshly ironed trousers, amidst automobile parts, waterpipes, fruit stands. We turn a corner swiftly, and I nearly break my ankle in a pothole the size of a well. Mohammed laughs and shakes his head: *amateur*! Then we are entering a tall gray building covered with dust and broken stone. In the dark interior we climb four flights of curving stairs, Mohammed turns a key in a lock and we are home.

The flat is a windowless dining-living room, two small bedrooms off to the left (rectangles of light), and a tiny foyer off to the right leading to a dimly lit scullery-kitchen and a dank little bathroom. In these rooms live Mohammed, his mother, and three brothers, one older, two younger; the father has been dead four years.

The house instantly encloses me: it is my grandmother's house, my aunt's house, my mother's house, all rolled into one. The rooms are scrupulously clean, filled with mismatched objects, conflicting patterns, flowered linoleums, antimacassars, green walls, pink walls, blue walls. The theme of decoration here, instantly recognizable to me, is: Everything should be clean and dry, warm in winter, cool in summer. Beyond that . . . what? Is there something *else*? The furniture in the dining room positively looms: huge, clumsy pieces of dark, polished wood—a high, thick sideboard on clawed legs, an enormous dining-room table, eight high-backed chairs—that leave only narrow spaces for walking and moving about the room; clearly, it is furniture that is *proud* to exist in this broken-down, crowded, ghetto street: large is good and more is better.

Mohammed's mother comes rushing out of the kitchen, and collides abruptly with the sideboard. Mohammed stares at her, raising a remonstrating hand, palm up, as much as to say: How many times have I told you to watch that? The small woman wrapped in a flowered housedress, a grimy apron, a dripping spatula, greasy black hair, and a grin in her black eyes, blushes. I move forward to greet her, twisting my body halfway around in order to pass between the sideboard and the table. At last we stand together in the entrance to the foyer. She lifts her arms to my shoulders and greets me with an embarrassed kiss on each cheek and a much repeated "*Salaam waleikum*," alternated with "*Marhaban, marhaban.*" I kiss her on each cheek, and wish peace on her, too.

From now until eight o'clock this evening I will spend with Mohammed, his mother, his older brother Wafik, his younger brother Kamel, and his baby brother, Galal. We will move—in varying combinations—from the kitchen to the dining-room table; from the table to a small group of easy chairs at the end of the room; from the chairs out onto the bedroom balconies; from the balconies back to the dining room; from the dining room out to the kitchen; then, back to the dining room; until finally, tottering on legs weak with the hours-long enclosure, Mohammed and I go out onto Shobra Avenue, now dark and lit only with the madness of five thousand headlights moving at each other simultaneously.

During all of these hours Mohammed's mother never stops cooking. When I arrive she is preparing lunch; later, she will spend two more hours in the scullery preparing a special sweet in my honor; before I leave she will prepare a tea; the day is structured by the ritual preparation and consumption of the food.

We wait for Mohammed's brothers to make their Thursday afternoon appearance, and the twenty-seven-year-old Wafik coming from his engineering job at the steel works in distant Helwan, the sixteen-year-old Kamel coming on the tram from his school in Heliopolis. Meanwhile, the mother keeps sweating in the kitchen, Mohammed sets the table with blue plastic soup plates, wide and shallow, and slowly the lunch begins to take shape on the huge dining-room table. Mohammed has questioned me carefully about the Egyptian foods I have already tasted, and the dishes that now appear on the table are all strange to me. There are cold pickled vegetables, flat strips of breaded lamb, crumbled meat beneath a flaky crust, eggplant in tomato-meat sauce, homemade *felafel*, and at the last minute Galal will come rushing through the street door with a bubbling casserole of cucumbers in a white sauce. (Mohammed explains that there is no oven in the house, and his mother sends casseroles down to the baker to be cooked in his oven, the timing carefully calculated in advance.)

Wafik comes in first: a warm, dark Egyptian, who says little and giggles with painful shyness; he looks nothing like Mohammed and I remember that he is the son of the mother's first husband. He immediately closets himself in one of the bedrooms and emerges shortly in a freshly ironed shirt and new pants. Within twenty minutes, Kamel has also appeared. Ah, *here* is Mohammed's brother. Small, quick, brown, his features are a sharper, thinner, longer version of Mohammed's. When he darts through the door Mohammed reaches out a long tender arm to hook his head and draw him close for a kiss. The adolescent Kamel laughs awkwardly and tries to avert his head, as Mohammed croons at me, "Kamel. Good brother. Good brother."

Galal comes rushing through the door with a stack of hot flat bread inside white butcher paper, and Mohammed announces, eyes rolling to the ceiling, "At last. We may now sit down to the daily feast. From which we must arise at least two kilos heavier than we sat down. Otherwise my mother must consider herself deficient in her duties." Galal laughs, nodding his own version of Mohammed's head, his hand on his skinny little stomach. He is thirteen years old but he looks eight. Quick, small, all clever eyes, he runs all day long for them. (As Mohammed says: "*I* ran. Then *Kamel* ran. Now Galal runs.") But Galal also *disappears* all day long, and very funny dialogues take place, while he's gone, about where he went to get whatever he's been sent for: how much easier it would be to weave the cloth for new trousers rather than wait for Galal to return with the laundered ones he's gone for, or buy a cow and milk it rather than wait for a carton from the grocery.

When we sit down at the table it is as Mohammed has said it would be: for twenty full minutes everyone shovels in the food, arms reaching across the table for bread, salad, meat, vegetables, everything piled together on the single soup plate, all tastes and textures mingling into one, a total dismissal of the many separate labors represented on the heaped-high table. But it's fun: gay, alive, the fun of poor people being reassured by the festival of food. It's every family dinner I ever took part in, and as I sit beside Mohammed, leaning always into him while he attentively angles for the best bits of food for me, I know him for the blood relative he really is; a secure, rushing weakness overcomes me, anxiety is released, my breath is drawn deeply, I have recovered an original, long-lost safety; it is as though the blood in Mohammed's wrist and forearm would flow into my own veins were he to lay his flesh against mine. I am home. I am back in the womb of my original idiom. I am where I deeply come from. And somewhere inside myself a whip of confusion is flicking at my brain: Why? Why do I feel an extraordinary sameness here as in the home in which I grew up? These people are not peasant immigrants, they are not Jews fleeing with all their possessions on their backs, they are not. . . . And, suddenly, I understand. *These Egyptians are immigrants in their own country.* The true meaning of immigrant is not that one has crossed an ocean and settled in a country not his own: it is, rather, to be dispossessed by the culture, even if one is born into it. Mohammed's native Moslem mother is surely as much of an immigrant, struggling to raise her dispossessed sons here in Shobra, as my Russian-born Jewish grandmother was, making the same struggle on New York's Lower East Side.

It is now four in the afternoon. The table has been cleared, the scullery wiped clean, the leftovers tucked out of sight (where? I wonder idly; there's no refrigerator). We are all gathered on small, hard easy chairs near the end of the dining-room table. Mohammed smokes a cigarette, Wafik reads the paper, Kamel leans over his mother while she sews a button on his school jacket, and Galal has disappeared. The radio is tuned to the BBC and Mohammed and I listen while the dispassionate British commentator details the hopeless machinations of the United States and Soviet governments to bring "peace" to the Middle East. In the middle of the newscast Mohammed reaches over and violently flicks the dial. American rock-and-roll floods the room; his mother raises her head in sudden alarm but soon smiles as she sees the look of pure pleasure on her second son's face. Wafik shakes his head slowly, and says to me, "I prefer Bach." These are the first words the painfully shy engineer has spoken to me all afternoon.

An hour passes. Mohammed speaks to his mother in Arabic. She rises from her seat, wipes her hands on her grimy apron and disappears around the table into the kitchen. As she goes each of the boys says something to her, and manages to touch some part of her body: an arm, a hand, the back of her neck. She, in turn, does the same: laughing, she cuffs one on the head, another gets pinched, a third is caressed. She is an ignorant old woman, full of love and humor for her four sons; the boys clearly adore her.

"She is going to prepare a special treat for you," Gandhi's grandson says to me.

"Oh, no!" I protest. "Enough with the *cooking*. Don't make her work anymore today."

"It is not *work*," Mohammed says patiently. "It is her pleasure."

He takes me by the hand and leads me through one of the bedrooms out onto the balcony for some air. The room we pass through is a tiny rectangle, crammed with cots, cheap dressers and a single bedside lamp. The linen is threadbare and spotless, the blankets thin and warm-clean, the little lamp shines. The balcony looks out over the "gardens" of Shobra: a dismaying heap of rotting junk and garbage, fallen among broken walls and caved-in earth; but the sun shines brilliantly in the blue Cairo sky, causing a stunning silence to fall on the depression down below.

In half an hour we return, blinking, to the darkened dining room, and Mohammed says to his brothers, "Let us help our mother." We all trot into the scullery-kitchen where the mother, working in the dim light of a single naked bulb, is pounding a large round mound of dough on the floured marble slab between the sink and the four-burner stove. On the stove: a large black pot half-filled with simmering oil, and a small deep saucepan filled with a colorless liquid that erupts periodically into little boiling bubbles. Mohammed explains that the dough will be shaped into little balls that will be thrown into the oil where they will puff up and turn golden brown; then each ball will be dipped in the colorless substance which is liquid sugar; then they will be drained; and then they will be *eaten*. And, he assures me, the kingdom of heaven will be attained with each mouthful.

The boys gather around their mother as she works quickly, expertly, and all lend a hand: Mohammed, next to her at the stove, turning the small balls of flowering dough in the deep oil—*intently*; Kamel, behind her, anxiously overseeing the liquid-sugar process; Wafik, in the doorway, simply adding his shy, benign presence. The mother, every now and then, almost absent-mindedly, pulls down the head of one of her sons for a quick, deep embrace, never missing a beat of her practiced expertise as she does so.

Suddenly, here in this scullery in Shobra, one can see the whole Egyptian mother-son life for what it bare-bones really is. Here, in the ghetto, the quality that infuses the power of this national family love becomes crystal clear: loving each other is all we've got. The son is the treasure; the mother, the only giver of value in a culture that does not reinforce. And does she ever *give* that value. She does not nag, she does not reprove, she does not demand. She guards, she serves, she consoles. "You are the sun in the heavens," she whispers fiercely, day in, year out, "the center of gravity, the star toward which all the universe is tending. And when you marry, and become the head of a *new* universe, you must take for your wife one who was trained to be your servant, even as I—unhappily, oh my son!—was trained to serve your father. And that, my Egyptian son, is your inheritance. That is your center, your nation, your government; that is where your intelligence will blossom, your will be asserted, your wisdom dispensed. That is your all, your suffrage, your manhood. From the lowliest kitchen in Shobra I can send you out to claim your one undisputed right in this disinherited dust that is our Egypt."

The boys puff with pride as each ball of dough becomes a perfect golden crisp, sleek inside its sugar coating, heaped in a pyramid on a thick white plate, left to cool while fragrant mint tea is prepared to accompany the heavenly consumption. We retreat to the dining room to await the golden moment, and in a very little while the perspiring mother appears with a tray of glasses full of tea, and the sweetness all have had a hand in producing.

"Magnificent!" pronounces Mohammed.

"*Aiwa!*" echoes Kamel.

"M-m-m," nods Wafik.

Galal bursts mysteriously through the door at precisely the right moment, his eyes glittering as he heads for the lovely tray.

The mother beams, bobbing her head eagerly at me, her hands urging me to try one more, just one more, of the delicious offering with which she binds her sons to her even as she nourishes them.

It is now six o'clock. The boys are preparing to go out for the evening. Galal is sent downstairs to have a pair of pants pressed for Wafik. Kamel scorns to spend any of his precious piastres in this manner; he will iron his own pants. Rapidly, he assembles all he needs to accomplish his task. He spreads a thickness of blanket on the dining-room table, warms the iron at an outlet in the nearest wall, and brings a cup of water from the kitchen. The electricity is weak and Kamel must wait quite a while until the iron is hot enough to strike.

Meanwhile, Wafik has begun to pace the floor. It is already twenty minutes since Galal disappeared with his pants; the child should have been back ten minutes ago. Where, Allah help us, has he gone to now? The tired mother snuggles down in her chair and laughs softly at her impatient eldest son. Mohammed sits talking and joking with me. Every five minutes he breaks through his own conversation to raise his eyes to the ceiling and to yell, moan, croon, implore, "Gal-aa-al!" The mother closes her eyes and giggles blissfully at her clever son. Kamel also laughs. Only Wafik does not laugh.

Now the iron is hot enough, and Kamel goes quickly to work. He brings his dark blue pants from his bedroom, folded neatly at the crease, and spreads the trousers on the blanket. He touches the iron with a wet forefinger, takes a sip of water and, making the most

amazing noise, transforms his mouth into a spray-bottle. No sooner
does the spray hit the pants than Kamel is busily ironing away. Only
a few strokes of the iron, and Kamel is spraying again. Whenever he
sprays, the same wild noise fills the room, making me jump violently.
Mohammed claps his hands gleefully each time I respond to Kamel's
spray-noise, and the mother gurgles with laughter. Shy Wafik only
smiles but his dark eyes grow bright with ill-concealed laughter.

The mother leans urgently toward Mohammed, speaking rapidly in
Arabic. He shakes his head at whatever it is she is saying; she
becomes annoyed, prods him with her finger and bobs her head
repeatedly in my direction. At last, Mohammed sighs and says to me,
"She wishes you to bring her some American vitamin B."

"What do you mean?" I ask, puzzled. "Can't you get vitamin B in
Egypt?"

"Yes, of course, we have it here in Egypt. But it comes from
France, and she does not think it is as good as the American. She is
ignorant, very ignorant, but nothing I say can persuade her."

"Why does she need vitamin B?"

"She is diabetic," says Mohammed, making the motion of a
plunging hypodermic needle with the fingers of one hand. The
mother has been watching us both carefully, her eyes having become
two little brown beads. Now, at the sign of the hypodermic needle,
she nods her head eagerly at me, and pulls her dress up to reveal a
pair of thighs hideously disfigured by innumerable puncture marks.

"Not only does she receive the needle every day," says Mohammed, "but also she must have much vitamin B. She is convinced that
the American vitamin B would help her more than our Egyptian
vitamin B does." He shrugs his shoulders helplessly.

"Well, I can't believe it can be any different, but of course I'll try
to get it for her. It will be some time, though, before I can get it."

"Yes, yes," sighs Mohammed. "I understand. Let us see if *she* will
understand. I am sure she thinks every American travels with a
two-year supply of vitamin B."

He explains what I have said to the mother. She stares in blank
suspicion at him for a moment; clearly, she does not believe what he
has told her; either he is lying, or I am lying, or we are both lying;
either he has not translated her request properly, or I have chosen

not to understand. Then she pulls herself together and turns, smiling, toward me. After all, I am her guest. She must accept whatever I choose to give.

A quarter past seven. I am stiff with food exhaustion, sitting exhaustion, listening exhaustion. Mohammed, I say, I want to go soon. That message, translated, seems to electrocute everyone; even Kamel stops in mid-spray.

"*La, la, la,*" says the mother, eyes closed, finger waving like a metronome.

"Another cup of tea, at least," Mohammed says softly.

"Yes-s-s, pliss-s-s," says Wafik in some distress.

"Okay, okay. One more cup of tea. And then I really must go," I say firmly, thinking: Lots of luck.

The tea is being prepared. Mohammed is smoking another cigarette, and Wafik is now pushing his fingers through his hair as he paces the narrow strip of floor. Just as Mohammed is about to raise his voice in another "Gal-aa-al" we hear Galal racing up the stairs, chanting "Gal-aa-al." He bursts in, trying unconvincingly to look as though he has experienced untold troubles in order to accomplish his errand, but Wafik only cuffs him on the head and snatches the black trousers from his childish arm. Galal laughs and escapes to the kitchen.

A fresh tea tray is brought in: full glasses and a plateful of bread triangles filled with white cheese and cucumber slices. "No," I say grimly. "I cannot eat any more." Absolutely no attention is paid; obviously I am being polite. A glass is placed in one hand, a cheese and bread triangle in the other. Everyone waits while I raise the glass to my lips and place the sandwich between my teeth. No one else is forced to eat or drink, but I, the guest, *must.*

At eight o'clock I am free to start making my actual good-byes. After twenty minutes of hugging, kissing, handshaking, and eighty-two *ma'salaams,* Mohammed is at last closing the door behind us, and I am descending the pitch-black stairs, my hand clutched tightly in his, into the nighttime chaos of Shobra Avenue.

The shops are all darkened or only very dimly lit; street lights are almost nonexistent; even traffic lights seem to be nowhere in sight. Nevertheless, thousands of people are milling about on the streets, shrieking, running, conducting business as though it were broad daylight. In the road hundreds of moving headlights indicate the jerking stream of traffic. We must cross the wide avenue, divided by concrete bus-stop islands; on the other side we will hail a taxi going in the right direction for me.

Mohammed has played the game of dodging the cars with me before, so now he drags me along behind him as usual when he suddenly leaves the sidewalk, plunging into the stream of traffic. But this time I'm out of my league: the pace is for professionals only. I become confused, my head is whirling, headlights begin to converge, I dart too quickly after Mohammed, or I hang back a few seconds too long. The other side of the avenue seems miles away. A dull panic begins to settle in my chest: I'll never make it. And then—incredibly —it happens. I'm hit by a car. My right leg is hit *hard*, and I'm thrown with thudding pain off-balance. I go careening wildly into Mohammed's back, causing both of us to double over, nearly hitting the ground together. But Mohammed rights himself before he touches bottom, turning with amazing agility in nearly the same instant, dragging me, his hands clamped on my arms just above the elbows, up with him, through the now-screeching traffic to the sidewalk that was only a few feet beyond our reach.

Oh my Mohammed. Something happens now that makes you mine forever.

In our relationship I am in every way the stronger of the two; Mohammed defers to me always, in shyness, ready to be chastised by the superiority of my years, my sex, my foreignness. At this moment, however, he has forgotten that I am the stronger. He knows only that I am in danger, and his feelings take control. He yanks me onto the sidewalk, his hands still on my arms, pulling me up and toward him, supporting my limp body. His eyes stare into mine, the horror in his own held in check: saving time. He probes my face as though to quickly search out there the true extent of the damage done.

"Are you all right?" he demands roughly.

I nod, no breath in my body to speak with.

"Examine your leg," he orders.

I can't. I start to shake when he releases his hold on me.

He throws an arm about my waist and kneels before me. We both look at my leg. An ugly bruise, swollen and discolored, covers the entire calf; but no more than that; the skin is not broken, there is no blood.

Mohammed stands, his hands once more in place on my arms. He stares again, wordlessly, into my eyes, and I see now the depth and strength of his feeling for me. I see, in this moment, that he loves me. I see that I might grow old, ugly, crippled before his very eyes and he would hold on tenaciously to the precious substance that is me, protect it with everything in him, every bit of anguished strength that is in him to act with. I see that it would be this way with anyone he treasured: mother, brothers, children, cousins, neighbors. I see the emotional gold of the man that is Mohammed.

Hours later, lying in bed in Mohammed Sidki Street, my leg throbbing unmercifully, that expression on Mohammed's face floats in the darkness above my upturned face; it will be there again tomorrow, and the day after that, and weeks later at unexpected moments, and years later, like a flash from another life, another incarnation, another time in an altogether other country.

My bedroom balcony faces onto the narrow, dirty Bab-el-Louk alley that is Mohammed Sidki Street. Four flights down, in the crowded road, donkeys bray, cars honk, people run back and forth in their *gelabyas* and turbans; to the left of the building in which I live is a cigarette kiosk; the old man in the kiosk turns away from his customers five times a day to kneel and face the East; to the right of the building is a hole-in-the-wall laundry service run by a Copt who never stops working, except for half a day on Sunday. Every morning a painted glass cart is drawn into the street by a man loudly selling *fetir*. Skinny, ragged, dark, laughing children dash about all day long, big ones pulling little ones, brothers protecting sisters, neighbors watching out for neighbors. The Koran blares down all day and all night on everything, as well as Om Kalthoum, whose voice floats down, a dream of national agony. Upstairs, at eye level, I am surrounded by the balconies of other flats. Sometimes I feel as though I could simply stretch out my hand and touch the balcony across the street where two laughing teen-aged girls perpetually lean over the railing, chattering away and watching every flat in my building like a pair of hawks. Certainly, I *can* touch Fatma Shanawany's bedroom balcony: it is no more than three feet from mine. And on the days when Fatma and I are both hanging out our wash we do drape our arms sometimes across each other's railings for an intimate across-the-laundry chat.

We all, on the street, oversee one another's washing. Each balcony is affixed with a network of clothesline within a wooden frame that extends off the railing into the air; this frame is inevitably loaded with the daily or weekly washing of the family within. Everyone who hangs off the balconies observes the pajamas of Mr. Shanawany, the sheets of Mrs. Lutfallah, the underwear of Miss Soliman, those little dresses of the American lady.

I use this balcony for sunbathing as though it were the balcony of a villa on the Mediterranean—and, like my neighbors, I wash my clothes and hang them out here in the burning sun that already, even now in mid-April, dries everything within minutes. And the pleasure I take from these sun-dried clothes is more than I can describe. When I bend over the line and remove the clothes, clean and dry and smelling so gorgeous, I feel some satisfaction of existence, some essence of simple, animal well-being that strikes so deep a note in me that it is almost as though I were not performing these actions for the first time; I experience a distinct sense of *déjà-vu*. Is it that in some other life I was an Egyptian housewife? I never *can* really identify the origin of the sensation that overtakes me in these moments when I stand here on this brilliantly sunny little balcony, my nose buried in an armful of clean washing as though it were the most fragrant bouquet in the world, an intensity of warmth spreading through my chest, a smile uncontrollably forming on my mouth. . . . So familiar, so familiar. . . . What *is* it? Why do I have this feeling? What is its origin? Nearly, the answer is within my grasp; I can see it, taste it, smell it; then, with the painful jarring of a half-remembered bit of melody, it is snatched once more beyond my reach.

This morning Fatma and I were both hanging out our wash. Clothespins between her teeth, her heavy brown arms bare (sleeveless dresses are permitted in the house), her black hair piled high on her head, Fatma worked quickly and deftly, the mountain of wash in her basket soon tossing lightly in the early morning breeze. I, with less experience and less wash to handle, worked slowly, enjoying the feel of each clothespin sinking into cloth, securing towels, underwear, blouses, pajamas.

"Tell me," said Fatma. "Do you wish to be in love?"

"Yes-s-s," I said slowly. "I suppose so." It was hard for me to concentrate on love at that moment.

"But," persisted Fatma, whose favorite subject is love, "do you wish love *with* marriage, or without?"

"I think without," I said.

"Yes, that is true." Fatma nodded solemnly. "Love without marriage. Much better."

"Tell me, Fatma," I said, "do you really believe these things you say to me?"

"No," Fatma said, sinking a pin into a pair of Walid's socks.

"Oh, Fatma!" I laughed. "You remind me of my mother."

And, suddenly, there it was. My mother. "You remind me of my mother." My own words were the source of the revelation.

My pleasure on the balcony, the sun-dried clothes, the sense of *déjà-vu*—they are all an evocation of childhood, my very own childhood. And this street—beyond question—is the street of my childhood: the backyard clotheslines, the children scrambling madly all day long in the alleys, the shouting, the corner grocery with its tubs of butter and blocks of cheese and bottles of milk, the candy store where I was sent to bring home five Lucky Strikes for my father in the evening; all this was the Bronx during the Second World War; all this is Mohammed Sidki Street today.

But more than anything it was the wash: my mother and the wash. How many times during those years before washing machines had I hung over the windowsill watching my mother's strong brown arms in the sunlight pushing freshly pinned wash out along the clothesline that stretched from our kitchen window to a thick wooden pole sunk into the concrete of the alley in back of our apartment house? How many times had I felt that curious, inexplicable little pleasure blossoming in me as I watched my mother re-create each week the wonder of clean white sheets unfurling in the sunny wind? How could I ever calculate the depth of peace and security this simple ritual of weekly cleansing had accumulated in me—a peace and security that the subsequent years had shattered beyond all redemption?

My mother hung her wash in the Bronx as her mother thirty years before her had hung her wash on the Lower East Side. Only I, the assimilated daughter, the first middle-class American, I did not hang my wash. . . . But here in Egypt, on this balcony in downtown Cairo, I have become the woman I would have been had I been my mother. Here, standing in sunlight directly on the other side of my mother's world, these thirty years so fatally different from the thirty years that stood between her and her mother, have somehow all locked together, in focused position, one behind the other, like the image on a camera lens. I have slipped inside her old skin and those round brown arms she bequeathed to me are now functioning as her original ones did, re-creating the ritual wonder of weekly cleansing right here at my own clothesline.

Oh, I could laugh! I could laugh out loud with the pleasure and wonder bursting inside me! The little crowing laughter. The warmth and funniness of it all. The "historical inevitability" of all my fucked-up wanderings.

But I controlled myself. Fatma was eying me nervously. I guess it had been a long time since my last words to her.

Last night I had dinner with Amr El Haman at Andreas' Restaurant out on the Pyramids Road. Although the handsome ex-naval officer and I have met for coffee once or twice in town, I've not really seen much of him for some weeks now. In fact, I've not seen much of any of the Hamamsys lately. To my own chagrin, the memory of Magdi—whom I have neither seen nor heard from since I left Garden City—dominates my sense of the entire family: I experience a slight shock of pain whenever any of them crosses my mind. So, like Scarlett O'Hara, I decided that I would think about it tomorrow. . . . But Amr has persisted in calling me, and finally, tomorrow has come.

At seven o'clock I climbed into Amr's old Cadillac and we drove through the spring evening out of downtown Cairo, onto the bridge at Roda Island, through Giza and onto the Pyramids Road. The velvet sky was streaked with the dying sun and the air filled with a kind of undulating bittersweet sensuality. I felt the weight of unused sexuality washing down through me as the warm light bathed my face and lifted my hair, and I grew so depressed I couldn't speak.

"What is the matter?" said Amr, all spruced up in a dark blue suit, maneuvering his car through the usual traffic exhaustion. "Aren't you feeling well?"

I looked quickly at him: What does he know? What does he suspect? Does he realize Magdi is on my mind now that I am in his cousin's presence?

"Nothing," I said restlessly. "Spring, I suppose . . . ."

Amr's bullish neck was smooth against the snow-white shirt collar, his face all olive warmth and beady dark eyes: stolid, impassive, self-contained. How absurd I was! Whenever I am feeling lost and hungry I project onto everyone about me that settled peace I so sorely want myself. What, after all, did I know about Amr? What reality did these terms of description actually reflect?

After thirty minutes on the Pyramids Road Amr turned the car onto a wide dirt lane parallel to one of the old canals that crisscrossed the land out there. The soft, lazy country scene filled my eyes: farmers jogging along atop carts filled with hay, barefoot young girls leading donkeys, green mossy trees swaying gently toward the soft dark water, jade-colored fields of short grass moving restlessly in the breezy light. I breathed deeply to calm my jagged mood.

Andreas', famous for its chicken—roasted in huge open pits and eaten in a garden that sits directly on the canal—was half-empty. Both Amr and I were pleased with the prospect of a quiet dinner and undistracted conversation. We seated ourselves at a small table near the water and ordered a drink.

"Tell me," he said when we had our drinks in our hands and the turbaned waiter was bowing away from us, moving backward. "Did something occur between you and Magdi?"

"Why on earth do you ask me *that*?" I said in a quick, alarmed voice, my eyebrows going up without my permission, my back arching itself, also without permission.

"You have been most distant from the family since you left the flat in Garden City," Amr said evenly, his eyes on two inches of

Scotch-and-water. "And Magdi himself will say not a single word about you."

"Why, what have you been asking him?"

Amr leveled a silent, unhurried stare at me; as much as to say what-sort-of-fool-do-you-take-me-for?

"It was just a matter of proximity," I sighed at last. "If those very kind, very naïve ladies, your stepmother's sisters, had not thought it the most logical thing that I take a room in that flat, I assure you nothing would ever have happened."

"All right, then," said Amr, tapping three efficient fingers on the wooden table. "You *did* take the room, something *did* happen, it was merely circumstances, those circumstances are now changed, there is nothing more to discuss. Why do you still seem worried?"

"I feel terrible about my own part in the whole thing," I said. Not *actually* to the point, I thought unhappily, but so much easier to say I acted a fool rather than I was made a fool.

"What did you do?" Amr asked, tugging at his tight white collar, never for a moment considering unbuttoning it.

"I was ridiculous," I burst out. "I did the very worst thing that a woman can do. I knew there was nothing, really, between us. That there never *could* be anything between us. But I couldn't stop myself. I became jealous, possessive. Demanded to know where he was going, *why* he was going . . ."

"You did *this?*" Amr threw down the napkin with which he'd been mopping his forehead. "With Magdi? How, how could you be so foolish? I thought you were different from Egyptian women. I thought you were strong. Sure of yourself. Really independent. Why, you're as weak as the rest of them. And, it would appear, no more intelligent."

I took a swallow of the burning liquid in my glass and stared out at the canal.

"You must surely realize," Amr went on calmly, "that you can never win by demanding something from, as you Americans say, a position of weakness."

I nodded ruefully. "Yes," I said. "I *do* realize. But always too late. Always too late."

"Then you *are* lost," Amr said, warming to his subject. He leaned toward me, and in a quiet voice: "You must never want anything.

You must be able to get along with nothing—nothing. Then, and only then, can you win. Because then you are strong, and your instincts are trained to obey you. In that way there is no such thing as 'realizing too late.' Your realizations are always on time."

"But that's absurd! One *always* wants. There is no way to *stop* wanting."

"Not true." Amr cut the air with the side of his hand, decisively. "I learned love was not for me when I was fourteen. I liked a girl. I found myself waiting for her. Worrying when she did not come. Anxious. Unhappy. I looked at the feelings, and at all those around me, and I was old enough. I *knew*. I decided then and there, I would not suffer this torment. Never. I trained myself. I suffered the pain. One thing I knew: pain cannot last. It must pass. I may suffer one year, two years, but one day, the suffering is over.

"And now, I find myself walking up and down. She doesn't call, she promised to call, I am thinking of her, I want her, it hurts. Finished. By the time she calls and I talk to her, when I hang up the telephone, *as* I am hanging up the telephone, it is all over. I do not *allow* myself ever to feel love. If I feel it coming I run."

"What about your wife?" I said, amazed.

"My wife?" Amr said blankly. "My wife. My wife has a mind but she does not use it. I have a mind and I use it. That's what gives me the power.

"I am not a man of sentiment. I give and give and give. She thinks I give everything. But I am giving nothing. And I want it that way. The most important thing is that she loves *me*, and she devotes herself to me.

"The whole trick in marriage is to keep your wife happy." Amr grinned. "*That* is power politics in Egypt. I will give you an example. Mirella wanted a hat. She loves these things. She loves the expensive things. I had the money in my pocket last week, but I told her, 'I have no money.' This morning we went shopping for food. We passed the hat. I say to her, 'You want it. Go. Buy it.' She thinks I have no money. She says, 'Oh, no. You have no money.' I say, 'It does not matter. I will manage.' We buy the hat. We buy underwear she needs. We buy material for a dress. She sees the money is coming, somehow. She is flying around like the happiest child in the world. We come home. She spreads everything on the bed. She never dreamed when she went out this morning she would have these things when she came home.

"I am planning, planning, planning. Always. I never even go to the movies with her without having planned it. So I know everything about her, backward and forward. She is, in a way, my creation. I keep her happy, and she is my *wife*."

Our chicken dinners arrived. Silence between Amr and me as the waiter spread many small dishes before us, and finally the crusty chicken halves themselves. We lifted our knives and forks, and Amr leaned forward obsessively before he began to eat.

"The important thing is to be in constant training to be strong," he said. "To know what you *want*. Never to be anywhere because *others* wish you to be there. Never to do anything or say anything because you have sentiment for others, or because you promised, or any of that nonsense. Remember: no one pays you back the good you do, never. *Trust no one*. Not even me. All will approach you. All."

We ate . . . in a manner of speaking. I felt that I would choke if I actually took a healthy mouthful of food.

As we were drinking our coffee, Amr suddenly said in the oddest voice, "You think perhaps from what I have said that I have no feelings? It is not true. I do have feelings. And yet . . . my feelings trouble me. I think they are abnormal."

I stared at him. He *was* a curiosity. A bit frightening, too.

"What are these feelings?" I asked in a calm, smooth voice, once more the working journalist. Amr didn't notice.

"Lately," he said, tugging at his collar, "in the last eight or nine months, I feel I want a virgin. I don't know why. But I feel I want to change a girl into a woman."

"A *virgin*?" I said. I couldn't believe my ears. Where could one even *start* with something like this?

"Yes," Amr sighed. "A virgin. Believe me, I suffer over it. I suffer too much." His face had undergone a transformation: his skin looked nearly gray, his eyes so creased with the pain of his own thoughts that it was almost as though I were no longer necessary to the conversation, his mouth seemed dreadfully agitated.

"First," Amr went on, "there is the question of my own wife . . . so young herself. Then there is the one whom I would be starting, and she would hate me for having started her on the way to

becoming bad. They *must* have it once they have begun, you know.
. . . And I am afraid. I became religious when I was in prison. I am
afraid of hell." He stared miserably into his coffee cup. Where was
the man of authority who only an hour ago had been instructing me
in the science of self-control? Amr seemed to have misplaced him.

I was out of my depth. I could say nothing. Nothing.

In half an hour we rose from our seats. Amr paid the bill and we
left the garden of Andreas. In the car, he recovered his self-posses-
sion and as he drove out of the restaurant's wide cinder-path
driveway, he said to me, "Remember. *No pain lasts.* Fight the pain,
fight it. It will make you strong. You want to love. *I* do not want to
love, but you do. Make yourself strong and all will want you, and you
can choose the terms on which you will accept."

Exactly as though we were allies in a war, and he was imparting
his fighting knowledge to me. After all, the *strategy* was legitimate,
and who knew? Perhaps I could make better use of it than he seemed
able to.

I leave my house at eight o'clock in the evening and plunge into
the dirt and darkness of Mohammed Sidki Street, suddenly overcome
by a rush of affection for Cairo, so grateful to be going out into this
city of night, unafraid, not feeling the tension of possible combat I
feel each time I leave my house after dark in New York. Whatever
else may threaten me here in Cairo, I have no fear that this night I
may end up face to face with psychotic rage: a knife at my back, my
bag wrenched from my arm, my legs forced apart in fear-silenced
darkness, a maniac's sudden spray of bullets, schizophrenic fingers
closing around my throat, my skull smashed in an elevator: all the
commonplace images of possibility that flit with lightning speed
through the ordinary New Yorker's mind as she prepares to embark
on a casual evening in the city.

Cairo after dark is like a village. The city is only dimly lit since the
1967 War. ("My brilliant countrymen," says my painter friend
Farouk bitterly one night when we are stumbling across Midan el
Tahrir. "They think the Israelis are flying around up there saying,
'Oh, where is Cairo? We cannot find it since the Egyptians put out

the lights.' They never heard of radar.") The semi-gloom encloses me, wrapping itself like a warm cloak about my senses, protective rather than sinister; the Cairo psychotics, as yet, still know their *place*; given another fifty years of progress they, too, will lose that conviction of reprisal that keeps most men passive in their derangement. . . . But, tonight, oh tonight! Cairo is *safe*: warm and snug in the dark evening buzz.

Farouk takes my arm and we cross three lanes of Midan el Tahrir traffic, heading for the glittering Hilton on the other side of the square's dense rushing and shoving that still has a good few hours to go before things start letting up.

"You will like Debbie very much," the young painter says eagerly. "Of this I am convinced. She is another American child like yourself, and she simply *adores* Egypt."

Already, I don't like her.

Debbie Lindner is an American graduate student. Her subject is American-Egyptian relations. She studies in Paris and makes periodic trips to Cairo to dig out of people what she cannot dig out of the Parisian libraries. Farouk met her two years ago on one of these trips, and he sees her whenever she is in Cairo. He has been insisting for weeks now that I must meet Debbie.

We stand just inside the door of the crowded Hilton café, searching the rings of faces gathered around fifty or sixty tables in the room. I come here rarely, and I enjoy it thoroughly whenever I do. A sense of expectant gaiety stirs in me whenever I walk into the Hilton: it always comes as a surprise, this feeling, reminding me with a jolt of how far from home I am, how deeply in an "other" place is the set of my mind and my responses as I go about my daily life amidst the streets and houses of Cairo, and how deeply repetitious are those streets and houses in some psychological manner, and with what a ridiculous uprush do I feel America and *variety* rushing through me no sooner than I walk through the vulgar doors of the Hilton.

"There she is," says Farouk, and steers me toward the center of the room where a young woman dressed in a blue pantsuit, blond hair streaming down her back, sits at a table for four, waving and grinning as we approach, her smile unmistakably that of an American "gamin."

"So you're Farouk's 'other' American," Debbie says to me,

hunching forward in an odd, tomboyish manner; she grins again, and now that I am sitting next to her I see that she is older than she looks from a distance, the lines around her blue eyes indicating thirty-odd years rather than twenty-odd.

Farouk orders beer from a passing waitress, and immediately launches into a rapid-fire exchange with the American graduate student. It seems Farouk has missed two previous appointments with Debbie, and he must now explain. I wait patiently for them to sort out the history of four days of aborted plans. It is a commonplace in Cairo, this opening conversation between people who strive to reduce through detailed explanation the chaos of communications that eternally surrounds the lives of Cairenes: the telephones are always out of order, the messages left are never received, the plans made are inevitably misunderstood. Someone is always waiting in vain near a telephone, in a restaurant, on a street corner. And when, at last, all parties involved manage to meet it is vital that the entire mess be minutely discussed and sorted out so that all concerned can reassure each other that every effort at civilized behavior has been made; then, and only then, is exasperation diluted if one of the persons is a Westerner, and satisfaction achieved if the other is an Egyptian.

Ten minutes pass before Farouk and Debbie are somewhat straightened out. By then the beer has arrived, the inevitable dish of peanuts is planted on the table, and we all drink and eat gratefully.

The Middle East is her "passion"; the Israelis, the contemptible enemy; anti-Semitism a faint, acrid odor that surrounds her "Jew-ish" references. She laughs and tells me that she is often taken for Jewish because of her name: the Egyptians can't tell the difference between a Jewish name and a German name. She'll bet a lot of Jews take advantage of *that.* I look wonderingly at her: Doesn't she know? Doesn't she even suspect? Marvelous! Here, with my own country-woman, do I taste for the first time in Egypt the bitterness of emotional hatred of Jews as such. . . . The conversation is a political travelogue: Lebanon, Syria, Jordan, the Palestinian guerrillas, the refugee camps, the archives at the American University, the current maneuverings of the Egyptian government, Sisco's impending visit, the cynical expectations of the people at *Al Ahram.*

She talks a dense, nervous, exhausting blue streak: the earnest, "informed" American college student whose words are bitten off with the kind of furious intensity that is wildly disproportionate to the observations being made or the opinions being exchanged. She is angry at everything. And then suddenly: the gamin smile and a disarming friendliness. Her emotions seem to ricochet like a taut spring bouncing off . . . what? Her response to my presence in Egypt—dense, nervous, overeager—is in keeping with the rest of her conversation.

"It's wonderful, your being here! Wonderful! You don't *know* how these people need you. It's just *disgusting* how ignorant people back home are about the Egyptians. They don't *know*. They just don't *know*. This country is tragic. *Tragic*. It breaks my heart every time I come back to Cairo. And all they know in New York is the latest clever thing that miserable old woman in Tel Aviv is saying! Or that other one-eyed wonder! Every time he farts it's all over the front pages of the *Times*. . . . But who do you know? How are you working? You must meet people. I know! You must meet Farid Wafa! He's just the man to help you. He's an editor at *Al Kahira*, he lives at the *pension* I stay at here in Cairo. He's a good friend, he's helped me a lot with my work. Farid knows everyone in Cairo. *Everyone*. I'll take you to see him. Are you free tomorrow night? He works late at the magazine. We can go to his office. . . ."

I feel like I'm going under . . . but how can I say no?

As we leave the hotel Debbie clutches at Farouk's arm. "Take me back to the *pension*?" she half-asks, half-demands—the smile on her face nervous, pasted-on. I stare at her, uncomprehending. We are all going in different directions. Taxis are cheap enough, God knows. Why should Farouk have to go out of his way to drop her at her *pension*?

It turns out she's terrified of traveling alone in a taxi late at night, and she's convinced the *boab* (porter) in her *pension* building is intent on raping her.

"I like this girl very much, Debbie," said Farid Wafa. "Very much! Thank you, my dear friend. Thank you for bringing her to me. I think she will do my poor country much good, and I am honored to be able to help her in her mission here."

Debbie Lindner and I were sitting on a leather couch in Farid Wafa's gloomy little room at the offices of the newspaper *Al Kahira*. The man behind the desk had been questioning me for nearly an hour about my purposes in Egypt, and now he seemed pleased.

"Ah, but this is very important, what you are trying to do, and you must get all the help you can. You must meet the right people. By the right people I mean a proper cross-section of Egyptians. You must meet a rich man and a poor man, a priest and a *sheikh*, a clever adolescent and a working-class child, a liberated middle-class woman and an enslaved middle-class woman, an artist, a doctor, a patriotic engineer, a lawyer who would sell his mother to get out of Egypt, a first-generation university student from the village, his father's younger wife, the servant in my house in Alexandria, a Nubian photographer, a girl here at *Al Kahira* struggling to become a journalist—all these are Egypt. All. And you must meet them all. And I will help you to meet them all. Now I promise you, I won't let you down. You shall meet them all. You must give me a bit of time, however. To think. To draw up a proper list."

I remained speechless throughout this recital, unable to grasp my good fortune in having been steered to this energetic, organized editor with whom I felt an instant affinity, and a freedom to be myself. There was a kind of affectionate cynicism between us: he wanted something from me (American sympathy), I wanted something from him (Egyptian information); we understood each other perfectly. Then just as I was getting ready to make full use of Mr. Farid Wafa he caught me off-balance by leaning forward across his desk and saying very softly to me, "It's for the children that I do it. These children growing up out of the streets of Egypt. These very intelligent children I watch every day of my life, with no future, no hope, no change coming for them. Do you know that seventy percent of all university graduates in this country remain unemployed? Do you know that the buildings are there but the children have no shoes to go to school with? Do you know what the infant mortality rate—*still*—is in this country? Perhaps your book will help them, yes? And perhaps I will help you to make the book that will help them, yes?"

These children. These very intelligent children growing up out of the streets of Egypt. . . .

"You know," says Soad, "when Ali Mahmoud was very young his father came to me one day and he said, 'I will bring a child from the village. She will live with us and she will be a companion to the boy.' So he comes with the child one day. And I take one look at her and I say, 'To hell! This is impossible. She is an animal!' And Ali Mahmoud's father says to me, 'Wait a bit. Clean her up and then let us see.' She was *vermin* from head to foot. Sores all over her feet, broken eyes, hair like some disgusting matted steel wool. And silent. And shrinking from every human touch. I shaved her head, soaked her for a day and a night, took her to doctors for a month. . . . And what a marvelous child she was! We had Italian neighbors. She would take Ali next door to play with the Italian children. Do you know, without anyone teaching her she learned all the words of the songs the Italian mother used to sing to her children. Gasbia used to recite her lessons aloud. This child could repeat the lessons better than Gasbia and she used to help Gasbia with them when she couldn't remember the next line! She grew up a wonderful woman, and she was married from my house. . . ."

Soad's eyes stare off into that private distance of hers. Her mouth crumbles into laughter. She recalls another tale about another child: "Once a boy was shining shoes here in the street below. An American came. The boy shined the American's shoes and then the American said, 'I only have a five-pound note.' The boy said, 'I'll go get change.' The boy went across the street and then he began to run. The American got up to chase him, and found his shoe laces tied together! He was astonished. And then even he began to laugh."

Farid Wafa. The fifty-year-old managing editor of *Al Kahira*. Very heavy. Very dark. A strong, clever, warm, gentle face. In a class all by himself. Two days after that first evening in his office Farid and I sat in the bar at the Sheraton Hotel. Suddenly, I blurted out, "I'm Jewish."

"I know," said Farid.

"How?"

"You are just like us."

He knew Nasser before he came to power, he lived through the revolution, he was managing editor of the ill-fated opposition paper, was thrown out of work for two years, and arrested twice: once three months in prison, once two weeks, the two weeks worse than the three months; they threw him into a pitch-black cell, took his glasses away from him, and screamed fearful piercing screams into the darkness as he crawled blindly about on the floor of the cell; periodically, an interrogator would appear, slap his face many times and yell questions into his terrified ear.

"Do you consider it strange that I live at the *pension* and my wife lives in Alexandria?" Farid asked.

"A bit," I said, "but I think I rather believe in part-time marriage. . . . Is that why you live separately?"

"Not exactly. We married three years ago, my wife and I. I had been a widower for many years. I have three children. My first wife died giving birth to the last child. Then, a few years ago I was visiting a friend in Alexandria. I rode up in the elevator and a woman rode up with me. I liked her. I liked her very much. I tried to exert my charm in the elevator. She resisted it very nicely. When I arrived at my friend's house I described this woman. 'She lives on the eighth floor,' my friend said. 'She is a widow. Forget it. She will never speak to you.' The next day I waited for her to come out of the building. I followed her. She turned on her heel, very angry. 'What do you want of me?' she said. 'I wish only to speak to you,' I said. 'Go to my brother,' she said very curtly. 'If he says you may speak to me then you may come to the flat.' Imagine a man of my age going to a brother! But I went . . . and finally I won her. However, she refused to come to Cairo. She has lived in Alex all her life. She would die, she said, if she had to live in Cairo. So it was agreed: she would keep her flat in Alex and we would live apart from each other for a few days each week. And it has been a good arrangement. She knows she can trust me, and I trust her, and when we are together we really enjoy each other."

Farid is dreadfully obese; indeed, a baby elephant, as Debbie has said. Also, his head is too narrow for his huge body, giving him the appearance of one about to lose his balance; his eyes swim behind thick glasses, his lips are like African rubber; he chain-smokes and ashes are perpetually tumbling onto his shirt front. Yet, when he speaks his appearance becomes literally transformed, and it is easy to see why he has had much success with women.

He has lived in many places, traveling as a journalist to Europe and Japan, and all over the Arab world; he's quick to pick up on a Westerner's allusions to the interior life; he has the most European sense of life of any Egyptian I have met.

"I love this country," Farid sighs as he lights a cigarette and sips his drink, "but it's killing me. There is no free flow of ideas here. So the intellectuals talk to themselves. An idea is born and it dies on the spot. No soil for it to root itself in. There is no revolutionary consciousness here. It never happened. The people were never transformed. The intellectuals are all Marxists, but they are totally disorganized. And what is a Communist without organization?

"There is no cause for the young or the middle class to draw its initiative or its ideals from. After the revolution there was nothing to believe in. For a people to find themselves there must be a free clash of opinion, and this was never allowed. Change cannot be imposed from the top. It never takes, never happens that way. So now everyone talks about change but no one *feels* it, no one understands it; and everyone grows bitter and apathetic. Every day the best brains of the country are leaving. If they criticize the government they are enemies of the state; if they keep their mouths shut they die inside. . . .

"I've got to get away from the Egyptians. I need to feel the free flow of human minds around me. You know, here we never write of anything until it is an established phenomenon. I want to watch a phenomenon germinating."

We spend hours together, comparing the lives that have brought us to this unlikely meeting. I show him my first impressionistic pieces on Cairo.

"It is wonderful!" Farid cries. "I feel as though I am reading Arabic! You have captured us completely. *Completely*." And then later: "I love your journalism. I love your womanness. I love your

Jewishness. They are all you. We will be good friends, *ya*-Vivian,° yes? You and I?"

Farid loves to have long, intense conversations about: me, Debbie, his wife; how he feels about each of us, how I feel, how Debbie feels, how his wife feels, on and on. I am his good friend, he says; Debbie is a child he must help, he says; he has spoken foolishly to his wife about Debbie and his enthusiasm for her work; he fears that his wife is becoming jealous. It's all so silly, a joke that makes me feel happy and ridiculous, and that he is absurd and strong at the same time.

"You must come to Alex soon," Farid says as I put him on the train one Thursday afternoon.

"Yes, I want to. Tell your wife about me. Ask her to invite me sometime. Don't make me illegal in your life, Farid."

"No, Vivian. Never. You will never be illegal in my life."

"You are going to Upper Egypt?" Farouk claps his hands.

"Ah, I wish I could accompany you," Amr says. "I am an expert on the ruins, you know. I could show you much the guides do not know."

"Now you must be very careful," Soad croons, holding my hands in hers. "You are a woman traveling alone, and you must keep your eyes and your ears *open* at all times!"

"Yes, go now, before the heat becomes unbearable," says the young Aischa. "And go everywhere in Luxor. *Everywhere*. Believe me, you will come back an Egyptologist. It is something marvelous to see, and something never to forget."

"Ten days," mourns Mohammed. "You will be gone ten whole days."

"When you come back I will be ready with my list," says Farid. "And then we will go to *work*." He looks steadily into my eyes. "Come back safely, Vivian," he says. "I care deeply for you."

"Good-bye, good-bye," says Fawzy. "Stay at the Old Cataract in

---

° *Ya* is a term of endearment that is always linked to a name; it is somewhere between "dear" and a diminutive such as Dickie or Janie.

Aswan. I had many marvelous days and nights there. Ah! You will never be the same after you have seen Upper Egypt."

South to Aswan. South to the heart of Upper Egypt. South to the upper reaches of the Nile. South to that part of the world where for more than a thousand years the Egyptian Nubians have labored patiently in the vast Sahara waste, and fished and sailed on the Nile. South to where, long long before the Nubians, were the Pharaohs who kept moving steadily up the Nile, leaving the great temples and monuments that testify to that extraordinary civilization alive here four thousand years ago. South to where now there are: the Russian engineers who built the High Dam, Egypt's bid for entrance on the stage of world power; UN workers laboring in the vineyard of the undeveloped country; Cairo public health doctors bearing gifts of contraception and vaccine; tourists gaping at the Pharaohs, the Nubians, the Russians and the doctors. South to where all are piled up together, none ever having successfully replaced another. South to where an amazing sociology of the living and the dead bears extraordinary witness to a complexity of historical life that is continually reaching backward, then jumping forward, then standing still: finally overpowering in its intimations of human destiny.

The train left Cairo at seven-thirty in the morning; it would arrive in Aswan sixteen hours later. This time I had a seat in a first-class car. I shared an upholstered double-seat chair facing another one just like it with three young Egyptian men, two of them chemistry students returning after a brief holiday in Cairo to their institute in Aswan, the third an engineer four years out of the university, "learning computer" in Aswan, also on his way back after a week in the city. The two younger men, Ahmed and Ashraf, were nineteen and twenty-one. The older one was twenty-eight; his name was Fouad. They were delighted to have me with them, and in broken English they plied me with sandwiches, cigarettes, tea and love. Sixteen hours is a long time to spend knee to knee. . . .

The railroad tracks followed the Nile, and for hours and hours we rode along the river, looking out beyond it to the stony desert spreading itself to the horizon, the earth-colored villages that seemed to rise right out of the land, the occasional farmed strips, the swaying palms, the bleak low sandstone hills that appeared like a surprise against the low skyline. It was a monotonous landscape.

"Beautiful, is it not?" said Ashraf, leaning across me to get closer to the window.

Yes, as only water and green in any shape can be to a people whose home is an unyielding desert.

The two chemistry students were a pair of puppy dogs. Like the soft dark dancing men on the streets of Cairo they cleaved together: clowning continually with each other, with me, and with the engineer. Ahmed would open a sandwich and, just as he was about to take the first bite, Ashraf would snatch it from him and bite into it himself. Ahmed would roll his eyes to the ceiling, slap his knee and fall, laughing and punching, all over his gleefully waiting friend. Ashraf would offer me a cigarette, and when I refused—out of politeness, they assumed—they would both hover over me, one with a cigarette, the other with a match, laughing and carrying on.

"*Ya-reiis!*" either Ashraf or Ahmed called all day long, and when the sixty-year-old waiter (*reiis* actually means "chief") who has spent his life swaying up and down the aisles of the Cairo-Aswan train bent his tired eyes to us, one or the other would say "*Shai*" or "*Ahwa.*" Then the other would shake his head and his finger, and a pantomime would begin about who wanted the tea and who wanted the coffee.

The engineer, sitting opposite me, smiled indulgently at the two young students, but only rarely did he join in to playfully cuff one of them on the head, or defend himself as another hooked a hand around his neck, or allow them both to pin his arms behind his back. (Physical contact! It is the lifeblood of this country.) Generally though, the engineer lay back in his seat, his features silenced by an expression of deep distraction.

"He is very sad," Ashraf whispered to me. "His mother. She has died two weeks past."

The engineer caught a few of Ashraf's words to me. His eyes clouded over and in German he said slowly, "*Meine Mutter. Sie ist tod. Plötzlich.*" I told him how very badly I felt, and he nodded, sinking back into his seat, his eyes trained on the window, his fingers groping for a cigarette. Unlike the two boys, the engineer was tall, with a beautiful Roman head, a cap of tight black curls, a long well-made body, shapely hands and strongly proportioned features. His pain made his beauty even more vivid.

"Are you from Cairo, Fouad?" I asked.

The engineer struggled to collect his thoughts. "No," he said, closing his eyes briefly. "I am from Montsoura. From the village." He smiled sadly. "I am the first in my family to go to the university." His eyes clouded over again. "And now I must to help my family." He grew very distracted, and lit a cigarette rather than go on. Then, after a long pause: "My papa. He is very sick . . . after my mother . . . he cannot to work . . . I must give money." He stared out of the window. He dragged his eyes back to me. "Thirty-six pounds. That is what I receive in a month. It is, *yani*, impossible to support a family on thirty-six pounds. . . ." His mouth twitched in an abortive attempt to form itself into a cynical smile, and very quietly he said, "What I will do?" He jerked toward the window, and then back toward me. He stared wordlessly into my eyes, and I stared back: both of us stricken by the hopeless little question. He lay back in his seat, like a man exhausted by fever, staring blindly out the window. Then his eyes brightened suddenly, and he said, "I must to America. They have need for good engineers in America, yes? I am good. Really, I am good." He grew disconsolate again. "Perhaps not so good as American engineers?"

"*Shai!*" Ahmed announced, handing around four large glasses of sweet dark tea as the waiter's tray swayed above us. We drank in silence. I turned to the window. The monotonous scene rolled swiftly by. The river was very narrow and dark here, and the desert seemed to fill the world. Villages rose up out of the earth and quickly disappeared. Often, a group of people stood silent and motionless near the river or beside a few earthen houses as the train went by; they, too, seemed to be made out of earth, molded from the same material as the desert and everything on it. I shivered with sudden revulsion. Imagine. What if I were to wake up tomorrow morning and find myself one of them instead of me!

The boys pushed food on me. I shook my head no, but they would not hear of it. Laughing, they shoved a sandwich at my lips. Consistency! It had a death grip on the Egyptian mind. I had taken half a sandwich an hour or so before; *therefore*, I naturally wanted a sandwich each time they offered, and if I said no it must be forced on me.

It was now late afternoon. Exhausted with the confinement of the train, our legs aching, our bodies cramped, we all stretched and dozed. Beside me, Ashraf was sound asleep with his stockinged feet in Ahmed's lap. Ahmed also slept, with his feet tucked beside Ashraf's thigh. Directly opposite me, Fouad tossed restlessly, his eyes closed. I, alone, could not lose consciousness. My eyes kept closing drowsily, and for moments at a time I seemed to faint sitting upright, but then I would jerk to, with my head lolling on my chest, dazed but awake.

I never could recall, afterwards, exactly when it all started, but once when I came suddenly awake I found Fouad looking intently at me. I started to look away, then found I couldn't. Some urgency in the young engineer's face held me. His eyes never left my face. He pulled out a cigarette and bent forward to light it, and still his eyes stared into mine. He began to give off a sexual tension that mounted like a flare. He seemed to toss, sort of, inside his skin, his head moved back, he loosed his tie as though he were choking. The long, beautiful body, alive suddenly with hunger and need, stopped the breath in me for moments at a time. I began to stir—against my will—inside; deep inside. . . . For months now I had moved in the atmosphere of Cairo's sexuality, powerful as a drug, abstract and full of porous hunger—feeling always as though I am sleeping with six men at once; faces merge, one behind the other, as a dark Egyptian takes my elbow and steers me tenderly across the street, the motion somehow an act of love, a drifting sensuality, a melancholic reminder of lust—and now, here on the train, I felt, suddenly, the force of pressure; pressure building unawares.

A world of anxiety seemed *caught* in Fouad's agonized body. And there began now a litany of pain, interspersed with the mounting sexual fever.

"*Meine Mutter,*" he whispered, and fell back again, his eyes on me.
I stared at him, unable to move, unable to respond, unable to . . .
He leaned forward. "I have *need* of you. Stay beside me tonight."
Everything inside me leaped up, like brush put to the match.
"No," I whispered back, my lips dry.

"*Please*," he said in a tight low voice. "I will come to your hotel in Aswan this night. You *must*."

"No."

His head fell back on the head rest; little veins trembled in his dropped eyelids like live, trapped creatures; his head tossed from left to right.

"I *must* to America," he said, his eyes flying open. "Can you help me? Tell someone in America I am good engineer."

What the hell, I thought.

"Stay with me," he moaned. "Just this night. Only this night . . . I beg you."

I couldn't even speak this time.

"Thirty-six pounds," he said calmly, leaning forward to take my hands in his. "What I can do with thirty-six pounds? Tell me, my American friend. What I can do?"

He laughed bitterly; and yet sweetly, youthfully. Then desire was draining the color from his face again, the muscles were tensing, exhaustion was etched in the fine eyes, the strong Roman nose, the full long mouth.

"Stay beside me this night," he whispered. "*Stay*."

He became one long flame of sexual need. Everything in him that was wretched, confused, desperate, longing, needful, all his anxiety named and unnamed, became sexual desire, a powerhouse of driven need, throbbing inside that beautiful young skin. It drained all the energy from me. I became limp inside my own still body, as though all the blood in my veins hung in suspension. If he had touched me then I would have flared into fire in an instant. Instead, he leaned forward suddenly, grinned and said licentiously, "You know what means *fuck*?" Fire turned to lead.

He leaned back silently, and the anguish rose in his face and in his body again, and the fire began to surge in me again. I felt as though a thick band, wide as our two bodies, invisible and smoky, held us together. His anxiety was a catalyst for my own: his so easily named, mine so easily disturbed. . . .

We went on like this for eight hours, to the point of utter exhaustion. He was such a wretched little prig! A hearty peasant on the train began to chant the Koran and Fouad said righteously, "This is no place for that." And later, he told me that Jacqueline Kennedy was no good because she had married again. And yet his need—intense, confused, conflicted—ennobled him. He reminded me of a man I had once seen beside the tram tracks in Heliopolis. The man was cleaning out one of the thousands of free-standing kiosks on the streets of Cairo made of wooden boards and slabs of warped glass that contain candy or cigarettes or some other slapped-together variety of goods: this one selling candy. He was rearranging all those hopeless stacks of stale biscuits and week-old candy into neat pyramids and solemn rows: very carefully, very patiently. Suddenly, his neck jerked forward and his head came up, for one moment scanning the tracks in the direction of Cairo. There was, in his motion, wild impatience, and a hunger beyond articulation. It lasted only a moment but it told all: of the still, gathered energy in him; the bewilderment sunk deep in the gut. I took a good look at the man then. He was in his thirties, very strong and dark. He should have been a factory foreman, or a merchant marine, or the owner of an electronics supply house, or a diesel engine mechanic; but here he stood—strapped, mute, chained into quiet, selling candy beside a tram track.

Fouad, like the man beside the tram track, began to seem like a figure in a myth: all the strength and manly capacity in him sealed off, bound inside this fever of sexual need that made of a man a child, forever chained, forever muted, a doomed infantilism, an unspeakable quiet.

Oh, this country! This country!

At seven o'clock the train drew into Luxor. The boys woke up, rubbing their eyes like children, stretching and yawning. People got off, others got on; ragged children in the station leaped on the train to sell peanuts, pocket combs, hard candy. Fouad stared gloomily out at them. He said, "Two weeks ago I took this train to Cairo. When I sat here on this station at nine o'clock, *exactly* as I sat here speaking with friends, my mother was dying in Montsoura. . . ." Again he tossed back in his seat. Again: agony, sex, futility.

"Fouad," I said, "don't you know any girls in Aswan?"

He looked at me as though I had suddenly become demented. "This is Upper Egypt," he said slowly. The following night in Aswan I went for a walk with him, and anxiety lit his face as we moved through the hot, dark moonlight, and I knew the depth of isolation in which this stupid, feeling boy lived. Not a girl or a woman on the streets of Aswan, never. A man never knows a girl until he marries her. To speak to her is to marry her.

And things weren't much better for him in Cairo: "I have a good girl in Cairo. I cannot marry her because I *must* to America. I *must*. So sometimes I pay a woman—one pound, two pounds—she stays the night beside me. . . ."

We arrived in Aswan at midnight and when I got off the train it was like July in New York: a blanket of sweet, dark heat wrapping itself about us. Exhausted beyond words, I extricated myself ruthlessly from the imploring faces of Ahmed, Ashraf and Fouad, and rushed for a taxi. Fifteen minutes later I was checking into a hotel on the riverfront, and twenty minutes after that I was deep in the sleep of the dead. In the morning I stepped out on a narrow balcony into the spectacular beauty of the Upper Nile Valley. Below me was the river, wider, darker, more vivid and far-reaching than I'd ever seen it before, the sun gleaming on its smooth, faintly restless surface. In the river were islands—one large enough to hold an entire Nubian village—and strange, prehistoric-looking rock formations. The far banks of the river, as well as the islands, were dense with palms and sycamores and foliage of various and wonderful greens, and on the horizon, low shapely hills of reddish-gold sand and broken sandstone. But what was most exciting was the brilliancy of the morning light, the clarity of the air, the primary-color look of the sky, the river, the trees, the desert. There was, as well, in the view before me the appearance of a developed resort: a long, arcing road and walkway that ran the length of the river, hotel boats lying at anchor, yellow, blue and white buildings of all sizes: hotels, flats, stores; on the walkway along the river: vendors, benches, trees; strolling peasants, tourists, workers. It was lovely and exciting, filled with promise as only a beautiful riverfront in summer can be. I watched for a long satisfying while, then set out to see the sights.

There was only one way to see the ancient temples and monuments of Aswan—as everything in Egypt requires official permits—and that was through an official tour guide. The tourist agent in the hotel—a handsome Nubian named Loutfi—couldn't do enough for the American journalist lady ("A bargain," he assured me in low, swift tones. "Only two and a half pounds for you. Everyone else pays five."), and he couldn't do it fast enough. Within an hour I was being hustled into a wreck of a 1955 Chevrolet along with an American lady named Alice (whose husband was an agricultural advisor in Turkey), her mother visiting from Seattle, and a bearded high school physics teacher from Amsterdam. When I expressed alarm over the overwhelming smell of leaking gasoline in the car, the Nubian driver said the car was blessed by Allah, and we went limping off to see the famous quarries from which the Pharaohs had hacked the stone they had used to build their temples.

The quarries were some miles out of the town in a kind of valley in the desert. When we pulled up into the clearing space before them there were half a dozen other cars looking just like ours, discharging many more tourists than ours did. There were eighteen Swedes, a dozen Germans, five or six Frenchmen, and a couple more Americans. The driver-guides all began delivering their travelogue spiels in the appropriate language—describing the quarries, the method of transport on the river used by the ancient Egyptians, the technology of using basalt to quarry granite, and finally a brief description of the huge unfinished obelisk lying directly before us in the quarry, a piece of work inexplicably abandoned by the ancient Egyptian workers. The tourists swarmed all over the place, and I along with them, all of us walking across the obelisk like a colony of ants. It was impossible, somehow, in this atmosphere of fast-talking, sweating guides and docile tourists to get worked up, and the sense of ancient Egypt eluded me entirely, as indeed it always had in the past when gazing at picture postcards and museum artifacts.

After a while, simply to get away from the yapping sound of Swedish-German-French-English ohing and ahing, I began climbing up over the rocks on the far side of the quarry to see if I could get a view of the river and the desert from some higher place than the one in which we all stood. I climbed and climbed until I came to a rough path that leveled off in the desert above the quarry. I followed the path to its end, then turned and looked down not on the river but on the basin of stone below me, and the obelisk lying within it.

It was a wrenching sensation—to suddenly see that thing lying there in its shallow grave, surrounded by the bleak ungiving sandstone, and to feel surging through me the unmistakable presence of fear. Fear that I knew was four thousand years old. Fear that was powerful enough to still make itself felt. Pure terror, I suddenly *knew*, was the only driving force that could have created the kind of energy men had needed to hack the stone out of this remote earth all that long time ago. Terror was at the backs of the men who had worked here, terror was before them when they stopped working, terror was etched in the vulnerable beauty of the stone tower lying patiently on its side all these helpless centuries. For the very first time in my life ancient Egypt came alive for me, and when I finally retraced my steps and came back among the tourists their voices had receded in strength for me, and for a while I was alone with my thoughts: moved and mystified by the sensation of dread I had so briefly but so intensely experienced.

We were herded back into the cars and driven another long way over the bleached and broken sandstone until we came down to a kind of inlet in the river. Here, we were all hustled into small rowboats and taken out onto the Nile. Luckily, Alice and her mother and the Dutchman were quiet, and the silent rhythm and depth of the beautiful river soaked through us as birds whirred in the sycamores on the shore; I leaned over the side of the boat. What a tremendously long way this water beneath my fingers had come, and for how many thousands of years had it been pouring out of mountains and deserts to get down here: to us.

And then we were there. The many rowboats gathered, circling in the water, around the magnificent Temples of Philae, the ancient temples now half under water whose salvage costs are just beginning to be assumed by the countries of the world. (Philae, like Abu Simbel, doomed by the High Dam to be flooded forever, is going to be removed to a safe and high part of the river shore.)

Looking at Philae, again that same uncanny sensation of looking at naked fear. The ancient carvings on the walls of the stone temple, full of complicated symbolism, images mingling with hieroglyphics; of portraits of the Pharaohs as gods, of the gods as beasts, of the two as each other; of battles and marriages and mythic fulfillment; of invoked protection and justified doom; of conqueror and conquered and swelled pride, with a telltale shadow of anxiety behind it. All, all seemed absolutely driven, so deep were the carvings and so pure their message. Driven by the fear of nothingness; driven by the fear of death and obscurity; driven by the conviction that earth and sky were all and men born to be extinguished; and in that drivenness, in that hunger, a defiance that made me love the Pharaohs, and an arrogance that made me go cold.

And then behind me, Alice's mother was saying to the Dutchman, "And on my last trip around the world. . . ."

In half an hour we were rowed back to the shore and our broken-down Chevrolet was limping along to another part of the river, where on high embankments we were treated to the wonder of the High Dam, water-driven electricity, Russian signs, and proudly delivered statistics.

Touring is a merciless business: one is continually being transported, but one is *never* being transported.

In the afternoon I cut loose. I wandered back to the riverfront, and started walking. At a certain gathering point for boats on the river a dozen men began to shout at me, enjoining me to rent one of their sailboats (dhows). I kept going, hoping to simply keep walking through it all until I got someplace quiet. A hand on my shoulder stopped me. It was Loutfi, the tourist agent.

"What happened to you?" he said.

"Nothing," I said.

"Would you like to go out on the river?"

"No."

"Come on, take a ride on the river. You'll enjoy it. The trip is on me."

"No, no," I protested, but I was already being hauled down the bank to the river dhows and being introduced to a small, thin, very muscular, very black man with calm eyes beneath a blue and yellow embroidered skullcap, and wearing a blue *gelabya* from which protruded bare feet and strong hands. His name was Ramadan.

Those two hours on the river with Ramadan were the best I spent in Aswan, and surely the most evocative. The dhow is a lovely boat, long and narrow with a very slim high mast and beautiful complicated sails, and the moment Ramadan unfurled, and started steering with the wooden stick at the back of the boat, I knew that the river is experienced in a very special way on a dhow. Although . . .

I don't know much about sailboats, I only know I'm afraid of them; but like roller coasters, I'm drawn to try again—even though I inevitably wind up, once again, scared and impotent: No sooner were we out on the water and I was suddenly facing into a rush of sparkling wind, gulping sweet windy air into my mouth, and the water alive with movement, and the sun streaking through the palms on the shore, and the desert a lovely golden hardness in the distance—in other words, I was *enjoying* myself—than the boat started to keel over on its side. With my shoulder six inches from the water, I involuntarily screamed, "I can't swim!" Ramadan looked bewilderedly at me, not understanding my words; but he caught my meaning a second afterwards, and started to laugh gently.

"*La, la,*" he said, and moving quickly, he gripped my hand, pulled me to the other side of the boat, and pushed me down on the seat. Then he went to work. He was like a cat, moving everywhere on that boat at once. He pulled ropes, he pushed wood, he used his hands and feet to steady things; he handled every single thing not as though he loved that thing, but as though he knew it better than he knew his own bodily sensations. The boat dipped again, and then again, and yet again. Each time it happened my terror decreased, replaced by my rapidly developing trust in Ramadan. By the fourth time, there I was, happily gripping the sides of a half-overturned dhow, waiting for Ramadan to make everything all right.

Loutfi had told Ramadan to take me to all the islands—Elephantine, Kitchener, there's a whole group in the river directly before Aswan's riverfront that have been turned over to the tourists—but as we approached Kitchener Island I saw three boatloads of Russian tourists disembarking and I said to Ramadan, "Forget it. No islands. Let's just sail on the river." Ramadan stared at me in disbelief; then his face broke into a wide grin; then he reached inside his *gelabya* and offered me a cigarette.

The dhow bent quickly to every slight movement of the water, every shifting air current, every tiny atmospheric disturbance, and when you learned to go with it, it created a voluptuous and exhilarating sense of rhythmic connection that was oddly muted,

oddly quiet, and most oddly reassuring. We moved swiftly through
the waters until soon we faced the far end of the town and we began
to curve away from it, going up the Nile a bit. Ramadan knew all the
secret, quiet places on the river and he began to make them available
to me. He used his boat like a master technician. It took him instantly
where he wanted to go, and so *silently*. After a while it was that the
quiet was inside him, the quiet on the river was inside the man . . .
or was it that the quiet inside the man was being transferred to the
river?

I began to feel myself in the presence of mystery. The world
became a place of gliding water, strange rock formations looming in
the river, whirring birds in the dense foliage on the shore, the desert
beyond and the sun just over the top: dazzling, blinding, sinister. For
the first time since I had been in Egypt I thought: I am in Africa.
There leaped into my stomach a sudden lurching desire to keep
going on the river. I felt the reality of Moorehead's books about the
Nile, a reality that seemed, incredibly, within my reach, and I
wanted to discover for myself exactly what those obsessed Eng-
lishmen of the nineteenth century had repeatedly come back here to
discover. What, after all, *was* it? After all the *words*, what exactly
was it out there? I wanted to keep moving up into the desert,
through the Sudan, past the rushing falls beyond, onto the Ethiopian
plateau and into the mountains, beyond to the source of the Blue
Nile at Lake Tana; or into the swamps and green heart of Central
Africa to the White Nile gushing out of Lake Victoria. At the very
least, I wanted to say to Ramadan, "Park the boat a minute, run into
town, get some food and blankets, and let's keep going until we get
to Khartoum." Khartoum. Imagine. The distance between Khartoum
and the place in which I now sat was less than the distance between
New York and Oklahoma.

Of course, we didn't go to Khartoum.

That night at the hotel Loutfi said to me, "Listen, the hydrofoil to
Abu Simbel hasn't been running for four days. Tomorrow it will run.
The tourists over at the New Cataract Hotel are tearing the hair out

of their heads to get on the boat—they've been waiting here all this time just for Abu Simbel—so everyone will say there is no room for you. But I will get you a place on the boat. Free," he ended triumphantly. The boatride to Abu Simbel is a four-hour trip across Lake Nasser—the lake created by the dammed-up river—and it costs thirteen Egyptian pounds (twenty-five American dollars). I looked at Loutfi, trying to gauge the exact meaning of his generosity and the possible consequences of my acceptance. What the hell, I finally thought, the guy's a born hustler. He loves wheeling and dealing.

"Okay, Loutfi," I said. "Great. Get me on the boat."

Abu Simbel is, of course, the two great temples built by Ramses II which were very nearly flooded by the High Dam. They represent a double marvel of engineering: to have built those temples four thousand years ago; to have removed them, piece by piece, from the cliffs in which they were embedded, and then put them back together again in another place on the river. The whole thing is entirely amazing: magic.

The pleasure and excitement one feels looking at Abu Simbel is rare and genuine—and lasts about twenty minutes if luck is with you. Abu Simbel is a place where one should be left to oneself for days on end: to come for a while and go away; to come again when the weather is different; to come for an hour, a moment; to *live* with a bit. Instead, as a tourist, one spends four hours on a boat with a load of boring, noisy Europeans who are "doing" the world; is hustled off for an hour and a half to gaze for a fraction of time at the four enormous statues of Ramses carved out of the cliffs of the Nile and rush beyond them through the vast carved temple rooms built by the boldest Pharaoh of them all for the fierce and dramatic contemplation of life, death, and the deification of man; and then hustled back on the boat. . . . Abu Simbel, for what exactly have you been saved?

When I got back to the hotel Loutfi was waiting. I was tired and wanted to go to my room, but I agreed to have a drink. In the bar Loutfi characterized the tourists for me: "The French are the most interesting. They know the guidebooks backwards and forwards before they ever get here, and they ask questions the guides can never answer. The Americans, they take pictures. The Germans, they like to be like the French because they like to be thorough, but really they also only want to take pictures." (You're not kidding, I thought, remembering the German who nearly pushed me off the boat trying to get a picture of the approach to Abu Simbel.)

In an hour or so I rose from my seat at the bar. "Well," I said, "I'm afraid this is good-bye, Loutfi. I'm dead-tired, I've got to go to bed, and I'm leaving on the morning train for Luxor."

Loutfi stared at me in disbelief. "You can't," he said softly. "You must stay another day. You must. I was planning . . . I was *hoping* . . . we would become friends. Good friends."

"Yes," I said. "That would be nice. But I'm afraid I can't stay."

"*Can't* stay?" he said petulantly. "You mean you don't want to stay."

He was right. Dead right. Don't *want* to stay. Don't want to stay, and don't *have* to stay. There soared up in me the strongest sense of separateness I have ever known. I was free. Free to come, free to go. Free to take the five o'clock train, the ten o'clock train, the morning train, no train. Never in all my wanderings in the United States had I felt it so clearly, so strongly, as here in this moment in Aswan—the perception of choice in this life, the capacity to act on that choice, the willingness to accept the consequences, whatever they be, of action taken—here in Aswan where there were no choices, where life was a caged animal, and alternative action an unknown concept.

"No," I lied happily. "That's not it. I really do have to get back to Cairo. I can't stay any longer."

"You *must*," Loutfi said.

"No," I said. And we just stood there, eying each other. Finally, I said to this Nubian Sammy Glick, "Look, Loutfi, there'll be another trainload of tourists in the morning. Forget it. You win some, you lose others."

The cynical laughter that filled Loutfi's eyes then was distinctly *Egyptian* cynicism. In New York the cynicism would have been lit from within by a brittle admiration for the contest acknowledged; here, it was overlaid with a warmth that was oddly sad and giving-over.

At six o'clock the next morning the train for Luxor pulled out of Aswan with me neatly tucked into a window seat in a half-empty first-class car. The morning was bright and still cool, people bustling about with the energy that would soon fade as the day went on and the heat collected. Just as the train was about to leave the station five young women, laughing and talking, rushed into the car, their arms full of straw baskets and packages of food. They dropped into seats all about me, one of them sitting beside me. She addressed me in Arabic and I replied in English.

"Oh," she said shyly in English. "I am so sorry. Are you English?"

"No, I'm American."

"American! How wonderful. We don't see many Americans here." And she patted her long dark hair self-consciously. She was very pretty, with a wide but slender body, heavy legs and bad skin, dressed in a blue nylon top and a black knee-length skirt. Her friends were all a variation on her theme. They looked like working-class secretaries in New York.

"Are you on a holiday in Upper Egypt?" I asked.

"Oh, no," the young woman demurred. "We are doctors in the public health service. We are all working in a medical unit in a village near Aswan. We have been here one year now. But we have two days of holiday now—we are Copts, it is a Coptic holiday—and we are going to Cairo."

"Is it worth it to make such a long trip for so short a time?"

"Oh, yes!" she blushed. "A few hours in Cairo are worth *anything*."

"Do you hate it here?"

"Oh, no. I do not hate it. I am serving my country. But you know, it is very depressing in Upper Egypt. I think," her eyes flashed mischievously, "it is much nicer to be a doctor in America." I smiled, and then as it was still so very early in the morning we both began to drowse, lying back in our seats, dreaming out the Nile Valley window. . . . Again, the earth-colored villages and the earth-colored people rose up without warning on the horizon, and then quickly were gone, leaving flash imprints on the blue-and-gold morning of a life frozen in time and space: startled to be thus caught, something like Lot's wife turning to salt: caught in the act of humans being transformed into an even more elemental material.

An hour passed, and the young woman beside me blinked sleepily and repeated, "Yes, I think it would be very nice to be a doctor in America."

"Why do you say that?" I roused myself. "There is much change occurring in Egypt. It is exciting to be part of change."

She stared blankly out past me, and once again demurred.

"Yes, there is change in Egypt. Yes, it is good that things should change. But we do not want too much change, you know. Some of the European social habits . . . I think they are very bad. The Egyptian social habits are very solid, you know. It will take much to change this." She smiled: very quietly, very dazzlingly. "And this is good, I think."

I had heard this sentiment expressed a thousand times in Cairo, but now it was as though I were hearing it for the first time. As the bleak villages of Upper Egypt rolled past the window, the words uttered by the young Coptic doctor ceased to be rhetoric and became living communication. Now, I thought, now I see why this country is melancholy instead of excited in the face of change. It is as Farid said: not a single revolutionist in Egypt, not one anarchist ready to plunge into chaos in order to risk the excitement of feeling new life. There is only anxiety, and the dreadful accommodation to anxiety. Only a constant straining backward even as one is dying of need.

From out of nowhere there flew into my mind: Did Nasser grow out of all this?

And six weeks later in Beirut I was thinking the same thing. An American newspaperman, trying to explain why the Lebanese considered the Egyptians effeminate, told me the following story (apocryphal or no, I cannot tell): After the 1967 War Nasser supposedly met with the Algerian president, Houari Boumédienne, and was asked by the Algerian, "How could you have given up so quickly? How could you have ended it all in five days? We fought for years!" And Nasser supposedly said to him, "I saw in my mind the Israeli bombers flying over Cairo. I saw them destroying hospitals and schools, everything it had taken us so long to build, and I saw my people dying by the thousands in the streets, and I could not take upon myself the heaviness of this burden." To which the Algerian supposedly replied, "Then you have no right to include the word 'war' in your vocabulary. You are unable to accept its meaning."

Listening to the newspaperman's story, I was struck by the pity and compassion of Nasser's words—as well as the soft, hopeless capitulation to anxiety. And I remembered the Coptic doctor on the Aswan-Luxor train.

About a hundred and thirty miles north of Aswan, Luxor is Thebes—once the capital of ancient Egypt—and here on both banks of the Nile lie some of Egypt's richest deposits of Pharaonic life. Here are gigantic temple ruins; the famous tombs of the kings, queens and nobles excavated out of mountains of desert stone only some fifty years ago; the wildest and most extravagant assortment of sphinxes, columns, monuments, statues, wall drawings, all preserved for more than four thousand years. At the same time that Luxor is a ruin of ancient glory, it is also a Nubian village, a Moslem town, a modern Egyptian eyesore.

Luxor lies on a part of the Nile that bends in broad, sweeping, snaky turns as far as the eye can see; on either side of the river the ever-present palms, the low sycamores, the palm-trunk trees with long hanging mosses that lean in green and tender silence toward the river whose banks here are steep and even, and whose waters are a highway of shining stillness on a bright clear day, or "liquid tin" (as Lady Duff Gordon once described the Nile) on a burning hot one. Luxor has the appearance of land that has not changed for thousands of years. For centuries—through tribal wars and Arab conquest and European occupation—men and women have come here to look at what the Pharaohs looked at, and now I, too, was standing here looking at what the Pharaohs looked at.

The riverfront of the village is linked from one end to the other by the great hotels that the British built in the nineteenth century when Luxor was a British watering place, and people like the doomed Lady Gordon (who died here of the consumption she had been fleeing, falling into genuine love with the Egyptians before she did so) were always passing through Egypt. Standing on the spacious terraces of the Winter Palace and the Savoy, one feels again the power of Victorian assurance in the desert, but seen within the context of the tiny sprawl of Luxor today, those English hotels—still widely in use—only add to the angry confusion of disparate elements that mark this historical bit of Upper Egypt.

In the direct center of the village stands Luxor Temple, built right on the river by many Pharaohs, each in their turn. In front of the temple stands a large and very pretty village green with stone benches, bright flowers, two summerhouse cafés. To the side of the temple and the square stands the town's large and prosperous-looking mosque, its minarets rising in yellow sandstone arabesque directly into the brilliant blue sky. Behind all this, the streets of Luxor are grouped in a dreadful peasant slum, and here for the first time I felt unrelieved depression gazing on Egypt's poverty. There is a desperate lack of variety to the poverty here, a kind of stupor of simplicity, an aimlessness that covers the people in a thick expressionless haze: fly-ridden children, women in black staring in hovel doorways, men somnolent on donkeys, listless peanut vendors, store goods covered with silent dust. And at the end of all this, a mile and a half out of town, the grandeur of Karnak Temple, one of the greatest temples ever built by the ancient Egyptians.

That first day in Luxor I decided to walk out along the river to Karnak Temple. In Luxor it was possible to avoid tours. I simply purchased a collective ticket to the monuments, and went on my way alone. As I walked, the open horse-drawn carriages of Luxor that cater to the tourists (one of the charms of the village is no cars) trotted beside me, their drivers unable to believe that I preferred to walk. Beside me marched a parade of Luxor's townsfolk: children riding donkeys, boys with schoolbooks under their arms, women with water jars on their heads, soldiers off a lone Army truck. My presence was noted by every man and boy—all calling, joking, inquiring, "You speak English? *Parlez-vous français? Sprechen Sie Deutsch?*—while the women hung back, wide-eyed, openly staring at me beneath their water jars, with their children dragging at their skirts. And over us, like a tremendous global cloak, the sun burned down, its heat dense and airless, enclosing us all in a kind of stifling membrane that seemed always on the verge of some fatal thickening. . . .

Suddenly, the sun disappeared and a wind off the river began to rise. In a split second the wind became furious and began to carry sand up off the riverbanks; in another few minutes I realized I was in a sandstorm. The wind and sand flew with increasing speed, the sky darkened, people began to appear as through a heavy mist; I began to bend forward against my will, and then I was almost flying along. I pushed myself toward a big tree and held on with my arms around it, hoping to beat the storm there. Sand flew into my hair, my eyes, my nostrils, filled up the creases in my skin and the open pores on my face. The river, the trees, the land, the sky all lost their original colors and became a universal brownish-gray, seen through a screen of sand; a haze of weather that had worked a magical transformation, aging the world a thousand years before my eyes, deepening the sadness and the loveliness of Luxor, which had endured.

As quickly as it had begun, the storm now ended. The wind stopped and the sand began to drift to the ground. At that instant I looked down into the river below me and I saw a naked boy of perhaps sixteen or eighteen emerging from the river. He moved slowly, as though he were lost in thought, head down, neck bent forward, his skin shining with wet, his hair black and matted. Something in the sight of that boy went right to the center of me, and I felt at the same moment both oppressed and elated. I am tempted to say he looked as though he had stepped from a Pharaonic drawing, but that really wasn't true, for surely he was his very own present self; but there was in the slow, thoughtful way he stepped from the river a sense of compressed time and inherited movement. His naked body, exposed to the elements, seemed unbearably vulnerable in its competition with air, water, and earth; and yet, strength and beauty and a strange courage that seemed to incorporate and transcend his vulnerability washed across his neck, his shoulders, his young back. Stepping out of that ancient water onto that ancient land, into that thick sandy haze, with all the poverty and beauty of Luxor in and around him, he seemed at that moment to embody the calm of hopelessness, a depth of *being* in a place where people had learned to submit to timelessness and destiny without ceasing to be human. He seemed a figure in a dream, and I couldn't be sure whose dream it was.

When I finally got to Karnak I hated it. It was a jungle of stone filled to overflowing with masses of sphinxes and statues and columns and obelisks, hieroglyphics and symbolic drawings, all for the greater glory of Ramses II and Seti I and six or eight others, all seeming to cover nearly an acre of ground. One wandered and wandered in this delirium of detailed beauty and massive assertion, and one could just imagine what a canyon of stone it had been when all its towering columns had been standing whole. The sheer obsessiveness of it made me ill—or was it the heat from which I was nearly fainting?—and then when I got lost I began to feel frightened. (As it happened, that day I kept missing one group of tourists after another and found myself alone nearly everywhere I went.)

I kept walking rapidly toward open space and, gratefully, I soon found myself out in an open stretch of the temple near the Sacred Lake, approaching a tiny group of tables and chairs set out near the lake. From a shack near the tables and chairs there unexpectedly whirled something that for a moment looked like a specter. It was a boy of perhaps twelve in a *gelabya*, tall and thin, very black, and with beautiful narrow Pharaonic features. He seemed wildly glad to see a potential customer and beckoned me toward the shack. As I drew closer I said, "Do you speak English? May I have a glass of water?"

"English! English!" he cried, dancing up and down in front of me. "Yes, yes. Come in, come in. Coca-Cola? You have Coca-Cola? Is gift. You no pay. You American? American? Ah, American good. Russian no good."

I didn't know what to say to all this, and was too tired to care much, so I laughed and nodded. Once inside the shack he suddenly pushed me up against the wall, chanting, "American good. American good. Wonderful people. Wonderful people," and tried to kiss me. I was so startled that all I could think to say, as I pushed his frail body from me, was, "How *old* are you?" He backed off, blinked at me, and said, "Twenty years."

Salah, the tourist guide at my hotel, also looked ten years younger than his twenty-five years (half the undernourished population of Luxor turned out to share this unhappy aberration), and he also loved Americans.

Within thirty minutes of our meeting Salah and I had established an undying friendship—the usual proposition in Egypt begins with "We are really good friends. *Good* friends"—and he was cementing it with his Confessions of a Nubian Tourist Guide, which consisted mainly of the distinctive ways in which French girls made love, and German girls and Danish, and English, and Canadian (Canadian???), and Italian, and Dutch, and Lebanese, and of course, American.

"But these American girls," Salah said thoughtfully, "I think they are all crazy. Yes, Vivi-yaan?"

"Why do you say that, Salah?" I asked politely.

"Well," Salah warmed to his subject, "last year I had one. She was good girl, liked love very much, very, how you say, *active.* One night she wake me up at one o'clock in the morning. Salah, she say, the moon is full, and I want to go to Karnak. Barbara, I say, we make love all day, I am *tired.* No, she say, we must go. And she begin to kick me and pull my hair and pull on my trousers. She must go to Karnak Temple and make love on one of the stone coffins in the moonlight. And she burns this *incense*, and she has a drum she beats. And you know, Vivi-yaan? We do it. She give me no peace until we do it. Two o'clock in the morning I am making love in Karnak Temple. I was scared! Crazy. She was crazy."

Salah shook his head slowly, concentrating on the memory of Barbara. "She was from Ohio," he said. "They are all like that from Ohio?"

The next morning I crossed the Nile from the East Bank to the West on a ferry boat that services the town. There I hired a taxi and drove through the blazing harshness of the Valley of the Kings and Queens, visiting the tombs of the Pharaohs, Queens, and nobles of the Middle Kingdom of old Egypt. This valley was once the ancient Theban necropolis, and here the power of the land in conjunction with its human homage to death was overwhelming. For here, we had moved miles into the desert away from the river, and the land rose up into small mountains of stark sandstone, bleak and glaring in the sun, enclosing and remote, entirely unyielding, entirely without interest in human solace. This was the true desert beyond the influence of the Nile, and here the ancient Egyptians made their City of the Dead. Here they cut tombs deep into the living sand rock, filled them with the treasure of their accumulating lives, tenderly laid their mummified leaders, and sealed the whole up, none of it to be uncovered until 1922 when a British archaeologist named Howard Carter ("Mr. Carter," as the Egyptian guides all call him) spent five obsessed years digging the tombs out of the tons of sandstone beneath which they had long been buried, and was rewarded with the glories of King Tutankhamen's famous entombed wealth, as well as innumerable, almost equally dazzling, earth-enclosed, riches-filled burial places.

The Valley of the Kings is entirely a tourist enterprise now, carefully run and supervised by the government. The tombs are all neatly numbered, carefully railed in, and surrounded by guides, guards and sellers of "antiques." Surrounded isn't the word. They *swarm*, and they pick at you like human flies, and you hate them, and you hate yourself. And all this going on beneath the bleaching, glaring sun in the midst of this godforsaken desert that dries up the energy of the foreigner and embalms the spirit of the native, in plain view of the remains of a people who narrowed their eyes against the sand and haze and shimmer, and grew powerful in their incomparable defiance.

I tramped on and on, from tomb to temple, from temple to monument, in and out of the taxi, moving deeper and deeper into the desert, from one railed-off space to another, from one group of guides and tourists to another, growing exhausted rather than exhilarated. Late in the afternoon I visited the tombs of the nobles, those small jewels set in this crown of kingly death. One of the tombs was located at the edge of one of the innumerable miserable villages that dot this entire valley, and as I approached the tomb, entirely alone this time, there darted from the village a man selling genuine antique mummy beads. They were very pretty and for the first time I decided to buy; that is, I took a deep breath and started to bargain. As I stood there, steadily offering two pounds less than the man was asking, a little girl began tugging at my skirt, begging for a piastre. I looked down at her—my first mistake—standing there in the wretched dust and heat, a thin little thing in prophetic black rags, barefoot and looking painfully old. She pulled and pulled at me, whining dreadfully, and at last I reached for my purse. As though at a signal, eight or ten more like her rushed from nowhere and surrounded me, all pulling at me from every side imaginable, their fingers scratching feebly at my arms and sides and neck. Panic rose in me and instinctively my hands flew to protect my face. I had the distinct impression that my entire body was being outlined by the clawing motions of the children, and I felt like some great helpless Gulliver overcome by the Lilliputians. I screamed. The children backed off and I fled, stumbling back up the dusty path to the waiting taxi. Twenty minutes later I dropped, exhausted, onto a seat on the ferry and within an hour I was back in the square in Luxor.

That night I did not leave my hotel. I took a shower when it began to grow dark and sat, clean and wet-haired, on the small balcony of my room, watching and smelling and listening to Luxor as night overtook the town. From this balcony I looked directly onto Luxor Temple and the town mosque, standing there side by side in the brilliant, vanishing light. I had wandered briefly through Luxor Temple in the morning and at one point had come upon a long row of sphinxes that ended at the wall of the mosque. I knew that these sphinxes had once formed an avenue that ran the entire three or four miles from Luxor Temple to Karnak Temple. Looking at the broken-off avenue of sphinxes in the morning I had been struck by the realization that the Pharaohs had built their temples and monuments to stand within the sweeping spaces of their limitless world, that the land and river and sky open to them had been part of their architecture, and now, broken off and hemmed in by Moslem conquest and modern squalor, entirely out of their element, the temples often seemed ugly, awkward, and irrelevant. But that night, on the balcony of my room, the temple and the mosque together seemed to have another meaning.

In Cairo, as everywhere else in the Moslem world, the muezzins send the beckoning sound of the Koran out into the air five times a day to call in the faithful. However, in Cairo, to hear it you must really be listening for it, as the noise of the city is so deafening, so various, so continuous that one hardly ever is able to distinguish the religious sound from all the other sounds that assault the Cairo airwaves. But in Luxor I had been continually aware of the distinctly separate sound of the religious chanting; perhaps, indeed, some of the sound *had* rubbed off on me in Cairo, creating without my conscious consent a residue of response in a newly educated ear. Whatever. That night on the balcony, as the Luxor sky streaked soft red, then soft black, and the velvet air of the Upper Nile Valley night washed away the dust and exhaustion of the day, the muezzin's call rose in a long thin whine, piercing the heart of the encircling world, speaking with painful clarity. It was the aching sound of a people who have lived close to the stolid earth and have eaten dust; the sound of men who are acknowledging the meanness of their passions, the frailty of their decisions, the cynicism of their wisdom, the contradiction between matter and spirit that runs rampant, like a blood disease, through the entire history of their efforts. It was a sound that seemed older than time and politics, a sound that felt the pity of life so deeply that its soul turned away from chaos, embarrassed to death by violence.

"All, all, we acknowledge all, O Allah," the muezzin keened. "We understand everything. We are beyond bitterness, almost we are beyond pain, and yes, still we are asking for compassion. We do not beg and we do not demand. We simply ask: Compassion, O Allah."

The sound of the muezzin floated through the ruins of the ancient temple built by men who had asserted the nobility of their being, and had decided they were more like gods than like men, looking to the sun rather than to the earth to identify the sources of reward and punishment, living a life of magnificent arrogance, giving no quarter and asking none in return.

The two parts of schizophrenic human destiny had met, here in Pharaonic-Moslem Egypt: not warring, not merging, only standing together at the edge.

Oh, it was good to be back in Cairo!

The men walking arm in arm, that dark, dancing, cleaving together . . . the whole country seeming, sometimes, to bend deeply into itself in a long embrace that curves backward, and projects forward, in time.

And Groppi's dark tearoom where thin middle-class Egyptian women drink lemonade while they work their mysterious eye-art on thin middle-class Egyptian men (Egyptian women being renowned for the sexual expertise with which they make their eyes operate), and fat middle-class Egyptian women eat ice cream topped with *marron glacé* and whipped cream, while their husbands look morosely over their black coffees at the lemonade on the next little round table.

And Lappa's, across the circle from Groppi's, all open white space and sunlight, the image of a French *pâtisserie*, filled with thin young men in tight shirts and pants, bobbing, smoking, talking, flirting.

And beyond the central squares the drab, dusty sameness of the endless Cairo streets: the narrow alleys and wide avenues alive with medieval poverty and that anxious, lurching, driven activity.

And along the Nile the armies of beggars now that it is warm, and whole families of peasants camped on the grassy islands that border the Corniche.

And out in Heliopolis scarlet and purple blossoms flaming to life in spring gardens.

And gnarled old men leaping around in front of me as I hail a taxi, breaking my heart, trying my patience, extracting a dull recognition from me as they put one hand on the door, and hold the other one out for three piastres.

I had missed it all. I could hardly believe it. I had missed *Cairo*. I was back from the burning land. Back from the harsh, brilliant, primeval South. Back in the city. Back where I belonged.

Debbie Lindner sat in Lappa's at ten in the morning with a cup of black espresso in front of her. She twisted her hands nervously on the table, and her face looked more American gamin than ever. I felt a guilty twinge: I didn't like this woman. Try as I might, I didn't like her. There was an American female hysteria in her I knew so well, so well . . . one that aroused no sympathy in me at all. ("A'tall," as the British Egyptians said.)

"Did you have a good time in Upper Egypt?" Debbie asked nervously.

"Yes."

"Isn't it marvelous? I mean, there's nothing in the world like it."

"Yes."

"Look, I'm sorry to lay my problems on you, but there isn't another American woman I know here, and I feel I have to talk about this to an American, and besides you know Farid."

"Farid?"

"Yes. It's incredible, what's happened. Incredible. I feel I'm going mad. I don't know what to make of it all."

"What's wrong?"

"Well, it all started almost the day after you left. His wife came from Alexandria. She's been staying at the *pension* with him. No sooner does she come than he stops talking to me. The first night she was there he passed me in the hall *as though I wasn't there*. The next morning, before she was up, he slipped a note under my door. The note said I should say nothing to him at the *pension*, but I should come to his office that afternoon. I was *furious*. I stormed into his office, yelling and screaming what the hell was going on, weren't we friends, didn't our friendship mean anything to him? He said yes, it meant a great deal to him, but that his wife was jealous and if she knew that we were seeing each other like this there would be a perfectly dreadful scene."

"Doesn't his wife stay only a few days when she comes to Cairo?"

"Ordinarily, yes! But *this* time she has remained. And he will *not* talk to me while she's here. . . . He slips me notes. . . . I go to the office. . . ."

I stared at her. What on *earth* was she saying? And then she said it.

"I think I want him," Debbie whispered, her eyes large, frightened, excited. "I'm going mad! Mad! He's an elephant! He's old enough to be my father! If his wife hadn't come none of this would ever have happened! . . . What will I *do*?"

Then came her kicker: "Farid's going crazy, too. He says he'll leave Egypt, he'll divorce his wife, and come to Paris with me. My God! It's all so *insane*. I don't want to be a home-wrecker. And what will he do in Paris? *Leave* Egypt? It's madness, I tell you, madness."

Today was *Chamonisimme*, Egypt's May Day, and the entire Hamamsy clan—accompanied by their friends and guests—went out to Salah's farm for a traditional holiday picnic, arriving in half a dozen cars, loaded down with enough food to feed a battalion. Soad and I drove out with Gasbia's youngest daughter on both our laps in the back of a Volkswagen station wagon driven by one of the teachers from Nahed's German school. Gasbia seemed to have invited the entire faculty: once out there I felt surrounded by Germans.

But it was the kind of a day, and the kind of a family gathering, in which you had only to wander off to another group if you didn't like the one you were with. Scattered all about the farm were Amr and his wife and son and a group of friends under the arbor; Monir and his wife and daughter Aischa on the roof of the pumphouse; Salah and a group of friends somewhere out in the beanfields; Leila and the Doctor and their daughters and neighbors not far from Soad's brood; Magdi and his Naha and Fawzy and Mona Amr across a small irrigation ditch near the pumphouse; each group with its own fire, its own food, its own entertainment. People wandered from one group to another all day long, as though at an amusement park. The culmination of the day's raucous laughter came when all the young men dragged all the young women, shrieking, toward the wide channel of water behind the pumphouse and swung them out, hammock-fashion, over the water and then, plop! I couldn't believe they would do it to me, too—but they did.

Food, as always, was the main event. No sooner did people land on their patch of sandy ground than out came the coal, the matches, the portable grills and fires were begun to broil the lamb, chicken and beef that was now marinating in beds of onions, tomatoes and lime juice inside dozens of hampers. Meanwhile, coffee, bread, cheese, boiled eggs and slices of fruitcake were passed about in abundance to ward off the hunger pangs that were sure to attack before the next two or three hours had passed, while coffee was dispensed from glass jars of all sizes, and tea was continuously being brewed by Salah's "boys."

Soad hugged me over and over again, in between her tireless serving, saying, "Vivian! I have not seen you in so long a time! What a bad daughter you are!"

But Naha snubbed me openly, and Magdi seemed to look right through me, cold and polite as though he had never seen me before.

The day passed from the morning dew glistening upon the green and gold of Salah's fruits and vegetables standing in the desert to the brilliant heat of shimmering afternoon. Everyone ate and drank and laughed and sang songs, and the Hamamsys let down their hair with gusto: Ibrahim blinked like a sleepy bear, Gasbia shrieked like a squealing pig, Soad nodded and laughed like a wise peasant mother, Leila fingered her blond wig nervously, the Doctor sat smiling as though his teeth were made of wood and his eyeballs vacant behind his glinting glasses, and Monir told dirty jokes, his wide sensuous mouth curving back in enormous appetite over his sixty-four-year-old teeth while the purple veins on his nose gathered as his nostrils flared. Beside me, on a stool not far from Soad's fire, Fawzy Amr said calmly of Monir: "With that man love is rape."

I clung to Fawzy all day long. Faithful to Magdi, the fat, beady-eyed little man who loved books nevertheless managed to remain my friend, assuaging with his keenly feeling attentions the terrible sense of outsideness that began to afflict me no sooner than Magdi allowed his eyes to rest, expressionless, upon me a moment, and then moved wordlessly away.

"I feel such a fool," I said recklessly, as Fawzy took my arm and led me away from the circles of family fire toward the open fields.

"Why, madam?" said Fawzy, immediately revealing his own distress. "Why a fool? Why should a beautiful, talented woman like yourself ever feel a fool? Why, madam? Why?"

"Magdi and I were friends," I said weakly. "I feel very foolish now, being here. He acts as though we have never known each other. And I feel a fool. A fool!"

Fawzy stopped in the midst of the glinting fields, and cast a baleful eye on me.

"Perhaps you *are* a fool," he said sternly. "Do you not realize there are men who when they cannot win the prize they simply turn their backs on it and pretend it does not exist? You are not the fool. *He* is the fool."

"No, I don't believe that, Fawzy. He has the strength to order his life as I do not. He holds himself together while I fall apart." I took his arm and started off again, walking through the sandy rows toward the tall thin mossy trees swaying hopelessly on the horizon.

"Is that strength? My dear Vivian, I would have expected better of you. Strength! The strength of one who defeats emotion by cutting it out of himself! The strength of one who puts blinders on and says, 'Only this which I choose to see is the real world. The rest does not exist.' "

"Yes," I cried. "That *is* strength. Better that than to bleat and cry and *need*. Better that than to feel rejection like a wound in the gut, and depression rolling in like fog. Oh yes! Better that. Don't you see, Fawzy? I feel *weak*. And helpless. All I *see* does not give me the strength to *act*."

"My dear Vivian, you put me in mind of Nietzsche who positively *enjoyed* pain. You have every dimension, every element, every necessary characteristic to enjoy life, and yet you are depressed. You want to seem *important* so you choose to be depressed. Of course, of course. Why else would you allow a circumstance to develop in your life that is certain to end in failure? Why else would you choose by appearances when you know all is useless?"

"But the truth is . . ."

"The truth! The truth! Man is a poor defective creature, hm-m-m? hm-m-m? He makes, therefore, poor defective symbols and crucifies himself on them!"

Fawzy mopped his sweating forehead and we walked on in the afternoon heat. He stopped again. His hands flailed out at the air, and his voice broke with agitation.

"I know very well the men you speak of. The Magdis and their sexual power. I know very well the value of their strength. And mine is greater! I have the light of understanding! Yes, they have the power of perseverance and concentration. But, my understanding is greater, and my feelings are sharper and deeper, yes. . . ."

And we stood there in the desert fields, the fat foolish Egyptian Vanya and the depressed nervous American Natasha, our eyes clinging together, reassurance coursing through our veins like new wine. Ah! The world was a cruel place and the sources of power lay far beyond us, but we were a better breed for all that. Yes, yes. Ah yes! *We* were what was worth saving in this beastly universe, and only we, each for the other, could know. . . .

From across the fields I saw Soad waving her arms in our direction and calling, "Vivi-yaaaan! Vivi-yaaaan! Come and eat! Come and eat!"

Fawzy rolled his eyes to the blue cloudless skies and slapped his thigh. "Food! Always it is food! Always it is come and eat. It never occurs to them that there are parts of the being that are not fed with lamb and rice. Ach! We are a gross people, my dear. A gross people!"

For more than an hour the Hamamsys—along with their infinitely more sensitive guests—gorged themselves on coal-roasted lamb and chicken and beef; on salad without end; on bread and vegetables and fruits and cheeses; on halvah and baklava and "European" cake; on coffee and tea and orange juice and Coca-Cola; and all of it tasting magnificent, laced as it was with sun and sky and desert wind and heat.

When the sun began to set everything was packed up and the families all returned to the cars they had left some eight hours before. This time Soad and I climbed into the back of Ibrahim's Volkswagen, with the three children tumbling all over us now, instead of only little Amal.

"Do you know the Naha?" Soad asked casually, as we drove out of the farm. "The Captain's lady? Ah, things are changing! When I was a girl one did not simply appear at our family gatherings with a young woman, *totally unexplained*. Ah, but things are not as they were, *yani*, when I was a girl. And thank God they are not!" She held her little granddaughter close to her, and shook with girlish laughter.

"Yes, I know Naha," I said. "She used to come to the flat in Garden City when I was there."

"She seems a decent girl," Soad said cautiously, looking out the window as she spoke.

"Yes, I am sure she is," I said. "Why? What do you think of her, Soad? How does she strike you?"

"Young," she said curtly. "Very young. And too clever by far in woman's ways."

"What do you mean?" I said, astonished.

"She will get him," Soad said.

"Oh no, Soad! Magdi *told* me he would never marry her. They are just friends for now."

"She will get him," Soad insisted. "Look how she sticks like honey to him. She will get him. She will make him think he is everything to her, and she will get him." She stared off, lost for a moment in that private distance of hers. Then she turned angrily to me. "Men are stupid! So stupid! And especially Egyptian men. All a woman has to do is know his weak spots. And then she has him." (Soad made a cup of her right hand and tapped its center with her left forefinger.) "Right here. She has him right here. You know, Egyptian men are like babies. They must have a woman. They cannot live without one. It is their nature. . . . And they must believe they are the master. . . . So she will get him. Watch. You will see."

An hour later I was dropped in front of the house on Mohammed Sidki Street, and the exhausting workers' holiday was at an end.

Farid sat behind his desk at *Al Kahira* holding court. His office was a dingy shuttered square through which, starting at ten in the morning and ending at seven or eight in the evening, there trooped an endless parade of people. They came from the offices of *Al Kahira* all around Farid's office, as well as from the offices of all the other newspapers and magazines to which this building, one of the three largest government-owned publishing houses in Cairo, gave a curious kind of protection. And they came for all sorts of reasons: reporters came—flushed, angry, wheedling—to argue with the managing editor over their stories; photographers came to insist that this, that or the other be done with their pictures; secretaries came to complain about their work load; the house doctor came to get away from his office; writers came to explain some insanely complicated circumstance that was preventing them from taking an assignment abroad; and friends came—businessmen, lawyers, actors, critics, minor politicians—to smoke a cigarette, drink a cup of coffee and unload their troubles or their entertainments, or often both at the same time.

I sat in the chair beside Farid's desk and watched the stream of demanding, cajoling, amusing, agitated Egyptians filing past the heavily-breathing, chain-smoking, harassed editor whom Debbie Lindner had recently described in such strange terms. As each one came in Farid would say, "You must meet my American friend, Miss Vivian. She is a journalist from New York. She needs to talk to someone like you." And the person in question would struggle to contain his or her agitation or distraction, and bend most courteously and often, even enthusiastically, over my hand, shaking it vigorously and saying, "Yes, yes, we must see one another."

At two o'clock Farid rose from his desk and prepared to leave for lunch; he would return again at five o'clock and continue to work until eight o'clock (the only time he got anything done, he said).

"My dear Vivian, I feel terrible, you are only just back from Upper Egypt, and I have no time for you . . . but this circumstance will not last long. It is only for the next week or so. You see, aside from my work here at *Al Kahira*, which as you can see demands my constant attention . . . I am suddenly involved in Debbie's work."

"Oh? How is that?"

Farid's eyes looked puzzled behind his thick glasses, and a smile of vague embarrassment played on his mouth. He shook his head and passed his hand through his hair. "I don't really know how it all became so complicated." He laughed. "But it seems now that Debbie finds me absolutely indispensable to her work, and I have promised to give it my full attention in the next week or so. So, whenever I am not here I will be trapped reading her manuscript, getting books for her, offering my criticism, and so on and so on. . . ."

"I see. Well, don't give me another thought, Farid. Whenever you are ready, I'll be here. You owe me nothing, and really I expect nothing. So whatever you can give me of your time or your help is gravy."

"Gravy? Is that not a mixture of flour and juices to be served with meat?"

"Yes," I laughed. "It is. It's also an idiom, meaning something extra, something over and above the necessities or expectations of life."

"You know, you really *are* a woman. This Debbie, she is such a child! Such a child!"

One of them was lying outright. Which one? My guess was Debbie.

On the other side of the Nile, on the bank that faces Gezira Island, adjoining Giza, is a section of Cairo called Aguza. Here, in a five-room flat filled with ornate molding and French provincial furniture, lives Sohair Kamel, an upper-middle-class Egyptian woman who divorced her husband many years ago. Sohair's position is a rarity in Egypt, even within her class—as, according to Moslem law, a woman has absolutely no right in the matter of divorce. An Egyptian woman may be informed that her husband is divorcing her through a letter that arrives in the mail, but she herself is forbidden to petition for divorce. She may be thrown out of the house with only the clothes she is standing up in, but never can she lock the door on her husband. She may (and often does) lose her children outright to her husband and/or his family, but never as long as they both live may she veto her husband's decisions in the matter of raising the children. While, of course, life in Cairo is far more sophisticated than the bare law would indicate—and thousands of women are divorced and raising their children and receiving child support and aid and comfort of all sorts from friendly though departed husbands—still it is rare for a woman to seek and obtain divorce, much less to do so in the manner in which Sohair did it. But then again, Sohair herself is rare. As is Soad. As were the movie stars I met so many months ago. In a country where women's lives are lived as though under water, these few are striking: for, unexpectedly and quite suddenly, it is as if they have left their comfortably submerged sisters, and have dived even deeper in order to shoot with speed and power to the surface, gulping the air so long denied them.

"I come from the village," Sohair says, pulling her long handsome legs up under her as she sits on the small couch in her foyer-salon. "We raised cotton. My father was a rich man, a very rich man. But he wore the *gelabya* all his life, and his peasants worshipped him. My father loved me very much. Very much. When I was a very little girl he said to me, 'Do not say to yourself I am so-and-so's daughter. That will not help you to explain your life to you. You must work hard to understand yourself, and then you must *be* that self.'

"My mother, she was a bad woman. Mean, bitter, envious of me. Now, she is very religious. She wears the white *milayeh* and she prays all day long. She wanted me to marry my uncle Esan. He was much older than me, already an officer in the Army. I was fourteen. I hated him. My mother said, 'She must marry him.' My brother said, 'She must marry him.' My father said, 'No. She is not for him.'

"But when I was sixteen my father died. And within the year they made me marry Esan."

The servant, a young girl with a long braid down her back and bare feet, has entered the room bearing a large silver tea tray. Sohair swings her legs to the floor and prepares to serve tea. She is a tall, large woman of thirty-five, handsome, with nothing youthful in her bearing, her face a striking mixture of the dark, downward-turning Moslem features and the queenliness of the Pharaonic caste. Her long nose draws a bead on the generous mouth that curves contemptuously, as she leans back in her seat, balancing her teacup on the pedestal she makes of her arm and hand, raises her beautiful black eyes, and says, "He was a *terrible* man. Selfish, stupid, degenerate. He never loved me, but he insisted that I love *him*. He would *torment* me, and then he would fly into a rage because I was afraid of him. One day when I was nearly twenty-one he looked into my face and he saw that I hated him. *Hated* him! And he grew afraid. And when he saw that *I* saw he was afraid he knew he was no longer master in that house. From that day on he became systematically cruel to me. He would hit me and scream, '*I* am the master here!' And I would say nothing. Nothing. I would only stare into his eyes, and he saw that if the hate could flow out of me it would drown him.

"We were living in Alexandria. I was twenty-two. I had the two children already. My house was filled with my wedding furniture, with crystal and china and fine linen that my family had given us. One day we all came to Cairo for a two-day visit. I dressed myself and the children and took only enough with me for the two days. I took nothing else. I left everything behind me. I never saw that house again.

"We arrived at Cairo and we stayed with my husband's sister. In the afternoon of the first day I said, 'Let us go to my brother.' I knew that if *I* suggested going he would not go. 'No,' he said, 'I do not wish to go to your brother.' 'Surely, you will not deny me a short visit to my brother?' I said. 'He has not seen the children in a year.' 'No,' he said, 'I will not deny you this. You may go to your brother. But you must return to this house at six o'clock this evening.'

"I went to my brother, and I told him he must help me. He was surprised, but he saw that I would throw myself in the river if he did not help me. . . . At seven o'clock Esan called my brother's house. 'When are you coming back?' he said. 'Never,' I said.

"That was thirteen years ago," Sohair continues merrily, looking fondly at her fifteen-year-old daughter Za-Za. "And, *yani*, we have done very well by ourselves, have we not, my Za-Za?"

Of course, Sohair can never remarry, or Esan would definitely take her daughter and her sixteen-year-old son away from her; as it is, Sohair says, he has been content to let her raise the children entirely alone with absolutely no help, or interference, while he has steadily degenerated over the years, living off his military pension, smoking hashish four or five times a week, sitting in Lappa's every evening, doing God knows what to satisfy his crude sexual tastes.

Sohair Kamel is Debbie Lindner's friend. We have come here this evening, Debbie and I, at Sohair's invitation, to discuss this "pig of a married man" who is trying to "get something for nothing" from Debbie. That's Farid as Sohair sees him.

"No, no," Debbie cries distractedly. "It's not like that at all!" But, of course, she has already supplied Sohair with the perspective that allows the experienced Eygptian woman to close her eyes, put up her hand and say, "Debbie, please. They are all animals. Especially Egyptians. Especially *married* Egyptians. There is only one thing they want. No matter *what* they say. And when they get it, finished."

I am mystified, upset, slightly sad; I begin to fear that perhaps Debbie is describing things between herself and Farid exactly as they really are. This afternoon, in my apartment, she paced the floor, flinging herself nervously down on the couch, then up onto her feet again, crying all the while, "I am mad! Utterly mad! What am I *doing*? He says he will leave everything and come to Paris. How can I let him do that? It's impossible! I don't even know if I love him! The man's an elephant! And yet." She leaned forward from the couch, her eyes glittering. "He's *magnetic*!" she cried. "The man's got a goddamn magnet inside him. But oh God!" She wrung her hands. "He's still passing me *notes*. And I can still only see him in his office. It's insane! Insane! I feel I am going mad."

To this moment Farid has said not a word to substantiate Debbie's tale of growing passion between herself and the managing editor of *Al Kahira*. But each meeting with the confused young American graduate student, whose words are consistently frantic, leaves me feeling: Maybe . . . ?

And now tonight, at Sohair's, we have become three women instead of two dealing with the stubborn "reality" of Farid's strange but indisputably guilty involvement with Debbie. The upshot is: Debbie runs around wringing her hands, Sohair smokes cigarettes and calmly announces Farid should be castrated, and I play mediator with no appetite at all for the game.

At ten o'clock I am weary and begin to suggest leaving. As I move forward in my seat to collect my purse and my cigarettes, the doorbell rings and the little servant girl is peering through the frosted-glass opening in the grilled front door. A broad smile covers her amazingly flirtatious thirteen-year-old face (Sohair's eyes roll to the ceiling: What troubles I have with this one!), and she flings the door open to admit a very slim young man with receding hair and a face of startling sensitivity.

"Nabil," cries Sohair. "When did you arrive?"

"A few hours ago," the young man says in a quiet, musical voice that is the absolute reflection of his face.

"My cousin, Dr. Nabil Kamel," Sohair says, turning to me and Debbie. "Meet two Americans, Nabil."

Dr. Nabil Kamel pulls up a chair and joins the circle of women, offering us all a cigarette from his package. We each accept a king-size Cleopatra, and the young man lights each one in turn with a black-and-silver lighter drawn from the pocket of his dark brown suit jacket. I settle back in my chair.

"Are you a medical doctor?" I ask.

"Yes," Nabil Kamel answers, "I am. A specialist in blood diseases. But now," he shrugs his narrow shoulders slightly, "I am simply an Army doctor, exiled from my beloved Cairo most of the time, treating sprained backs and sore feet and stomach flu out in the desert. I fear that by the time we see actual combat with the Israelis I will have forgotten even the meaning of the words 'blood diseases.' "

The young doctor leans fully toward me as he speaks: a thin, brooding face; very smooth skin; luminous intelligent eyes; a sensitivity in the face so fine that the eyes seem almost to strain as they rest intently on the face of the person being addressed; aristocratic—an aristocracy of the spirit—is the only word for Nabil Kamel.

We speak for two hours or more, falling oddly into an idiotic conversation about women's liberation: me defending, Debbie attacking ("I *like* being feminine"), Sohair nodding wisely, and the doctor interrogating. The doctor is more conservative than Debbie in his argument against the liberation of women as I have defined it, but clearly more intelligent than my compatriot. He reverts continually to the authority of "nature," speaking in eloquent, rather wistful terms of the integrated parts of the community, of man's need to be at one with his world, to live within a context and to fulfill the functions of happiness within that context. He breaks off suddenly to ask with some intensity if I believe in God.

His arguments are absurd to me, and yet something elemental in his tone, some coded message in the straining hazel points within his black-brown eyes, some communication in the smooth skin, some perception in that sensitive face belies the meaning of his actual words and says to me: We are friends, you and I, not enemies. We are utterly human together, you and I. We are bound in recognitions.

I am drawn to Dr. Nabil Kamel and later—when we have left Sohair's house together, and together we have dropped Debbie at her *pension*, and he turns to me in the darkened taxi—I see that he is drawn to me also.

"No," I shake my head in answer to his unspoken question. "We cannot go to my flat."

"Let's have a coffee at the Hilton then," the thirty-two-year-old doctor of blood diseases says softly.

At one o'clock in the morning Nabil Kamel and I sit in the golden Formica quiet of the Hilton café. Not far from us sits a noisy group of Lebanese men and women.

"They are a vulgar lot," says Nabil, his narrow face poised and aristocratic. He laughs. "But they enjoy life. More, I am afraid, than we Egyptians can."

The doctor asks me many careful questions about myself, noting that although he speaks English he cannot infer as many things about me as he could with only a very few words between us in Arabic. His perception makes me melancholy and I in turn question him closely. He tries to come toward me; slowly, with that soft, dark, delicacy of his, he tells me many things. But I, like him, cannot interpret. I can only listen:

"I was raised in the Kasr-el-Ainy district of Cairo," Nabil begins. "But we traveled a great deal, as my father was a visiting farm inspector. Thus, I knew what it was to be a twelve-year-old racing along the beaches of Alexandria, a fourteen-year-old lusting after my first woman in Ismailya, a seventeen-year-old in the feudal mystery of Assiut. I was the apple of my father's eye, although I had a brother above me and another below me. My father took great pleasure in my bent for learning, and delighted in sending me to medical school. All went easily and well for me. So much so that a few years ago I was already on my way to being an established doctor. I had a clinic, another special practice with a doctor friend of mine, and I was doing blood research. Also, I was sleeping with two girls at the same time. They were two girls who worked at the Nasr Motor Company. Everything was fine between us. I slept with both of them alternately, we all knew each other, we were all good friends.

"Then came 1967. You cannot imagine what it was like here then. What went on. I became depressed. Very depressed. I stopped sleeping with the two girls. I left my practice and my clinic. I gave up my research. I joined the Army. And I became religious. And when I became religious it took up all my emotions. All those emotional dissatisfactions and confusions were taken up—all, all—in the larger emotion. Women, the war, my work, the life: all were immersed in the larger circle. I prayed, I read the Koran, I went to the mosque. And you know? It was a very comfortable life. For a long time I continued in this manner. I was sealed into a circle of the deepest comfort, the deepest order, the oldest method of dealing with worldly pain man has known. I felt as I had as a child in my mother's bed.

"Then I fell in love.

"It started with a wrong number. She called the wrong number and I answered at the Army hospital in Cairo. I don't know why it was, something in her voice, something calling suddenly to me out of an old place in my mind. . . . I began to joke with her. And she began calling back. Finally, we met.

"At that time we began to meet once in every ten days. She told me she was engaged. We said we were only friends, we were doing no harm. We continued to see each other." Nabil looked around the café. "We used to meet here," he said and his mouth winced.

"After a while she told me that actually she was married, but not yet deflorated. (You know this custom of ours? The three steps of marriage?) I told her to get divorced. I began to grow frightened. I felt myself being sucked in.

"At that time I said to her, 'My love now is like a coal that has become red. I hold it in my hand. If I wish, now, I can let it go and it will fly out of my hand, and it will leave a scar that will take a little while, but it will heal. If I continue in this way with you my love will become transformed into a gas and if I open my hand then it will fill all the space around me, and surround me, and I will never get free of it.'

"I asked her then if I should continue in this way of love, or let the red coal go. She said yes, I should continue.

"So we continued in this way. We would meet here at the Hilton, or in the Gardens, or in Manyal Palace, or at the Omar Khayyam. I could never reach her. I must wait always for her call. I grew thin. I could not work. I forgot to pray.

"And then one day she told me it was impossible, that we must stop, that she was pregnant and could not leave her husband. I cried then. For the first time in my adult life, except for the times when I am facing my God, I wept. Because the coal had become a gas and I was no longer free. I could not retrograde then. No matter what happened I could not go back.

"We continued in this manner up until two months ago. We left each other many times, but always one or the other of us came back almost immediately. And each time we reconciled we were closer, warmer, with more and greater understanding of each other.

"But she is terribly afraid of her father. Not her husband. Although her husband is a government minister, and if I told you his name you would know it. But it is her father she fears with a terrible fear. It is him she has not the courage to tell.

"Now I have told her, 'I can no longer go on this way. As a man it is disgusting to me to be in this position. You must decide, and this time it is for good. . . . She will decide to divorce or not in the next two months.

"But do you know? I feel a crack in my love this time. I feel that even if she goes through with it now, it will be bad, it cannot work out."

Nearly at dawn the gentle doctor delivered me to the house in Mohammed Sidki Street. He shook my hand solemnly; his straining luminous eyes searched my face.

"I return to the desert tomorrow," he said very softly, "but I am once more in Cairo in seven days. I hope that I may call on you at that time?"

"Of course." He turned away into the darkness of the narrow cobbled street; almost gone, he turned quickly back.

"Wait for me," he whispered. "I have need of you."

And I? I thought, staring after him. What do I have need of?

Today, with Mohammed, a long-planned-for visit to the "prosperous" cousins in Heliopolis.

The apartment is large, with two shades of green-and-white molding. The usual dark rooms with the glinting spring sunlight locked out, and the heavy furniture, in large rose-print this time. The family consists of three fat sisters from forty to fifty-two, one gray husband, six or seven children of varying ages. A few years ago they all lived within walking distance of Mohammed's mother. Now that the husband is office manager of a petrol company in downtown Cairo they have made the crucial move to Heliopolis. . . . And here comes Mohammed: peering in the window of the cousins who have escaped Shobra.

The day is full of cooking and eating, laced with a crude humor and an even cruder affection. Drunk with the effects of a meal of orgiastic proportions, the family begins to let down its hair with the

American guest. They act as peasants in the village would never act, the peasants being possessed of a natural politeness the climbing lower middle classes have long lost.

The sisters gape at me; openly take my measurements; finger my clothing; demand to know the difference between American and Egyptian materials; announce, without consulting me, my opinions on Egyptian men, women, fashions, food, houses, marriages; they *know* what Americans think; the father met an American business-man once.

As the day wears on things definitely degenerate. The seventeen-year-old daughter, whispering and giggling with her cousins, sud-denly dashes across the room and pushes her face into mine: "How old you are?" Everyone laughs as I jump.

Someone else booms. "You like *felafel*?" The children stamp on the floor, and laugh until tears run down their cheeks.

Now people are running at me:

"*Maṣa'ah!*" °

"WELCOME!"

"You like this?"

"You like that?"

"No?"

"WHY?"

Against this good-natured boorishiness, the counterpoint of Mo-hammed's moodiest time and our most intimate day. Looking more than ever like Gandhi's grandson, Mohammed is in a private tender gloom as we hustle onto the bus for Heliopolis in the hot dusty bus terminal in Tahrir Square, surrounded by fat hairy legs in scuffed plastic wedgies and dust-covered *gelabyas*. The bus is a filthy, crowded, tin trap that hurls itself along with people hanging, clinging, lunging, pulling back inside, me standing with my back to the metal partition that separates the driver from the passengers, Mohammed in front of me, his skinny body tense with the effort to hold himself upright against the violent swaying of the bus, his hand periodically slamming against the metal above my head in a last-ditch effort to remain standing. Nevertheless, he stands over me, yelling his most private thoughts over the din, secure in the

° An eggplant dish made with fried onions and a meat-tomato sauce, and then baked in a casserole.

knowledge that we are certainly the only two English-speaking people inside this moving cage.

"The people," Mohammed mourns at the top of his voice. "They do not give my mi-i-ind rest. I think in a few years they make me crazy, mad, I will not bear it. Always the people, my close friends, they say these things to me: 'You go to her flat, no? Why you do nothing? It is a *chance* for you.' And I say to them, 'Sex is not everything. Can you not understand friendship?' Why I am friends with you? Not for sex. 'Why I must be friends with her for sex?' I say to them."

Uh-oh, I say to myself.

Mohammed stares gloomily out the window, the armpit of his blue cotton shirt soaked with sweat, the veins working inside the skin drawn tightly across his temples; his eyes, when they turn back to me, filled with a soft spreading pain.

"Sometimes I like someone," he says. "And I want to be with them every day. And sometimes it is best when I do not see someone for a long time. Or rather, a long *short* time. And I do not know. How can I have both at the same time? It is impossible! And which do I need most? But I cannot choose!"

Silence; and then over the crash: "What it is—I do not know what I need. That is the whole thing that is pressing in my head, always. I do not know what I need. That is the whole thing in the *life*." His eyes search my face frantically. "Do *you* know what you need?"

I look at him for a long silent time. I'd give ten years of my life at this moment to answer him as he wishes to be answered. Suddenly, I feel immeasurably tired.

"Only sometimes," I say quietly. "I'm sorry, Mohammed. I'm not the one to hold out much hope for the future to you. Only sometimes do I know what I need."

And we both know then, as we hold onto each other with our eyes: That is why we are here together. That is why we are friends. That is why there is this closeness between us. Mohammed, in the dusty bewilderment of his twenty-three-year-old Egyptian life, does not know what he needs. And I, his sophisticated American lady, I also, do not know what I need.

As the day drags on it is clear his feelings for me have taken a leap ahead. He now openly wants love from me. He wants me to confirm his dreams, certify his longings, wash Shobra away in a cleansing desire. He *wants* it. Oh, he wants it! He may not know what he needs, but this he knows he wants. And when I am difficult this day, or unresponsive, or feel hateful toward his relatives he dissolves in desolation, practically hitting his delicate head against the wall.

But he has begun to irritate me with his continual *sensitive depression*, which is real enough, God knows, but oh how he milks it! He tells a joke. The whole family laughs. A look of pain comes over his face and he says to me in English, "Always I am laughing, laughing. I cannot stand it. I need to cry. I have not cried in three years. I must cry." And there is a waiting silence while I'm supposed to be registering once more his tragic condition.

In the middle of the day his left leg begins to hurt. By evening he can barely walk. I hate him. I feel him begging for sympathy. I hate him. I withhold. I withdraw. We are both miserable.

At ten in the evening we travel back to Cairo by the electric tram rather than the bus. The ticket-taker who passes up and down the aisles, selling and checking tickets, is young with a runny nose and long sad eyes. He wears a tattered Army overcoat, and seems stupefied as he travels endlessly back and forth on this tram that will never arrive for him. He cannot remember if we have shown him our tickets, and he plants himself silently before Mohammed twice, three times, an unbelievable four times, waiting like a disappointed child. . . . At last, Mohammed sticks the tickets halfway into his shirt pocket and points ironically at them each time the ticket-taker passes us. We laugh softly together, and the tension between us breaks. In the weak yellow light of the tram filled with tired Egyptians, a rush of silent feeling passes between us and we are caught without warning in the sorrows of unconsummated love, bound up in some inexplicable way with the swaying tram and the stupid ticket-taker and the silent Cairo night.

We cannot part. Back in the city at eleven o'clock, Mohammed limping painfully along, the depression, the love, the sad and confused longings are real enough. We sit drinking a coffee in the Bab-el-Louk square. Mohammed looks ready to cry. He condemns himself for the "mistakes" in his character: he is jealous of the time I spend away from him . . . the pain in his leg increases . . . I am exhausted unto death. He cries out violently, "I do not know what I want from you! Do I want friendship? Do I want love? Or just the experience?"

I realize the same is true for me: I don't know what I want from him, either. He is twenty-three years old; he is devout, tense, spiritual; his capacity for self-loathing is just this side of hysteria; if I were to draw closer he would surely turn on me; but the distance I keep between us has begun to strain. . . . I feel for both of us, but I want out. I am weary of all this Egyptian melancholy, fearful of Mohammed's intensity, lost in a shadowy hunger of my own.

At the gate of my house Mohammed shakes my hand correctly, mockingly; and goes limping off to catch the last bus back to Shobra.

A tall woman sitting near Farid's desk stands up as I enter the office, her hand outstretched toward me.

"How do you do?" she says. "I am Leila Soliman. Farid has told me much of you. I am so happy to meet you at last."

Farid has spoken of Leila Soliman to me also. Of her intelligence, her ambitions as a writer, her dissatisfactions with her work as a business reporter on one of the magazines in the *Al Kahira* building, her travels, her modernness. Nevertheless, her appearance is a surprise to me—she looks like an Italian *contessa*—and my first question is "Are you part-European?"

"Ah, my dear!" Leila Soliman laughs. "Is there an Egyptian who is *not* part-European whether or not the blood of a European actually runs in his veins? But no, I am actually part-Turkish. And this Turkish blood is indeed a strange and capricious thing. In me it has surfaced violently with this white skin and these blue eyes; but in my brothers and sisters it is only a hint, and often it is scorned entirely. Africa comes up, strong and dark, in my family. It is only I who give perpetual life to my Turkish grandfather."

"What a pleasure!" Farid beams, perspiring happily behind his desk. "To have two of the most beautiful and intelligent women in Cairo in my office at once!"

Leila Soliman's aristocratic blue eyes rest thoughtfully on Farid for a long moment. "Yes," she says, turning to me, "it is always a pleasure to an Egyptian man to have two women, or better yet *three* women, or five women in his presence. It is his unfailing belief that we are there to adorn his life, to increase his powers, to testify to his value. Have you not found this to be so? Even in the short time you have been in Egypt?"

What have I got here? Egyptian female gold! I love her. I must know her. This woman is all the Egyptian women I have not been able to find.

"To tell you the truth," I say, leaning forward in my seat, "I have found Egyptian men to be just like the women in my own country."

Leila Soliman's eyebrows fly up into the brown waves resting on her forehead. Her eyes widen, and then quickly narrow. "Tell me," she commands quietly.

"They are nervous. High-strung. Filled with an extraordinary intuitive intelligence. Gripped by an emotional anxiety that is common in American women and almost never revealed by American men. They approach me in order to make love, but in reality they wish to talk more than they wish to make love. I am a woman, true. But more important, I am a Westerner, and a *stranger*. The talk comes pouring out of them as though they have been locked away from the world for centuries with no one to talk to, certainly not each other. That is exactly what Western women are like. And oh, that fever in them. That fever in the Egyptian men! Blind, unintellectual, the fever of a developed consciousness strangling in its own energy. Exhausted with the frustration that comes of having no outlet, no way in which to express itself. That is *exactly* what the women of my country are now groping toward, moving up out of that internal darkness in which they have passed the entirety of their lives . . ."

Leila Soliman stares at me. Farid stares at me. *I* stare at me. We are all startled by my outburst. The aristocratic Egyptian woman speaks first.

"You have learned a very great deal about my country in a very short time. All that you say is true. Painfully true. And of course, it says a great deal, as well, about the women of my country. The women who are still placid like the gentle hopeless cows grazing in the Valley of the Nile."

"Exactly." I nod my head vigorously. "The women are placid because they aren't even in the running. It is only when one is fighting for one's life that one experiences anxiety."

"I must protest." Farid holds up his hand. "What is happening in Egypt now is *not* this battle you have described between men and women for conscious development, but rather it is a battle between the old and the new."

"That is true," I concede. "What is really most striking in Egypt is the incredible combinations of the modern and the conservative that I find in endless variety in every Egyptian I meet."

"That is what I tell my daughters." Leila Soliman smiles. "I tell them that in our block of flats alone one finds the sixteenth century, the seventeenth, the eighteenth, and, if one looks very hard, the nineteenth as well!"

The lady rises from her seat, and comes around to my side of the desk to clasp my hand warmly. "I must go now," she says. "You will come to my house for lunch. We must go on with this conversation. And you must delight my family as you have delighted me. Friday at two. I will take nothing but yes for an answer."

I agree happily, and Leila Soliman moves gracefully toward the door of Farid's office. As she is about to disappear through it she turns and says softly, "Remember your promise, Farid. I *must* have that letter."

Farid nods his heavy head at her, and swears solemnly that she shall have what she wants from him within a week. When the door closes behind Leila, Farid sighs and wipes off the beads of sweat that collect perpetually on the end of his generous nose.

"Ah, she is a wonderful woman," he says, "but she will drive me to distraction!"

"Why? What does she want?"

"She has been invited to East Germany. She wishes to go. For some reason our government will not grant her an exit visa. She wishes me to write a letter to a minister who owes me a favor. I will write the letter when I think the time is right. She cannot wait. She comes every day and she *reminds* me that I must write that letter."

"Why won't the government grant her an exit visa?"

Farid stares at me. He shakes a cigarette from the package on his desk. He lights it carefully. He stares at me again.

"No one knows," he says. "It happens all the time. A visa is requested. It has been granted before. There has never been any trouble. Suddenly, the visa does not come. The government does not say no. The visa simply never arrives. No one knows why. No one knows what he has done. There is no one to appeal to. From the government, only silence. Not a single office in any ministry knows why this is happening. It is simply happening. And now it is happening to Leila."

We are quiet for a long time. The telephone rings, and Farid sits listening into it for five full minutes. I leaf through the papers and magazines on his desk. The thirty-year-old "boy" brings coffee. We drink in silence. Twenty minutes pass.

"How's Debbie?" I say casually. "I haven't seen her for a week now."

Farid observes me in silence.

"You know, don't you?" he says at last, in a voice so heavy I understand immediately: he is really in distress.

"What's going on?" I ask softly.

"I wish I knew," Farid cries unexpectedly, pushing his fingers through his thick black hair. "I wish to Allah I knew!" He bites off these words as though he has difficulty in getting them out; his huge bulky body heaves in its seat; he lights another cigarette with unsteady fingers; I remain silent, waiting for him to go on as I know beyond question he will. At last:

"I still don't know exactly how it started. My wife came to Cairo. I realized when she came that I had spoken too often of Debbie and her work, and I had made her jealous. She is a wonderful woman, but she is something *fierce* when she is jealous. I did not wish to have trouble. I sent Debbie a note, telling her not to speak to me at the *pension* in the presence of my wife. If she wished to see me she should come here to the office. I thought it was the best way, and besides my wife was only to stay in Cario four or five days.

"Debbie came to the office. She was very upset by the note. She demanded to know what it meant, how I could treat her like that, weren't we friends, *special* friends? And suddenly, she seemed to go mad. She jumped up—she was sitting right there, right there on that chair facing you now—and said she couldn't go on like this, she didn't know what was happening to her, she thought she was in love with me, she felt mad, absolutely mad.

"I was stunned. I thought she was a *child*. I didn't know what to do with her, what to say to her. I calmed her down and told her to come back the next day and we would talk the whole thing over. I thought she would think over what she had said and done and regret it, and that would be the end of that. But no. She came again, and again she said the same thing. And she seemed even more desperate than the day before. . . . I didn't know what to do. I began to believe her. I felt she *needed* me."

Farid is looking more and more distracted: a painfully confused and red-faced fat man.

"*Ya*-Vivian, I have been married three times. I never dreamed . . ."

"*Three* times?" I interrupt. "You told me twice."

"Yes, I know. I lied. I was ashamed. Your American eyes were so direct and so sincere. It seemed so bad to me, to be married three times. I thought: twice is enough for her. But now I will tell you the truth, the entire truth. I have been married three times. My first wife did not die in childbirth. She is still alive here in Cairo. And so is my second wife. And, Allah help me, so is my third wife. I have had plenty of experience. More than enough. I thought it was all behind me now. And yet, this Debbie, she has done something to me. I do not know what it is, but I feel myself responding to her, and it disturbs me. I do not wish this thing now at my stage of life. I do not wish it at all. I find myself saying the most fantastic things to her, and I am dreaming of a new life, away from Egypt. It is *insane*. I know it is insane. And yet. . . . And my wife refuses to return to Alexandria . . . she knows something is wrong. . . ."

My head is reeling. Is this actually Farid speaking? I had not realized the extent of the literal belief with which I have been listening to this man since the first day I have known him. . . . Debbie! Little Debbie *Lindner*? This prize American hysteric? What is happening here?

"I don't know what to say, Farid."

"I have disappointed you, my good American friend? Your strong Farid is turning to jelly before your very eyes?"

"No, no, Farid," I say hastily. "Not at all. I am only surprised. No, no. Listen, Farid, emotion is still the ultimate mystery. There is no question of weakness or strength involved. Only the mystery."

Farid heaves himself to his feet. He would love to go on speaking to me, he sighs, but he has work to do. Work he has been unable to face for days now, days. He extends his hand to me. I extend mine. Sometimes I think what I love most about Farid is that I know when I touch his hand it will be sweating. A handshake is the automatic greeting in Egypt, and often the hand you shake is perspiring. I never cease to feel an uprush of wonder and gratitude when I experience a sweating hand in Cairo because my own are *always* wet and clammy, and in New York, where every hand seems warm and smooth, I will do almost anything to avoid shaking hands; whereas here, in this wonderfully nervous, self-doubting country, I can stretch my hand out—eagerly, warmly, a friendly American lady, secure in the knowledge that the hand I shake is likely to be as moist as my own. Especially when I am shaking hands with Farid, whose hand is invariably dripping.

On Sunday morning Amr called and asked me to have lunch with him. Something odd in him lately; something altered in his voice when he speaks with me; some irritated urgency, almost; it was there again on Sunday morning.

We met at two and went to a *kabob* restaurant somewhere off the Twenty-sixth of July Street. The restaurant stood on a corner, its two outer walls an endless continuum of squares of wooden frame filled with window glass, rising at last into graceful arches of glass. We sat at a table covered with a white cloth in the room flooded with light, a potted palm at my back, and dark boys with doleful eyes in red *gelabyas* and red skullcaps delivering the ritual meal to our table.

"How are you?" Amr said with a heavy lightness.

"Fine," I said automatically.

"And your social life? How is it progressing?" Funny. He *did* say social life, but I could have sworn he was saying love life.

The meal was eaten with an awkward, indefinable strain between us. Something in the air, definitely, but what? Something on Amr's mind, but what?

As we left the restaurant Amr asked me to accompany him to his office; he had some few minutes of work to do.

We drove to the building on Galal Street where Amr's business was housed in two rooms on an upper floor. Two young men jumped to their feet as we entered the inner office.

"Hamdi! Abdul!" Amr greeted them joyously. They all clapped each other on the back, and Hamdi and Abdul shook hands gravely with me. All three then fell into chairs, Hamdi and Abdul in the ones they had been sitting in, Amr in the one behind the desk—and all flung their legs up on the desk. As I was wearing a dress, I sat with my legs demurely crossed.

"Have you just come back from the Pyramids?" Amr asked Hamdi. Hamdi blushed and twisted about in his seat. Abdul roared with laughter. Amr's eyes twinkled maliciously. I looked inquiringly at Amr.

"Hamdi has a mistress who lives out on the Pyramids Road. But he blushes in polite company when she is referred to."

"Not at all," Hamdi replied hotly. "It is only that you two are such beasts. You roll everything through the mud."

"Of course," Amr said mockingly. "She is really Snow-White. The Virgin Queen. If it wasn't for us . . ."

"No," Hamdi cut Amr off, "she is not Snow-White, but she is a good girl, and she is very good to me."

"Why don't you marry her?" Amr went on mercilessly. Hamdi drew a blank. He sat—his mouth half-open, ready to retort—silent.

"Now you have gone too far," Abdul said softly.

"Why?" I interjected. "Why *don't* you marry her?"

Hamdi went "Tst-t-t" and shook his head once, an Egyptian gesture meaning: No, no, it is impossible, there is nothing further to discuss.

There then followed a lengthy conversation about wives and lovers, with these three good Moslem men turning their most serious attention to the weighty matter of what kind of sexual experience is acceptable in a woman they might marry. Every conceivable combination was examined, but in the end: if she sleeps with them, forget it.

And yet. Hamdi longed for a soulmate.

"I want to marry a woman who can share my life and my work with me. A woman who can give me *understanding*, not this slavelike devotion most Egyptian men want. But how is that possible? It is *not* possible! For if a woman has understanding, then she has experience, and if she has experience . . ."

"Then how can she be a pure, pure, pure girl at the same time?" I finished.

"Exactly!" beamed Hamdi.

Amr and Abdul laughed out loud, and Hamdi peered at me.

"You are mocking me, yes?" Hamdi said. "It is easy for you Americans to mock! You do not know what it is like to live in the Middle East!"

"Nonsense," Amr announced. "A man must marry a good girl. That is the most important thing in a marriage. And it is *impossible* to know if they are good, any of them. She may be good with me, but who knows what she has done with others? It happens all the time. A man marries a girl he believes to be good, then one day he meets a friend who has a friend—finished. He discovers she has been with the friend of the friend, and God knows who else! No, no. For myself, I say: If a girl goes out with me *alone*, it is finished. Because I *know*. Four or five times, and I take her to the bed."

"Ach, Amr, that is too strong!" said Abdul, the most dashing of the three.

The expression on Amr's face was extraordinary: malevolent, grudging, furious; as though he were in the grip of some powerful and disfiguring emotion. I felt suddenly that I was seeing him for the first time as he really was: beady-eyed, sweating in his flesh, an Egyptian businessman with delusions of spiritual grandeur, enslaved by appetites he feared desperately, a narrow frightened mind, cunning because he *had* married his seventeen-year-old virgin.

"I have to go, Amr," I said.

"Yes, we must all go," sighed Abdul.

"Ach!" Hamdi smacked his forehead. "Work, work, work. I have a mountain of work on my desk."

As Amr drew up into Mohammed Sidki Street he said lightly, "May I come up for a cup of coffee?"

He had never asked to come up before, and I looked inquiringly at him; but his expression now was so utterly bland and his manner so simply lonely that I stifled my nasty suspicions and said, "Sure, come on."

We rose silently in the elevator. Silently, I turned the key in the lock. Silently, I turned the lights on in the perpetually darkened apartment. That was the last silently.

Amr grabbed me by the shoulders, jammed me up against the foyer wall, and pushed his face into mine. I struggled and heard my own voice call out, "Amr! For God's sake, *stop this*. Stop it!" But it all began to seem far away; I felt as though I were going into a trance, so dreamlike and repetitious was the quality of what was happening. Amr began to snort and breathe heavily. He buried his head in my neck and moaned my name. His hands were like a steel vise on my rigid arms, but I could feel *his* arms trembling. His mouth, seeking mine, mashed itself repeatedly into my cheeks as my head thrashed from right to left. His face was white and his eyeballs seemed about to disappear into his upper lids. I thought he was going to faint. At that moment I remembered the under-secretary, and how I had wondered then: When was the last time he has been with a woman? I saw that it was the same now with Amr, and I realized that I was, both times, in the presence of sexual hysteria. It was the terror of what they were doing that so transfixed these men. The pursuit of illicit desire had become the very need of their souls, and compelled as they were, they were being driven onto the swordpoint of conflicted longing. Here in Amr's face—possessed! lost!—the battle raged: there was virgin goodness to the left, and black passion to the right; the peace and safety of the Egyptian bride, the beckoning allure of the American whore. And somewhere in the confused distance—which road to take? which road? oh, quick!—at the end of the long, dark tunnel, there glimmered the light of moral grace, as well as the fires of hell. But too late, too late—ah, the quick pain!—*pinned* by the denied and devouring flesh.

"Stop it, stop it, stop it," I screamed.

And then all was still. We remained frozen: me jammed up against the wall, Amr's hands on either side of my head, our voices silent, our eyes locked into each other's. The expression in Amr's eyes haunts me still. Terror and disbelief were there dancing about inside the black brilliance: the hunter had become the hunted; the aggressing man the retreating child; the desire of the flesh now the fear of retribution.

I saw so clearly then the terrible and complex longing for innocence that is Egypt. The fear of consciousness, and the weight of original responsibility that comes with consciousness. For, to be fully conscious is to lose innocence; and to lose innocence is to risk hell. How on this godforsaken earth could Amr acknowledge me, how not transform me into some profoundly foreign "other," how not make of me a source of temptation that attacks from the outside like malarial fever, how and still remain as a child? These men were literally buying back their innocence, their purity, their redemption from hell through their obsession with female virginity. For, to possess the virgin wife, daughter, sister, is to be wiped clean; is to hold before one's black self a shield of whiteness behind which the cunning of passion and the malevolence of original knowledge will never be discovered. Is to stand before one's God and deny that one has entered the game of life. Is to say, "Oh, no. We were just *fooling*. We weren't really in the game at all. We just *looked* for a while there as though we were playing. But see? I'm still the good child I always was, long before I was even supposed to enter the game. See? No sex. No love. No maturity. Just me and my little virgin here. We weren't doing *anything*."

And I saw then with equal clarity the true enslavement of these Egyptian women, the stunning force with which they are pressed into selflessness: nonexistent except as symbols of male purity. And my mind burned for the women, and my heart hardened against the men, and I was lost in the grievous gutlessness of this whole twisted agony: this fear of standing alone, this national terror of the loss of childhood.

PART THREE

An odd moment: a steaming hot night, crossing the Kasr-el-Nil Bridge in a taxi, caught in grinding traffic. Suddenly I am overwhelmed by the memory of a passage from John Steinbeck's book on Russia, a moment when, after a few months in the postwar Soviet Union, Steinbeck is seized with longing for the chic and material goodness of New York. I realize: I am feeling the same thing. A hunger for Lexington Avenue; the glitter of Fifty-seventh Street; First Avenue and Sixty-eighth Street; Fifty-ninth Street and the Park. Something I have never felt before in my life: a distinct sense of the pleasure and added goodness of material life. Cairo seems unbearably drab tonight, *stiflingly* drab. A bleak and leveling city; an unbroken expanse of dust and poverty; a hopelessness of the future.

Nabil Kamel and I became lovers two weeks after the night we met. The young doctor was oddly without sexual energy, and our lovemaking was neither intense nor genuinely arousing. But it seemed not to matter to me, I felt neither annoyance nor dissatisfaction, so drawn was I to the gentle Nabil, and to the anxiety he radiates. He seemed, in some curious way, to be psychically exhausted—although boyish and lovely—and I was touched.

Afterward, in ritual obeisance to my female insecurity, I said timidly, "Will I see you before you leave?" Nabil seemed astonished. "Of course," he said softly. "Tomorrow." And I felt a rush of surprised affection: so good, so true, so faithful to the moment did he seem.

And that is how it has gone. He is naïve, amazingly boyish sometimes; often—in response to my own demons—I am hurt and feel rejected, but always, to my gratified astonishment, he returns with an answer that confirms the steadiness and faithfulness of his feelings—whatever they are—toward me; or rather toward our intimacy. And when I question him about those feelings it is his turn to seem astonished.

"Don't ask me questions," he says with a soft wonder in his voice. "These are not things one can answer with the tongue. Don't you *feel* me? Don't you know what I feel for you? Don't doubt me. . . ."

One day Nabil says of Egypt: "What most foreigners do not understand about Egypt is, it is the *most* sympathetic country in the world. Nowhere else will you find such a sympathetic country. And this sympathy, coupled with terrible ignorance, makes it a dangerous place. But never as dangerous to others as it is to itself. It *feeds* on itself, it eats itself alive. Yes" (pain in his eyes, irony on his mouth) "very much like one of my blood diseases. . . . My country is a raging blood disease: flaring up with heat and false life, dying down for want of the precious cellular balance. And we are all—all of us—dying with her."

He is a profoundly middle-class Moslem, an unintellectual man possessed of that rare healing intelligence that occurs in sensitive and reflective men who become doctors in countries like Egypt. I will not fall in love with him, but he moves me deeply. In him the anxiety of Egypt is luminous, alive and changing, almost radiant at times. It strains to the breaking point, and there is in him a fullness of longing that breaks my heart.

A week after we had begun I told Nabil that I was Jewish. He had a pain in his stomach just as I was telling him. He barely blinked at me, and went back to the pain in his stomach, saying, "I thought so."

I loved him then! And only then did I realize how very nervous I had been about telling him.

But he brooded on it, and the next night when we returned late to my apartment from his cousin's house, and he had his doctor's case with him, and the gateman, not recognizing him, had yelled after us into the darkness of the wire-cage elevator, "Where are you going?" and later Nabil and I had made hasty love upstairs, and he had to leave in the middle of the night, as he was dressing and I lying on the bed watching him, he suddenly seemed to turn guarded and some indefinable element of suspicion softened his voice. He recalled a snatch of conversation about "the political situation" we had been having at Sohair's house, and he said now to me, "Why did you say, 'We will always be enemies'? Are you then an Israeli that you say 'we' to me?"

"I *never* said that. You're imagining things."

"You *did* say it. I heard it distinctly. My ears registered shock."

"Why on earth would I say such a thing? Do you know me so little that you could think I think in those terms? Or is it that we all look alike to you?"

He stared at me in the mirror as he stood knotting his tie. Then, very slowly, he said to me, "You are Jewish. As well as American. As well as a journalist. You know it is *illegal*, as long as I am in the Army, to know you. Yes? You know this?"

"Yes," I said quietly. "I know it."

"This limits my courage in coming here," Nabil said.

I lay naked on the bed, watching this slim, dark-suited stranger who only moments before had shared my nakedness. Now, still in his presence, I felt alone, exposed, bewildered. Out of the corner of my eye I could see the contours of my own body, round and full, infinitely *Jewish*. An idiotic impulse nearly overtook me: I wanted to laugh. Instead of experiencing the anxiety that would have marked the situation "tragedy" I found that I wanted to laugh: it felt like farce. What was I doing here, anyway? Was this a part I was playing? Let's ring down the curtain on this act, it's a lousy play. We'll start all over again. Ladies and gentlemen, please. . . .

I could not escape the feeling that it was not me inside my body, this body that lay here so theatrically, so inertly responsive to the action that was being played out without will or consent. That uncanny sensation of distance from my Jewishness began to overtake me again. Distance, but not dissociation. I felt rather like a Jewish hostage in a story from another age, only I couldn't get the part straight. Was I Esther? Was I Salome? Or perhaps Moshe Dayan's illegitimate daughter? Was I vulnerable? Was I impregnable? Was I the betrayer or the betrayed? *What was happening here?*

"I said it limits my courage," Nabil was saying. "I did not say it abolishes it."

And then the most extraordinary thing happened. As I stared at Nabil's image in the mirror it seemed to me that I saw him in a military uniform. Suddenly I understood: the politicalness of life bore down on me. I was a Jew in Egypt. Bound in some irrevocable way to the nationhood of Israel—whether I willed it or no. That was a political fact of life. No conscious decision of mine—no place, no person, no experience within the boundaries of this country—could overturn its meaning. In the act of intimacy it was almost as though Nabil and I had become collaborators. I realized then that I felt this numbing "distance" from the word "Jewish" coming up strongest in me during the moments when I felt closest to one Egyptian or another.

And then I went fearful-cold, and felt anger and death inside me. All right, I thought. That's it. The hell with him. I'll cut him out right now. I don't really give a damn. I'm in bed with raving fantasy, anyway. Who is this man? It's not as if I loved him. But then I looked into his face. The uniform was gone. The deathly cold inside me thawed. The radiant anxiety of Nabil's face came up strong and clear. This was *Nabil*! Not some political abstraction!

"What are we doing?" I wailed. "We barely know each other. We can hardly communicate. Our conversations are full of misunderstandings."

He said, and I felt his hands on my face, "To love and to marry, yes, one must communicate fully. One must know one's partner by heart. But to take those first steps toward love, to feel those sensations, one need not have much communication. We *have* those sensations, you and I. Let us experience them."

And I felt again—recalling how he had shivered in my arms one night over the remembered taste of freedom I had brought into his life and would soon take away with me again—that he was a better person than I, more faithful, more courageous, more willing to risk the moment: less dogged by fantasy and the bittersweet taste of projected melancholy.

I sat drinking tea with Fatma, gloomy over Nabil. The doorbell rang and Fatma rushed to embrace a young woman standing in the open doorway. It was her schoolmate, Zeinab, just returned from four years in America. Zeinab was delighted to make my acquaintance. She amused, and then intrigued me. Once again: the sudden Egyptian illumination from an unexpected quarter.

Zeinab. Very thin, a large hooked nose, magnificent eyes, long black hair, alluring in a vulgar red velvet dress with puffed sleeves and a band across the center of a V-neck opening. She looked thirty; she was twenty-four. Nervous. A bit melancholy. Sudden flashes of lit laughter. A crooked smile (the right half of her upper lip climbing higher than the left half) that gave her a look of cynical tragedy. Despite her transparent vulgarity, in fleeting moments she seemed haunted. She spoke with a voice whose soft inflections were a piece of cynicism against the starkness of the words that began to pour out of her no sooner than we mentioned America.

"My husband, when he say to me, 'Do you love me?' I laugh, and I say, 'Love? What do I know of love? Have I ever experienced it? How do I know the difference between you and love?'

"I was sixteen. Very beautiful. Not like now, now I am finished. Men in the streets turned to look at me. I spoke French very well. Ten men came to my father, to marry me. He, my husband, was one of them. My father chose him. Directly I came out of school I married him.

"Is this right? This is not a life. This is not a meaning between a man and a woman. And do you think he loved me? No. No one marries for love in this country. I was beautiful, educated, my family good, my father rich. He *marry* me.

"I want to be free inside myself. How can a man and a woman live together like this? How? It is impossible! This is not a way to discover what your feelings are. How can I ever know my feelings? Or he?

How he knows his feelings? He does not. So he thinks he has none. . . .

"The Egyptian woman, she is nothing. She is afraid, always afraid, inside herself. She never talks, never speaks her mind. He will *leave.* Always she is afraid he will leave. When her husband comes home she sits in another room, never with him. She does not go out, not even to the cinema with her friends. My husband, even in Canada, he goes out many nights, has girls for friends. I, I must sit at home, talk to no one, go nowhere. . . . The woman is nothing. She never forgets that the Moslem can take four wives. This is always in the back of her mind, and it influences *his* emotions.

"I want to fight for the women of my country. I want them to be different than me.

"I hate men now. Really, in my heart there is something cold, like stone, for men. . . . In Canada I had a good friend. Young! She was so young. . . . She killed herself over a married man who told her he loved her. . . . She was *dying,* and he would not come. . . . Why he tell her he love her? Why? I mean, why *love*? If he wanted sex I am sure she was easy. Why this love that makes the women to kill themselves?

"My husband, he lies. He lies, like all Egyptian men. If they go to the corner for cigarettes they must tell the woman they go the other way for newspaper.

"Yes, I love my husband. I stay with him eight years. I love him too much. But I do not wish to *marry* this way! It is not the life. It is for animals, cows, not for people."

I stared in silence at the Egyptian woman, ten years younger than I, infinitely older. I realized, looking at Zeinab, that it is not the harsh life in Egypt that ages the women: it is the loss of virginity. Virginity is all that they have in this life: the single card they can throw into the game. Once they've played it, that's it. Egyptian women are most beautiful in those last years of ripening sexuality before virginity is lost: it is a moment of gathered courage, of excitement and energy. It is everything on the edge of expectancy. The leap is about to be taken; the momentum is gathered; the lungs are filled to bursting; the eyes are shining. *Go!* Gone. If she marries at eighteen, at twenty-one she is faded, and at twenty-four she has the harsh, shadowed look of one whose choices are long behind her; the look that is Zeinab's at this moment.

And now they seem to be crawling out of the woodwork, these Egyptian neurotics who all hasten to assure me that they are *not* the typical Egyptian. From out of nowhere, diminutive Samir Abdel-Rahman, brother to the man whose apartment I am living in, and copy editor on a woman's magazine. This long-lashed, green-eyed Egyptian faun comes bearing two ridiculous bunches of funeral lilies on a hot, lonely night: nervous to the point of imminent screaming violence—self-inflicted or otherwise. Homosexual? Immaterial: a true New York hysteric out of Cairo; depressed, lonely, tearing flesh from the inside out; a slow, bleeding vapor of disconnection, a growing sense of being switched-off; and yet—like all of them—responding to me like a starving beggar, pouring out life story, confession and pain, wistful observation, hated longing:

"Oh my dear Vivian! But the Egyptians are so *complicated*! You must stay longer than four months if you wish to understand them at all! They never say what they mean. At the same time they hold nothing in, all their misery is right outside. You can meet someone and five minutes later she is saying, 'Why aren't you married, a nice man like you?' It is funny, yes? And do you know? They never fire anyone because he is bad at his work. *Never.* They say, 'The poor man, how will he live? How will his children live?' I say to them, 'This is no way to run a business!' But it does no good, no good at all.

"They are warm, yes. Full of feeling, and will speak very easily to you immediately. But they do not know *why* they feel, or what they *really* feel. They never look *inside* themselves. And immature. Oh, my dear Vivian! They are so immature! How can it be otherwise? No experience. They have no experience. Everyone lives at home until he is married, the girls marry strangers, no independence at all ever, and without independence there is no experience, and without experience no maturity. Is that not right, Vivian? Is that not right?

"Oh, I don't know! I am abnormal in this country. I do not live with my mother, I am not happy, I cannot find some good way to live, no one understands how I feel. . . . It is terrible to live alone, it eats at me. But what can I do? So I feel, how shall I say it? I feel *disconnected* from Egypt.

"I studied English literature at the university, and there was a man I read. Oh *what* was his name! Do you know a book called *Far from the Madding Crowd*? Thomas Hardy, that's it! Well he did something to me, this Hardy. He was not an intellectual, but oh a true writer, a true writer. He had in him some deep misery, some deep sense that we are blown about in this world, that whatever we do, *yani*, it comes to nothing. Oh, Vivian! I don't know, but you know? It crept inside me what this Hardy said, and it began to tear at me. . . .

"My father was intellectual, my mother was not. She was one of those women, clothes and good times, that's all she cared for. And you know, when a man is intellectual and a woman is not, he is more sensitive than she, and so he suffered, and he was beaten down, and he *seemed* weaker than she, but really he was not.

"So we lived, with this misery, and I *hated* it! And when he died she began to fight with me, and I didn't know why, and I said, 'Oh, *this* I cannot stand. This I *really* cannot stand. I'm going to leave your house, my mother.' And do you know? When I came home she had packed my bags. So I left. With no money, and no place to go.

"Then later I met a Greek woman at a party. She was older than me and had a child, a boy who was sickly. I told her my story and she said, 'Come live with me.' Really, I was shocked! Do you know how long I stayed with her? Eight years. . . . And then she left. Her child grew very ill and she went back to Athens and left me. All alone. Really, I could not believe it, that she would leave me. But she would have given the whole world over for that child. . . .

"And now I am alone. And it is all no good. Oh, why is the life so *sad*, Vivian! One wants to have fun, and one doesn't. One looks for the good times, the good feelings, the good friends, the one who will love you, really love you as you are—and one doesn't find it. It is all loneliness. And who is there to tell this to in this Egypt?

"A doctor? Oh, *no*. Here, that is the last resort. They must bring in a dead man before the doctor talks to him, one who is foaming at the mouth as you Americans say. I cannot go to a doctor, *yani*, for my loneliness. I cannot go to him, *yani*, and say, 'Doctor, I am old. *Yani*,

I am not *young*, and still I am lonely, I do not feel in harmony with the world.' No, no. This would never do. To tell a doctor I am not in harmony with the world and this is making me sick! That would really be strange, Vivian.

"I cannot believe you are American. No, really, I cannot believe it. You are so *tenderhearted*, you must be Egyptian. I met an American in Geneva once. Really, I was afraid! 'Are you going to be violent?' I said. But he was so sweet! Really, it was strange!

"I have not spent two hours talking like this, I cannot remember when. Or with whom."

The tablecloth is ivory-colored cotton, crocheted to look like lace. It covers a long oval of polished mahogany, is surrounded by eight high-backed, darkly carved chairs, and stands in the center of a square dining room filled with light that comes from a block of unshuttered windows whose right-hand corners are filled with the distant minarets of one of the largest mosques in Cairo. If it weren't for the mosque in the dining-room window I would have thought I was eating lunch in an apartment on New York's West End Avenue.

This is Leila Soliman's home: a large, comfortable apartment filled with books, music, sewing and esoteric arts. Leila's two teen-aged daughters speak German, French, and English, study botany, mathematics and Arabic history, and make quilts and raise hamsters. Leila's husband is a lawyer and an amateur astrologist with an impressive library of books on occultism and the black arts. Leila herself does a great deal of elegant sewing, and the book-lined study in which we will later drink small cups of semi-sweet Turkish coffee is brightened by her graceful flower arrangements. The entire atmosphere is one of wholesome, somewhat academic, middle-class culture. . . . But let me not forget that this is Cairo, not New York, and this is the Egyptian middle class, not the American.

Leila's husband, Mahmoud, is about twenty-five years older than the tall, lovely reporter: a little man with a Santa Claus fringe of white hair surrounding a bald head; kind, patient, a bit silly; the sort of man who wins a woman like Leila by seeing her endlessly through her troubles. And sure enough, it turns out shortly that she married him in the wake of a tragic love affair: Leila loved a Copt for many years, and could not bring herself to surmount the pressure of family disapproval. She married Mahmoud who had been her sympathetic confidant throughout the entire affair. (Lord, this business between the Copts and the Moslems! What I have discovered in Egypt is that the Copts—ironically the first Christian descendants of the Pharaohs —occupy the same moral and emotional space in Egypt that Jews do in the West: they are the feared, admired, distrusted minority of Egypt, and they have risen by dint of brains, diligence, insinuation, and colonial reward. When Nasser took control of Egypt one of the first things he set about doing was replacing every Coptic officer in the army with a Moslem, and it quickly became one of the aims of universal education to raise the IQ of the average Moslem child to that of the average Coptic child. If it weren't for the war with Israel Jews would receive no more attention in Moslem Egypt than any other strand of the great Arab mix. But Copts! Ah, that is an altogether other matter.)

But more significant than Mahmoud's sympathy during this crisis of passion in Leila's life is the little lawyer's infinite loyalty throughout many years of illness. The lovely Leila has a long history of accident and sickness: a broken spine, gangrene, diabetes, lung ailments, kidney ailments, falling spells, scars, rashes, skin diseases, the list is endless and, indeed, horrifying. And the faithful Mahmoud has been there through it all.

"I have nearly died so many times," Leila sighs, pouring coffee in the study, "that I cannot get excited, or fight with anyone, over anything anymore."

Curious that Leila should have said that, for during lunch it became astonishingly clear that this complicated woman whose intelligence is genuinely interesting is also a domineering power-house of middle-class housewifery, with a finger in every family pie, an opinion on everything and, apparently, not an instant's hesitation over interfering in other people's lives when she is convinced she is *right*.

The telephone rang while rice was being spooned onto everyone's plate. Leila answered and seemed to be repeating the word no very firmly a great number of times. When she hung up, she spoke quickly in Arabic to her family. Everyone laughed and shook their heads solemnly, and without further ado Leila turned to me and said:

"That was my brother, Farouk. He wishes to bring his wife here this evening. That is, he wishes to *deposit* his wife here this evening. I told him no, no, no. But it does no good. He is forcing my hand, and this I do not like."

"What do you mean? What's this all about?"

"Farouk has been having an affair with the wife of my uncle. I have discovered the affair, and I have insisted that he put an end to it. I told him that otherwise I would go to the entire family. He is frightened, naturally, that I may do exactly as I have said I would do, and he has been pleading with me for time. He says he will end the affair but I must give him time, he cannot simply walk away from her. Now he calls to ask if he can bring his wife here this evening while he goes to visit his mistress. He feels guilty about leaving his wife home alone. I said no, no, no . . . but in the end it was yes. I warned him, however, that if he did not end this entire business within a month I will do exactly as I have said I would do."

"How old is your brother, Leila?"

"Forty."

"Don't you feel a bit strange about interfering in the life of a forty-year-old man?"

"Not at all. He is my *brother*. And besides, I like my sister-in-law very much, and I dislike the wife of my uncle very much, and I think women who like each other should help each other. Who else is going to help us? Why *should* he be allowed to treat his wife so badly? Who else will protect a wife if it is not another wife?"

"Is he actually going to leave his wife with his sister in order to go and make love to his mistress?"

"No, no. They do not make love in the evening. He only visits with her and her husband then. They make love in the morning when the husband is at work and so, supposedly, is Farouk."

"How do you know all this? How did you discover the affair in the first place?"

Leila leaned forward, propping her face against her cupped hand, her eyes glittering with amusement and the pleasure of a good story.

"I invited the entire family here one day for afternoon tea. I had made some orange juice. The oranges were sour and I put sugar in the mixture. My uncle and his wife were among the first to arrive. She drank some of the juice and said, 'There's *sugar* in this.' Later, Farouk and his wife arrived. Farouk drank the juice and said, 'This is delicious.' My uncle's wife smacked Farouk's hand with the glass in it and said, 'Don't drink it. It has sugar in it.' Later, I offered Farouk some more of the juice and he said, 'No, I won't drink it. It has sugar in it.' And I thought to myself: But he drank it before and said it was delicious. What is happening here? He takes orders from *her*? Why? Why her?

"After that, I had only to watch and to wait. One morning I had an appointment at the Gezira Club. I walked into the club and there, sitting in a corner, were Farouk and my uncle's wife. They did not see me. That night I called Farouk and told him I knew everything. He was so foolish. I knew nothing. I was only guessing. But he admitted all immediately."

Leila's husband and daughters listened to this tale as intently as I did, as though she were re-creating it anew for them at this very moment. . . . She is the absolute queen of this beehive. Later, when she spoke on the phone with a friend whose husband had just died and she began to cry, the whole family sat watching her attentively, waiting with sympathy and concern for her to regain her queenly composure. She suffers, she laughs, she feels, she observes; she is the most beautiful and interesting person in the room—and also the most iron-willed.

At seven in the evening Leila's sister, Awatif, came down from her apartment on the floor above; with her was her thirteen-year-old son. Shortly afterward, the bell rang and Farouk and his wife entered the room. Everyone in the room—including all the children and the visiting stranger—knew that he had come to deliver his wife to his family in order to visit his mistress.

Farouk, a tall solid man with flashing eyes and a weak mouth, was very jolly and very attentive to his docile, pretty, sad-looking wife. The entire family sat in a large circle in the salon, drinking tea and eating oranges. Farouk sugared his wife's tea, lit her cigarettes, peeled her oranges, fluffed a pillow behind her back. She preened softly, sadly; and an almost visible tautness overtook the people in the circle. At last, Farouk stamped out his cigarette, slapped his thigh and said he must be going. The tautness snapped: bad character was infinitely preferable to the awful suspension of "perhaps he won't go?" Leila sighed, and rose to see her brother to the door.

Later, when the children were making a great deal of noise, laughing and running in and out of the salon, and a fresh pot of tea was brewing, Farouk's wife said to Leila, "That honey is *rotten*. And Farouk won't let me throw it out."

"But that is absurd!" Leila pronounced at once—turning softly to me to say, "*She* gave them that honey"—and then back to Farouk's wife, who was picking ruefully at the hem of her skirt. "*I'll* throw the honey out, and if he says anything send him to me."

And an hour later up she marched to Farouk's Garden City apartment to take down the rotten honey; returning to the car where Mahmoud and Awatif waited to accompany her on a visit to the *sheikh* to get advice on what to do with Farouk. Awatif had to come along because Leila is suffering from all this, and her delicate health is a matter of great concern to the entire family. It seems that Leila is so sensitive that she becomes ill when there is trouble: her stomach grinds, like some mystic Geiger counter, when anyone in the family is quarreling.

A description of Upper Egypt taken from the diary of a French soldier during the Napoleonic expedition of 1798: "A region of that tranquil monotony which is never disturbed by the shock of a single novelty, of that calm which leaves a length of time between each event in life, of that quiet where everything succeeds peaceably in the soul, where little by little an emotion becomes a sentiment, or a habit a principle, where, in a word, the lightest impression is analyzed; and this to a degree, that, in conversing (with the inhabitants) one is altogether astonished to find in them the greatest niceness of distinction and the most delicate sentiment, in company with the most absolute ignorance."

Fatma's warm, fat fingers press into my arm, her dark eyes widen and her beautiful mouth opens: Where have you gone? Whom have you seen? Famous people? Nightclubs? No, my dear! Not *really!* Tell me. Tell me all.

Fatma drives me crazy with the persistence of her questions. There is not a single night that I return before midnight that she does not open her door as the elevator reaches our floor and draw me inside "only for a single cup of tea, come, my dear, come," and then, of course, I am in for a twenty-minute grilling. I feel the startling hunger in her through these questions, the shut-in quality to her life, the amazing avidity with which she longs for news of the glamorous world. But still there is the strong, steady depth of Fatma's friendship, and I love her, and am ashamed that she rouses irritation in me.

On this particular evening as we sit drinking "only a single cup of tea," Walid, just returned—at eleven P.M.—from his evening clinic hours, joins us. He is delighted to see me, as always; the deep lines of fatigue carved into his face smooth out a bit, his eyes light up. I am an intellectual treat for Walid. He enjoys the liberty of thought that passes between us, and holds me as having the legitimate right to think and do as I please. Of course, this is not so for his wife, who is infinitely more real to him as a woman than I, the Western anomaly, can ever be. Walid and I discuss the nature of freedom as equals. Fatma is *loved* throughout all this, but clearly the choices involved in the question of freedom will never apply to her: she is an extension of her husband.

Walid excuses himself to wash and change out of his military uniform into his pajamas; then he will return in comfort to us. Looking at the uniform, I am reminded of Walid's peculiar distinction in Cairo. He is one of twelve doctors in Egypt trained at the Royal College in London. Now a cancer surgeon, recently promoted to the rank of colonel, the Egyptian Army will not let him go.

Fatma shakes her head as she watches her weary husband retreat into their bedroom. I remember the night she told me: "He aged overnight in 1967. When the war broke out he was at Ismailya. They brought him to Port Said, to Suez, everywhere. He was one of those who carried a white flag onto the field to recover the dead. He operated day and night for three weeks. He saw terrible things, terrible things. He never forgot. They made him nearly crazy, my dear. When he came home he had this gray in his hair, and the hair at the center of his head had all fallen out; it has never come back. Terrible. It was really something terrible. When he came through the door I did not recognize him and when he told us who he was my daughter cried and said, 'You are not my father!' Really! Could you believe it?"

When Walid returns to the little salon in which we sit a fresh cup of tea is poured all around. We chat about this and that for a bit. But something has been nagging at me, and I wish to hear Walid on the subject.

"Walid, could you explain something to me? I have heard lately in a number of different places that Egyptians prove to be excellent doctors abroad but they are lax or incompetent here at home. Is it true? What does that mean?"

Walid thrusts a tired hand through his gray hair, smiles that deep, comforting, intelligent smile of his and replies:

"First of all, you know, there is a saying that no man is a prophet in his own land. And to some extent this is true for the Egyptian doctor. But really it is not true that we are so very terrible here, or that we were so very wonderful abroad. We all think here that we are geniuses, but it is not true. The Egyptian, quite simply, can do what *any* human being can do in the proper circumstances. He goes abroad, he is eager to do everything, try everything, learn everything that he comes across; naturally he does well. Then he returns home. Here, he finds no facilities. Or the facilities he finds are old-fashioned. Then he finds his education resented by the old administrators and those who have been doing things the same way for all these long years. He struggles awhile. Then he gives up.

"For instance. There was a certain instrument necessary for purifying the blood during operations. I tried to get that instrument from 1964 to 1971. I never got it. Even if I were to get it today it would be useless. It has already become obsolete.

"Yes, we read the medical journals. But you know? I do not read the journals as though I were going to make use of things I read of. I read as though I am reading of distant curiosities. And when I am tired I do not read. After all, it is only intellectual curiosity, anyway. . . .

"The only doctors who really make money, who are really

respected here, are those on university staffs. And those doctors do not care about their patients or their students; they care only for the research that will increase their names. It is really a sad and strange contradiction.

"I have been an Army doctor now for fifteen years. At first, I grumbled, it is true, and I thought I had made a great mistake. But since the 1967 War I do not feel this way. I was at Suez then, and I will never forget it. I treated men who needed me, who were doing something for my country, and they still need me, and they are still doing something—however hopeless—for my country. Now I am very glad to be an Army doctor. . . . But if this bloody war should ever end I will be glad to leave. Yes, then I will leave."

It is all over between Farid and Debbie, and God help him, it is just beginning for Farid.

Five days ago Debbie called me at three in the afternoon. "I'm at the railroad station. I'm leaving for Alexandria in fifteen minutes. Farid is waiting there for me."

"*What*?" I didn't even know that Farid wasn't in Cairo.

"Yes. Yes. I'm going. I don't care. I don't care what happens. I must go. I feel mad! Mad! But I must go. He is waiting for me. We'll be together. I don't care *what* happens anymore."

Forty-eight hours later she was back in Cairo, a changed woman. The fever had drained entirely from her. She was satiated, triumphant, free. It had been marvelous, wonderful, exciting—the man was a fantastic *animal*—all those hours locked up together in Alexandria's poshest hotel. . . . And now she *knew*, and wasn't it a bit sad, but after all, it was better to know, wasn't it, than not to know, and yes, she definitely would have gone through with it, despite everything, despite her parents and her boyfriend back in the States and the institute in Paris and well, just *everything*, but it was really of no use, she didn't love Farid. That was definite, now. She did not love Farid. And, oh yes. She was leaving for Paris in a week.

And what of Farid?

Suddenly: shattered by Debbie. Wretched, shallow, uninteresting Debbie! Acting out of her own hysterical need to believe herself special she has, in the process, convinced Farid that she needed his love. And, presto! She has touched some terrible fantasy lying around inside him like an exposed nerve, and he has fallen apart before my very eyes. But fallen apart like I've never seen before. All is out: his shabby, weak life; his three marriages—first to an Egyptian Jew ten years older than himself, next to an ambitious actress who married him for his connections, and third to a brutal, smoldering sexpot, a woman who is all shrewd instinct and coarse sexuality; his need—oh God, can I feel for *that*—to be needed, to be adored, to be looked up to, to seek oblivion in sensation; his need to believe that he can *still* be loved; the terrible weakness at the center of this man who looks more and more like a sad elephant each day; his feverish fixation now on having Debbie; his mad, mad plan to go to Paris and "fight for her and win her."

Farid clings to me with his eyes and his words. "Don't leave me," he pleads. "I have no one but you. Whom do I dare speak to? Whom would I tell this to?"

He feels himself lost, and his life passes daily before his dulled eyes.

"Really, I don't know what it is, but I feel this girl is mine, that I must have her. . . . You know, at my age and with all my experience, I never thought I could be loved again. Yes, that is the truth. I did not imagine this could happen to me again. And when she came, and she sat right there on that chair facing you, and she made me believe that she loved me, and later when she came to me, and I gave her the ticket for Alexandria and she said, 'I am mad, absolutely mad,' still I could not believe it. But after that night in Alex I must believe it. And now I must *have* it. . . .

"We passed eighteen hours together that really were among the happiest in my life. And when I remember how she was sitting with her head against my back, so contented, so full . . . and then later . . . I do not understand, Vivian, how could she be acting this way now? What is she? Is she a child? Or a woman? Or what? That night she was completely a woman. She kissed me all over, my hands, my face, my back, and in the morning she came to me and she said, 'Farid, you are a master. You can do anything you want to do.' She knew I was weak, but I tell you it was after *everything* that she said to me, '*Ya*-Farid, you are a master.'

"I must have her. I don't care anymore. I don't care about anything. She is mine. She belongs to me. . . ."

His eyes are a haze of watery film and his thick lips tremble; the cigarette ash falls unheeded onto his white-shirted chest; the heavy glasses slip down on the sweating bridge of his nose.

But there is more to this than an infantile American woman passing through Cairo, and on the day that Debbie leaves for Paris Farid and I sit in the welcome cool of Shepard's lobby and he digs deeper into his life than he ever has before with me. For years now he has inertly remained "a number-two man, a routine man," he has long ceased to do any work of significance, he has given over too many times, he has forgotten how to think, how to write, how to go after a story. Part of the reason he finds himself in this position is political. Nasser always appointed the editors of all the magazines and newspapers in Egypt. The word always went out from the president's office on who was to go up, down, or out. Farid was always to be kept, but to be kept number two. To this day there are two managing editors at *Al Kahira*: Farid and a man who is a Communist of the regime.

Debbie, he thought, was his last chance to make a genuine life for himself.

He stares hopelessly at me across the cool light streaming through Shepard's long arched windows. I see in his eyes the dreadful desire to conquer himself coming to panicky life out of all that painful spiritual sluggishness surrounded by all that symptomatic obesity. . . . He has it in him to put up a struggle. I *know* he does.

"I must leave this country," he says. "I must get away from all this. If I don't go now I will get used to it, and that is the end."

I nod my head hard at him. "Yes," I agree. "You must. You must get out of here. Go to Europe or the United States or even some other part of Africa. Go where you will be alone, and you will have nothing but yourself to fall back on. If you can, *go. Go.*"

"Promise you will take me with you when you go," Farid says. "No, not to the United States. But only out into Europe. I will make my way somehow after that. Only make sure I leave Egypt when you do."

I stare at him in astonishment. Then: "Yes, Farid. I promise. I promise you will leave Egypt when I do. We will fly together into

Europe and I will stay with you until you get your bearings. I
promise you this."

We are so excited suddenly that nothing will do but to make
concrete plans. We put our heads together and consult a calendar.
We talk about money, his wife, how long it will take to wrap up his
affairs at *Al Kahira*, how much longer I can remain in Cairo, and we
settle on a date: July tenth. On the tenth of July Farid and I will fly
out of Egypt together.

We stare at each other. We have arrived at a finality that seems so
sudden! But is it really? Is this "sudden" decision in actuality not
merely the conscious recognition of an emotional event that has
already taken place—in both of us?

"You really mustn't leave the Middle East without seeing another
Arabic capital," the *New York Times* man said. "In fact, it would be
best to leave Cairo, and then return here. The perspective will be
invaluable for you."

I had come to him one day in distress, suddenly feeling closed off
from the world, a dreadful muffled sense of being off the map, sealed
into Cairo, cut off, shut away from the action. The intelligent,
reserved man behind the desk in the Immobilia Building had smiled
a weary diplomatic smile and said, "You don't know what a closed
city is. Try living in Moscow sometime. Cairo is the most open city in
the world after that. But if you think Cairo is closed, travel a bit in
other Arabic countries, then see how you feel."

I decided I would do as he suggested, and on May eighth I began
to plan a trip into Lebanon, and perhaps also to Syria. I would see
how things went.

Soad and Gasbia were more excited than I at the prospect of a trip
to Beirut. They themselves had never been out of the country. We
drank tea on the now-blooming balcony in Zamalek, and they gave
me a list of things they wanted brought back from the Lebanese city
they both despised and hungered to see.

"Remember," Soad sniffed. "When you go to buy in Beirut under
no circumstances are you to accept the price that is given you!
Remember! They are all thieves in Lebanon. *All*! Not one is

straightforward or honest. It is the aim of their hearts and their minds and their bodies that you should leave their country with not a single penny in your pocket. Whatever they say, you offer one-half, and then pay one-quarter. Remember!"

"But," Gasbia shrieked softly, "bring back a whistling teakettle. I have wanted one for so long! And a bathing suit for Nahed. And a silk blouse for me."

"And three brassieres for me," Soad added demurely. "And mail a pair of shoes to Ali Mahmoud. There is nothing in America like Egyptian leather. I will buy them here and you will mail them there. It is better that way. The customs in Beirut will not be as difficult as they are in Cairo."

And, and, and . . . The contained consumer hungers of Cairo go wild at the mere mention of Beirut, which exists in the Egyptian mind as a delectable mixture of Sodom and Babylon: a glittering marketplace where everything—oh isn't it terrible! isn't it wonderful!—*everything* is for sale.

The clerk at the Passport Control Office in the Mogamaa was not quite so overcome at the prospect of my making a trip to Beirut. She sat behind her grimy desk fingering my visa renewal form for the hundredth time, while for the hundredth time I stood before her, my brain straining to read her face, my stomach muscles beginning to tense.

My relations with the Mogamaa had troubled and angered me; they nagged often at the back of my mind as I went about my daily business in Cairo. But it wasn't until now, when I sought an exit visa from Egypt along with the reassurance of an untroubled return, that they had begun to assume Kafkaesque proportions in my mind.

I entered Egypt originally with a tourist visa issued by the UAR Interests Section at the Indian Embassy in Washington; although I had announced my intention of remaining in Cairo for four or five months the visa was marked "good for one month only." When I questioned the UAR in Washington about this I was assured that it was only a matter of formality for me to renew my visa each month in Cairo up to a period of six months. However, once in Cairo, matters had not proceeded quite so smoothly as I was led to believe they would. Within a week of my arrival in the Egyptian capital Magdi took me down to the Mogamaa (the word means "collection of agencies"), the great semi-circular municipal building that stands in Tahrir Square. Here, we climbed the tremendous spiral staircase that fills the center of the building to a dingy little room where a man in dark glasses and a uniform received my visa and Magdi's application formally registering me as a foreigner residing at his address. The man behind the desk was quick and extremely polite to "the Captain" and me. He told Magdi that all I had to do was return in three weeks' time and I would automatically be granted a visa renewal.

Three weeks later, Fatma Shanawany took me back to the Mogamaa to reregister me as now residing at the house in Mohammed Sidki Street (the first order of business is that the Egyptian government should at all times know exactly where every foreigner in Cairo is living), and we then entered the visa renewal office. Here, in another dingy room, this one divided by a high counter on one side of which were three desks and on the other side never fewer than twenty-five people at a time scrambling for the attention of the occupants of those three desks. Fatma spoke to a heavy young woman with thick glasses dressed sloppily in shapeless black and slippers. She sat behind one of those desks, nodding tiredly at everything Fatma said. (Egypt's civil servants, overemployed, underworked, depressed and ignorant, without any sense of participation or hope in the system under which they live, are sluggish, stupid, officious, bewildered.) Finally, the clerk asked me if I had bank receipts worth thirty pounds. Yes, I said. She then pulled out a long form printed in Arabic and directed me to fill it out. With Fatma translating, I answered all the questions and returned the form. The woman behind the desk scanned it lazily, looking up only once to say to me in faltering English, "But you have write in *none* for religion. You are Christian, yes?" I told Fatma to explain to her that all Americans are atheists; we never identify ourselves by religion. Fatma (who did not know I was Jewish) looked queerly at me, but translated what I had said. The clerk and Fatma stared at each other. Fatma shrugged her shoulders as much as to say: These Americans are primitives. What can one do? The clerk nodded her head, made one or two marks here and there on the form with a thick black pencil, and told me to return to this office in ten days.

Ten days later I returned to the Mogamaa and was told that there was some delay in the matter of my visa renewal. The clerk did not know why; no matter, she shrugged her shoulder; it was surely of no importance; come again next week. Since that day I have returned once a week on schedule to this office. Each week the woman in the black dress smiles cheerfully at me and says, "Come back next week." Each week I say, "What is wrong? What is holding up the renewal?" And each week she replies, "Nothing. Only some small complications. The ministry has not yet returned your renewal form. You must come next week, please?" "What ministry?" I say. "What complications? If you would just tell me what is wrong perhaps I could clear it up for you."

At this point she no longer understands my English, and the conversation is at an end. But when I look over her shoulder at my original application form lying on her desk I know something is wrong, terribly wrong (but what? what?). The pencilled writing on the form has increased, the slash marks, the inked rubber-stamping . . . and I know from Fatma that the police have been to the house, questioning everyone about the American woman on the fourth floor: What do they know about her? What is she doing here? Why do they think she wishes to remain in Cairo? . . . I turn away from the clerk in the Passport Control Office and walk slowly out into the hall where I am immediately swamped by the fearful crush of people that at all times fills the corridors of the Mogamaa.

From the very beginning I have always felt that the place was like some great DP camp during a national siege. The look in the Mogamaa is of thousands of refugees milling endlessly through dirty green offices occupied by slatternly women and dull-witted uniforms behind scarred desks, all shuffling along in the Middle-Eastern version of the "revolutionary bureaucracy," hiking up their slovenly black hems, peering meanly through their glasses: withholding the stamp, the card, the signature that everyone so desperately seeks. Meanwhile, out in the corridors and on the other side of every counter in every room on every floor: hundreds of people who look as though they've been sitting here for three days, and expect to go on sitting for three days more. Every now and then some peasant

woman in a black *milayeh* seems about to faint or scream; but the
confused and beset-upon man in the *gelabya* standing beside her will
speak intently into her ear for a moment; her exhausted black eyes
register comprehension and she pulls herself together. Another six
hours pass and once again the ritual of exhaustion and patient
resuscitation is enacted. And still the official they must see has not
come, the forms they are waiting for have not arrived, the office they
stand before is not unlocked.

Now, I stood once more in "Room Number Ten—Passport
Control" before the by-now rather kindly woman in the black dress.
I was at this moment illegally in Cairo, and had been for two months.
The woman behind the desk began automatically to shake her head
at the sight of me walking through the door. I ignored her motion,
and said, "I want to go to Beirut for ten days. I need an exit visa and
the assurance of permission to return to Cairo."

"*Hamdulallah!*" she said in a low voice, and began looking
bewilderedly about the room. She then extracted my by now
well-thumbed application from her file, looked seriously at it for a
moment, frowned, and said, "Take it to that man over there."

I took it to that man over there. He was short and breathless, also
wearing thick glasses, and looked altogether as though he didn't
know what the hell was going on at any given moment in the day. He
listened to my request, frowned at the form, read it over twice, his
lips moving, and said, "Take this to Room 47."

Room 47 looked like a Soviet official. But he also only read the
form over twice, glared fiercely at it, and then looked up with
masklike neutrality to say, "Take this to Room 82."

Room 82 was thin, dark, moustached, and looked like Egyptian
Intelligence. He stared at the form for a long time. A very long time.
And he frowned *heavily*. Now, for the first time I began to feel
frightened. The conviction began to grow in me that this thin, dark
man was going to look up and say, "You're under arrest." My heart
began to beat so quickly I was afraid I wouldn't hear him over the
noise.

But what am I guilty of? I found myself thinking. What? What?

(When I repeated this sequence of events to Farid he said, "Every
time an Egyptian wants to leave the country can you imagine what
he goes through? A country in which every citizen is constantly

under the kind of scrutiny designed to make him feel guilty? I used to go through this for weeks over an exit visa. Every week I'd go, and then I'd begin to tremble when I just passed the Mogamaa. One day, an official I knew called me aside. He said, 'Farid, I see you are very nervous. Let me give you some advice. When you come to apply for a visa just put it in your mind that you are not going to get it. After that everything will be easy.' ")

Then, suddenly, for no reason at all, I was granted an exit visa—good for two weeks—with the assurance that the Egyptian Embassy in Beirut would grant me a reentrance visa with no trouble whatsoever. I prepared to leave Cairo. What the hell? I thought. Someone would bail me out if there was trouble in Beirut.

May thirteenth: Nabil came last night at eleven o'clock, standing in the hall, thin and dark, his eyes luminous. Full of feverish excitement: there had nearly been a coup within the last twenty-four hours and the government had just sacked Ali Sabry, the pro-Soviet vice-president, and eight of his chums: the minister of the interior, Field-Marshal Mohammed Fawzi, and a string of others whose names I could barely register. Nabil was delirious with joy.

"Things are going well! This Sadat! What a reasonable man! We will be friends, your country and mine! These vulgar, stupid buffoons will be gone!" Nabil sits on the bed, untying his tie, and in a quieter, more bitter tone: "And at last, we will be able to breathe again. . . ."

He clasps me to his thin, hot, nervous body. So many things make him feverish tonight: the political situation; his favorite aunt is suddenly possibly cancerous; his doctoral research; that godforsaken desert in which the days of his life are draining away; the few snatched hours with me. It is a compendium of current and continual crisis: Egyptian crisis.

The entire city is swept up in the excitement of the near-coup and the extraordinary promise of Sadat's midnight speech to his people. Everyone is instantly aware of the enormous implications of the removal of the so-called Soviet hatchet men from the government and Sadat's announcement that a new life is about to begin in Egypt; in the most effective speech to the people that Nasser's successor has yet made it is announced that: the treacherously undermining surveillance under which the Egyptian people have been living is about to end (i.e., the thousands of telephones that are tapped will cease to be tapped and the tapes will be burned); free elections to the Socialist Union will begin; the United Arab Republic will no longer be the name by which the Egyptian people will call their beloved Egypt; from this moment on the country is to be called the Republic of Egypt.

In the streets of Cairo a state of happy confusion. People are marching and demonstrating everywhere; truckloads of farmers are sweeping into the city; chants of "Viva Sadat!" are heard on every street corner (from this day on a remarkable visual change in the city: whereas before only Nasser's picture was plastered everywhere, now Sadat's picture will also be plastered everywhere); in every office in Cairo men and women embrace and exclaim, "Isn't it wonderful? Isn't it wonderful?" In the offices of *Al Kahira* it is almost as though a national holiday has been declared. The paper is being ripped apart to make way for new articles, new pictures, new profiles, new plaudits and new denunciations. A reporter about to leave for London pumps my hand vigorously and says (and I swear there are *tears* in his eyes), "For the first time in twenty years I am proud to be an Egyptian. I go abroad *proud* of Egypt. You cannot imagine what it feels like! To imagine that we will breathe freely again!" He has used almost the exact words that Nabil spoke last night. . . . For the first time since I have been in Cairo it begins to dawn on me that it is not the disinherited rich who have really hated Nasser, but rather the bourgeois liberals who have not their money to lose but the freedom of thought inside their heads that cannot *live* while they fear the knock on the door at three o'clock in the morning. . . .

Three weeks later the euphoria will have passed, and the joke around Cairo will be: "Of course, they burned the tapes. They were all used up. They needed new ones."

Beirut lies tossed out in a long, narrow arc along the glittering shore of the Mediterranean; behind the coastline, the city reaches out, climbing, climbing up into the foothills of the Lebanese mountains at its back. Threaded through its hilly back districts are the old Arab ghettos, but along the shore of the glimmering sea Beirut is pure Miami Beach: a stretch of hotels, bars, cafés and clubs that all look as though they went up yesterday. Sharp, clean and plastic: the result of all the European and American wealth that, since socialism came to Cairo, has transformed Beirut from a pretty Arab-Christian village into the international business center of the Middle East. The price the city has paid for its incredible welcome of Western wealth is a confusion of Arabic identity that is extraordinary to behold.

You can feel it instantly, the moment you step from the plane, the difference between Beirut and Cairo. It is there in the slightest Lebanese motion, the subtlest tone of voice, the chic details of dress, the abrupt politeness with which business is conducted, the vicious speed of the cars, the quick jerky quality of the Arabic spoken. The atmosphere of Beirut is like that of Europe or the States, as alien to the slow warmth of Cairo as Rome or New York is. This Arab-Christian city—like the cities of the West—is guarded. Guarded and ambitious. For after all, there is something to guard here: money. And even more important than money itself: *the prospect of making money.*

I wander the streets of Beirut for seven days. In my wanderings I meet Egyptians, Germans, Syrians, Americans, displaced Palestinians. The Westerners are all here making money, the Easterners are all in economic or political exile:

A Palestinian who knows only that I am American takes me on a tour of the Palestinian camps that are located all over Beirut's outskirts. Thousands of people are crowded together in these camps that are tin-shack villages without plumbing, without electricity, without transportation, without, without. . . . I know why I have been brought here.

"I've seen worse in Upper Egypt," I say belligerently.

"That is not the point," the Palestinian says with great dignity.

An American I meet one day says to me, "I've got to get my family out of here. The dirt is incredible. We just can't take it anymore." I stare at him in amazement. To me Beirut is a miracle of shining cleanliness.

The bars along the shore's "downtown" district are filled with Egyptian B-girls—immediately distinguishable from the Lebanese girls who are thin and chic in contrast with the Egyptians who are buxom and sensual. They say in Beirut that the girls come pouring in from Egypt; their families back home think that they are working as governesses or domestics; of course the girls never return to Egypt.

I have dinner one night at the home of an Egyptian neurologist and his American wife; the neurologist works at the American University in Beirut. Except for the fact that their home is a villa clinging to the side of an elegantly climbing street with a magnificent view of the Mediterranean, we might be sitting in the California suburbs: the rugs on the floor are Navajo in design, the kitchen is out of *House Beautiful*, the wine is French, and the tableware is Danish. The people at the table are Lebanese and immaculate; the conversation is as immaculate as the people. I feel restless and out of place.

I sit in a café on a wide boulevard near the sea drinking coffee out of an elegant white earthenware cup. All around me, at the pretty yellow and orange tables scattered across the café's tile-covered terrace, sits the entire collection of Beirut's motley population, dominated by the slim Lebanese men and women in European mod clothes, pretending to a worldly boredom they have carefully studied on the screens of the sleek movie houses they pack each night. The sun shines blindly, the sea glimmers, the sky is blue and cloudless; on the white beaches men and women in bikinis and dark glasses made in France lie sunning themselves.

But, somehow, the dust of Cairo rises up before me, obscuring my vision. . . .

I stroll along the streets passing from residential neighborhoods filled with lovely, well-kept houses behind wrought-iron gates whose open spaces are filled with thick green foliage and flowering bushes dancing in the cool, bright sun into business districts whose sparkling windows abound in tasteful displays of the goods of the world: fruit from Switzerland, dresses from France, appliances from America, cheese from Holland, coffee-grinders from Germany.

I want to go home runs through my mind. And with a start I realize I am thinking of Cairo.

Cairo! That filthy, sprawling, passionate city out there in the middle of that godforsaken desert, struggling to get to its dusty knees. What on earth am I doing here in the midst of all this ersatz gleam? I feel uneasy, immoral, more wretchedly dislocated than ever.

His name is Abdul Mohammed Levenson. He is an American Jew who converted nine years ago to Islam and, until the 1967 War, lived within the shadow of Jerusalem's Wailing Wall—on the Arab side. After '67 things were a bit difficult; he became known as a renegade Jew working for the Jordanians, someone Israeli Intelligence was just a bit too interested in. He now lives in Beirut, making his living as the editor of an English-language newspaper.

Levenson is my age exactly; he is Jewish; he is from New York City; we have many mutual friends, and—although we have never met until this moment here in Beirut—we have worked for the same New York newspaper. Yet, it is a vital difference, rather than these easy similarities, that has governed our lives, his and mine: whereas I was raised in the immigrant working-class ghetto of the Bronx, Levenson grew up in Scarsdale, the son of wealthy middle-class Jews who had climbed farther up the ladder of assimilation than my parents working three lifetimes could have climbed. Exactly how and why this difference operated to make Levenson take on a variety of political passions—ranging from Eisenhowerism to the drug culture —during the last fifteen years of his life while I remained stubbornly scornful of *all* political passions is difficult to say; but operate it surely did, and we have traveled in multiple ways down different roads—confused searchers in the ill-fitting cloak of defensive behavior—toward this curious moment: two Jewish children of the displaced New World meeting here in the heart of the Middle East, Levenson clasping the Moslem prayer beads he carries at all times, me looking with hot eyes at every Arab walking down the street. ("Tell me," says Levenson. "Do they do it like they pray?") Levenson and I stare at each other. I see suddenly that I, like he, also respond to the Middle East out of some rooted need; some root of fantasy is touched for both of us by the Arabs: I sexually, he religiously, both erotically. . . . It dawns on me that the sex with Nabil is bad because it can never be good; there is no substance between us, only the fabrications of mysterious longing; to sleep with him is to drink at the well of fantasy. . . . Who *are* we, Levenson and I? And *where* are we? Are we home? Are we in exile? Are we allies? Are we enemies? What is the connective thread that forces Levenson (I cannot bring myself to call him Abdul) and me to find in each other some abortive attraction to an original memory that would surely never have been triggered had we met in New York?

We talk endlessly for two days, especially me. To be able to tell a New York Jew (to hell with the prayer beads) what I have found in Egypt! To watch his quick response, and even quicker comprehension. To be able to tell so much while explaining so little: half an idiom here, half a gesture there, he understands everything, everything.

But we are not kind to each other, Levenson and I. Not kind at all. One night I return to my hotel to find a large folded card of white pasteboard with a red-foil mosque cut into its center; inside the card a message from Levenson:

> Although it has taken two years to crawl from here to the Holy Cities of the Hijaz and back as an act of piety and the cuts and open sores on my knees and elbows will make a mess of the upholstery . . . nevertheless, I must have you.
>
> Overpoweringly yours,
> Zaim al-Adat Sittat

The next morning over coffee I say to Levenson, "What's this all about?"

He stirs his coffee nervously; crosses his legs nervously; and nervously he says, "I'm offering you temporary marriage."

"Why?"

He looks steadily at me for a long moment. Then he sighs. "You're bubbling at the source."

"And you are reminded of an older life," I say without pity.

I do not realize how frightened Levenson has made me; I only know that I am angry and contemptuous. I reject him coyly . . . he flinches before my indirection . . . then it's his turn.

We sit late one night in an Arabic restaurant in the old town. Our table is at the far end of the restaurant, against a mirrored wall that makes of us four instead of two; the place is bathed in a brownish-yellowish light; we eat a cream dessert; the Arabic waiters are dressed in European black-suit; a Syrian journalist enters and salutes Levenson.

Levenson the mystic has become Levenson the historian. He sits explaining the *true* causes of the Arab-Israeli war to me: it is a case of economic determinism that Levenson argues with an acuteness so informed, a disinterest so melancholy, a sense of fate so Marxist, a love of facts so spiritually encompassing that he stirs something old and deep inside of me. I feel what I feel with painful rarity: that I am in the presence of the deepest, the most familiar, the most thoroughly accepting; that here, with Levenson, I may not be loved but more important—oh, infinitely more important!—I am "known." I feel what I have not genuinely felt for more than a moment in life since I was a little girl, sitting at that kitchen table in the Bronx with my parents and their socialist friends, drinking tea while my father cut large slices of pumpernickel bread spread with thick butter and they all explained to each other the "real" meanings of the New Deal, the Russian pacts, the purge trials . . . and I, excited by the words and the richness of their rhetoric and the longing behind their analyses, felt *safe*, as I have never since felt safe. . . . Now, I sat across a table in Beirut from this boy from Scarsdale fingering Moslem prayer beads and I wanted him never to come any closer, never to retreat any farther. I wanted him always to be there, exactly where he was, saying what he was saying, and I always to be where I was, feeling safe and at peace, protected by his presence and his words. I wanted us to remain suspended in time and space, for I was feeling again the lost warmth of those people and those days, of that time that came so early and lived so briefly, and left in its wake a welter of panic and loss and confusion of the soul. Oh, Levenson! Did any of this ever happen? Is it something I dreamed? Some fabrication of grievous longing? Some manufactured memory of nurturance in this wilderness of obscurity and isolation? No matter. It drifts through a tunnel of time and has come to rest in me, and here at this moment it is awakened with force.

When we return to my hotel Levenson says, "Let me come up."

"No," I say.

No, Levenson. But don't go away. Yes. But don't come any closer. I need something from you, Levenson. But I don't know what it is. And I don't know what price I'm willing to pay for it.

"Fuck you," says Levenson, and turns away into the gray dawn of Beirut.

I stare after him, knowing that I will never lay eyes on him again, and I am reminded—with more force than ever—that I will come away from Egypt knowing only that in that desperately anxious country where everyone is in need, and no one can identify his need, I feel myself at one with the people.

And now I want to leave Beirut. Fast. But not yet to Cairo, not yet. . . .

An Egyptian journalist offers to drive me across the Lebanese mountains into Syria and spend a day in Damascus with me. I have been eager to go but a bit nervous, and am grateful for the Egyptian's reassuring company. I agree, and we plan to rise early the next morning and leave before the heat sets in.

The Lebanese mountains are not quite like any other range I have traveled in. Their steepness is cut by a deceptively wide rolling appearance, and as one travels deeper and higher into them the green of the wooded mountainsides gives way to a white sunny rockiness that is reminiscent of volcanic land. . . . There is in these mountains some especially sweet recklessness I cannot properly identify, but bound up somehow with the Lebanese peasants in the many mountain villages who look queerly displaced—as though they should be Bavarians, not Lebanese—but *gay*; and reckless.

We drive for two hours across these mountains in the back of a hired car, coming at last to the Syrian border. As we approach the customs shacks set up on both sides of the mountain road patrolled by soldiers of Lebanon and of Syria my Egyptian friend leans over and says quietly, "Remember. You are a Protestant American schoolteacher." I nod, grateful and nervous at the same time that the American passport lists neither occupation nor religion.

The Lebanese barely flick an eye in my direction. The Syrians make a bit of a to-do. They consult a large list tacked to the wall of the customs shack, arguing over it among themselves. At last the Egyptian explains, "There is a different customs fee for each nationality. As you can imagine, my dear Vivian, your country commands the highest fee. However, you are to be here less than twenty-four hours. So one of them is saying, 'It is not fair to charge so much for so little a time.' The others are saying, 'Rules are rules.' You can imagine who will win out."

"What is the range of admissions prices?" I ask.

"As little as fifty cents for a Saudi Arabian, as much as eight dollars for an American."

"Eight *dollars*! That's outrageous! That's . . ."

My Egyptian friend is nodding calmly, exasperated by the Syrians but also equally exasperated by me. The last time he crossed this border Nasser had just done something the Syrians didn't like, and he spent forty-eight hours in jail. Why the hell am I complaining about eight dollars when he may wind up at the police station if the headlines change within the next few hours?

We give the Syrians my eight dollars, and we're off, pushing on down the road, now very close to the ancient capital that is our destination. On the road we pass truckloads of Syrian soldiers: thin, ill-clad, young, dark, they look like juvenile delinquents. The trucks look like covered wagons. The weapons look like surplus from the American Civil War. My heart begins to sink.

A day in Damascus leaves me with a set of fleeting impressions that are alive with contradictions. St. Paul called Damascus the "city of fragrance," and indeed when one drives up into the hills above the city and looks down, Damascus is a marvel of tall thick perfumed green in a mustard-colored valley surrounded by the gentle Syrian hills; but on the streets the green trees are hidden, sealed off in walled gardens, unavailable to the pedestrian, and the city looks bleak, hot, biblical; oddly barren and with a loneliness unknown in Cairo. The center of the town is an incongruous mixture of wide newly laid concrete roads with steel-beamed street lights hanging over them, and ancient cobblestoned streets, narrow and dark. The women on the streets look like walking death's-heads: a black diaphanous cloth pinned to the tops of their heads and dropping down over their faces and over the backs of their heads into their black ankle-length shrouds is the uniform dress of three out of five (I remember wistfully that Syrian women are reputed to be possessed of the finest strain of Arabic beauty). In a narrow overarched street I am jostled by three men in military fatigues with bayonets strapped to their shoulders: fighters in the Al Fatah; in a distant Coptic neighborhood, suddenly, an overpowering sense of medieval Europe: streets narrow and harshly clean, high garden walls with open gates leading to tiled courtyards and splashing fountains, stone churches and men in long black dress with golden crosses swinging from long chains.

But what is most depressing in Damascus, and most memorable, is the silence: that ancient silence of a forgotten city that dominates its streets, its bazaars, even its cafés. . . .

The next day in Beirut, with glad heart and purposeful stride, I board the plane for Cairo.

Cairo. *Great* Cairo. Oh, this city that has remained alive and continuously lived in for more than a thousand years. The mercurial solidity of life that has flowed beneath the invasions for all these many years. Desert routes and caravans may come and go but Great Cairo remains alive; Sudanese tribes, Turkish Ottomans, European commissioners: all may come and go but Great Cairo remains alive—and Egyptian. Again, the overwhelming sensation of men in the Lawrentian sense: doe-eyed, sloe-eyed men in a loose embrace moving at an angle, almost floating in the air, through the flooded human streets of Cairo. The noise, the dirt, the rush. The passionate longing. That is what gives Cairo the right to still be called great. It was good to be home.

Over coffee in Lappa's, Leila Soliman listened to me speak of returning to Cairo and she said, "Two years ago I was in Russia. I did not enjoy the Russians, and the time passed slowly. One night in a club they knew I was Egyptian, and the musicians played an

Egyptian folksong in which a young man is calling to his sweetheart, Shelabiyah, to come and sit with him under the lemon tree, and in the song he calls her his *bet*. Now, you have to know that when you hear the name Shelabiyah you are among Egyptians of the lowest class (it is a name given nowhere else). And when an Egyptian says *bet* it is a lower-class corruption of the word *bent* for girl. And now that we are in a period of rediscovering our folkloric past this song which has been sung for hundreds of years is being played all over Egypt. And when I heard this song that night in Moscow I wanted" (Leila closes her eyes and her hands fly to her breast) "to run back to this Egypt and smell the dust and the mud and the filth once more! Oh, I can't tell you!"

And yet, I stood one night in the middle of one of the bridges looking down at the Nile, and out at the winding Corniche to the left of me, and the Giza skyline to the right, and I felt suddenly as though I were being buried alive, diving down into some soft, doughy center that was Cairo itself. And I wanted air, I wanted to surface, I wanted to swim, fly, run, walk away from it. I saw then that New York and Cairo are, indeed, emotional polarities: New York a glittering, defensive cold in which one walks alone with a wide space around the self, while Cairo wraps itself round in a thick, warm, soft band, clinging to the dissolving separateness. Within these contexts, of course, people's personalities emerge: they battle, and rage, and submit, and struggle to be themselves—but always and only within the given context. . . . I was gripped then by a terrible hunger for New York: for what was deeply my own, for that place in which I could most successfully struggle to be myself, for that brutal idiom which alone could truly define my experience.

What a misery! For I know I will mourn the warmth once I am back in the brilliant cold.

In the flat in Zamalek all was confused excitement. The Vivian was here with presents from Beirut, and Soad had caught a bird.

"I was writing a letter to Ali Mahmoud," Soad confided to me, her hand a loose fist in her apron pocket. "When suddenly. With no warning a'tall. This little thing flew into the window and settled on my desk. Oh! I thought to myself. This is good luck. This is *really* good luck. And I put out my hand ever so gently, ever so silently. And I caught him in my hand." She withdrew her hand from her pocket. In it she held a small yellow-brown bird, chirping madly. The children danced around Soad, reaching up for the bird.

"*La, la,*" Soad said. "Go get the cage. You will frighten the poor thing to death." They ran out of the room and returned in a moment with a beautiful bamboo cage into which the little bird was placed. It hopped onto the bar inside the cage and blinked idiotically at the children who crowed with laughter and clapped their hands.

"What a beautiful cage!" I said. Everyone nodded.

"It costs seventy piastres," mourned Gasbia. I stared at her. She was like a French *concierge* whose head could calculate loss and gain faster than any cash register in the world. Sometimes it seemed to me that Gasbia would one day lose her reason under the pressure of that rapid adding and subtracting that continually dinned in her mind.

"That's not so very much," I said. "Forget it. Look how beautiful the cage is, and how much pleasure it gives the children."

"Yes, pleasure, pleasure," Gasbia shrieked softly. "Everyone must have pleasure and I must pay for it!"

Soad spoke sharply to Gasbia in Arabic, and then turned to me.

"*Ya*-Vivian, you must not take notice of Gasbia today. She is overexcited as the issue of Za-Za's marriage has come up again."

"What is the issue of Za-Za's marriage? Isn't everything settled?"

"Yes," Gasbia murmured. "All *too* settled."

"You see," explained Soad, "the arrangements are as follows. Upon agreement that two people shall marry the groom is required to bring two hundred pounds to the bride's father. The father of the bride then supplies approximately three hundred pounds and with that money the bride's gold is purchased plus all the furnishings that are required for the proper preparation of a flat. Now in the case of the marriage of the Za-Za, her father, who is an old man in the village, is incapable of giving the money. So the burden falls upon Dr. Ibrahim. The groom brought only one hundred and fifty pounds to the father. The old man then took fifty of those pounds for himself, and turned the rest over to us. So all we had was one hundred pounds. With that" (Soad went on, eloquently turning fingers, one by one) "we had to buy the gold, the furniture, the silver, the china, the curtains. Really! It is ridiculous!"

At this point Gasbia seemed to go into a frenzy. Her breath came quickly, her eyes rolled wildly around in her face, her mascara began to moisten. She slapped the side of her left thigh and screamed, "They think we grow money in the garden, these crazy people! They think all we have to do is ask, and the money appears. And they think it is all coming to them! *She*. This stupid girl. She does not think she must wait and work and pay for her marriage herself. No. She wants to marry and *we* must pay." Gasbia was nearly tearing her hair out of her head. Clearly, she thought about the money she was forking over for Za-Za's marriage day and night, and she burned today, a year after these negotiations had begun, as brightly as she undoubtedly had on the very first day. She rushed over to me, the heavy pancake makeup on her face beginning to sweat, her hands beating the air.

"Two pounds a day it costs me to live," she shrieked into my face. "Two pounds! Do I get it in the street? Where do I get it? Where?"

"That is enough," Soad said sharply. "Hold your tongue before you say something you will regret the rest of your life."

Gasbia stared wild-eyed at her mother; at that moment she bore a striking resemblance to a horse who's just been shot in the head. But she remained silent, and slowly her large breasts stopped heaving, her breath came more evenly, the sweat dried on her face. She shrugged her shoulders and grinned at me, her considerable store of kindliness coming at last to her aid. "Ach! It is all so silly, is it not? Come, let us have a cup of tea and forget all this nonsense."

Little Amal climbed up onto Soad's lap and lay sucking her thumb with her head against her grandmother's breast. Soad rocked her and buried her nose in the child's rich black curls. After a while she said to me, "How many have I given suck to! How I would love to suckle this child as well! When I was nursing Gasbia my youngest sister was one year old. When I was gone from the house my mother took Gasbia onto her free breast, and when she was gone I suckled my sister. And she was a *devil*. Really! She sucked and she sucked and she sucked at me. Until she had *fully*. And *completely*. Taken into herself and absorbed every drop of milk in me. . . . Ah! She is *still* hungry, that one!"

When tea was served Soad raised her cup and sipped at the rich brown mint-flavored liquid, her eyes off in the distance. She seemed to be thinking still of those dead and gone days of her young life. But when she spoke she looked directly at me and she said, "Well, it is done. The Captain has married the Naha."

My cup nearly fell from my saucer.

"You must be joking," I said. "How? When? I don't *believe* it."

"Believe it, my dear," Soad said dryly, "believe it. It is done. While you were in Beirut."

"My God! How *could* he. The fool. The bloody fool."

Soad looked sharply at me.

"Forgive me. I had no right to say that. I hope they will be very happy. Send them my congratulations."

She nodded correctly, her old wrinkled eyelids coming heavily down across her eyes. Now we had satisfied the demands of convention. We remained silent, both of us. Then Soad said to me—in rapid bitter bursts—what she would never have said to anyone in her family:

"The Captain's first wife was a woman of independence. No matter what he has told you. She was a woman of *independence*. A lovely, high-spirited, intelligent girl, mature and with a mind of her own. He could not stand this. No, *this* he could not stand. He needs a slave. They all do. The independent woman will always suffer and be cast aside. It is the slaves who win. Each and every time."

Nabil took me home last week to his family. Incredible.

Ten out of the fifteen flats in this building in Giza are occupied by the members of Nabil's family. In one flat lives Nabil and his parents and his younger brother. In four others live Nabil's aunts and their families. In the remaining ones live a bachelor uncle and four grown cousins now married and with families of their own. Life among these people is a circus, with doors continually opening and closing, an endless stream of aunts, uncles, cousins flowing in and out of each other's flats, with emergencies arising every thirty minutes that involve at least three to five people in the interlocking subdivisions of this corporate existence. "Extended family" isn't the *word* for what goes on in this building.

Seeing Nabil here, in the bosom of this huge clumsy family, has burst the fantasy that surrounds him in my mind. Here, he is no tragic hero. Here, he is the bright, favored boy: "my son, the doctor." Everyone pulls at him, everyone wants his attention, his knowledge, his expertise. No sooner do we walk in the door than a cousin rushes in to announce that an uncle on the floor above is dying, Nabil must come quick. Before he can get his bag his mother demands that he just take a look at this cut on her arm, his father wants his opinion on a document he holds in his hands, his brother complains of a sore back, a young cousin wants advice about a family quarrel in which she is one of the principals.

"I'll be back in a moment. I must see to my uncle." Nabil shakes his head and smiles ruefully at me. "They watch from the windows," he says. "When they see me coming they all start getting sick at once." But he collects his things and makes the rounds of the house just the same, and I see that he is really happy to be doing so. He is tied to the family life in ways he cannot even acknowledge.

For the next few hours people will rush in and out of the flat: laughing, talking, sighing, complaining. Every conversation is interrupted to acknowledge the newcomer, the children rush around creating a din, the cousins inspect me, the mother makes tea, the father peers at me from behind dark glasses. Nabil's father is strange: a tall, thin, gray-haired man with weak eyes, he wanders around his house like an intelligent ghost. He sort of glides in an orbit of abstraction. Some part of him is already gone from this household, turned off in the midst of the racket. He is quite capable, in the middle of someone's sentence, of suddenly flinging himself to his knees, his head turned eastward, so religious has he become in his declining years.

Once again, there flashes across my thoughts: How depressing is Egyptian family life up close in all its dreary, stifling particulars. And how it gets transformed into waves of love in the streets, in the people, in the dust, the air, the history, the politics! The true deranging madness of love is here; the inexplicable chemistry of life; the reverse technology of the East.

At nine in the evening Nabil says to me, "Come, we will visit my uncle."

We walk down three flights of stone steps and knock on a door in the darkened hallway of the family-owned building. The door is flung open and a handsome middle-aged man dressed in blue pajamas stands framed in the light.

"Ah, Nabil," the man cries with pleasure. "And this must be the American young lady I have heard about." He bows low before me, and his face half in light, half in shadow, seems suddenly twisted to me. Involuntarily, I press against Nabil who stands behind me; he laughs softly and pushes me gently forward.

"Do not be afraid, little one," the man in the doorway says in a parody of the evil rake; but somehow I am not relieved, not convinced of the parody.

And when we come fully into the light of the room I am shocked to discover a full affirmation of the instinct that made me draw back: the face of the man in the blue pajamas is ravaged and degenerate, the eyes cynical and hysterical, the mouth loose and stained, the cheeks slack and discolored with the purplish veins of broken blood vessels. . . . This is Sohair's ex-husband: the man she fled from so many years ago.

We sit on pillows on the floor of a room with low tables and an unmade bed in it, and Nabil's uncle says, "She is prettier than the German girl, Nabil." His voice rises in a high-pitched giggle. Nabil blushes and murmurs to me, "He is speaking nonsense."

Nabil's uncle rises and says, "Come, we shall eat and drink wine and do one or two other things." He winks heavily at Nabil. I feel alarm rising in me. Nabil presses my arm comfortingly and says, "*La, la.* Do not be nervous. Nothing terrible is about to happen to you."

The uncle retreats to the kitchen and comes in shortly with arms loaded with wine, bread, and cheese. He arranges the dishes on the floor all around the pillows on which we sit and urges us to eat, although he himself only sips from a glass of wine. After a short while—filled with Arabic conversation between the two men, interspersed with the uncle's high-pitched giggles and Nabil's refined blushes—the uncle rises heavily and excuses himself. I turn to Nabil who only places his finger silently across his lips.

The uncle returns with a large charcoal brazier in his arms. He sets it down in the space before the arranged pillows, kneels and sets fire to the coals sitting in the small grill. He tends the coals carefully for a few minutes, then rises, retreats once more to the tiny kitchen and returns with a contraption that I at last recognize as a water hookah. The mystery is at an end: we are going to smoke hashish. I stare at Nabil, shaking my head slightly. He shakes his head back at me, vigorously. We cannot insult his uncle. I am to remain calm, and simply do as the others do. And I am not to worry! It is all entirely harmless.

Nabil's uncle is preparing the waterpipe. He places some of the hot coals on the small round surface of the hookah; then, upon the coals a wad of sticky black tobacco into which the hashish has been evenly mixed; when the mixture begins to smoke he places the reedlike attachment that extends from the hookah in his mouth and sucks in rapidly; the water inside the hookah begins to bubble; all is ready.

And now, as though at a signal, the doorbell begins to ring. One by one, four of Nabil's uncles troop into the room. Ah, it is a family affair. I begin to feel easier, expecting some of the women to follow. When none does, I inquire of Nabil. He is horrified. "Oh, no," he says quickly. "The women *never* smoke." Then why am *I* here? He looks blankly at me. "You are different," he says innocently. "You are an *American*." In other words: you are not actually a woman.

The pipe is ready. The men all settle onto pillows in a circle on the floor. Slowly, the pipe is passed. Each man sucks deeply at the reed and passes it on. When it comes to me I want simply to pass it on. Nabil urges me, and Sohair's ex-husband positively frowns at my recalcitrance. I place the reed between my lips and suck. A hot rawness fills my lungs. I know before I even start: I am not going to get high, I'm going to get sick. Another Egyptian "delicacy" I must fake. . . .

The men in the room are all fat, middle-aged, and weary-looking. They are two engineers, one school administrator, one retired naval officer, one factory foreman. One of the engineers is the husband of Nabil's favorite aunt. The husband is home on a two-month leave from Saudi Arabia. He is even heavier than the others, with an uncommonly round and childish face. As he smokes, his face grows even more childlike and he begins to speak sentimentally about his wife, assuring me repeatedly that she is the most wonderful woman in the world and he couldn't live even a single hour without her.

"Ours was a real love match," he says, and his eyes begin to water. "True, she was my cousin, but nevertheless I was mad for her. I *had* to have her. I followed her around day and night from her sixteenth birthday on, until finally she said yes."

"And now that you are in Saudi Arabia ten months out of the year you can still say you have a very happy marriage," mocks Nabil.

"What are you saying!" cries the round-faced engineer, but his cheeks flush and he giggles uncontrollably.

(Later, out in the cool of the suburban spring night, I ask Nabil if the engineer and his aunt are indeed a love match. "No," says Nabil dryly, "they are miserable. They have always been miserable." "You mean he was lying?" I ask. "No. He thinks he speaks the truth. He doesn't know *what* he feels.")

As I predicted: I feel myself going hot, cold, and nauseated with each inhalation of the pipe, while all around me the men grow peaceful and joke gently. My throat feels raw beyond endurance, and I want to pass each time the pipe is handed to me, but my host urges me, almost fiercely, to inhale yet once more. I don't know what he is expecting will happen to me, what exotic response to the hashish these good Egyptian burghers are yet hoping to observe in the American naïve, but my conviction grows stronger and stronger that it is something freakish they are hoping for, some American wildness they have been encouraged to believe in, something pornographic in the soul of this odd creature in their midst. And my anger comes up raw and hot as the foreign strength floating through my throat. Damn them all! Damn their mean little souls, damn these wretched little men whose oily politeness barely disguises a frightened contempt for the person they cannot immediately place: the Western woman who to them is neither woman nor male authority, neither conquered nor conqueror, neither slave nor master. Where shall we place her? We cannot. Therefore, let us despise her. . . . And I feel myself a stranger, alone for the first time in Egypt among those I *know* to be my enemies.

Farid understands. He nods his head rapidly as I sit beside him at his desk, railing against the men of Nabil's family, and the contempt implicit in their invitation to smoke hashish with them.

"Yes, yes," Farid says gleefully. "They are brutes, these men. Absolute brutes. Egypt is full of them. They are the respectable middle class who will go on treating women like despised possessions until the end of time. There is no changing them. Ah! Poor Vivian. What a time you are having in this bad country of mine! Nah, but soon you will be gone and you must endure the Egyptian men no more. No more the poor little girl so good, so open, so *trusting* in a circle of wolves."

"Knock it off."

"Nah, nah. And they all have a piece of you, all whom you spend the time with . . . this Nabil you give your body to . . . they think they have you. But no matter, in the end I shall win. In the end *I* shall go out of this Egypt with you. Not they. Not any of them. Only I."

"How are things going, Farid? What's new on the getting-out-of-Egypt front?"

Now Farid is flying high. He tells me he has openly split with his wife, he has begun divorce proceedings, and he has told her he is leaving the country: "She said to me, 'I am tired. Very tired. For three years I have been jealous and I can't go on living this way anymore.' I told her, 'Very good. I want to leave the country. I am a routine man, a second man. This is my last chance. If I don't go now I will get used to it, and that is the end.' She was very happy, really she was. I am leaving the country as well as leaving her so it will not look so bad, and all will turn out for the best."

On the last day of May Fawzy Amr and I spent the afternoon together. It was a hot Saturday and Fawzy was recovering from his weekly visit to his mother whom he hated. We took a tram out to Ma'adi, the loveliest and richest of Cairo's suburbs. Fawzy mopped his sweating forehead and cursed the dominating mother who could still get under his forty-three-year-old skin.

"My dear Vivian, there is nothing on this earth quite like the Egyptian mother. She has nothing but her children, especially her sons, and these she will not let go free from her embrace even if that embrace proves murderous. She controls in the subtlest of manners. Each statement is an implicit criticism. Each criticism is a blow to the heart. Each blow is a link in the chain that binds one to her *forever*."

"Fawzy, you are describing the Jewish mother."

"Oh? How can that be? You seem so free. I cannot imagine you tied to your mother as I am to mine."

"We put up a better front. And besides, we don't *see* them so damned often. Why do you visit your mother every week if you feel that way about her?"

Fawzy stared incredulously at me.

"She *needs* me," he said.

I stared incredulously at Fawzy.

"Ah, my dear Vivian! Understand. When I walk through the door her face is transfigured. A look of sublime happiness and inconceivable relief passes over her features. She is transported in that moment to the center of absolute well-being."

"This happens *every* Friday?"

"Without fail!"

We wandered in Ma'adi amidst lovely villas and in streets lined with tall trees from which hung weeping moss, and everywhere the rich dazzling purple of lilac bushes and bougainvillea and clustered blossoms hanging from trees like ripe grapes, and the streets filled with Russians and Americans who were more at home in Ma'adi, the suburban refuge of foreigners, than Fawzy would ever be.

Later, we took a tram to a Greek Orthodox cathedral where we sat out on a stone terrace, smoking cigarettes, and Fawzy told me the story of his Czech love.

"I spent a year in Czechoslovakia, teaching English. And I fell in love. She was a nurse, a lovely girl, full of spirit. I was ill in the hospital. No one could speak any language I knew. I lay there like a dog, weeping with sheer loneliness. She came and sat beside me and spoke English. And that night she wanted to crawl up into the bed with me. Later, I had dinner at her house and we went to sleep separately, she in her bed, I on a couch. I awoke and she was beside me. We were together nine glorious months. Never in my life have I loved anyone with such total happiness as I loved her. The *time* flew with her. We went everywhere together, everywhere. . . . And yes, I loved her body. And she, she was crazy devoted to me. She washed my feet with her own hands and kissed them and said, 'Never in my life have I done this for anyone.'

"But she was an orphan, and her friends convinced her not to come to Egypt with me. . . . At the plane she wept, the tears cascading down her cheeks, and said, 'No, darling. No, darling. Don't kiss me at the airport. What will people think?'

"She wrote to me later. My mother kept the letter from me for two years. . . . And I married Mona."

Oh Fawzy. What would have been if you had taken a spirited European wife?

"Dear, lovely Vivian," Fawzy moaned as we squashed our cigarettes and prepared to leave the stone terrace. "Do you wish to know what my life is? What my life *really* is?

"I rise at seven. Take a coffee. Read my paper. Wash, and finally the car comes, and I go to work. At the factory we seem to do nothing for a long time. Then the president sends for me, we talk, and finally, for no reason and on some arbitrary signal, we go to work. We work for some hours and at three o'clock I go home. There I eat a perfectly huge meal and lie down—most unhappy that once more I have overeaten. I rise at seven or eight, speak to my wife and children, and they retire at ten. Then, if people come I speak to them until one or two in the morning and go to sleep. If they do not come I read from ten or eleven until three or four, sometimes five in the morning. Dear Vivian. These are the only happy, *really* happy hours of my life."

PART FOUR

Yesterday afternoon I became violently ill in the street. Nausea suddenly rose in me, wave upon wave in a direct line between my gut and my brain, and my legs began to buckle. Luckily, I was only in Soliman Pasha Square and managed to get home in seven minutes. I fell upon my bed and lay there, the shutters of the room drawn, for nearly three hours.

Today, ill again. And again: struck down in the streets at three in the afternoon. Suddenly, it dawned on me: it was the *heat*. I looked around then and realized, with equal suddenness, that the streets were almost empty.

The June heat has struck Cairo with a force unlike anything I have ever experienced. It is a dry, airless, oppressive heat that stuns the brain and nauseates the stomach. Nothing in the American desert can compare with the relentless attack that is this mountain of heat pressing down, down, down upon the population of Cairo. Now the streets are literally empty between three in the afternoon and seven in the evening. Every Cairene I know lies prone in a darkened room, and for the first time I understand why the shutters are drawn all year round: the memory of this heat is enough to convince anybody that one should be in preparation at all times.

Somehow, the heat has created an atmosphere of pathos I have not clearly felt here until now. Some dreadful drying-out from within that turns the bones to dust, and the mind to helpless confusion, and within whose context the crippled condition is suddenly seen plain. The thousands of people of Cairo who perform useless made-up tasks: the three people to tie up a package in a store; the old men who run to open the taxi door or roll down the window after you've gotten the taxi yourself; the man who gets five piastres for watching someone's car, or running for coffee and cigarettes; the six people sweating in a government office where three would do; the servant who pays a child three piastres to go for the bread and cheese; the boys who sling water onto the streets to dampen down the rising dust; the sixty-year-old "boy" who brings Coca-Cola on a tray. . . . The sharing of this filthy hopeless poverty is enough to break the heart and transform the soul.

Lunch at Soad's. I feel I am about to faint: the heat has altered the eating patterns of this household not one jot. Out comes an enormous meal. The heat catches at the grease with which everything in Egypt is prepared (*samna* it is called, a fat made by rendering butter); the air reeks of the stuff, making me practically gag at the table. But everyone else seems oblivious to the smell.

"Soad," I say weakly. "The heat . . . shouldn't the meals be lighter?"

Soad stares uncomprehendingly at me. Lighter? What could be lighter than this simple meal?

"A salad, perhaps . . ."

"But here is *salat*. Here, have some."

"No, no . . . I mean *only* a salad."

"But my dear! One must keep up one's energy."

I look at Gasbia, who is eating as usual, sopping up the gravy in her plate with slices of bread drawn from a package no one else is using. Gasbia has been on a diet since I arrived in Cairo, but she still looks two hundred pounds to me. She glances up and catches me looking at her. She laughs embarrassedly.

"This is special bread," she says. "You can eat as much as you want and you won't get fat."

I look closely at the package. It is a loaf of American diet bread.

"That's silly," I say calmly. "Bread is bread. This only means that the bread in this package is a few calories less than ordinary bread."

"No," says Gasbia in that hoarse shriek of hers. "Ibrahim says I can eat as much as I want. He *knows*."

Ibrahim smiles calmly, a contented baby bear, says nothing, and continues to chew away.

"No, he doesn't," I say, my voice growing sharper.

We have a ten-minute exchange of this "Yes, I can," "No you can't" nonsense about the bread, Gasbia continuing to spout the most incredible nonsense about how one does or does not get fat, citing Ibrahim as her authority in residence, and me growing more and more American irritated, angry, insistent.

Soad, meanwhile, continues to eat: spooning up her food, almost shoulder-level at the table, like a child, lost in bliss, her eyes, as she eats, off in one of those private distant places of hers (it's always like this when she eats), every now and then laughing and rocking back and forth as I keep telling Gasbia that Ibrahim doesn't know what he's talking about.

"You see," says Soad at last, "Ibrahim is fat. He knows that he has no chance of reducing *his* weight. Now, she is trying to reduce *hers*. So he brings her this bread and tells her she can eat as much as she likes and she will get *thinner*." And she laughs and laughs and laughs.

But I persist. *Determined* that Gasbia will see what an idiot she is. Finally, Soad says, "Nah, nah. *Let* her go her own way." And she laughs and laughs.

At the newspaper offices of *Al Ahram* one day, wandering down the wrong corridor, looking for a reporter I know, I meet Abdelaziz Megally, and suddenly another friendship—swift and carrying with it the urgency of *no time, no time*—flares up.

"Who are you? Where are you going? An American! Ah! We must talk. We must talk. Here. Quick. Into this little lounge. A coffee. Only a coffee. We must talk. . . ."

Later, I could understand why Abdelaziz felt such urgency toward me, but when I thought it over, it was curious that somewhere I also felt the urgency, as though without articulation I knew my time in Cairo was running out: my emotional time.

He is thirty-three years old: a beautiful Roman-Graeco head, full of delicate power; a receding cap of black curls; eyes, a bit beady, full of darting light: quick, serious, pained; in his laugh hidden child's laughter; a twelve-year-old boy's cunning trapped in the disheveled confusion of adulthood.

A passionate Marxist, Abdelaziz was arrested at twenty-one (this was in 1959) in his third year as a history student at Cairo University. He spent the next five years in prison: two years at Abuzabel Prison just outside of Cairo, three in the dreadful desert of the New Valley (the Egyptian Siberia). Now, a "fully restored" citizen, he is the token Marxist in the history department of Cairo University.

"Ah, my dear!" Abdelaziz says in the coffee lounge. "Your Hemingway was a very great writer, a very great writer. He said, 'Life kills us all. But first of all, it kills the good, the brave, the gentle. You may be very sure if you are none of these things that it will kill you too. But there will be no great hurry.'

"We must live, my dear, we must *live*. There is no *time*," Abdelaziz hisses, "no time. We must live. I am very fast in everything now. Since the concentration camp I am fast. If I have a strong feeling I act on it. Don't you see? There is no *time*. There, in the desert, I confronted death every day, every day. I never thought I would emerge from these tortures. But I said to myself: If I do come out alive I will *live*."

For the next few weeks Abdelaziz and I will meet often: at four in the afternoon, at nine in the morning, at eleven at night. We will walk the length and breadth of Cairo, drinking coffee, eating *kabob*, going to Egyptian movies, taking boatrides on the Nile, sitting at two A.M. in the railway station: talking, talking, talking. As though we are two people at a besieged frontier snatching hours to trade oral histories: Let there be a *record*. Let it be known that we two lived, that we met, and we understood each other. Let our existences not pass without recognition into some great flowing wash of life-denying time.

Abdelaziz was born and raised in a large town in Upper Egypt. Of his past he says, "We are Copts, you know. My brother was very handsome, very handsome. He made many sexual adventures. The women in our village all wanted him. And I? I stayed in the house, and read books, and Marxism. Then he became a priest and I became a Marxist. But it is something funny: I am religious over Marxism, and my brother is a good man with a materialist soul. . . .

"They came to my house in Upper Egypt, and they arrested me. The man with the gun was trembling. *I* was being arrested, but he was trembling. He looked at my books and he saw *Feudalism and the Bourgeoisie.* Aha! A Communist! I told him, 'It's about the French Revolution. It's one of my university books.'

"For eight months I was in the terrible Abuzabel. The first night six men came and beat me. I thought I was going to die, really to *die.* The guards were like men who had become machines. The entire prison was a machine. Imagine!" Abdelaziz's eyes pop wildly, and he smacks his forehead. "To die in a second, surrounded by a machine!

"Ah, this Egypt was a terrible place in those days. When Nasser put us in prison he said the Egyptian Marxist movement was receiving its orders from Bulgaria. What *Bulgaria?* Who Bulgaria? None of us ever met a Bulgarian in our lives. . . . And then, when that was over, he said we were receiving our orders from Rome!"

Abdelaziz has the naïve, alive soul of the romantic: at the same time that he pines for revolution he keens after Islam, after Arabic music, after the old and the beautiful of the desert life. He takes me on all the working-class trips of Cairo. He feels Om Kalthoum deeply, and he resents the sophisticated intellectuals who reject her as the opiate of the people; he knows that her music reflects the inarticulate pain of the Arabs, and that it heals. He takes me one night to El Fishawy, a historic Arab café in Khan Khalili where old men drink tea and smoke the waterpipe. The intellectuals of Abdelaziz's stripe gather there to feel their roots, and themselves. I sit in this café with Abdelaziz, and as I watch him talk seriously with the old men, and wave delightedly to friends, and explain the *meaning* of various antique artifacts on the wall, for the first time, and for one moment I wish that I were Egyptian. I am pierced in a quick, needlelike motion by the desire to experience Egyptian-ness as Abdelaziz does.

Abdelaziz is always wearing a suit. In the worst heat, a suit. Unlike a number of the *Ahram* journalists—self-assured bourgeoisie who dress like Americans: *appropriately*—Abdelaziz is forever the boy from the provinces who must dress *respectfully*. His suits may be rumpled, crumpled, damp with sweat, but they are suits. His eyes pop, his hands move nervously through his hair, his gait is awkward and lunging, his words come in a rush . . . but he pulls his jacket tighter, straightens his tie, smooths down his collar, and assumes he is passing for white.

"One needs the stability," he says one night as we are walking across one of the Nile bridges. "One needs the *stability*. Here, in Egypt, the passion does not come. But one cannot work without the stability, without the tenderness. . . ." He stares off.

"So we marry," he says heavily.

Silence.

"But we do not stop *feeling!*" he cries miserably. "We cannot stop responding to the passion! To the need for deep feeling."

He turns to me as though he is about to make a political point, and he says, "Love is the inflaming reality. Ah, my dear! The compass of our feelings points to the inflaming reality, the gathered power, the tension of maleness and femaleness. . . . You complain to me that you are overweight. Yes, you would be more fashionable if you were thinner. But this weight, this volume of yours, it bears the pressure of femaleness. The *pressure*.

"The life is cruel, cruel, something terrible! After I married I fell into deep love with a woman, a colleague. She is well known here. She is married to a Marxist professor, and at present she takes her doctoral in Europe. . . . She began to come to my office to talk. Every day we talked, and every day I felt that we are more and more like one another. You understand what I am saying? It is terrible, something terrible! To feel that another human being is exactly like you!

"But we did not express our feelings for each other. She feels love, and I feel love. But we do not express these feelings. Here, in the Middle East. . . .

"And then all around us they began to talk. A colleague says to himself: Something extraordinary is happening between these two animals. And I began to fear for her, and I said to her, 'We must make compromises.'

"Her marriage was arranged. She did not love her husband, and he loved another woman, but their parents said, 'It is good that they shall marry.' So they married. And now she cannot leave him. And I? I took my wife when I needed the tenderness, the stability. How can I leave my wife now that I need another? How?

"But I must have the deep feelings! I cannot live without them!"

Abdelaziz remains thoughtful, silent, for a long moment. Then: "We must trust life. We do not trust *life*. I do not, and she does not. . . . Ah, the life is *incroyable, incroyable*. To defeat the *incroyable* of life! We must."

Most of what Abdelaziz says he says in answer to my questions. One day he looks feverishly at me and, his eyes popping, he bursts out, "Information! It is the need of your soul to have information. For information I think you would give up your mother. Really! You love information better than anything!"

Another day, knowing I am Jewish, he says, "The Jews. The only thing I know first-hand about the Jews is this: In the concentration camp there was a Jew. A young innocent student from the university. Not a Marxist. He wrote something while at school—a comparison of Marx and some Egyptians, perhaps. Nothing. It was absolutely nothing. He was arrested. He knew nothing of politics. . . . Well, we were together, all of us political prisoners. And one day a rumor spread that the guards were going to attack us when we went out into the yard. All around us everyone began stealing blankets and others' clothes to wrap around their bodies under their uniforms. I did not. I thought: Well, if they attack us, even if I die, I must not let them defeat me in this way. And I thought to myself: I do not think the Jewish boy will put on extra clothing. The Jews have more courage than that. And sure enough: all the politicians went out wearing blankets and clothes, and only the innocent Jewish student and I did not."

And yet, and yet. . . .

He comes to my flat one day, and he stands in the center of my room, and he stares and he stares, and he says, "You live alone here in this flat. It is *terrible*! To live alone is terrible. If I left my wife, and made many sexual adventures, and I did not have the one I love, and simply waited for another deep feeling. . . . No, no. I would be lost!"

He survived prison for politics, he experienced passion after marriage, he longs for world revolution, he is a tragic Egyptian hero . . . but he cannot live alone. That, oh my dear Vivian, that is *really* the unspeakable!

From the popping confusion of Abdelaziz to the nervous placidity of Nabil.

We sit one night in an open café on the Nile: Nabil and I, Sohair and her daughter. Nabil wishes a bottle of beer. The waiter apologizes profusely: the beer has not come. It was due to be delivered one hour ago, but it has not come.

"*Malesch.*" The waiter shrugs his shoulder.

We order ice cream and lemonade.

"You know this word of ours, *malesch*?" Nabil asks me.

"Yes. It means sorry, or excuse me."

"Yes," Nabil sighs resignedly. "Sorry or excuse me. . . . If a man bumps into you on the street he will say *malesch*. If he kills your father he will say *malesch*. If you wait three days in a government office and your life hangs in the balance the man behind the desk will say *malesch*." Nabil passes a weary hand across his face and grins softly at me. "*Malesch*," he says.

I feel tonight the psychic drain in the young doctor more acutely than I have in weeks. He seems exhausted in some primal part of himself: thin; without the necessary energy to respond; weak; ill with resignation.

The manager of the café paces up and down not far from where we sit. He chews a cigar. The veins in his bald head are bursting. Finally, he rushes to the phone on a nearby desk and starts shouting madly into it.

"What is he saying?" I ask.

"*Allah yekhreb beitk!*" Za-Za replies, nearly collapsing into her ice cream with laughter.

Nabil's eyes hardly register response—either to the words or to Za-Za's laughter. Abstractedly, he says to me, "He has just said, 'May God destroy your house' to the man responsible for delivering the beer."

For the rest of the evening he stares off in the direction of the darkened water just below us. Sohair tries to cajole him into laughter, Za-Za openly adores him, I sit close to him. But the young doctor of blood diseases is beyond us this night: thin and wan, inert in some deep part of himself, exhausted.

"*Malesch*," he smiles softly at all of us.

Leila Soliman introduced me to a movie actor one day, saying, "You really should know something of the Egyptian movie industry. It is very important throughout the Middle East, you know. Perhaps they never heard of Hamid in New York, but he is all the rage in Ankara."

Hamid El Din, a man in his forties, currently enjoying a burgeoning reputation in Cairo as a strong character actor, proved to be strangely good-natured for an actor (or was it that he thought all American journalists work for *Time*?), and offered to take me out to the movie studio for a day of shooting on his new movie.

We drove at two in the burning afternoon out of Cairo, down the Pyramids Road, onto the banks of one of the old canals, to a movie studio that looked like pictures of Hollywood studios circa 1927. The movie that was being shot was a dramatization of a popular Egyptian novel. The story, briefly, is as follows: Five men meet aboard a houseboat anchored on the Giza side of the Nile in Cairo. They come regularly, once a week, to this houseboat to smoke hashish. They are, variously, a banker, a lawyer, a journalist, a retired general, a businessman. What they have in common is their decadent ennui. One night they break their routine and meet to go out on the town. As they are driving back to Cairo late at night after a long round of bar-hopping, their car goes out of control and they hit a bicyclist. In a hit-and-run panic they drive away from the scene, leaving the man dead in the middle of the road. The following week they meet as usual aboard the houseboat, sick with fear, panic, and self-reproach. But the general consensus is: they will do nothing. They will smoke hashish and forget. As they sit smoking, the houseboat is suddenly torn away from its moorings. The men on board the boat are not aware of what has happened. The boat goes drifting down the Nile.

"You cannot imagine what a triumph it is to be making this

picture," said Ahmed Sadek, the actor who was playing the lawyer. "Until now it has been forbidden to portray a policeman as a thief, a diplomat as corrupt or stupid, and so on and so on. So Egyptian movies, which after the revolution should have become a great neo-realistic force, remained propagandistic soap operas. But now, it looks as though things may begin to be different. After all, this movie is essentially about the decadence of middle-class society in Egypt."

Yes, I thought uncharitably, and it looks and sounds like every arty Spanish and Italian movie of the last twenty years. Where in all that ersatz European existentialism is the authentic voice of Egypt?

Later, and with a bit more passion, I thought again about the authenticity of Egyptian movie art. Only this time: strapped to a chair with leather arms and beneath glaring lights; helpless.

Hamid El Din, thinking to do me a good turn, and to demonstrate his influence at the studio at the same time, insisted I have a makeup job from "the best makeup man in Egypt. Yes, really. The best. He is going to the United *States* in a few months."

There was really no way out. The makeup man, a short man with thick glasses and a toupee, sat me down in the black leather and white enamel chair, beneath powerful cosmetic lights, and worked over me for an hour, breathing "Beautiful, beautiful" every fifteen minutes or so. The man labored diligently, and I gave myself up to him entirely, except once to strenuously insist he *not* tweeze my eyebrows. When he finally whisked away the towel draped around my shoulders, withdrew with his pots of paint and pencil brushes, and whirled me toward the glass to behold the magic he had wrought, I saw staring at me in the mirror: the face of a forty-year-old tart, circa 1953. I stared speechlessly at the horror that was my own face, and when I opened my mouth to speak I thought I had lost my voice. But when I was able to breathe again, and I could stop and think about it, I realized: They *all* look like this. All the housewives and the well-taken-care-of ladies on the streets of Cairo have exactly this look, fulfill exactly this twenty-years-out-of-date notion of Western fashion; this is chic in the emerging middle class.

Mohammed and I continue to meet. Weeks and weeks of more brooding conversations, more endless speculations on the evil of the world all around him, more twenty-three-year-old angst—until I grow so bored and so irritated I can hardly reply at times. And yet I always rally—because I love him, and because, like all spiritual beings, he is really alone. The horror of Shobra is not the poverty; it is the spiritual loneliness: "Laugh, Mohammed! Life is *money. That* is the problem."

One night we were eating our supper on the river bank on the Giza side. Mohammed prepared the long, fresh "french breads"; slicing them down one side and stuffing them with cheese and cucumbers. We sat at the top of some stone steps that led down to the water. Behind us, in the hot moonlight, a family was camped on a grass island in the middle of the wide Giza avenue. The man was asleep, the woman wrapped in silent black, the children miserable. I said to Mohammed, "Is she going to sit there all *night*?"

Mohammed glanced at the woman, then went back to preparing our bread and cheese. In a few moments he handed me a sandwich, and he said, "No. Her father is coming soon with the car to take her home." He leaned back against the stone balustrade, staring at me with mock contempt, and I began to blush and laugh uncomfortably.

"Okay, okay," I said softly.

I bent over my sandwich. Mohammed laughed. A sudden silence. Then I heard him saying to me, "Have you slept with many men since you are in Egypt?"

My head came up with a jerk. Gandhi's grandson sat looking into my face. His eyes flickered as though he were about to receive a slap in the face. But he remained steady. Oh, so steady.

"Two," I said gravely.

Mohammed said not another word. He bent over his sandwich, taking an immensely long time. . . . We ate in silence.

After we had finished, we walked toward central Cairo along the river, coming at last to the Sheraton Hotel and the Kasr-el-Nil Bridge. We walked slowly across the bridge talking about nothing: the boats on the river, the peanut vendors, the nighttime summer crowds. We decided to stop for a coffee in Night and Day, the café of the Semiramis Hotel.

As we sat in the pleasant hotel restaurant where *cappuccino* is served with a scalloped napkin between the saucer and the cup, Mohammed—who had been brooding ever since I'd given him a straight answer to his question—suddenly looked weary beyond words. With the weight of the world on his shoulders, my friend from Shobra abruptly said to me, "I feel you are like a waterfall rushing toward a lake. Bits of wood stop your progress for a while, but you push them aside and rush on. The men in your life are the wood. . . . And," he whispered, "I am afraid of the lake."

I stared at him. Such a flattering view of me this child had.

But a few days later Mohammed said, "I want to be honest. I want to tell you what I am thinking. Because when I am alone I think of making love to you. I see you all ways on the bed. Then, when we are together, I feel you are my deepest, truest friend. So I wish to ask you what is on my mind. Have you come here to make a sexual study of the men of Egypt?"

I could barely control an astonished "Wha-a-at?"

But the words cut deep, and they rankled in me. That night I had threatening dreams about Mohammed: I dreamt that he had gotten into my flat, somehow, and was coming toward me in the bedroom. I managed to get him to the outer door, and just as I was about to lock him out, the door began to break apart in my hands. I found some large sheets of plasterboard in the hall near the door, and quickly began to slap them up over the shattered door. I got them all into place, one above the other, so that they created a fine, boarded-up doorway. Then the sheets began to crumble, one by one. And there stood Mohammed on the other side, smiling a sinister smile, and stepping over the crumbled plasterboard, coming toward me.

For weeks after that dream I did not want to see Mohammed, an especially sour taste coming into my mouth whenever I thought about his fantasizing about me sexually, and then coming to me, all friend and spirit, all righteous disapproval, all longing and pent-up Moslem desire. . . . I had a vision of Mohammed lying on his bed masturbating, his head twisting in an agony of illicit pleasure, reaching for the Koran no sooner than he came to orgasm; then the entire cycle starting all over again. Of such stuff are psychotics made, I thought, and began to frighten myself.

In a beautiful, carpeted office filled with classic green-felt-and-glass-topped furniture, at the end of a carpeted hall full of guards and aides in the Arab Television Building, I have a conversation with a man who is Mohammed's polar opposite. Tahseen Basheer, the "most important man" I've talked to in Cairo, the Spokesman for Egypt—the official post that is the equivalent of the American Presidential Press Secretary—is a stocky, gray-haired, urbane man, a graduate of Harvard University, and a world traveler.

Basheer leans across his desk, lighting my cigarette and then his own, and leaning back in his leather swivel chair, releasing a thin stream of smoke, he says lightly, "You must be careful not to take everything you hear too seriously. Egypt is a very emotional country. Everyone in Cairo is a tragic hero. The Egyptian weeps and moans about his tragic life, but it is all an act. It is all false indulgence."

Basheer is on my wavelength immediately, as interested in love and anxiety as I am, and in the interminable argument about love, sex, and marriage—East and West—he proves to be illuminating.

"In Arabic," the busy official tells me, "there are thirty-five meanings to the word 'love,' and not one of them expresses the singleness of man-woman love. The whole idea is really nonexistent in the growth of Arab culture. One loves in many different ways in the East, and those ways may *include* romantic love, but never do they concentrate on it."

Yes, I argue, but on the other hand this means the difference between a diffused tenderness, and the capacity to experience genuinely deep feeling.

"The Arabic way of love," Basheer returns, "is a series of adequate and satisfying substitutes. It produces another sense of love, and another experience."

What I'm getting at, I say grandly, is that the Western encouragement of one-to-one love encompasses self-love, which means self-discovery, which means the capacity to experience oneself. It indicates the enormous risk the culture of the West has opted for.

Basheer peers keenly at me. "It is a terrible gamble," the Spokesman for Egypt says softly. "One in which most people lose. In the East the choice of family love is a higher guarantee to provide the mass of men with those forms of sympathetic expression they can handle, whereas the West encourages a level of life that only a very few can profitably embark on so that the mass of men are caught by an idea that can only destroy them."

A young man walks into the office. He is introduced to me as an aide, a man recently returned to Egypt from Harvard.

"Now here is a *perfect* example of the efficacy of what we have been discussing," Basheer announces with satisfaction. "Ahmed here has a wife of one year who has been studying for the last nine months in London. Now, what man of the West would allow that? *Could* allow that?"

I realize suddenly that Basheer has made an important point. All these months in Cairo that I have been observing these marital separations—the wife or the husband is in Kuwait or London or Saudi Arabia for months or years—I have been scornful deep within myself of the lack of romantic love that alone allows for such a condition. Suddenly, I see that the diffused love, which is the deepest lesson of the East, has within it the seeds of nonpossessive love. And with a surprised weariness I remember my own country. For God knows, those clutched, nonseparating marriages of the West don't indicate *love*.

Once, speaking of the Suez Canal, Farid said, "When I feel lonely I go to the front. It is a way of washing myself clean. I go and I see enemy soldiers sitting there on the other side of the water and it gives me new energy. I can't explain. There is something about seeing enemy soldiers on a piece of land that is a part of your country that renews your desire to strengthen yourself, and to work, and to recover what is yours."

Suez, and the Canal, and the Israeli flag and moving figures across the water, and an entire day of desert and burning heat, and me moving through it all with a numb heart and a headful of turmoil, and a sense of dislocation so deep as to make me feel a sickness almost unto death. . . .

On a morning late in June I presented myself at the Arab Press Center and took my place in a carful of journalists heading for the front. We were an odd lot: one Egyptian, two Poles, two Sudanese, and me. The Poles, a newspaperman and a television cameraman newly arrived from Warsaw, spoke not a word of any language but their own. The Egyptians and the Sudanese, of course, spoke perfect

English. I became friendly with one of the Sudanese, a tall, gloomy man named Abdullah. Abdullah had had his own news agency in Khartoum—until the recent revolution. After that, the agency was confiscated by the government, and then he was offered his own job back, working for the government. He refused. Abdullah crossed his legs calmly in the back seat of the car and said directly into my ear, "Egyptians will tell you they refused government jobs also, but they're mainly lying. The Sudanese is not."

The car hurled itself along the desert road into a brilliant haze of thick sun, shimmering heat, and the breathtaking sight of sand everywhere as far as the eye could see and to the last horizon in any direction. The desert stretched endlessly before us, its compelling monotony broken only by the regular sight of soldiers encamped every mile or so along the road we were traveling on. They squatted over campfires, they emerged from tents, they faced each other in checkpoint position, they drove trucks and jeeps. In short, this was the Egyptian Army on permanent maneuvers on the road to the Canal . . . and God knows where else.

In two hours we approached the town of Suez.

Suez was one of the loveliest of all Egyptian towns. A French-Arab town of wide, white, desert-clean streets and lovely houses of many shapes: the French-style red-tiled roofs and whitewashed walls of the old Canal Authority houses; the worked-metal arabesque balconies of sand-colored villas; the neat gardens of English bungalows; avenues of palm trees; brilliant blue sky; burning sun; and in the distance the water of the Canal, a clear shimmering green.

Now Suez stood, bombed-out and evacuated. The people all gone, piles of rubble in the streets, the houses looking like the standing dead, riddled with shells that have torn them apart: caved-in walls, shorn-off roofs, blasted windows, wiring hanging out: guts that have burst the skin; not a single house intact, not a single garden but torn and withered, not a shop open, not a child playing. A thick, burning silence hung over the town, and it buzzed in my stomach and reached up into my throat and filled my head. After all the years of the *literary* experience of war I stood now for the first time in my life in a war-torn city. I turned and turned in the silent, rubble-filled streets of Suez. I looked up at the shattered houses, down at the dead and dying gardens, and I could feel the wild flight of the people. The warm life in my body began to fade; I grew cold in my fingers, in my legs, in my upper arms. To think: Jews did this. And in all this world there seemed at that moment no single place where I could feel the legitimacy of my existence.

We stood before a group of Egyptian soldiers quartered in a half-standing villa near the Canal. When they were told that I was an American one of them spoke to Abdullah, and the Sudanese journalist translated the soldier's request that I inform President Nixon that they were ready to fight to the last man, woman and child in Egypt to drive the Israeli invaders from their land. I stared at the soldier. He was a boy of perhaps eighteen. He stood there in the sad silent sun, his uniform shabby, his face callow, his body ignorant, his position desolate. And I thought calmly: This is a madhouse. I'm in a madhouse. Only I can't tell if I'm an inmate or one of the keepers.

I turned away from the soldier, and looked across the street. There stood a tall building, the roof and two walls gone. In a room on the second floor whose front wall had been blasted away a soldier sat typing. It looked like a scene in an experimental movie. On top of the building there floated a banner that read "UN Headquarters."

We stood on a balcony directly on the Canal and looked through powerful binoculars at the Israeli soldiers inside their sandbag bunkers on the other side, the familiar blue-and-white Star of David almost within my grasp. I looked around. On either side of me stood the Polish journalists. What was I doing there? What the fuck was I doing there with *Poles* on either side of me? I turned back to the Israelis. One of them was polishing a rifle. Of course, I said to myself. If this should be the moment when one of them decides to blow the Middle East sky high, and aims his gun in this direction, of *course* the bullet will hit me.

In the evening, back in Cairo, Abdullah and I sat on the terrace of the Nile Hotel, drinking weak "whiskey-and-soda" (as the Egyptians call every mixed drink), and the somber Sudanese asked me if I thought the Egyptians looked ready to fight. I stared dully at him. It had been a disastrous day for me, I could hardly keep coherent track of what he was saying.

"I don't know," I mumbled. "I just don't know."

"Never," Abdullah said.

"How can you tell? You didn't really see anything."

"They will never fight," Abdullah said bitterly. "Never. I know them. They will never fight."

"You hate the Egyptians, don't you?"

"Yes. I *do* hate them. I realize that as an American you find them charming. Well, it's easy for you to do so. You simply have no way of knowing them as *I* do. You are not black, for one thing. And you are not an African, for another. Believe me, I speak for ninety-five percent of the Sudanese when I say that. The Egyptians have always interfered in our affairs. Khartoum is run from Cairo. And for what? What are we getting out of it? Our one cash crop is cotton. And what are we buying with the cotton? SAM Ones, SAM Twos. What the *hell* do we need those things for? Is there any *real* possibility that Israel will attack Khartoum? Not bloody likely! That's all Cairo's doing. All Cairo . . .

"I don't trust any Egyptian!" the Sudanese said with the first burst of passion I had seen in him. "They cheat. They lie. They're insincere. They don't care at all about lasting friendships. They'll do anything to gain the moment. Do you know? I've never been invited to an Egyptian journalist's house? After *years* of working together!"

Oh God, I thought the next day when someone told me a political joke, the earth is going up in flames all around them, everyone in the world hates and despises them, and they *make jokes*.

But then, I shrugged my shoulders, what else should they do? What the hell else should they do? And I reminded myself of what I already knew: that the ability to make jokes, with oneself as the butt, is the salvation of a helpless intelligence, a sign of spunky, even heroic life.

The political joke is like breath itself in Cairo. It is everywhere, continuous, and a dependable barometer of how well the city is surviving. I could never understand the joking all around me, of course, but whenever I demanded a translation I would listen, open-mouthed, thinking: *It's all so Jewish.* The jokes are filled with a half-proud, half-despairing self-mockery that is the very heart of Yiddish humor, and grow out of a pervasive national sense of the self that is half "Schmuck!" and half "Prince of the earth."

One day, when I was on a bus with Mohammed, a man in the back of the bus lit a match that flew sparking out of his hand. People flinched but no one seemed terribly surprised. (The Egyptians call their uncontrollable matches "our national rockets.") The man with the match cursed. Across the aisle, another man said, "Don't be so hasty. We're an underdeveloped country. In ten years our matches will serve us better." "Yes," said the first man. "In ten years our matches will have solved the population problem by killing off half the population."

A joke that was current around Cairo while I was there went as follows: A man seeking to buy a brain for purposes of transplant comes to a laboratory where he is given his choice of three brains. The first brain is Chinese and costs five pounds, the second American and costs ten pounds, the third Egyptian and costs thirty pounds. "Why is the Egyptian brain so expensive?" the man asks in astonishment. "Brand new!" he is told proudly. "Never been used!"

After President Sadat announced that no Egyptian could hold two jobs because no one could perform two jobs at once, the joke around Cairo was: President Sadat goes to the bathroom to urinate. While he's standing there his penis erects. He slaps it and says, "Lie down, schmuck! You're only supposed to be doing one job at a time."

But the jokes that contained the most vicious self-mockery and the most despairing laughter were the jokes that surrounded the name of Gamal Abdel Nasser. Some of them went like so:

1. Nasser always said, "We need the right man in the right place." Supposedly, when he died, half the Egyptians said, "Now the right man is in the right place."

2. Mrs. Nasser is walking down the street and a man rushes up to her and says, "Mrs. Nasser, do you have a vagina?" Mrs. Nasser thinks: The man is mad. She continues on down the street, and one after another, people come up to her and say, "Mrs. Nasser, do you have a vagina?" Finally, she comes to a friend and she says, "Why are all these people asking me if I have a vagina?" The friend replies, "Because your husband is fucking us all."

3. Nasser said over and over again, "We must wipe out every

trace of the Israeli invasion." One day Nasser's servant comes on him furiously washing out his undershorts. The servant says, "What are you doing?" and Nasser replies, "I'm wiping out the last trace of the Israeli invasion."

(Nabil told me this last joke and when I responded only mildly he said pointedly that this joke was the most powerful of all, that it came directly out of the soul of Egyptian culture, that everyone from the gateman to the professor felt it, it was the heart of Egyptian humor.)

On the other side of the world from the place in which political jokes are told—yet still in Cairo—the Zar is held. The Zar is an ancient voodoo rite in which women alone take part, and which Nasser attempted to wipe completely out of Egyptian life. Many people in Cairo will tell you, if you ask, "The Zar? Nonsense! It is a thing of the ignorant, superstitious past. What have *we* to do with all that?"

In a building that looks rather like an adobe barn, somewhere at the end of an alley in the densely populated district between Midan Bab-el-Louk and the Mosque of Sayeda Zeinab, about two hundred women dressed in black *milayehs* and the shapeless housedresses of the urban poor gather each Tuesday and Sunday evenings to exorcise their devils. For eight hours at a time, within the sweating walls of this barn, the drums beat insistently with a wild, culminating beat that sends the women into the whirling, fainting frenzy of the dervish. There are different dances for different devils, and each woman in the room waits for the particular rhythm to which her own body is responsive, leaping to her feet only when the right beat is suddenly heard. Then round and round she goes, skirts flying, head thrown back, eyes closed, limbs jerking to a final paroxysm of purging ecstasy. Often, half the women in the room fall over, nearly in a dead faint, while the other half scream with urgent, frightful pleasure and grasp those fainting in their arms. In the next dance, the roles will be reversed. Those in Cairo who admit to the existence of the Zar say knowingly, "They use the Zar for sex." Fatma is one of those who says this but she agrees to take me to one all the same.

Fatma and I sit with her schoolmate, Zeinab, in the front row of the squashed-together chairs set up all around the central open space, watching the dancers. But the room contains all sorts of action aside from the dancers: Off to the side, reclining on shabby red velvet pillows sits the one-legged *sheikh* who took our ten piastres when we came in and shook a lantern of incense at our legs, our arms, and our heads. Off to another side stand two women pleading with a young man whose blue shirt is torn and whose eyes are wild. They attempt to restrain him; clearly, he wishes to join the dancers; it is forbidden; the women scream and pull at him; all three are the picture of disheveled fear. In yet another corner a woman sits on a chair, eyes closed, teeth clenched, fingernails dug into the sides of the chair. She utters not a sound, but her body jerks fearfully. Another woman stands over her, her hands clasping either side of the sitting woman's head. Zeinab leans across Fatma to whisper to me, "That woman is possessed. They fear she will injure herself."

"Dear God," says Fatma calmly, wiping the sweat from her forehead.

The room is alive with the gathered stench of sweat, fear, and erotic exhaustion. The beating drums dominate the atmosphere. The sound fills the room, climbing the walls, digging itself into the dirt floor. I feel it moving inside me, gathering speed and power; a drunken kind of abandon begins to take hold. A wild man, naked to the waist, dressed in feathers and decorated ropes of leather and silk, stands suddenly before me, dancing madly to the beat of the drums; he beckons me with a cunning finger, a wily eye, a mocking mouth. Another moment and I think I will leap to my feet, whirling out toward the center.

"My dear, I wouldn't if I were you," Fatma says, somewhat alarmed by the possibility of my joining the ladies on the floor.

"Don't worry, Fatma," I say. "I've been going to American Negro revivalist meetings since I was in college. I've never yet succumbed."

We sit thus for two hours until Fatma, who has not left her seat once, looks suddenly as though she is about to lose consciousness. The sweat, the noise, the airlessness, the madwomen, the shrieking, the beating drums: either one has a revelation or one passes out.

As we rise to go, a woman who has been sitting next to me

throughout the entire time we have been here (except for those times when she jumped to her feet with a piercing shriek and joined the swaying, jerking women on the floor), suddenly offers to give us a lift home. I look at her. Clearly, she is a servant somewhere. Her filthy dress hangs on her body. She is having delusions, I think. She laughs and says, "Wait only a moment. I shall return, and take you wherever you wish to go." Fatma and I stare at each other. Then Fatma nods, and I tell the woman we will wait for her. She disappears behind a curtained section at the back of the room. In a few moments she returns to us, dressed now in a short green dress with matching shoes and handbag, and a platinum watch clasped to her wrist. It seems that the lady is the wife of an Army officer. She lives in Heliopolis, and her car is just outside. It will be her pleasure to drive us to any destination we name.

"Yes, I come often to the Zar," the lady says as we step through the earthen doorway out into the alley beyond. "I find it *so* refreshing."

On June twenty-fifth I call Farid—hysterical. I'm screaming my head off about the heat, the running after people, the life I've been leading, I'm finished, I'm through, I'm exhausted, I'm being buried alive here, a journalist's life is a whore's life, the Middle East is living death, I've had it with Cairo. I want out, out, out. You must leave with me on July first. You *must*.

A moment of silence while my screaming voice reverberates along the telephone wires. Then: "My dear, today I have no time for your nervousness. Everything is a mess here at *Al Kahira*. The editor is sick in Alexandria, my foreign affairs man is off somewhere in Fayum, and my art director is celebrating a new love."

I break off suddenly. "Your art director? A new love? His wife just had a *baby!*"

"My dear, this has nothing to do with anything."

"Jesus!"

"Now, my dear, you must take it easy. You must stop all this fooling yourself—you know very well what you are feeling—and pull yourself together. Concentrate and *work*. After all, you didn't come here for this nonsense, did you? Are you going to waste the time in this nonsense emotion and sensitivity?"

Ah, Farid! My dearest Farid! My trembling baby elephant. My Egyptian Good Soldier. My rescue mission in the Middle East. My descendant of kings and masters whom *this* Jew is going to take out of the land of the Pharaohs. My dear friend. Now that *I* am crawling around, bleating like a sheep and falling apart inside, you come through like a trouper!

Yes, Farid. I will forget all this nonsense emotion and sensitivity. I *will* stop acting like an Egyptian. I will concentrate and work.

But it's no use. I begin to feel that my life in Cairo has become a broken record, with the needle hitting the same grooves again and again. I see nothing new, hear nothing new, sense nothing unfamiliar. I learn no more. My emotional energy is gone. I can only imprint now.

One night Abdelaziz Megally took me to the home of a well-known critic. The room was filled with journalists and their wives. The men were mainly Marxists—three out of four had spent five years in prison. Although they all knew each other, many of them—as is common in big cities—had not seen each other for some months. I was struck by their greeting of each other, and full of jealousy for the men.

The women remained demure at all times,. reserving for their method of communication the Egyptian woman's famous use of her eyes: long, dark, measured looks full of who knew what? Promise? Appraisal? Acceptance? Theirs was a mysterious communion.

But the men, ah the men!

As each man entered the room he spotted another man he particularly wished to see. His eyes lit up, the two men embraced heartily, kissed each other on both cheeks, slapped each other on both shoulders, and entered the circle of conversation. As the evening progressed, one or another of them, often in the midst of the most heated political exchange, would reach across the room in sudden irresistible affection to poke or pat or pinch a man's stomach, or back, or cheek and say jubilantly, *"Izaik, hebibe?"* ° Throughout the evening the men clowned around; they hugged, and slapped, and grabassed, and wrestled, and tousled, and comforted, and generally reassured one another with the physicalness of their love. And this between young and young, old and old, young and old.

And I thought of New York, and I felt the cold wind blowing.

And now Abdelaziz is gone—for a month to Moscow and North Korea. By the time he returns I shall be gone from Cairo. We had so little time together, but really I feel his loss. What didn't we do in those few short days we knew each other! We:

Talked feverishly in Abdelaziz's office of Policy, Feelings, Existential Love, the Communication of Distant Souls.

Had tea and beer and cheese and bread in a lovely "casino" on the Nile as the day died away, and the soft Cairo evening came.

More of the same the next night, in another casino on an even more beautiful part of the river, on the other side of the Nile down near Roda Island.

Abdelaziz, all the while, sweating and popping and laughing and lunging and falling and stumbling all over himself, torn between the agony of Marxism and the agony of passionate connection, alternating between "policy" and sex. (I can see his brows gathering in pain now: Oh Vivian! Do not say *sex*. It is *love* I speak of, *love*.)

Went to Heliopolis and walked. Ate *kabob* in a restaurant that reminded me of an American diner and returned for a drink to this "special flat" in El Dahar, an ancient neighborhood behind the railroad station where Farid Wafa grew up, the streets all looking a few hundred years older than any other part of Cairo, and the people in them also looking ancient. The flat belongs to Abdelaziz's dearest friend: a Marxist who loves women. "Oh," croons Abdelaziz, "he is a lovely man, a deeply good and innocent man. But he loves *women*. He is terrible. He makes many adventures."

Walked in the hot, moon-filled night at two A.M. to the railroad

° "How are you, dear?" *Hebibe* is the male form of dear; *hebepte* the female.

station where there's always lots of action: boys from Upper Egypt selling grilled corn, *koshry* carts all lit up in painted glass and white frames; the police taking away a drunk who keeps trying to kiss the youngest cop; taxi-drivers gathered around their Fiats, laughing, talking. We sat in the station buffet, drinking tea and talking until dawn.

Met at nine in the morning to take a ride up the Nile on the riverbus. Without my knowing it, Abdelaziz was taking me to the Delta Barrages. When I realized where we were going I stared at him, and said, "It's illegal. It's illegal for me to go to the Delta Barrages." Abdelaziz stared back at me, his eyes popping, his hand smacking his forehead. "I forgot!" When the riverbus arrived at the fabled gardens and bridges of the Barrages we saw how really dangerous our position was: soldiers *everywhere*. Abdelaziz said, "Let me think." Then: "You look Egyptian. Take my arm, and do not speak, above all do not speak."

He had decided to leave the gardens without returning on the riverbus (who knew who had overheard us speaking English?), but none of this did I know until it was all over. We kept moving up out of the gardens toward the great bridge of stone that Mohammed Aly built. Abdelaziz wanted to say to me: Walk faster! But he did not. Some boys on the bridge watched us walking, close together, arm in arm, and later Abdelaziz told me they had said, "Those are the people who are alive!" A soldier called up to us from a position beneath the bridge, and Abdelaziz stopped. Suddenly, a cold snaky fear began crawling up my arms. Abdelaziz said a few words to the soldier and, his fingers clutching hard at mine, we kept walking. *Oh do not walk too fast, do not walk too slow, but keep walking!* At the end of the bridge we were suddenly in a town. There would be a train back to Cairo in two hours. Then a man at our elbow was saying to Abdelaziz, "Want a taxi to Cairo?" We followed him and jumped into his car, with three workers asleep in the back seat. A long, hot, dusty ride with the driver going a maddening thirty kilometers an hour. Abdelaziz feigned sleep and we spoke not a word all the way back into Cairo. But the driver had caught a single English phrase, and remembered. "Sorry," he said to me when he bumped my arm, and he winked at me. Once inside the city limits we caught a trolleybus, and I insisted on hugging Abdelaziz because we were so relieved and it had been such a close call, but he was shy on the bus all the same, looking around to see if people were watching us.

Walked the length and breadth of Cairo one night from the El Husseiny quarter to Zamalek, sitting in the garden of the Omar Khayyam Hotel, walking across the bridge and down the Corniche talking, talking, talking, the romance of Abdelaziz's Marxism piercing me through and through.

"I am a Marxist," he said, "because I long for liberty and for justice. God knows there's little enough of either in the world I find myself in. Perhaps it is all hopeless, everything we do here in Egypt. We are nothing in the world: shabby, absurd, almost beside the point. But if I give up Marxism I lose my soul. And," he grinned at me, "I am sure to burn in hell."

But his eyes grew anxious, and he pulled his rumpled, sweat-stained suit jacket tighter about his waist, and thrust his hand nervously through his black curls.

Really, I feel the loss of Abdelaziz keenly. He has aroused in me memories of a life I was one generation too late for: the comradeship of the poor and the intellectual bound together in an ideal of revolution; that passionate life of the immigrant radicals that was already dying in my infancy, but which I nevertheless feel my roots in; those memories that haunt me of working-class Jewish boys and girls, handsome and fragile in a way none of us is anymore, wearing V-necked navy sweaters, close-fitting polo shirts, no makeup, and *intensity*; those men and women with work-blackened hands and intelligent eyes who operated sewing machines in New York's garment district, or drove bakery trucks, or laid wiring, but were introduced to me by my parents as writers, poets, *thinkers*, and whose ignorant devotion to "a better world" sunk a hook into me. . . .

To think: it took a romantic, feeling, disheveled Marxist from Upper Egypt to speak to the deepest longings of a daughter of the East European Jewish socialist ghetto.

Before he left for Moscow Abdelaziz held me close and we kissed each other many times and he said, "I have spoken to you as I could to no Egyptian woman. Really, it is destiny that we have met and my cruel fate that I should lose you." And I felt the same, I felt the same.

The afternoon is drowsy, the country is half-asleep, the time is drawing nearer.

Ibrahim the Bear and Soad and I are having tea. Soad sucks thoughtfully at a slice of lemon. The Bear lights a cigarette and sits blinking into the afternoon heat. I sit and wonder. . . . A dialogue takes place:

THE BEAR (*speaking to me*): "You must not exaggerate our faults. And you must not use names. You must write your impressions and say only good things about us."

SOAD: "Why must she say only good things? She must say what she feels."

THE BEAR: "No. She must listen to our impressions and know us as we know ourselves."

SOAD: "Nonsense. She must write what *she* feels, not what you feel. You do not know your faults. Only other people know your faults."

THE BEAR: "No. We know our faults."

SOAD: "You do not know your faults."

THE BEAR: "We *know* our faults."

SOAD: "You know *nothing*. So keep quiet. If you knew your faults you would have changed years ago. Half the remedy is to be able to name the disease. To *understand* the cause of our faults. That is our whole problem here in Egypt. We do not know ourselves. We know this is wrong and, *yani*, that is wrong. But why? Why is this and that wrong? We are never able to look deeply, really deeply, into ourselves and know what the cause of our problems is." (Soad looks as though she is turning something over in her mind; she shrugs her shoulder briefly; she will speak anyway.) "Yes, even with Gamal it was the same. He thought he would change Egypt in a day. And he didn't know how to do it. He could see what was wrong but he was unable to know why. And when things went wrong he began to *accuse*. He accused and he accused and he accused. Hundreds of people he accused. And he made enemies. Deep enemies. Serious enemies. Important enemies. And all around him they said: Listen, you are losing. But he could not hear." (Soad turns on the Bear.) "So keep quiet and don't speak stupidly to her. You know nothing."

Soad purses her lips, folds her arms across her breasts, and her eyes retreat into that private distance of hers. Ibrahim falls silent. I raise the teacup to my lips.

Everything has fallen apart: Farid cannot raise the money he must have if he is to leave Egypt.

For weeks now it has been the same: It is coming. The money is coming. Today, tomorrow at noon, absolutely Wednesday at three o'clock, a signature is necessary from the bank in Alexandria, I spoke to the man, beyond question, in my office tomorrow at ten o'clock sharp. . . . His friend Ali keeps promising him the money . . . his brother in Algeria . . . *Al Kahira* . . . nothing materializes.

I am reminded of the money he owed (and still owes) me, and I feel the panic that precedes anger thudding against my breastbone: A number of months ago I lent Farid a hundred pounds. He needed to give his wife the money in order to obtain her consent not to contest immediate divorce proceedings. "It is only for two weeks," he said. "You will have the money back in two weeks." A month later, when I needed the money to plan my trip to Beirut, I still did not have it. For days and days it was: tomorrow, next day, the signature from Alexandria; on and on in a sweat of breast-beating, brow-wiping, desperate feelings, ashamed meetings. I left for Beirut without the money. At the airport Farid squeezed my hand between his two sweating palms and swore, "My dear, on June first you will have a hundred pounds."

On June first he appeared with thirty pounds; I took the money and said nothing. Weeks later, twenty pounds; a month later, five pounds. At least three times he has had all the money in his pocket but has never considered it a binding debt on me that he should simply hand it over. There was always something more urgent, something more immediate that prevented him from paying up. Inside, I burned. When I finally spit it all out, how I felt about this matter, he looked at me, all blinking innocence, and said, "Why, you know, I guess I thought of you as I do with my own friends. If I owe one of them money, and I have thirty pounds, I give them thirty pounds. When I have twenty I give twenty."

I was convinced that he really believed all this, and I knew to force him to see the truth of the matter as I saw it would be to lose our friendship; though God knew I was so full of anger I would probably have plunged into that emotional anarchy if I hadn't held myself in iron check.

Now, watching him thrash around over *another* pile of money, while the days slip by, one by one, in a limbo of waiting, knowing in my gut it will all come to nothing, I try to sympathize with his wretched position, but I cannot. Anger surges up in me. Anger over the lying, the manipulating, the ineffectuality, our wrecked plans.

Day by day, hour by hour, glance by glance, I feel—no matter what he says—that he is closing off from me. That now that I am no longer "the most important thing in his life"—that is, he knows although he will not say, that he is not leaving Egypt with me—he is drifting off into his own bitter dreams.

Yesterday, while speaking absentmindedly about his bank in Alexandria, he said thoughtlessly, "My wife called this morning . . ."

"Your *wife* called?" I shot back at him. "I thought you haven't seen or heard from her in weeks. I thought you were divorced by now. You *are* divorced, aren't you?"

He stared hopelessly at me, and slowly shook his head. He's been living continuously with his wife. He has never even started divorce proceedings.

"Well, at least I will never let you down. . . . Well, anyway, I never let you down." This is Farid's continual refrain now, in these our last moments together, and it becomes unbearable to me. My pent-up anger bursts its skin, and in a voice that could cut through steel I fling at him, "What the hell have you done for me? You introduced me to the people who walked into your office. What else?"

Even as I am speaking the hateful words, and watching him harden into unforgiving fury before my eyes, I am thinking: *Oh Farid. I am unfaithful. Unfaithful.*

"All right," Farid spits at me. "Nothing. I have done nothing. Forget the whole thing. Now you have thrown it all away."

He turns a stiff and unyielding back on me; but I see his hands quiver as he tries to light a cigarette.

Thus ends the great exit from Egypt. I will leave him here, after all. Will he ever get out? Will I ever forget him? Will we ever forgive each other? Will we ever, either of us, change?

Good-bye, good-bye.

Good-bye, Fawzy: "Dear lovely Vivian! Never in my life will I forget our conversations. Never! I will feed on the memory for *years!* Go, now. Go, *quickly*, dear. If you must, go!" Good-bye, Fatma. Good-bye, Walid: "You will return, yes? You will come again to this filthy Cairo, this peculiar Egypt. Once more, yes? We will not say good-bye, only *auf Wiedersehen*." Good-bye, good-bye. Good-bye, Leila. Good-bye, Abdelaziz. Good-bye, Sohair. Nabil, oh Nabil, good-bye! Good-bye, Zeinab. Farid! What is this? Pressing forty-five pounds into my hands! Oh Farid, good-bye, good-bye! Good-bye, Engineer Anwar. Good-bye, Lizette. Good-bye, Samir Abdel-Rahman. Good-bye. Good-bye, all you Hamamsys. Oh, Soad! My Soad. Quick, our hearts are breaking. One fast embrace, no tears, no admissions, lots of false promises, Ibrahim, *watch her.*

Good-bye to Zamalek. Good-bye, Giza. Good-bye, Mohammed Ali Mosque. Good-bye, Bab-el-Louk. Good-bye, El Husseiny. Good-bye, Shobra. Good-bye to the Nile, dear God, *how* can I say good-bye to the Nile! Good-bye, good-bye.

Good-bye, Cairo.

July tenth. Early morning. The plane leaves at one. I am racing around the apartment, packing clothes, books, records, paying bills,

sorting what I've borrowed from what I've brought with me. . . .
Mohammed follows me around from room to room.

He has come to make it up between us—too painful to come any
sooner than the very last possible hour—and, at last, to put a surgical
end to the sympathy between us we have so long denied. He stands
silent in the doorway—for the first time in this flat—his eyes soft
with pain.

"Standard Stationery," he says, his voice nearly failing him.

We sit in the little salon amidst the square ugly furniture, the
glass-topped tables, the red velvet curtains, the light streaming in
through the open shutters: stricken, forlorn, afraid to face the sorrow
of this parting. Mohammed speaks of our last terrible meeting.

"You know," he says quietly, "sometimes you have feelings. You
don't know what they are. You grab at anything, any thread, maybe
it will lead you to your feelings."

I nod. I believe. I cannot speak.

The time is going. I start racing, distracted, through all the rooms,
picking up, putting down, I don't know what I'm doing, I can't look
at him, I can't look away. Misery and anger are boiling together in
me. Where am I? What have I done? Where am I going?

Mohammed, too, is helpless. He explains into the void. He
defends, he amplifies.

"I give and give and give," he says. "Men are evil . . . I have a
God . . ."

He has broken the barrier in my chest, the thickness that is
choking me. Elated, I turn viciously on him.

"You *think* you give, but you are always counting up what you
give. You do not know your own feelings, and what is worse, you do
not know that you do not know. I came to Egypt angry and I'm going
home angry, but at least I know my salvation lies in ridding myself of
my anger, in knowing myself. You do not even wish to know that it is
your own self that is the enemy, not Shobra, not Egypt, not the evil
in other men. You are the ultimate coward."

Mohammed stands motionless in the bedroom, a suitcase in his
right hand. I stand, equally motionless, a pile of books in my arms.
We stare, horrified, at each other. After a long moment Mohammed
speaks. Sadly, ironically, wistfully.

"I want to preserve my innocence," he says.

"Exactly!" I say triumphantly.

But even as I hear the words, and the literary puzzle of Egypt falls into place, satisfying my intellectual greed, my insides are tumbling and tumbling in great overturning waves, and I am sinking.

Oh, my anger! Oh, *my* preserved innocence!

Oh, Mohammed! I hold on to my anger, I hold on. I also fear the loss of fear. I would not lose the infuriated anguish. I will not come to consciousness. I, also, seek my lost childhood. I, too, would remain innocent.